V&R

Alexander Thomas
Eva-Ulrike Kinast
Sylvia Schroll-Machl
(Editors)

Handbook of Intercultural Communication and Cooperation

Volume 1: Basics and Areas of Application

With 23 Figures and 14 Tables

2nd Revised Edition

Vandenhoeck & Ruprecht

Translator: Charlotte Weston-Horsmann
Proofreader: Megan Hayes

Translator's note: I have tried to include the pronouns for both genders (he/she) as far as possible. However, in translating longer passages and for purposes of clarity, I have used only the "he" form.

Bibliografische Information der Deutschen Nationalbibliothek

Die Deutsche Nationalbibliothek verzeichnet diese Publikation in der Deutschen Nationalbibliografie; detaillierte bibliografische Daten sind im Internet über http://dnb.d-nb.de abrufbar.

ISBN der gedruckten Ausgabe 978-3-525-40327-3
ISBN der elektronischen Ausgabe 978-3-6475-40327-4

Satz: Satzspiegel, Nörten-Hardenberg
Druck und Bindung: ⊕ Hubert & Co, Göttingen

Gedruckt auf alterungsbeständigem Papier.

Table of Contents

II. Areas of Application

Introduction

Internationalization and globalization have become an integral part of our society and continue to increase in importance. Our contact with culturally diverse individuals whether in the workplace, educational institutions or in our daily lives, is increasing steadily. For many, job-related international cooperation at home or abroad has become the norm. The international media covers events worldwide and easily accesses geographically and culturally distant countries.

In today's world, a sound basic knowledge of international affairs is a prerequisite to operating in a global network. The ability to contribute qualified and informed opinions is central to international business and constitutes an integral part of a person's self image. In order to be taken seriously in the global arena, a person must have a well-founded understanding of environmental issues, European, transatlantic and transcontinental security, rankings in global economic competition and the worldwide struggle against poverty. Business leaders can no longer afford to lag behind in their grasp of international politics and global developments, regardless of their position in the corporate hierarchy or whether they are themselves only indirectly involved in international business. A minimum of international competence is required in either case.

The challenges faced by many echelons of society with regard to internationalization, globalization and the strategies required for dealing with these issues are central to the 21st century.

Seen from a historical perspective, these developments are certainly not new. History has shown that there have always been times when transcontinental movement for political, economic, expansionist, religious and other reasons was on the rise. Diverse intercultural encounters were a natural outcome.

It was always a question of one dominant power exerting influence over another and securing strategic power bases, countries, cultures and continents. The most recent research into the significance of overland trade routes (e.g., Silk Road, incense, spice, and salt caravan routes) or sea routes (e.g., The Northwest Passage, Straits of Malacca, the Transatlantic Routes, Bering Strait) has shown that religious beliefs were disseminated in the wake of trade and conquests (e.g., Hinduism, Buddhism, Christianity and Islam). This development continued on into modern times with the spread of political and ideological systems (colonialism, Marxism, capitalism). Trade and the exchange of ideas throughout the world used to progress steadily over decades or even centuries. It was not until much later that historical research uncovered the global networking processes involved in the movement of people, goods and ideas. The people themselves remained largely oblivious of events outside their immediate sphere of influence, having no information network through which they could grasp the extent of transcontinental developments.

The rate at which the age of technology has progressed over the last century has lead to readily accessible sources of transportation and information, and contributed to a qualitative increase in internationalization processes. As a result of modern scientific and technological know-how, information can be instantaneously sent and retrieved from around the world and is available to everyone at a relatively low cost. International co-operation and travel, as well as access to information gathering, is no longer a privilege of the well-to-do, but long since available to the general public as well, at least in First World countries. The Information Age is here to stay, offering undreamt-of international and global mobility. The question arises, however, if individuals directly or indirectly involved in these developments have the necessary psychological makeup to absorb and process (perception) information adequately. Given this ability, are they able to analyze and evaluate (thought patterns, judgment) newly gained insights, manage emotions (feelings and sensations), plan and implement (application) these in a way that satisfies individual needs and leads to mastering the given challenges? Social and technological developments in a number of areas offer a range of choices for accessing individual potential and lifestyle preferences. However, just as many people who might benefit from such a wide range of choices do not, simply because they are unable to for reasons of heritage and/or personal background. This is a common phenomenon where sophisticated technology is used. An example is in the construction sector, where highly developed machinery and technical components are designed for multi-functional use, but only operate at 50% of their capacity. The reason for this is that persons operating the equipment are either not aware of the full scope of available options or choose not to change the problem-solving strategies they have developed over the years or which have traditionally served them. While users rely on the equipment as such, its full potential is not fully exploited.

In the technical field, the realization that multi-functional operating equipment is not fully exploited often leads to an initiative to train and qualify the users. The result is an overall improvement in the problem-solving process, requiring all those involved to reorient and reassess their original approach. The problems and possible problem-solving strategies discussed in relation to the handling and use of development potential inherent in increasing internationalization on the macro-social (societal level) and on the micro-social level (individual life planning and career development) are similar.

The following examples from different centuries and cultural regions shed some light on the gradual development of intercultural competence through the ages.

Assessing Intercultural Experiences

In the introduction to his book "Chinese Characteristics", published in 1900 in Germany, Arthur H. Smith mentions the enormous difficulties confronting Westerners in their dealings with the Chinese: "Sir Robert Hart, the inspector general for Chinese maritime customs who lived in the Middle Empire for forty years, speaks of the exact same phenomenon. 'China is a difficult country to understand. A few years ago, I thought I had finally reached that point and grasped something about its inner workings, which I attempted to bring to paper. Today, I feel like an absolute beginner again. If I were asked to write three or four pages about China, I would not know where to start. One thing sticks in my mind, however. Where I come from, we tend to say: do not bend, even if you should break apart in the process. In the West, it is considered a virtue to adhere to one's convictions and value concepts, even at the risk of becoming socially alienated. The Chinese, on the other hand, as Sir Robert Hart noted, believe the opposite to be true: bend freely but do not break'". Adhering to individual convictions, values and norms might be important, but only as long as they do not lead to a break with the closely-knit family and social network. The ability to intuitively grasp cultural differences and adapt behavior accordingly in an intercultural encounter with Chinese business partners may very well have a positive, long-term effect on the business relationship in terms of communication and sustainable cooperation. The opposite is true if business partners remain largely oblivious to cultural differences and insist on pursuing their own agenda from the perspective of their own cultural orientation system.

Other-culture Experiences

The CEO of a large German industrial corporation with business operations worldwide recounts his experiences in East Asia and the US: "After having worked in East Asia for three years, I was sent to the U. S. In Asia, I was struck by the cultural difference from day one. It takes months to discover anything vaguely familiar behind the foreignness. My experience in the U. S. was quite different. At first some aspects seemed foreign to me, such as urban planning. However, the differences were nowhere near as striking as in Asia. I always tended to see things in relation to Germany. I used to ask myself, sometimes hopefully, but more often with trepidation: When will we be seeing this sort of thing in Germany? The question in itself points to certain similarities between Germany and the US! I got along quite well with the Americans at first: 'People like you and me', I thought. The longer I stayed, however, the more dissimilarity I discovered. From today's perspective, I would still say that I experienced far more difficulties in communicating with my Asian partners. Nevertheless, there were moments in the U. S. when nothing seemed familiar. Things simply did not proceed as I expected them to. A significant difference was certainly my approach to both the American and Chinese cultures: In Asia I expected otherness and was surprised to find similarities. In the U. S., I expected familiarity and experienced much that was foreign to me".

According to an American trainer who prepares executives for international assignments to Germany: "Most Germans underestimate the differences between the U. S. and Germany. Americans, on the other hand, have little information about Germany through the media and often fall back on a number of clichés. We are not entirely free of feelings of mistrust due to events surrounding WWII and post-war history, current developments in right-wing radicalism and xenophobia. U. S. executives sent to Germany on overseas assignments frequently miss the point when dealing with their German business partners. They believe they are superior, from a technical and especially from a moral standpoint. It is no secret that a number of well-known German firms have experienced difficulties on the U. S. market over the past years. This was largely believed to be a result of the fluctuating exchange rate and similar unpredictable events. Meanwhile, it has become evident that much of the misfortune on the U. S. market was due to the approach in dealing with American business partners. Since then, there has been some reassessment of appropriate and effective behavior in doing business with Americans". Expectations of the other person and the personal assessment of a given situation inevitably shape other-culture perception, which include experiences of similarity and dissimilarity, cultural distance and conclusions drawn from these. A certain degree of willingness and the ability to reflect on everyday encounters with dissimilar others is necessary for developing an awareness of intercultural learning and ultimately understanding the factors underlying appropriate and effective behavior in an intercultural encounter (applied intercultural ability). This constitutes intercultural competence.

Intercultural Incompetence

A German engineer received the following mail from his Nigerian client: "Dear Mr. X! Thank you very much for your support. We have decided that Mr. Y will leave Nigeria tomorrow. We feel that there is little sense in continuing his assignment. Regarding his return to complete the assignment, we feel that we need another specialist from Germany, one who is more tolerant and cooperative and is better able to communicate with people from a different culture. Such a person should not only be expertly versed in mechanical processes but also be able to get the job done. In case you do not have a replacement for Mr. Y, we prefer that you do not ask Mr. Y to return. We are prepared to begin production with our own crew. Please send me the contractual conditions for Mr. Y's replacement. Thank you very much".

Know-how and technical specialization alone are apparently not enough to ensure success in global business. Customers are demanding intercultural sensitivity, understanding and the willingness to adapt to other-culture customs, rules and general social norms. Those who are unwilling or unable to meet this challenge are likely to forfeit their long-term competitive edge in the international market place. Terminating an international assignment prematurely and finding a replacement is costly and likely to damage the company's image in the long run in terms of trust, as personal failure can cast doubts on professional competence.

There is convincing evidence that there is a dire need for more awareness of culture-specific differences and the ability to deal appropriately and effectively with dissimilar others in international communication and cooperation. In spite of this observation, underlying cultural influences are regarded as academic hypothesizing rather than a factor worthy of serious consideration. An encounter with cultural otherness does not automatically lead to an analysis of culturally-based causes of unexpected or contrary behavior and the desire to understand intrinsic cultural factors.

In contrast, with increasing internationalization, countries tend to converge and adopt other-culture characteristics more readily (e.g., McDonaldization) and downplay the significance of cultural diversity. A certain degree of convergence is certainly due to modernization, assimilation and adaptation and is reflected in consumer habits, the workplace and in management styles. A closer look, however, shows that forced adaptation is not evenly distributed. More influential nations, societies and internationally active groups impose adaptation on less influential players. The more pressure there is to adapt, however, the greater the tendency toward cultural divergence, e.g., the (re-)discovery of and emphasis on cultural differentiation and self-determination. Along with the awareness and acknowledgment of cultural diversity, such tendencies stand in contrast to mass standardization. Thus, the convergence theory can hardly qualify as an argument against culturally-based differences and the necessity of training relevant specialists and leaders.

Regardless of whether perceived cultural differences are considered a burden or an enrichment, and dealt with accordingly, it does not change the fact that they exist and that they influence our perception, thinking, feeling and behavior and that ultimately, they impact communication and cooperation between individuals from different cultures. Individuals who intuitively grasp what is going on in an interaction between themselves and the dissimilar other and who understand why events unfold one way and not another, are able to synergize cultural dissonance in a way that leads to achieving a mutual goal. Understanding the dynamics involved in a mutually satisfying cooperation in the international/intercultural arena leads to a more sustainable approach to dealing with cultural otherness. Needless to say, intercultural competence enhances the competitive edge. This reference guide is designed to support and promote the success of such relationship-maintaining, human and materialistic interests.

The credo underlying this guide relative to successful interaction and co-operation between culturally diverse individuals is taken from a three thousand-year-old Chinese proverb: "Only he who knows the dissimilar other a n d himself well, can succeed in situations involving communication and co-operation".

It is not enough to grasp, study and understand other-culture values, norms, customs, rules of conduct and world views, in short, their unique system of orientation. Moreover, it requires a conscious grasp of, reflection on, comparison and understanding of one's own cultural system of orientation on the basic level of daily work and private life. Most often, this is taken for granted and only the rare individual is consciously aware of his daily routine. This aspect is key to developing "intercultural competence in action". The standard of quality worth striving for, however, is not reached until both partners, with their respective systems of orientation, manage to pool their potential in a manner that leads to goal attainment (effectiveness) and improved quality of life (satisfaction). This work of reference combines a practical approach, underlying theory and methodological tools for dealing with problem analysis and solution processes.

The first chapter deals with the basic theoretical concepts of intercultural communication and cooperation. This includes a discussion of the definition and description of culture and cultural standards, upon which this book is based, as well as the relationship between national and organizational structures. We will take a look at the dynamic triangle of applied interculturalism, which concerns aspects of self, otherness and the intercultural element. The last chapter in this section deals with the basic building blocks of core concepts such as cultural dimensions, acculturation, intercultural perception, communication and cooperation, intercultural identity management, intercultural learning, applied intercultural competence and intercultural research.

In the second chapter, we will examine a number of relevant practical examples from the corporate world: intercultural management, intercultural human resource development and intercultural marketing.

The third chapter explores the complex connection between the concept of applied intercultural competence, the development of applied intercultural competence and the effect of intercultural training and coaching on applied competence, including the evaluation and assessment of such measures. Within this context, we will provide an overview of and insight into different forms of intercultural training, education and coaching. We will deal with the advantages and disadvantages as well as the possibilities and limitations of the development of intercultural competence from a professional standpoint.

The fourth chapter deals with central management themes in an intercultural context. Here, we will take a look at the following subject matter: debating (rhetoric), negotiating, conflict management, project management, leadership, team development and work groups. Further, we will shed light on the complexities involved in joint ventures and acquisitions in international management, forms of modern corporate communication, the challenges employees and their families face on international assignments and finally, the role of women in international management and job enhancement opportunities.

Chapter five concludes our discussion on a strategic plan for comprehensive interculturalism in corporations.

This guide may be of assistance for those wishing to learn more about themselves and the many different facets of intercultural communication and cooperation or for specialists in the field of human resource development with an interest in practical application. Scholars and scientists may also find it helpful for an in-depth study of the theoretical foundations and methods for analyzing and dealing with core aspects of interculturalism.

Trainers, coaches and consultants will find interesting approaches and ideas with regard to the development of culture-general and culture-specific trainings and workshops.

The second edition, co-authored by Alexander Thomas, Stefan Kammhuber and Sylvia Schroll-Machl, "Länder, Kulturen und interkulturelle Berufstätigkeit" (Countries, Cultures and Intercultural Careers), offers insight into a number of different intercultural fields of application apart from the strictly corporate context and explores culture-specific behavioral patterns among individuals from different countries (cultural standards). The series "Handlungskompetenz im Ausland" (Practical Application for the International Assignment) contains additional training material for self-study and serves as a basis for intercultural trainings.

Sylvia Schroll-Machl's book "Die Deutschen – Wir Deutsche. Fremdwahrnehmung und Selbstsicht im Berufsleben" (2002) encourages reflection on the specifically German system of cultural orientation.

In closing, the authors sincerely hope that the information and recommended reading provided here will facilitate in-depth self-study and greatly enhance the reader's insight into the subject matter.

I. Basics

1. Theoretical Basis: Intercultural Communication and Cooperation

Alexander Thomas

1.1 Culture and Cultural Standards

1.1.1 A Private Conversation

"Say, Mark, what do you think of this? Last Friday, my boss gave me a book with the comment, 'Have this read by Monday, will you, so you can be prepared!'"

"What kind of a book, I mean, what's it about?"

"I'm supposed to lead a pretty high-ranking delegation of industrial engineers from Peking around the plant next Wednesday. The title of the book is 'Dealing with Chinese Business People'. That's ridiculous, what on earth for? I mean, I don't intend to become a China expert."

"But it can't hurt, can it, to learn a few words of Chinese? Just imagine the impression you'll make when you pick them up at the airport!"

"No, no, it's not a language text book. It's a sort of listing of do's and don'ts, like a recipe for correct behavior. It was written by some guy who did a short stint in China. Perhaps that would be something for Henry. He's the one who is going to China to join the joint venture for three years. This really isn't my thing. After all, people are people and the Chinese can't be that different from us!"

"I wouldn't be so sure about that. I'm sure they have different work habits and other ways of doing things. For one, their eating habits are different from ours."

"That's fine with me! But if they fly over here to visit our plant, I expect them to adapt to our ways. We aren't backward, you know! Anyway, friendliness and a warm smile should do the trick. Most importantly, I'm sure they'll be impressed by our quality and the history of our plant, especially the multi-media part. Oh, by the way Mark, what I wanted to ask you: Do you know our new corporate promotional film 'Mobility-Global 2000'? Let me tell you, it's great. The music and visuals are simply fantastic!"

"Is it suitable for our Chinese guests though? They might be used to totally different visuals."

"Oh, stop being difficult! People are the same all over the world. Anyone, anywhere can distinguish between quality and trash."

"Did it occur to you that no two individuals can ever be alike? There never was and there never will be an exact replica of you. You are unique!"

"I like the way you say that. How come I get along with you and others well enough if I am so unique? I spent my last holiday in Thailand. One day, I took a bike trip around the countryside. I can't speak Thai and the people there don't speak English but I was able to communicate with them all the same. I smiled constantly like they do and gesticulated a lot. They could tell that I wanted something to eat or drink or go shopping. They could even give me directions. So much for each person is different. You can't believe how many similarities there are!"

"Yeah, I guess you're right. So differences and similarities can exist side by side. 'All people are similar' and 'each one of us is unique'."

"Alright, so stop philosophizing and tell me what you think of my boss giving me this book. I'm not going to turn into an expert on China just because a few visitors from China will be running around the premises."

"Well, I'm afraid our opinions differ. I can understand your boss quite well. The Chinese not only have other customs and conventions, they have also developed a culture that is entirely different than ours."

"What do you mean culture? We're not interested in organizing some concert or art exhibit, nor is the Chinese state circus arriving with some sort of cultural agenda. All we are talking about here is a simple visit to our production facilities ... something that happens on a daily basis around here. The only difference is that these visitors aren't German, but Chinese, and that they are not staying for one day, but for four. What does that have to do with culture? Even in the book I mentioned, they refer to cultural differences, comparisons between cultures, intercultural learning, understanding culture, cultural influences and so on in every other sentence. You know what? I'm not at all worried about this visit. I've actually been looking forward to it. It'll be a pleasant change from some of the American or European visitors we get with their persistent questions. I've heard that the Asians are very reserved yet really friendly. But since my boss showed up with that book and now with you going on about culture, I'm starting to feel a bit edgy. I'm not even interested in going through with this anymore. It just means more work. I'm tired of hearing about all this culture stuff. I think I'll go over my presentation again and make sure there's enough tea. That should do the job."

1.1.2 What is Culture?

In cultures that differ radically from each other, human interaction develops along the lines of entirely different rules of conduct and regulations. Not knowing the rules, or understanding how to apply them, inevitably leads to misunderstandings in a given country. The rules we are speaking of here are nonnegotiable. They constitute a generally accepted mode of behavior in a given culture, are respected and adhered to. Most importantly, they impart an intrinsic sense of belonging to members of that culture.

There are many definitions of culture. By 1952, Kroeber and Kluckhorn had found over 150 and began comparing them.

The American psychologist Harry Triandis, for example, defines culture as "the human-made part of the environment" (1989, p. 306). The Dutch cultural psychologist Hofstede (1991) defines culture as "the collective programming of the mind". All researchers dealing with the concept of culture on a theoretical basis agree that culture covers a very broad field. The scope reaches from man-made objects, tools, etc. to values, ideas, worldviews, languages and philosophies, including the way in which animate and inanimate things, subjects and objects are treated.

A more practical, albeit narrower, definition of culture as applied, for instance, in the case of optimizing the conditions for cooperation between individuals from diverse cultural backgrounds postulates:

Culture is a universal phenomenon. All human beings live within a specific culture and contribute to its development. Culture creates a structured environment within which a population can function. It encompasses objects we created and use in our daily lives, as well as our institutions, ideas and values. Culture is always manifested in a system of orientation typical to a country, society, organization or group. This system of orientation consists of specific symbols such as language, body language, mimicry, clothing and greeting rituals and is passed on to future generations from the respective society, organization or group. This system of orientation provides all members with a sense of belonging and inclusion within a society or group and creates an environment in which individuals can develop a unique sense of self and function effectively. Culture has an influence on the perception, thought patterns, judgment and action of all members of a given society. The culture-specific system of orientation creates possibilities and motivation for action, but also determines the conditions and limits of the action (Thomas 2003).

The ability to orient in the world and to be able to rely on one's sense of orientation is a basic human need and central to a *system of orientation*. The need for orientation is met when an individual is equipped with an adequate amount of reliable knowledge about the material artifices and rituals of social interaction that define the particular environment and has the experience and ability to implement this knowledge efficiently and effectively. In an effort to obtain orientation, "culture", as defined here, allows us to find meaning in the things, people and objects that surround us, as well as in complex processes and the consequences of our behavior.

Under normal circumstances, we are not conscious of what "makes sense" to us, thus we perceive and process relevant information automatically. It is a uniquely individual experience that does not occur spontaneously or by coincidence, but is directed by collective, culturally relevant and binding social norms and rules.

Under "normal" everyday conditions, a person living in a culturally familiar setting is likely to be understood and accepted by other members of the collective who share the same cultural background. In special cases, clarification may be required to create rapport and understanding. However, the common culture-specific background knowledge is generally enough to facilitate mutual understanding without further clarification. In the course of each person's socialization process or the "absorption" into the society of a given culture, one is faced with the task of developing individual as well as socially relevant behavioral patterns and experiences in interactions with others. In this sense, the individual does indeed grow into the social network. This socialization process is not limited to early childhood nor to certain life phases, but continues to develop throughout life. Specific, socially relevant behavior must be learned during each developmental phase in order to deal effectively with difficulties in a given societal setting. The success of this socialization process or *inculturation* becomes evident when an individual acts in accordance with his worldview and this behavior is shared, understood and accepted by other individuals within a given social network. In this sense, culture provides a common frame of reference.

Once a person has passed through such a socialization process, he knows the ropes and is aware of what is acceptable and what is not. Appropriate behavior is acknowledged by society when the person acts according to existing norms and rules. Inappropriate behavior, on the other hand, results in direct or indirect disapproval and a sense of failure because efforts did not lead to success. If the socialization process in a particular field proves successful, then perception, thought, judgment and behavioral patterns are internalized to the point where general cognizance of the function, dynamics and consequences of these processes is no longer required. They have become part of the individual's operating behavior. Awareness of the processes sets in when unexpected and repeated events or reactions occur within the familiar social setting or in similar situations. Such a re-evaluation may occur on its own under favorable circumstances or through outside help. The situation is "reviewed" and subjected to critical censorship. This may result in a transformation of the familiar thought/action pattern and require a new system of socially relevant information processing. The individual learns new coping skills or "tools" (theories, methods, norms, rules etc.) with which to survive and reorient. These tools help in adapting to existing conditions in a natural social setting as well as to changes in existing situations. The benefits are twofold: on the one hand, individuals are able to adapt and on the other, to innovate.

The culture-specific system of orientation with it's sense-giving function and the tools required for adaptation that have been acquired during the course of an individual's socialization process do not apply if the interaction partner comes from another country, organization or group. The other-culture partner has developed a different culture whose members adhere to a different system of orientation, apply other adaptation and innovation tools and have internalized other norms, values and rules of behavior. This condition leads to a so-called critical interaction, in which either one of the partners, but most often both partners, are confronted by unexpected behavior and reactions, the meaning of which is not clear to them and which cannot be deciphered on the basis of their respective and familiar cultural system of orientation.

1.1.3 Cultural Standards

If culture is defined as a national and linguistic entity, which provides its members with a sense-giving system of orientation, then the question arises which culture-specific orientation signals come into play for persons of different cultures when the encounter takes place under particular circumstances such as conflict resolution or managing specific, work-related tasks. Observation and relevant research of German-American work groups (Zeutschel 1999) came up with the following results: During the product development phase, Americans tend to consider the potential customer and how the product can best serve them. Next, they determine effectiveness and customer advantage. After much discussion and mutual feedback, they get to work on the technical details involved in production. German technical experts, on the other hand, indulge in in-depth discussion about technical details and how to develop a near-perfect product according to the status of state-of-the-art technology. The goal, after long and detailed discussions on this topic, is to get a clear idea of the "problem" involved before getting to work on production. These different approaches are not coincidental, but rather a result of different culture-specific systems of orientation. On the one hand there is the effectiveness and customer orientation, and on the other, the emphasis on facts in connection with technical perfection. No doubt, both the German and the American project teams are equally goal and performance oriented. However, each is convinced that their problem-solving strategy is the more successful: a "trial and error" approach together with much feedback from the consumer and mutual support as opposed to "a search for meaning" and the central question of "what holds the world together", coupled with clearly assigned tasks and a high degree of initiative and responsibility.

Since these different behavioral patterns are not limited to specific project teams involved in a specific task under specific work conditions, but can be observed in typical American and German patterns of orientation related to complex problem solving, it can be assumed that different cultural standards apply in this situation.

In general, cultural standards can be defined on the basis of the following five indicators:

- Cultural standards are forms of perception, thought patterns, judgment and interaction that are shared by a majority of the members of a specific culture who regard their behavior as normal, typical and binding.
- Own and other unfamiliar behavior is directed, regulated and judged on the basis of this cultural standard.
- Cultural standards provide a regulatory function for mastering a given situation and dealing with people.
- The individual and group-specific way of applying cultural standards to adjust behavior can fluctuate within a range of tolerance.
- Forms of behavior that exceed this specific range are not accepted or sanctioned by the respective collective.

One can ask individuals from other countries what, in particular, they notice about their encounters with Germans and what difficulties they encounter repeatedly. For example, they find it difficult to understand their behavior and their reactions under certain circumstances and what factors seemed to contribute to complicated interaction? The information gleaned from these *critical interactions* lends itself to comparisons between countries and can be evaluated and analyzed on the basis of cause-and-effect in such difficult situations. The results point to a large consensus on a number of behaviorally relevant indicators, which can be defined as German cultural standards. Other indications of a German culture-specific worldview can differ depending on the perspective of dissimilar others. From the perspective of such culturally different countries as France, England, Spain, the Czech Republic, the U. S., China, Japan, Korea and Indonesia, German behavioral patterns in all areas of life are determined by its cultural standards (Thomas 2000a).

Seven German cultural standards and orientation patterns become evident on the basis of this research and emphasize:

- task orientation (tasks are more important than people)
- rules and regulations (structures and rules are held in high esteem, adhered to and expected)
- directness/truth (low-context communication style. There is right and wrong and very little in between. The most direct path is always the most goal oriented and efficient.)
- interpersonal distance (don't get involved in the business of others: keep your distance and be discrete!)
- internalized control
- time management (time is a valuable commodity and may not be squandered. Planning and scheduling are essential.)
- separation of the personal and public domains

If such culture-specific, in this case German, cultural standards are validated by other scientific disciplines such as literature, philosophy, sociology, ethnology and religion, in addition to studies in comparative culture, then it can be assumed that these are core cultural standards. Core cultural standards can be defined as such because they come into play not only in specific problem situations or a narrowly defined scope of action, but tend to mirror overall culture-specific orientation patterns. These standards become the unmistakable and characteristic behavioral patterns of individuals of a specific country or cultural environment.

In the example of the visiting Chinese delegation at the beginning of the chapter, the German host refuses to deal with the Chinese culture and his guests' cultural characteristics. After arguing with his colleague, he decides to concentrate on improving his presentation slides and "getting the job done". Again, the emphasis is on the task rather than the people involved. In this scenario, the German cultural standard of "task orientation" kicks into gear since the German expects to be successful if he behaves "normally", that is he welcomes his guests in a friendly manner, focuses on the facts and his task of hosting the delegation and presents highly sophisticated information. The Chinese guests, on the other hand, expect their German hosts to go out of their way to organize, facilitate and direct procedures in order to create an atmosphere of utmost social harmony and build a basis for mutual respect, trust and acknowledgment, especially since this is the delegation's first visit. The Chinese themselves are accustomed to such formalities and, as guests, will attempt to support their hosts in achieving this goal. Thus it is extremely important that social standing be emphasized in public, at meetings and dinner engagements. The social hierarchy becomes evident when high-ranking individuals are addressed first, receive sufficient praise and acknowledgment and are seated according to their rank. According to their specific cultural standard of "maintaining and giving face", the Chinese will attempt to simplify matters for the host by appearing modest to the point of self-effacement. They will compliment their host frequently, bring appropriate gifts upon their arrival and show profuse gratitude whenever possible. This show of modesty and discretion clearly does not indicate that they have nothing to say or do not have an opinion. Although they express gratitude at nearly every turn, it does not necessarily mean that they are overly impressed by their German partner's organizational ability with regard to the management of the site visit. All these gestures have to do with giving face in an attempt to create harmony and build trust. From the Chinese point of view, this behavior is a part of their natural etiquette and is expected in the presence of high-ranking hosts. If they were to behave differently, they would feel guilty and socially incompetent. Most likely, the head of the German delegation will remain oblivious to this aspect of his guests' behavior. From his purely task-oriented perspective, he will be aware of only a fraction of the efforts being made on the part of his Chinese partners to ensure an atmosphere of harmony. The behavioral aspects that he does notice, he will probably regard as unnecessary beating around the bush and irrelevant chitchat. His judgment and rejection of this behavior is based on his conviction that it has nothing to do with "the task" at hand and that there is no concrete reason for the exaggerated praise for task-related performance.

The example of comparisons between core cultural standards such as "task orientation" from the German perspective and "giving and maintaining face" on the part of the Chinese can also be observed in individuals from different national cultures in identical areas of task-related actions. Behavior can be documented and evaluated according to the differences and similarities observed, including the extent to which it differs. In the case of the previous example involving the different approaches to dealing with complex problem situations preferred by the German and American work teams, the domain or department-specific cultural standards become evident and can be defined. This makes it possible to predict and explain the observed individuals' behavioral patterns. In contrast to core cultural standards, domain-specific cultural standards require a specific task framework in which to operate, such as in the example given above involving complex problem-solving strategies in workgroups. Thus, they are goal, task and context bound and, as such, are relied on for orientation and applied by individuals who operate within this context.

Relevant studies (Thomas and Schenk 1996) indicate that aside from core and domain-specific cultural standards, something resembling contextual standards can also become operational. What is meant here is culture-specific basic orientation that obligates or even forces individuals of a given culture to act according to a very specific and narrowly defined basic behavioral pattern. This basic orientation operates holistically, that is, on all three psychologically relevant levels (cognitive, emotional and behavioral). According to Confucian teachings, the elderly are treated with reverence and special respect not only within the own family, but also in all aspects of public life, regardless of their social status, personal fame or personality (Thomas and Schenk, 2001). This form of "seniority orientation" is responsible for the profound transformation that takes place when a much older person joins a group of younger people of nearly the same age and begins to get involved in the social happening. The entire situation, the ambience and the social setting undergoes a shift. Everything changes. The operational frame of reference and the dynamic change as the focus shifts to the older person. Without having to speak or act in any particular way, all those present must reorient. Through activation of the contextual cultural standard "seniority orientation", new action impulses and possibilities arise but also impose limitations. Much of what occurs in the group after the older person arrives is the cultural standard in action, which, upon closer analysis, can only be understood within the context of the entire social setting.

1.1.4 Identifying Cultural Standards

Much research has been done in an effort to identify cultural standards (Tiandis 1995; Brislin et al. 1986; Landis and Bhagat 1996; Thomas 2000b), all of which attempted to analyze the so-called critical incidents. The goal here was to identify those cultural differences and special characteristics that came into play during an intercultural encounter. The most practical and frequently used approach is to interview a large pool of candidates with experience in diverse encounter situations, for example within the context of student and youth exchange programs, field experts assigned overseas or international experts working on assignments in Germany. The questions asked relate to the difficulties and problems they experienced repeatedly in dealing with foreign partners, which different, unexpected and inexplicable reactions they typically encountered on a regular basis when dealing with their other-culture partners and what explanations they had for unfamiliar and unexpected behavior. For instance, German managers in France were asked to describe encounters with their French partners, in which they frequently experienced unexpected behavior. In this example, the situational context, the Germans' own goals and expectations, as well as their observations, considerations, intentions and actions were noted. The French reaction to unexpected behavior on the part of the Germans and the Germans' assumptions about the underlying causes for the reactions were also documented.

Consequently, it is not the description of a particular situation, but rather about a prototypical interaction process that characterizes French behavior from the German perspective. After interviewing a large number of people, a single sentence that contributes to the critical interaction can be identified. This sentence is then analyzed in order to filter out the cultural standards that come into play during the interaction. The analysis is conducted by experts in the field of comparative culture studies, who are indigenous to and well versed in both cultures. A detailed analysis of the results is compared to earlier research findings based on comparisons, for example between German and French behavioral patterns, and provides insight into French cultural standards. The same holds true for German cultural standards upon analysis by French experts.

Cultural standards identified in this manner, say eight to twelve core cultural standards, are in no way indicative of an entire culture. Nor does a network of such cultural standards provide insight into what makes up the respective culture as a whole. They are, however, helpful in navigating and accumulating knowledge about the other-culture system of orientation and serve to explain unexpected and unfamiliar behavior on the part of the interaction partner. Such orientation aids also provide a point of reference from which to become aware of one's own system of cultural orientation and a basis for reflection.

The network between core cultural standards, their relevance to analyses based on cultural heritage and the context in which they arose can be combined with prototypical critical incident case studies to provide the basic background material for developing intercultural trainings. The goal of such trainings is to sensitize and prepare individuals for working with dissimilar others. At the same time, understanding that other-culture cultural standards have created their respective systems of orientation paves the way toward mutual respect and acknowledgment and lays the foundation for intercultural competence.

An ancient Chinese proverb states, "Only he who knows his opponent well can be victorious in a thousand battles". With reference to the challenges of an intercultural encounter, this wisdom could mean, "Only he who knows himself and his other-culture partner well can achieve mindful and productive cooperation". Well-founded knowledge of cultural standards together with the ability to deal with both own and other-culture standards, improve the chances of realistically perceiving other-culture behavior and of adequately reading characteristic signals of own and other-culture systems of orientation. Furthermore, they can be applied when initiating, directing and controlling behavior in an intercultural encounter. On the intentional level, such behavior is determined by cultural sensitivity. On the reactional level, it is determined by a high degree of intercultural understanding.

The actual encounter does not aim to adapt perfectly to the other-culture system of orientation nor does it attempt to force one's own system of orientation on the partner. Instead, the intercultural encounter is influenced by the intent to initiate and maintain an interpersonal cooperation based on respectfulness and esteem for cultural diversity. This allows both parties to deal with cultural differences productively without one-sided dominance and loss of orientation.

References

Brislin, R. W.; Cushner, K.; Cherry, C.; Yong, M. (1986): Intercultural Interactions: A Practical Guide. Beverly Hills.

Hofstede, G. (1991): Culture and Organization – Software of the Mind. London.

Kroeber, A. L.; Kluckhohn, C. (1952): Culture: A critical review of concepts and definitions. Cambridge, 47 (1).

Landis, D.; Bhagat, R. S. (Eds.) (1996): Handbook of Intercultural Training. Newbury Park.

Smith, A. H. (1900): Chinesische Charakterzüge. Würzburg.

Thomas, A. (2000a): Globalisierung und interkulturelle Managementkompetenz. In: Fahrenhorst, B.; Musto, St. A. (Eds.), Grenzenlos. Kommunikation, Kooperation, Entwicklung. Berlin, pp. 162–174.

Thomas, A. (2000b): Forschung zur Handlungswirksamkeit von Kulturstandards. In: Handlung, Kultur, Interpretation – Zeitschrift für Sozial- und Kulturwissenschaften, 9 (2), pp. 231–278.

Thomas, A. (2003): Psychologie Interkulturellen Handelns. 2nd ed. Göttingen.

Thomas, A.; Schenk, E. (1996): Handlungswirksamkeit zentraler Kulturstandards in der Interaktion zwischen Deutschen und Chinesen. Regensburg, unveröffentlichter Abschlussbericht Projekt Nr. II/673621 Volkswagen-Stiftung.

Thomas, A.; Schenk, E. (2001): Beruflich in China. Trainingsprogramm für Manager, Fach- und Führungskräfte. Göttingen.

Triandis, H. C. (1989): Intercultural Education and Training. In: Funke, P. (Ed.), Understanding the US – Across Culture Prospective. Tübingen, pp. 305–322.

Triandis, H. C. (1995): Culture specific assimilations. In: Fouler, S.; Manford, M. (Eds.), Intercultural Sourcebook (Vol. 1). Yarmonth.

Zeutschel, U. (Ed.) (1999): Interkulturelle Synergie in Arbeitsgruppen. Lengerich.

Alexander Thomas

1.2 National and Organizational Cultures

1.2.1 Problematic Issues

The headlines in the daily *Frankfurter Allgemeine* newspaper read, "Mr. Schrempp, why don't you just sell the whole mess!" Susanne Preuß, of the same paper, further states: "Reuter's scheme is outdated and problems are escalating at the automobile manufacturer, Daimlerchrysler. Reuter was blamed for his lack of technological know-how and market savvy (MBB), for misjudging profit forecasts and follow-up costs (AEG), for the incompatibility of corporate culture and poor cooperation between top management (Fokker), for granting too little influence to minority shareholders (Dornier) and inadequate information policies on the part of the holding company. The company names are interchangeable: Smart, Adtrans, Chrysler, Mitsubishi and Hyundai. The criticism could apply to Schrempp point for point. In retrospect, the Reuter era and Schrempp's performance during this time confronted both him and his team with nearly insurmountable challenges" (2000, p. 21).

Aside from the "hard facts", estimates relative to market and technology factors, revenue and profit calculations, and "mutually incompatible corporate cultures" played and still play a central role in the problems faced by national and international mergers and their management. According to a consensus of opinion on research findings by economist, over half of all national and international mergers do not meet the expectations with which they started out, fail within the first four years and then disappear from sight (Cartwright and Cooper 1992; Gomez and Weber 1989; Buono and Bowditch 1989; Hofstede 1997).

"The importance of the cultural dimension for the development and implementation of strategic goals in general is also widely accepted and empirically tested. Somewhat less acknowledged, however, although hardly ever disputed, is the potential impact, both positive and negative, of cultural aspects on the success of M&A activity. Such dimensions are often simply ignored, for example, in the pre-integration phases of acquisitions, or hardly ever considered (specifically and consciously) during due diligence and the integration phase" (Forstmann 1998, p. 57).

Assuming the definition of "cultural dimension" in this context includes successful management, then we are speaking of at least two levels of culture: the corporate culture, on the one hand, and national culture including the interdependencies among them, on the other.

1.2.2 National Cultures

We can assume that culture can be defined as a system of orientation that provides individuals from the same country with meaning and, to a great extent, defines their sense of belonging. The respective culture-specific system of orientation influences each member of a social network at the very basic psychological level of experience and behavior (perception, thought, feeling and action). Moreover, each member is actively involved in the further development of this system of orientation. On the basis of this assumption, the influence national culture has over so-called corporate culture becomes evident.

National culture can be defined as the culture a population is born into, the development of which they have contributed to and which they consider to be binding and essential for survival. National culture can be said to embody the collective consciousness of a people, more specifically, values that have been passed down through the generations (norms, behavioral rules, customs, laws and traditions) and ethical-moral beliefs (religion), which combine to determine their view of the world.

Research studies in the area of social sciences regarding the development of values and value changes within a society unanimously indicate that self-actualization in professional and private life is a central, value-laden goal. The realization of this goal, however, is only possible in a culture that encourages and rewards thinking and acting in relation to self-actualizing. Self-actualization is unthinkable in a national culture whose members are convinced that everything they think or do is predetermined, is in God's hands or depends on the whims of gods and spirits. Anyone belonging to such a culture and who strives for self-actualization sets himself apart from society and might even be accused of conspiring against it.

Self-actualization has to do with equal opportunity, responsibility for oneself, freedom of choice, self-sufficiency, social equality and social acceptability. An entire network of values, norms, attitudes, and rules of behavior must be present in a national culture and society for them to be accepted, supported and developed further. These features are a prerequisite if self-actualization is to become a worthwhile and basically attainable goal. The modern ideal of self-actualization is deeply rooted in the Christian faith. "Love thy neighbor as you would thyself." The postulate is a central theme in Christianity that allows for, even demands, self-actualization, provided it is socially acceptable. "Thy neighbor" here refers to all individuals regardless of gender, race, religion and origin.

Far from being static, immobile structures, national cultures are continually developing. At any given time in every given national culture and society, problems and obstacles must be overcome while simultaneously devising, introducing, testing and implementing a huge variety of solutions. An example of such a long-term transformation in Western society over the last one hundred years is evidenced by the shift of gender-specific roles. We have moved from a gender-specific distribution of rights and duties to a gender-unspecific version, which has dramatically changed the norms and roles of the past. This continual development permeates all aspects of society. A comparatively open and dynamic society nurtures individual life preferences and encourages creativity. Under these circumstances all forms of gender-unspecific roles are possible. There is much experimentation, praise and pseudo-commitment and just as much is rejected after a short time. What little remains is accepted, acknowledged and recognized as binding by a clear majority within a society or an influential minority group. It is integrated into the culture's system of organization and is passed on to the next generation in the form of values, norms and rules of behavior.

Referring to a German national culture, for instance, sounds very abstract and irrelevant to everyday life. If one were to speak in more concrete terms about significant characteristics of a German national culture, such as self-actualization and equal rights, then broader issues might crop up which would include other-culture individuals. In any case, the term "national cultures" is too intangible for it to be relevant to daily life.

Empirically based research (Thomas 2000; 2003) has attempted to explore the experiences of individuals from different national cultures upon meeting and cooperating with each other and to identify some of the typical characteristics of national cultures (see chapters 1, 1.1).

The manager of a prestigious German bank in China, with whom he had been employed for eight years, mentioned in an interview that he experiences cultural differences on a daily basis with his Chinese wife, who happens to run her own business. Although he has gotten used to the differences, he is still acutely aware of them. He is, however, able to react in such a way as to avoid serious miscommunication. Hence, the lasting and binding effect that cultural orientation systems have on even a longstanding and close relationship becomes evident.

1.2.3 Corporate Culture

In both business and the sciences, problems related to cultural differences and culture-specific cooperation problems occur most often on the level of national culture rather than in corporate culture, the culture of an industry, a department or work group-specific culture. If culture manifests within "a nation, society, organization or group-specific system of orientation", then it makes sense to differentiate between the cultural levels before analyzing the nature of their interrelatedness. Everything mentioned in relation to national culture above, its development, characteristic and effect, also applies to subcultures, where individuals grow into or group together in a collective, either voluntarily or involuntarily, and think, feel and act as members of a social community. If such social structures could, or in fact do, become personally meaningful in terms of life preferences, or career development, then specific systems of meaning and orientation emerge within these communities, allowing specific cultures to develop. Such subcultures cannot be uniformly and systematically specified and labeled. Both categorization and definition are relatively arbitrary. However, beneath the so-called national culture, two extreme poles of a subculture emerge: corporate and organizational culture and the dyadic group culture. Regardless of their size, corporations and organizations inevitably form cultures that intrinsically influence the behavior of their members, in other words, in their interaction with other members of the organization, and also outwardly, or in encounters with people outside the organization. Furthermore, there are job categories (e.g., technicians and retailers), business and economic sectors (e.g., the automobile industry or construction industry) and even broader business segments like the trades and manufacturing, all of which evolve their own specific cultures. These cultures impact the thinking and behavior of individuals who grew into and identify with the culture. In Germany, for instance, the trades have their own traditions and are very different from the culture of industry. During their years of training or apprenticeship in an industry or a trade, the trainees are imbued with different values, norms and rules of behavior to the degree that an employee, highly qualified in his field, finds it difficult to move from a culture of the trades to that of industry and vice versa. Within the industry itself and even between departments or in work teams, the job-related and culture-specific differences between salespeople and technicians are so pronounced that they find it not only difficult to communicate, but hardly seem to speak the same "language". They tend to prefer fundamentally different problem-solving strategies and are often incapable of cooperating on performance and quality evaluations. Most individuals grow into such career and job-related cultures and have, during the course of their job-related socialization, acquired and incorporated its value system, its norms and regulatory system in order to conform as closely as possible to its standards. The dyadic group culture on the other end of the spectrum shows a high degree of cultural independence in their development. The smallest conceivable group is a two-person dyad. Two individuals who fall in love with each other and proceed to enter into a close, long-term relationship are, in a socio-psychological sense, a group (small group). They agree on common norms and values, insist on maintaining their own habits, but also adapt to their partner's habits, make compromises and develop a set of specific and often new values, norms and rules of behavior. This might go as far as creating completely new means of verbal and nonverbal expression. They develop an independent group culture based on the interests and needs of this specific dyad.

The corporate culture has undergone a varied and contradictory development in the economic sciences and in business practice (Höh 2000). There have always been times when what was believed to be "corporate culture" was held in high esteem, and times in which the emphasis was on dominant qualitative features of the "corporate structure". Process-oriented economic scholars disqualified the idea of corporate culture and used the term to explain factors that defied definition. Still, Schein's (1985) suggested definition of corporate culture, and the three-level-model that builds upon it, provides the basis for the academic analysis of corporate culture. Schein defines corporate culture as "a pattern of common basic assumptions which the group has learned in the course of overcoming problems of external adaptation and inner integration, and which have proved to be successful. Over time, the patterns became binding and were passed on to new members as a rational and emotionally correct approach in dealing with such problems (1985/1995, p. 25)." Schein's three-level-model is shown in Figure 1 below.

Material and immaterial artifacts based on Schein's three-level-model are easily identified by observation. It is difficult, however, to decipher and interpret the effect they have on the behavior of corporate employees. Values, norms and rules of behavior shared by members of a corporation can be identified on the underlying level, the effects of which can be experienced to a certain extent. In part, the members are also aware of these effects or can be sensitized to them. Such values, norms and rules of behavior influence experience and behavior to a greater degree than the above-mentioned artifacts. Values which are largely accepted and which have proven successful in the attainment of corporate goals evolve into generally shared basic assumptions (collective consciousness). Basic assumptions or premises are essentially the central building blocks of the corporate system of orientation. Members of a corporation have internalized the values to

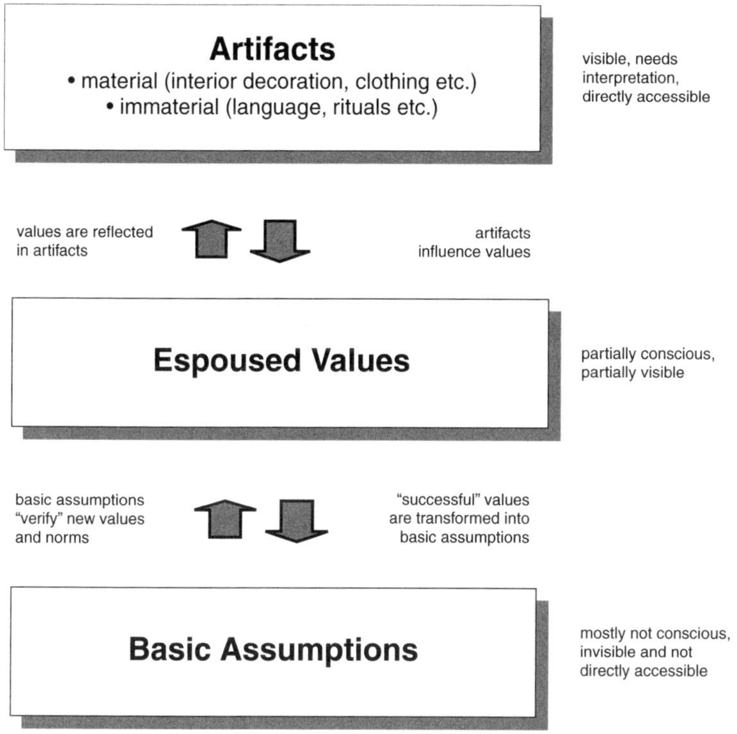

Figure 1: The three-level-model of corporate culture (according to Höh, p. 19)

the point where cognition is no longer required and as such, they are no longer at the forefront of critical analysis. They do, however, strongly influence the members' sense of perception, thought patterns, judgment and action. Once the corporation and its members identify with the basic assumptions, their behavior and work-related activity manifest an understanding of the corporate culture. Against this backdrop, a corporation can be seen as a miniature society, to which all members contribute in terms of development, design and legacy. The corporate-specific system of sense-giving, knowledge-providing and personal meaning has been created in the process of daily interaction between members and is a fundamental aspect of corporate culture, creating a common basis for its members, allowing them to share a common perception of themselves and their environment and accepted orientation guidelines for their behavior (orientation certainty). According to this understanding, a corporation does not represent a given reality. Rather, it is subjective and interactively created through social norms and values shared by all members of the corporation.

According to Kasper (1987), corporate culture can be identified by ten characteristic features: corporate culture is created by human beings, determines behavior, is the result of collective action and its basic premises are acknowledged by all its members. Corporate culture is passed on and can be learned through symbols and modeling. It is adaptable to changes in the environment and demands of the organization. In principal, members are aware of all aspects of the corporate culture. During the working day, however, these characteristics remain below the surface of consciousness. In fact, they are generally not required for routine working-day activities and are not readily accessible. Consequently, they can only be experienced once the message has been decoded. The corporate culture can be perceived in terms of both the result and the process of corporate-specific development. Proceeding from this more interpretive understanding of corporate culture (corporation = culture), different subcultures within a common corporate culture become specified and begin nesting into each other while remaining interconnected within the system. Seen from this perspective, the corporation itself can be defined as a subsystem of the national or societal culture (see Figure 2).

This box model illustrates a number of characteristic features:

1. The larger systems and the subsystems influence each other. The national/societal culture influence corporate culture to a great extent (Ogilvie 1992; Scholz and Hofbauer 1990; Hofstede 1991) on the one hand, and on the other, the corporate culture influences the national culture. As mentioned earlier, the industry itself also impacts corporate culture and vice versa (Schulz-Gambard et al 1997).

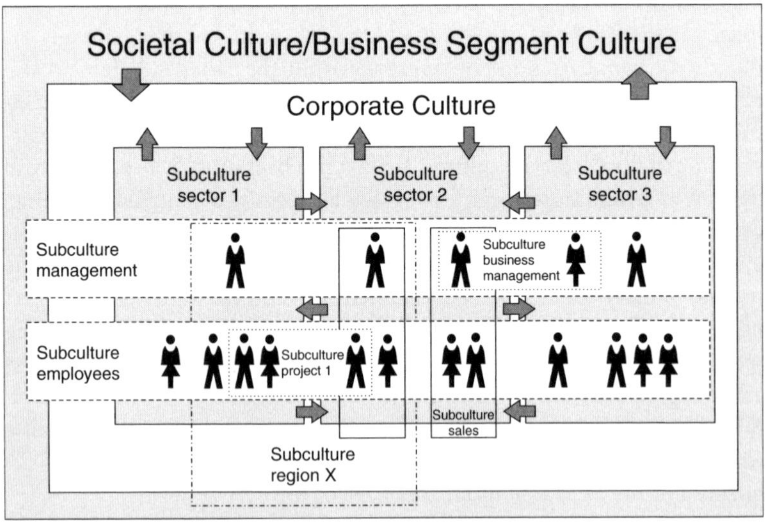

Figure 2: The Cultural Boxes Model (according to Höh 2002, p. 30)

2. The respective subsystems exist in interdependent relationships. Thus business sector 1 and business sector 2 influence each other. The subcultures, represented by management and employees, also exist in interdependent entities (Schwarz 1987).
3. Each member of the corporation automatically belongs to several subcultures. A person can be a member of the Marketing Department and belong to its corresponding subculture. At the same time, this person could be a senior manager in a related subculture while belonging to the job culture of business management and be a member of a project group that has developed its own specific subculture. Moreover, the person is still a part of the culture of the corporation and a member of a certain national culture (Berthoin et al. 1993).

Change processes within and across subcultures are possible. Assuming new functions and positions within the corporation changes the relevance of the respective subcultures and the relationship between them. The process also affects the relationship between the subcultures and each of its members in terms of proximity and shared interests.

1.2.4 National Culture and Corporate Culture within the Context of Internationalization

Internationalization in all areas of society such as in politics, economics, the arts, cooperation in developmental aid, and working with young people always results in cultural encounters on different levels. Individuals from different cultures come together in work groups, which are composed of national or multinational members and are required to cooperate. Departments, companies and organizations composed of different national cultures collaborate, form alliances or fuse across national and cultural borders.

Figure 3 differentiates between three cultural levels: the group culture, the corporate culture and the national culture. This clearly simplifies matters compared to the factors that actually come into play. As mentioned earlier, industry, job and status-specific factors have a considerable effect on the work environment and within what is here defined as corporate and group culture.

The individual is interactively linked between these levels and takes an active part in influencing and creating such cultures, has grown into these cultures in the process of individual socialization and has incorporated the

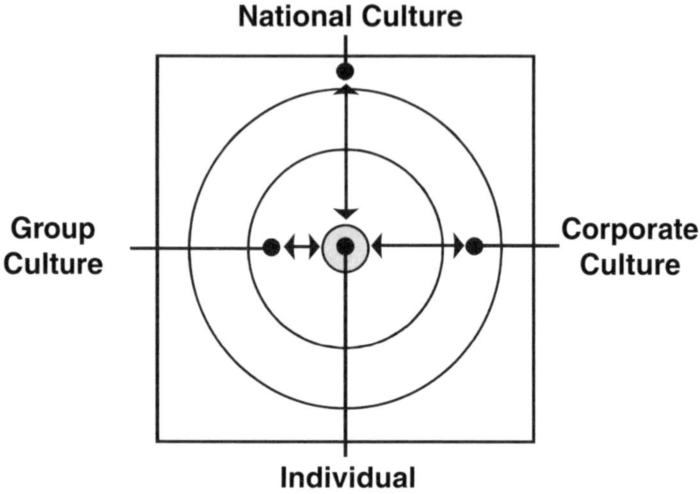

Figure 3: Intranational Cultural Level

culture's socio-relevant values, norms and behavioral patterns. Respective cultural orientation systems provide the individual with a sense-making mechanism and a guide for attributing meaning. Moreover, the different intracultural levels exert an influence on each other. Values which have determined behavior over decades in an organization, and which are lived and propagated, influence organizational group culture while operating safely along the lines of a national culture's orientation system. This applies as long as the corporation abides by a national culture orientation in theory (e.g., leadership clauses) and practice (e.g., social behavior in employee interaction).This can change if employees and leadership is made up of different nationalities, i.e., are internationally aligned.

Regardless of whether cross-border mergers or international teams are involved, there can be no "clean slate" or neutral point of departure devoid of all previous developments and cultural conditioning. During such a beginning phase there is much talk of corporate vision, new starts, paradigm shifts and pioneering new horizons. The assumption seems to be that all employees of the new organization will perceive the change as such, which is rarely enough the case, considering that each participant stands within the relative continuity of his life development and corporate history from which he has drawn and continues to draw his values, orientation, positive and negative experiences, as well as his convictions about the world around him. New developments brought on by international project teams, mergers or joint ventures affect participating employees on all levels, at best, by enriching their experiences in tackling formerly unknown tasks and challenges and offering opportunities for further development. The experience, however, also involves dealing with new challenges. Opportunities arise when groups come together and create a new social reference and new standards of evaluation, offering the chance to compare concepts of performance, ability, opinion, norms and rules of behavior, which enables the individual to broaden his social identity and access entirely new possibilities.

Every international joint venture is dependent on the development of the employees' manifested identification with the new joint operation, which, over time, replaces identification with the original organization with a more meaningful and dominant model. Joint ventures and mergers have failed repeatedly in the past, due to the inability to sever ties with the old structures and to create stronger identification and bonding with the new organization. This process requires concrete measures and work on identification issues (Vogl 2000; Höh 2000). Employees must be able to recognize and experience first-hand that their basic needs are being met. These include a sense of security regarding orientation, individual responsibility and enhancement of self-worth, all of which may have been taken for granted in the original organization. Employees must recognize that these basic qualities are guaranteed and are just as reliable and possibly better in the new work environment. The new corporate and group culture, while it is still in its developmental stage, must offer considerable incentive in order to move employees to integrate corporate values, norms and rules of behavior. Applied consistently, the old, familiar patterns will in time be replaced by the new standards. Not everything will be new. Much of what was proven successful in the past, such as rules and norms, which are inextricably entwined in the orientation system of the national culture, are carried over, as they must be, so that a sufficient sense of security regarding appropriate and acceptable behavior is maintained.

Leadership in international mergers requires considerable foresight in deciding what essential elements from the former corporate culture need to be incorporated into the new order and what new values, norms and rules of behavior will have to be accepted, learned and developed in order to deal successfully with new responsibilities. Both the old and new systems must be brought together in a new corporate culture, the modus operandi of which must be communicated to the employees in such a way that it is understood and accepted by everyone involved, is learnable and can be experienced in such a way as not to interfere with the familiar work environment and the sense of security provided by the former system. A gradual transition will facilitate the identification process with the new corporate culture.

References

Berthoin, A.; Dierkes, M.; Helmers, S. (1993): Unternehmenskultur: Eine Forschungsagenda aus Sicht der Handlungsperspektive. In: Dierkes, M.; Rosenstiel, L. v.; Steger, U. (Eds.), Unternehmenskultur in Theorie und Praxis. Konzepte aus Ökonomie, Psychologie und Ethnologie. Frankfurt a. M., pp. 200–218.

Buono, A. F.; Bowditch, J. L. (1989): The Human Side of Mergers and Acquisitions. San Francisco.

Cartwright, S.; Cooper, C. L. (1992): Mergers and Acquisitions: The Human Factor. Oxford.

Dierkes, M., Rosenstiel, L. v.; Steger, U. (Eds.) (1993): Unternehmenskultur in Theorie und Praxis. Konzepte aus Ökonomie, Psychologie und Ethnologie. Frankfurt a. M.

Forstmann, S. (1998): Managing Cultural Differences in Cross-cultural Mergers and Acquisitions. In: Gertsen, M. C.; Soederberg, A.-M.; Torp, J. E. (Eds.), Cultural Dimensions of International Mergers and Acquisitions. Berlin/New York, pp. 57–83.

Gomez, P.; Weber, B. (1989): Akquisitionsstrategie: Wertsteigerung durch Übernahme von Unternehmungen. Zürich.

Hofstede, G. (1991): Culture and Organization – Software of the Mind. London.

Hofstede, G. (1997): Lokales Denken, globales Handeln. Kulturen, Zusammenarbeit und Management. Nördlingen.

Höh, S. (2000): Entwicklung eines methodischen Rahmenkonzepts zur qualitativen Erfassung von Unternehmenskulturen. Eine empirische Feldstudie. Regensburg. (Unveröff. Dissertation).

Kasper, H. (1987): Organisationskultur. Über den Stand der Forschung. Wien.

Ogilvie, E. (1992): Die Kulturperspektive von Unternehmungen. Eine Analyse aus wirtschaftspsychologischer Sicht. Frankfurt a. M.

Preuß, S. (2000): Herr Schrempp, verkaufen Sie den ganzen Schrott! Frankfurter Allgemeine Zeitung (FAZ) vom 25.11.2000/275: pp. 21.

Schein, E. H. (1985): Organizational Culture and Leadership. A Dynamic View. San Francisco. (Dt.: Unternehmenskultur. Ein Handbuch für Führungskräfte. Frankfurt a. M./New York 1995).

Scholz, C.; Hofbauer, W. (1990): Organisationskultur. Die 4 Erfolgsprinzipien. Wiesbaden.

Schulz-Gambard, J.; Altenburger, R.; Breitenstein, U.; Schwarz, A. (1997): Führungsstile und Unternehmenskultur in deutschen Unternehmen. München.

Schwarz, G. (1987): Kulturelle Einflussgrößen des Projektmanagements. Zeitschrift Führung und Organisation (zfo) 4: 241–248.

Thomas, A. (2000): Forschungen zur Handlungswirksamkeit von Kulturstandards. Handlung Kultur Interpretation. Zeitschrift für Sozial- und Kulturwissenschaften (9) 2: 231–279.

Thomas, A. (2003): Psychologie interkulturellen Lernens und Handelns. In: Thomas, A. (Ed.), Kulturvergleichende Psychologie. 2nd ed. Göttingen, pp. 433–485.

Vogl, C. (2000): Deutsch-chinesische Joint Ventures unter besonderer Beachtung interkultureller Aspekte. Eine empirische und theoretische Untersuchung. Regensburg. (Unveröff. Dissertation).

Alexander Thomas

1.3 The Self, The Other, The Intercultural

1.3.1 Individual Perspectives

The American psychologist, Harry Triandis, observes the unsuccessful cooperation between an American manager and his Greek colleague in an American subsidiary in Greece in his book "The Analysis of Subjective Culture" (1972). He lists the dialogue in the column "Behavior" and the communication partner's corresponding thoughts, intentions and feelings in a second column entitled "Attribution", which occurs when one partner attributes causal characteristics to the other partner's behavior. Figure 1 depicts the course of interaction.

In this diagram, the cultural overlap becomes evident. That is, both partners are caught between two different systems of cultural orientation, which can be more or less clearly perceived, and are thus unable to act according to one specific system. The encounter between the American supervisor and the Greek employee within the context of a supervisor-employee relationship creates a situation in which there is a cultural overlap and which calls for conditions and motivation for action, but also limits it. Both cultural characteristics must come into play while developing a new "third" culture in the course of their interaction that combines thought patterns and behavior of both parties (Breitenbach 1975).

The following scenario is played out: The American supervisor was raised, so was socialized and educated in the United States. Being a successful specialist in his field, he was chosen for an international assignment. His Greek employee grew up in and was educated in Greece and, like his American supervisor, has enjoyed a successful career and was consequently hired by an American subsidiary in Greece. If he were not considered qualified, he would not have been assigned to complete the complicated report in such a short time period. Both parties do not seem to be prejudiced in any way.

Both the American boss and the Greek employee accept the hierarchical relationship they share. Neither one of them is aggressive. They are friendly towards each other, willing and cooperative in an effort to achieve a common goal. Apparently there are no language barriers. Both understand the issue at hand: a report must be written and completed by a certain deadline.

Table 1: The American supervisor and his Greek employee

Behavior	**Attribution**
American: How long will it take you to finish this report?	*American:* I asked him to participate.
Greek: I don't know. How long should it take?	*Greek:* His behavior makes no sense. He's the boss. Why doesn't he tell me? *American:* He refuses to take responsibility. *Greek:* I asked him for instructions.
American: You are in the best position to analyze time requirements.	*American:* I press him to take responsibility for his actions. *Greek:* What nonsense! I'd better give him an answer.
Greek: Ten days.	*American:* He lacks the ability to estimate time; this estimate is totally inadequate.
American: Take 15. So it's agreed, you will do it in 15 days?	*American:* I offer him a contract. *Greek:* These are my orders: 15 days.
	Actually, the report required 30 working days. The Greek employee worked day and night but at the end of day 15, he needed an additional day.
American: Where's my report?	*American:* I'm making sure he fulfills his contract. *Greek:* He is asking for the report.
Greek: It'll be ready tomorrow.	Both attribute that it isn't ready.
American: But we had agreed it would be ready today.	*American:* I must teach him how to fulfill a contract *Greek:* The stupid, incompetent boss! Not only did he give me the wrong orders, but he doesn't appreciate that I did a 30-day job in 16 days.
The Greek hands in his resignation.	The American is surprised. *Greek:* I can't work for this person.

From: Triandis, H. C.; Vassiliou, V. (1972): A comparative analysis of subjective culture. In: Triandis, H. C. (Publisher), The Analysis of Subjective Culture. New York, pp. 299–335.

These are all optimal conditions for a productive cooperation. Still, the Greek employee hands in his resignation at the end of the episode: "I can't work for this person!" The American is taken by surprise by his employee's behavior. Why?

Both partners think and act from the perspective of their own cultural understanding (mono-cultural), although they are actually in a situation of cultural overlap. Both are thoroughly convinced that they are right and acting in accordance with achieving the set goal. They are just as convinced that the other partner is in the wrong, acts contrary to producing effective results and that his behavior makes no sense. The partners are not aware

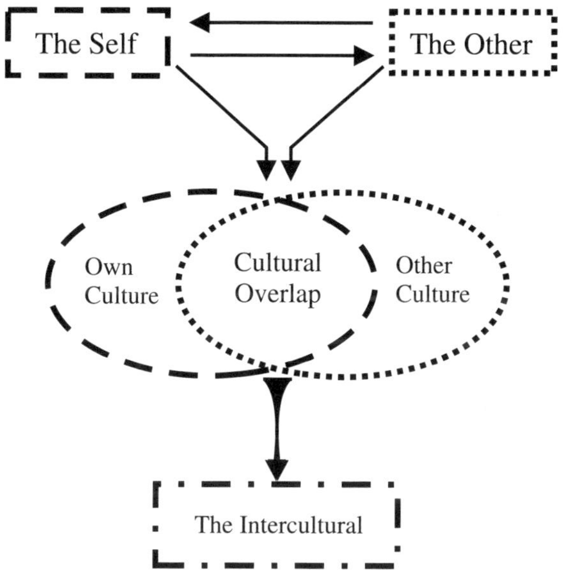

Figure 4: The dynamic in situations where cultural overlap occurs

of their own system of orientation and are oblivious to the other's. Moreover, they do not realize that in the given situation of cultural overlap, their behavior requires an intercultural "savoir faire" for each to feel comfortable with the transaction (Figure 4).

As can be seen from Figure 4, cultural overlaps occur when otherness impacts own-culture perspective and when interaction occurs between dissimilar others. Ambiguity, vagueness and novelty fill a gap that opens up between familiarity and the encroaching other. The ambiguity can be experienced as threatening or stimulating. In idiomatic terms, this is where you risk "putting your foot in it", when you submit to otherness but are oblivious to other-culture characteristics or peculiarities.

Under favorable conditions, interactive behavior can be alternatively determined by one's own culture and the other culture (alternate adaptation). If otherness dominates, however, the opposite is true (one-sided, forced adaptation). The interaction depicted in the above example between the American manager and his Greek employee points to the development of precisely this dynamic. Dissimilar culture-based behavior stands in continual contrast without ever reaching anything resembling a synthesis and creating something new as a result of the intercultural encounter (Thomas 2003b).

Research into the dynamics occurring in overlap situations (Bochner 1982) have found four different types of behavioral rules:

- *The concept of dominance:* Own-culture values and norms are considered superior to those of other cultures and must dominate the interaction. Thus, in the example, the American concept of leadership should be valid for the Greek employee, as the Greek concept of hierarchy (paternalism) should apply when cooperating with an American supervisor. German work ethic, Western methods of conflict resolution, Asian crisis management and French problem-solving strategies, among others, are preferred and considered to be more appropriate and are therefore routinely enforced over methods of solution-finding developed by other cultures. The partner is put under pressure to adapt until he submits and learns to adopt the dominant partner's cultural standards.
- *Concept of assimilation:* Other-culture values and norms are readily accepted and integrated into personal behavior patterns. The tendency to adapt to the other culture can become pronounced to the extent that one's own cultural identity risks becoming a part of the other culture. Individuals adapt to the dominant culture's national and company-specific norms and values in an effort to avoid criticism of their behavior and to minimize the pressure to adapt. They may even feel that the other-culture system of orientation is superior and try hard to adapt to it, as is the case in extreme forms of xenophilia (love of otherness). Assuming an other-culture orientation system and the willingness to assimilate frequently occur for purely pragmatic reasons, in order to minimize the pressure that arises from the experience of constant discrepancy between one's own and the other culture.
- *Concept of divergence:* Values and norms of both cultures are considered meaningful and effective. Many elements are incompatible, however, and continually contradict each other. The inability to integrate these elements leads to divergencies that cannot be resolved, causing a continual back-and-forth between own- and other-culture orientation systems. This development becomes particularly evident during the beginning phase of intercultural collaboration and may result in identity vulnerability and doubts about the validity of values, norms and modes of behavior within the context of the collaboration. Low morale and motivation, weak group cohesion and loss of commitment are likely outcomes in the long run.
- *Synthesis concept:* The partners are able to extract meaningful elements from both cultures and to combine them in a new high quality entity. The result is then no longer based on cultural preferences, but rather on a new concept, involving a creative synthesis of different cultural approaches and resources. This new understanding forms mutually binding norms so that, under favorable circumstances, cultural synergizing can take place.

In the example of cooperation between the American boss and the Greek employee, the synergizing effect obviously does not occur. Each partner fails to grasp the other's point of view during the course of the encounter. The American supervisor's leadership style calls for participation, assuming that the Greek employee is willing and qualified to contribute to planning tasks, organizing his work, scheduling and taking responsibility. This style complies with modern American management methods and with the American concept of a dedicated employee. In contrast, the Greek employee is used to much more supervision and involvement by his supervisor where interrelated task assignments are concerned. He expects his supervisor to give clear and informed instructions on the basis of his understanding of the assigned task. The Greek employee needs these instructions from above to which he can adhere and upon which he can depend. He almost certainly assumes that his supervisor is specially trained and qualified for this job, and that this is the reason for his higher salary. He is unable to comprehend why work organization such as time management, workload and the time it takes to complete a task should be his responsibility. The example illustrates the different behavior patterns shown by both partners, including the way each person interprets the other's actions and can be understood in light of the respective concepts of role distribution, that is, the role of supervisor and that of an employee. The respective role characteristics are derived from a corporate culture-specific and, to a larger extent, from a national culture-specific foundation. Seen from this perspective, the partners' behavior makes sense. During their encounter, the partners are not aware of this underlying national and corporate culture-specific premise, which would explain their utterly different and unexpected behavior. Instead, each interprets the other's behavior as inappropriate. On the one hand, the supervisor's behavior is interpreted as incompetent. The employee, on the other hand, is seen as poorly organized and reluctant to assume responsibility. The next section will deal more closely with the underlying psychological constellation and conditions for this behavior.

1.3.2 Special Challenges in Intercultural Cooperation

The dynamics between experience and behavior in situations of cultural overlap creates several different challenges. Dealing successfully with these challenges is a difficult undertaking.

Requirements of Own-Culture Orientation

Individuals normally assume that the way they behave is also the way others all over the world behave. They feel justified in their assumption because, as a rule, they share a great deal of similarities and interests with others belonging to the same culture and often also the same subculture. For this reason we are generally spared conflicting interests, misunderstandings and unexpected reactions in our interactions. Overall, we cooperate and get along with each other. If it becomes evident that certain individuals in the familiar setting are not behaving according to familiar mental scripts, then this is cause for concern. In particularly important or reoccurring situations, the person in question tries to find out why his partners are not behaving in a familiar fashion according to his expectations. He might try to find out more about his partner and consults confidants in an attempt to analyze cause and effect. Most individuals believe that the way they perceive the world, the way in which they evaluate themselves and their environment, and the methods with which they try to direct and influence others are acceptable and appropriate. Dissimilar perception, evaluation and influence, experienced first hand and reflected upon, is judged as inappropriate, not quite right, incomplete, primitive or deliberately manipulated.

Another important factor is the way in which one's own-culture orientation system retrieves and processes information and how it evaluates and reacts to unfamiliar behavior, all of which have become second nature to the individual during the course of his unique development (socialization). Under normal circumstances, our routine activities have become largely automated and no longer require acute awareness. Only when things go contrary to expectation, and the familiar routine is interrupted, do such anomalies merit closer scrutiny and might be brought up in a confidential discussion. Quite often such deviations from the norm are interpreted from the perspective of habituated mental scripts (expectations, habits, e.g., assimilated) or they are accepted as an inevitable part of life, thus weakening the impact to the point where a counter-reaction becomes unnecessary and is more or less willingly endured. Partners in mixed marriages and partnerships perceive dissimilar elements about their partners on a regular basis even after years of living together. Time and time again they are perplexed by particular reactions, but have learned to interpret and process them adequately.

In their everyday behavior, individuals within a relatively closed, same-culture environment are so habituated to their familiar patterns of perception, thought, judgment and behavior that they are no longer consciously aware of them. At certain points during an individual's development, these patterns were at the forefront of consciousness and could be consciously activated again under certain conditions. For example, conflict-laden events and a partner's unexpected reactions in a crisis can certainly result in such extreme discomfort that those involved resort to a conscious cause and effect analysis. The self, habit and things we take for granted become an issue when observing children, old people or foreigners who deal with objects and people differently, or who behave contrary to familiar patterns. There are readily available explanations for the behavior of children, old people, the handicapped and foreigners. For example, children have not yet learned certain behavior, old people can no longer apply it, handicapped people are no longer capable of accessing the "right" reactions due to their particular handicap and foreigners have not learned how to behave "correctly" because they are not familiar with the culture.

A particular challenge is posed by the unique culturally habituated mental scripts of human beings everywhere, which are considered axiomatic, accepted and appropriate and generalized to include all others. In combination with intercultural learning, understanding and behavior, we could say that:

Own-culture conditions of perception, thought and behavior must be broached, reflected on and acknowledged in their conditional constellation. In addition, communication processes and factors underlying our judgments must be understood. This requires knowledge of one's own-culture orientation system and its behavior-regulating functions (Thomas 2003a).

Requirements of Other-Culture Orientation

Any German who has not ventured beyond his own cultural setting and is then sent on an international assignment where he is singled out as German and confronted with presumed stereotypical German characteristics or prejudices suddenly, and often quite unexpectedly, finds himself in a situation which he experiences as insulting and embarrassing. He knows, of course, that he is German but has never really given a second thought to what it actually means until he interacts with dissimilar others. He is familiar with German history and is proud of his country's cultural heritage. He knows about the darker sides of German history, which affect or even shock him. But these factors have a different quality from what he is now experiencing with individuals from another culture, who relate to him on the basis of his affiliation with German culture and history and perhaps even hold him responsible for it. The fact that a foreigner should inquire about particular events and developments in German history or politics, or question the reasons for the Germans' particular and, from their point of view, unusual behavior, often leads to considerable irritation since the person himself has never considered himself accountable for events that seem to intrigue the foreigner. Clearly stated, it is not until the German travels abroad that he becomes aware of his nationality and how it is interpreted by others. Such an experience can lead to the awareness that specific knowledge and skills, acquired over years, are now perceived from the standpoint of the dissimilar other and no longer considered applicable.

Without doubt, individuals from other-culture religious, social, value, legal and economic traditions have developed different forms of perception, judgment, feeling and behavior. They have grown up under different geographic, economic, political, social and religious conditions and experience a different cultural consciousness over many generations. They have developed different survival and problem-solving strategies and forms of social interaction. Certain similarities between one's own and other cultures may exist which, seen from a historical perspective, are not entirely a result of interaction. More likely, events developed parallel to each other without reciprocal influence. Even geographically distant cultures distinguish themselves through a high degree of individualistic or collectivist patterns of orientation. Hofstede, for example, in his extensive empirical study, compared over 70 cultures on the basis of the degree to which they showed characteristics pertaining to particular behavioral dimensions and divided them into groups of very similar and very dissimilar cultures (Hofstede 1980; 1991; 1993) (q.v. Ch. I, 1.4).

Naturally, individuals socialized in other cultures assume that their behavior and the way in which they react to people and objects is "the right way" and will ultimately lead to success. Accordingly, they assume that everyone else behaves in the manner they deem appropriate. Returning to the example of the American manager and his Greek employee, both are able to communicate effectively in many aspects. The Greek employee, for instance, understood that he is to produce a report by a certain deadline. Furthermore, he knows what information and materials he needs and how the work schedule is to proceed. Striking differences become apparent where time schedules and deadlines are concerned. The issue is further aggravated by misunderstandings as to who is in charge of deciding on roles, functions and responsibilities pertaining to scheduling and performance supervision and the reasons with which each partner justifies his behavior. The misunderstandings and interaction static build up steadily until there is little choice left but to terminate the relationship.

In order to avoid such ineffective and emotionally draining interactions, it is necessary to be able to recognize conditions underlying other-culture perception, thinking, feeling and acting. The following requirements are based on this understanding:

- Learning to understand and acknowledge other-culture conditions and strategies for life and problem management and to accept that these forms are equally sensible and meaningful.

- Accepting other-culture systems of orientation, like our own, is only one option among a large variety of possible cultural systems of orientation.
- Developing an understanding of how to deal effectively with other-culture systems of orientation and the consequences thereof.

Requirements of Intercultural Orientation

Often individuals from diverse cultures meet and compare differences in their patterns of thinking, judgment and behavior. They find the differences interesting, exciting and exotic in contrast to the accustomed norms, without having such otherness affect their own thinking and behavioral patterns. Traveling with an organized group, for example, and exploring foreign countries together with an experienced guide allows you to observe and experience the other culture from a distance; to enjoy its exotic elements and be emotionally moved by it without having to actually deal with the foreignness on a deeper level. Personal involvement sets in once you are required to cooperate with individuals from another culture in reaching a common goal. Compared to a tourist, an executive of a German firm, for example, who is charged with successfully managing a business enterprise with foreigners and international employees in a foreign country, depends on smoothly running operations and productive cooperation with the other-culture partners. Moreover, the company's image and existential future are at stake. Without the cooperation of local nationals, the operation cannot be successful. Disinterest or lack of commitment on the part of local employees will render any specialist or executive helpless, regardless of expertise.

In such a case, it no longer suffices to reflect on one's own identity-based behavior and to merely take note of other-culture mental scripts. Substantive cooperation compels both parties to meet the following challenges:

Own and other-culture mental scripts must, for the sake of intercultural cooperation, be mutually adaptable and integrated into shared meanings. The process leading to such a trade-off requires distancing oneself from habituated mental scripts and a change of perspective to include possible courses of action and limitations within the personal system of orientation. New opportunities must be recognized and exploited while acknowledging and respecting new boundaries in the process. Difficulties in connection with these developments will be treated in more detail in the following section.

1.3.3 Consequences of Intercultural Cooperation

"Only he who is thoroughly familiar with his own and the foreign system of orientation can be successful in intercultural cooperation!", states a slightly modified version of a Chinese battle strategy. If respective systems of orientation are experienced as highly divergent among partners, then the question arises as to who adapts how and to what extent to the other's system. In many cases, a mutual understanding between partners develops naturally during an intercultural encounter, without extraordinary effort due to outside circumstances. When, for example, a Frenchman picks up a German company representative at the Charles de Gaulle airport in Paris, then he knows exactly what he has to do: he has to identify him among the other passengers, greet him and drive him to the conference location and on the way there, he must engage the visitor in some small talk. This is what the German visitor expects. Should the Frenchman, however, arrive noticeably late and, after a long search-and-find episode, try to cover up for the embarrassing situation with particularly polite behavior without justifying his "mistake", and to top it off, insist on having a leisurely lunch instead of rushing to the conference center, then the German visitor is likely to become extremely irritated. For his part, the German representative is continually plagued by the thought of missing something that may be important for business. This behavior creates a divergence in expectation, judgment, decision and action, which, as a rule, cannot be ascribed to outside circumstances, but rather to individual divergent behavior, although culturally contingent differences may also play a role.

Here the question arises again of who should adapt to whom in order to avoid a disaster at the very outset of such an encounter?

Different consequences arising as a result of even an everyday intercultural encounter between own and other-culture systems of orientation become evident:

Cultural Convergence and Divergence

If the intercultural encounter is understood as a process determined by the participating partners' intentions, expectations, wishes and hopes, then the following steps for action must be clarified and substantiated:

1. Does cultural divergence become evident and to what extent is it consciously and reflectively experienced? Or do we merely surmise the extent of own and culturally other overlap?
2. To what extent and with what regularity does one's own culture script

deviate from other-culture patterns, e.g., what quality of convergence can be expected?

3. To what extent can own-culture scripts and other-culture scripts co-exist without leading to serious conflict, e.g., can cultural compatibility be created?
4. Do own-culture and other-culture patterns contradict each other, e.g., are they essentially incompatible in terms of choice, inevitability or factors that seem immutable?

Cultural Transformation

1. If divergence between one's own and the other-culture systems of orientation becomes evident and is deemed modifiable by the parties involved, then they must deal with at least three consequences: what elements can, must or should be modified from one's own-culture script in the direction of the other-culture script?

The German company representative at the Charles de Gaulle airport, for instance, could have appreciated the French style of problem solving by thinking to himself, "Finally I can lean back and enjoy the French lifestyle" ... relaxed yet still somehow productive.

The core question is: how far can and should such adaptation go? Complete reluctance to adapt usually leads to considerable problems in dealing with dissimilar others. This sort of behavior can be perceived by other-culture partners as arrogant, dominant and disruptive. On the other hand, complete adaptation to other-culture patterns would not ring true either, as from his perspective, the partner expects a certain amount of cultural authenticity, that is other-culture behavior. A German who has been socialized in his own culture, can try to adapt to Chinese or French culture, he can integrate elements from the other-culture orientation system to enrich his own and can thus react more adequately and with more flexibility to culturally dissimilar situations. However, for all his efforts, he will not become authentically Chinese or French. The attempt in itself to adapt entirely to other-culture standards risks crossing over into the ridiculous.

2. How can other-culture standards be gradually modified to comply with own-culture standards? This can occur by pointing out one's own feelings and behavioral nuances to the other-culture partner, in the hope that he will be prepared to recognize and acknowledge the differences, and may gradually be willing to approach these unfamiliar behavioral patterns. If individuals represent an economic, political and social minority in a foreign culture, they are most often forced to adapt to life in the host country.

Groups of individuals belonging to an economically, politically and socially dominant minority in a country, such as experts from industrialized nations in a developing country, while not exactly forced to adapt, are nevertheless bound indirectly to the other-culture system of orientation in many respects in order to cooperate successfully.

3. If one considers an encounter between own-culture and other-culture as representing an intercultural encounter and if both parties are convinced that an appropriate and effective cooperation can only be achieved if a high level of mutual esteem and ambiguity-tolerance accompany the interaction, then it must be verified to what extent both partners can or are willing to alternately adapt; which culturally-specific characteristics of both systems of orientation are most efficient at any given time and in solving particular tasks, and to what extent the combination of both systems of orientation can create cultural synergies.

Far from being static structures, cultural orientation systems are extremely dynamic and flexible. As the anthropologist Arnold Gehlen (1958) correctly observed, human beings are "specialists for the nonspecific", each intercultural encounter promising the opportunity for creating a new culture and a new system of cultural orientation. For the moment, the value of this development may pertain only to synergetic cooperation. However, in the long term, the effects may also be felt by other individuals, groups and organizations.

The failure rate for international mergers can probably be traced back to one of the partners expecting and insisting on an unreasonable amount of one-sided adaptation. Neither top management nor the organization itself had the time or necessary skills to build a new, third corporate culture out of the original that could be efficient and above all acceptable to both parties. On such a basis, a common corporate identity allowing for shared meaning, values and norms could flourish.

1.3.4 Developing Interculturality

That which is culturally familiar to us, no longer requires our conscious attention and is perceived as intrinsically appropriate and proper. Cultural otherness is perceived as irritating, basically illogical and generally in need of improvement.

Cultural otherness is most often experienced in interactions with dissimilar others, the otherness generally being perceived and judged as a personal flaw. This complies with the so-called corresponding tendency (Ross and Nisbett 1991), a well-documented phenomenon related to the theory of attribution in the field of social psychology. According to this theory, an individual's observed behavior is attributed exclusively to the agent's characteristics while overlooking, underestimating or ignoring the situational factors influencing behavior. In the case mentioned here, the persons involved are oblivious to characteristics of the other's orientation system and are entirely insensitive to the importance of such systems. They are simply not in a position to recognize the flawed judgments resulting from the corresponding tendency relating to the dissimilar other, much less to remedy it.

Interculturality can only be created where one partner is dominant and the other is subordinate, and only with the means and resources (e.g., own-culture orientation system) that have been available in the past. Under all other circumstances, new awareness must be accessed and further developed.

Clearly all cultures have developed culture-specific forms of dealing with otherness and have more or less developed an intrinsic collective attitude toward dissimilar others. In economically and militarily dominant nations, and in those in which a cultural identity has been developed over centuries and even millenniums, forms of cultural orientation evolved which are determined by superiority and little flexibility with regard to otherness. In contrast, a nation whose country's history was influenced by intermittent periods of independence, dependency and forced adaptation tend to be less resistant to otherness. Seen from this perspective, the partners are by no means free to develop their own adaptation dynamic while in a situation of cultural overlap. Instead they are bound by their own cultural premises. Under such conditions, building an intercultural base geared toward creating cultural synergy is extremely difficult. It is essential for the partners to have developed a certain degree of ambiguity-tolerance, that is, they are able to withstand and accept unclear or contradictory situations and behavior. They must feel a certain amount of intrinsic esteem and respect for different life styles, forms of life management and social interaction and contribute a healthy sense of openness, curiosity and ability to innovate to the intercultural encounter. If this ability is lacking, they will not be able to venture beyond their own system of cultural orientation or they will fall back on the latter as soon as a culture-based conflict arises during an important interaction (q.v. Ch. I, 1.8).

Societies and cultures in which the process of internationalization permeate all facets of social interactions are called upon to include executives and specialists who are able to build a sustainable intercultural framework. On the one hand, those responsible must have a clear concept of their own cultural orientation, and on the other, have attained knowledge and understanding of other-culture systems of orientation. Moreover, they must have the necessary intercultural competence to recognize and be able to evaluate the synergy potential inherent in intercultural encounters and interaction. Such qualifications do not develop on their own as in "learning by doing", but require qualification measures, such as culture-general and culture-specific orientation trainings and intercultural coaching (q.v. Ch. I, 2.4).

Literatur

Bochner, S. (1982): The social psychology of cross-cultural relations. In: Bochner, S. (Ed.), Cultures in Contact. Oxford, pp. 5–45.

Breitenbach, D. (1975): Interkulturelles Lernen und internationale Verständigung in der Internationalen Jugendarbeit: Eine theoretische Einführung. Saarbrücken.

Gehlen, A. (1958): Der Mensch. Bonn.

Hofstede, G. (1980): Culture's Consequences: International Differences in Work-Related Values. Beverly Hills, Ca.

Hofstede, G. (1991): Cultures and Organizations: Software of the Mind. London.

Hofstede, G. (1993): Interkulturelle Zusammenarbeit. Kulturen – Organisationen – Management. Wiesbaden.

Ross, N.; Nisbett, R. E. (1991): The Person and the Situation. New York.

Thomas, A. (Ed.) (2003a): Psychologie interkulturellen Handelns. 2nd ed. Göttingen.

Thomas, A. (Ed.) (2003b): Kulturvergleichende Psychologie. Eine Einführung. 2nd ed. Göttingen.

Triandis, H. C. (1972): The Analysis of Subjective Culture. New York.

Gabriel Layes

1.4 Cultural Dimensions

"So what are the people like there?" Individuals who have lived abroad for a longer period and are asked to report on their experiences in the host country are probably familiar with questions of this nature. In answering, one might hear statements such as: "... they are incredibly superficial when dealing with people, even with friends ..." – "... they don't respect personal boundaries, talk constantly and loudly and are always touching you ..." – "... women have no say whatsoever. They always have to keep quiet ..." – "... they are so prudish and uptight ..." – "... everyone is friendly and willing to help ...".

Such answers have a two-fold purpose: On the one hand, the person answering tries to interpret certain behavioral patterns on the basis of his interactions with people from the host country that he believes to be typical. On the other, one tries to describe the behavioral patterns in terms that are plausible to both oneself and the listener. Scientists searching for so-called "cultural standards", in effect do little else. When referring to cultural standards in intercultural research, researchers base certain behavior on underlying cultural patterns.

The quest for so-called "cultural standards" goes a step further, however. At this point the question arises whether particular cultural standards can be traced back to and identified as certain basic dimensions of human behavior. This can be illustrated in the following example: A German manager, on an international assignment in Japan, might easily get the impression that Japanese business consist of very inflexible hierarchies and authoritarian relationships between superiors and subordinates. He might further conclude that something like "authoritarian hierarchy" is a cultural standard in the Japanese corporate world, while considering himself to be part of a more "cooperative hierarchy" on the basis of his experiences. Let's imagine further that the same German manager had the opportunity to interact with Danish and French business colleagues. In view of these new experiences, he might possibly change his mind on the basis of a comparison between the French and Japanese and conclude that the Japanese do have a rather co-operative style after all. He might also believe himself to be far more authoritarian than he thought he was, compared to the Danes. Based on these new experiences, the German manager might conclude that dealing with hierarchical relationships involves fundamental cultural dimensions with extremes of either "highly authoritative" or "highly cooperative". All cultures could be pinpointed along such a range of parameters.

Researchers engaged in the study of comparative cultures are convinced that the German manager's observations are, in principal, quite valid, which means that it is possible to identify fundamental cultural dimensions and to localize cultures along this dimension. Then the question arises as to how many cultural dimensions exist and how they can be labeled.

A pioneer in this field and in related research is the Dutchman Geert Hofstede. In order to complete his extensive study, which in its sheer breadth is the only one of its kind, he (Hofstede 1980) developed a questionnaire to interview a total of 116,000 employees of a multinational computer company. The questionnaire was translated into 20 languages and, as a result, could be administered in 53 countries. The questionnaire measured "work-related values" and contained questions to determine aspects of job satisfaction (e.g., "How satisfied are you with your current job?"). Other questions involved the evaluation of job requirements (e.g., "How often does your supervisor expect you 'to go the extra mile'?") or personal work-related issues (e.g., "How important is a high salary to you?") and more. Hofstede subjected his findings to correlation statistical and factor analytical evaluation, on the basis of which he identified four fundamental cultural dimensions:

Power Distance. This dimension examines the extent to which a culture accepts unequal power distribution. In cultures with a high power distance, members experience power differences in institutions and organizations as unproblematic and therefore expect them. Commensurate with Hofstede's findings, very complex and impermeable hierarchical systems develop here. In cultures with a low power distance, members experience the distribution of power in institutions and organizations as problematic and they will tend to resist. According to Hofstede, this will eventually lead to the development of very flat and permeable hierarchical systems.

Individualism/Collectivism. This dimension shows to what extent the members of a culture define themselves as part of a social network and how committed they are to this network. Members of collectivist cultures perceive themselves as members of a relationship-oriented in-group, and try to align and reach personal goals in accordance with the group. Members of individualistic cultures perceive themselves as autonomous individuals and try to set and achieve personal goals apart from the interests of their reference group.

Uncertainty Avoidance This dimension shows to what extent unclear and ambiguous situations create feelings of insecurity and anxiety in a culture. For members of a culture with strong uncertainty avoidance, rules to regulate private and public life are binding, causing them to react to unclear circumstances with disorientation or even aggression. According to Hofstede, very complex and rigid social regulatory systems develop, which, if ignored, result in a form of reprimand. For members of a culture with weak uncertainty avoidance, rules to regulate private and public life are not binding and they react to unclear or even chaotic circumstances with relative ease. According to Hofstede, very flexible social regulatory systems evolve here.

Masculinity and Femininity. This dimension shows to what extent gender roles are delineated and predefined. In masculine cultures, men and women's roles in society are clearly designated. The masculine role is defined through performance, assertiveness, dominance and materialistic pursuits. The feminine role is defined through solicitousness, modesty, subordination and warm-heartedness. In feminine cultures almost all roles in society can be assumed by either men or women and the gender roles are not limited to clearly defined characteristics.

Hofstede later amended these four dimensions by a fifth. He deemed this addition necessary after the findings of a group of researchers in China (Chinese Culture Connection 1987), who had conducted a replication study:

Long-term Orientation. This dimension shows to what extent long-term thinking is valued. In cultures with a high degree of long-term orientation, long-standing traditions influence the present and today's actions are binding for the future. According to Hofstede, this mindset creates very stable and binding social structures over generations and resists change. In cultures with a lesser degree of long-term orientation, traditions hold nostalgic value at best in the sense of "here today, gone tomorrow". In such cultures, claims Hofstede, social change is easily mobilized. The resulting social conditions, however, tend to be correspondingly unstable and noncommittal.

The terms developed by Hofstede and the mindsets underlying these cultural models are very practical. This is probably also the reason why Hofstede's work is acknowledged beyond the field of academics and has found much resonance with individuals active internationally.

The same is true for the work of the American researcher, Edward T. Hall (1985, 1990). He chose an entirely different approach and, like Hofstede, came up with specific cultural dimensions. Hall approached his topic from an anthropological perspective. He attempted to identify fundamental dimensions of human co-existence pertaining to human beings in all cultures. According to Hall, these are dimensions of space, time and communication. Every culture is forced to develop specific standards of action based on these fundamental dimensions. The concept of space, for instance, applies to cultural differences in terms of personal distance and the way in which it is automatically applied in interactions with friends or business partners.

In the *time* dimension, Hall distinguishes between two patterns of time that govern different cultures: *monochronic* time and *polychronic* time. In monochronic cultures, time is experienced and used in a linear fashion, prescribing a consecutive order in which specific activities occur. This orientation demands a high degree of self-management in terms of planning and reliability on a personal level, as well as in managing public systems and structures, as in the public transportation system for example. Accordingly, monochronic cultures tend to have a lower tolerance threshold when it comes to changes in timing, scheduling and other interruptions. In contrast, polychronic cultures span many different levels in pursuing their intended communicative action, any number of which can occur simultaneously.

This orientation requires a high degree of flexibility and consequently, individuals from these cultures tend to have a high tolerance with respect to time/schedule overlaps and interruptions.

Hall differentiates between the so-called *"low-context"* and *"high-context"* communication. The adjectives "low" and "high" refer to the extent to which the nonlinguistic context in a given situation is included in a conversation. In "low-context" cultures, an effort is made to render all information as explicit as possible leaving the listener little room for interpretation. In contrast, cultures in which "high-context" communication dominates, the prevailing atmosphere surrounding a situation, including nonverbal signals, is perceived as an essential part of the communication process. That which is actually verbalized is full of insinuation, ambiguity and metaphors, and can only be understood within the context of the entire conversation.

In his popular scientific work (Trompenaars 1993), the Dutchman Fons Trompenaars, an international business manager and consultant, added to Hofstede's, Hall's and other authors' models by developing a model of cultural dimensions based on his own professional experience. According to his model, there are cultural differences in three fundamental areas of life: (a) the relationship of human beings to *time*, (b) their relationship to *nature* and (c) in their *interaction with others.* According to Trompenaars, one cultural dimension can be derived from man's relation to time and nature respectively, while a total of five cultural dimensions can be derived from the different possibilities of man's interrelation with others. In this way, Trompenaars arrived at a total of seven different cultural dimensions. Like Hofstede, he refers to one of these dimensions as "individualism/collectivism". To Trompenaars, this dimension constitutes one of the five cultural dimensions by which the relationship between human beings can be described. His description is nearly identical to that of Hofstede, so that only Trompenaar's remaining six cultural dimensions are mentioned here in more detail.

Universalism/Particularism. This dimension shows to what extent universally valid laws and regulations prevail in universalistic societies. Regulations are written for everyone and must be upheld, even enforced, in a culture to structure human co-existence. In contrast, individuals in particularistic societies are more focused on the nature of a given circumstance and are reluctant to follow strict and predetermined rules.

Neutral/Affective. This dimension shows to what extent the public expression of feelings and emotions is prevalent. In neutral cultures, efforts are made to suppress feelings in public and to follow protocol as strictly as possible during negotiations or discussions. In affective cultures, the expression of spontaneous feelings is socially acceptable, even in negotiations and discussions. It is considered normal if "human" reactions such as loud laughter, angry desk pounding or shock are openly expressed. Certain parallels to Thomas' cultural standard of "task orientation" become evident here (q.v. Ch. I, 1.1).

Specificity/Diffuseness. This dimension describes the situation in which individuals interrelate. In specificity-oriented cultures it is quite common that individuals meet exclusively in defined areas of life, for example at work, at sports clubs and teacher-parent events at school. Although these encounters may be frequent and sincere, in specificity-oriented cultures this does not mean that those involved wish to socialize with each other in other areas of life. In diffuse cultures, on the other hand, individuals who have become more than just acquaintances are generally granted access to all areas of a person's life. Frequently, business partners are invited to join in common outdoor sports events in an effort to get to know them better outside of the immediate business setting. Occasionally, such "getting acquainted" rituals are a prerequisite to business relations.

Ascription-Achievement. This dimension shows what factors determine social standing in a culture. In a culture in which achievement is held in high esteem, personal success through demonstrated competence attained throughout the course of life, for example, as a result of professional or athletic accomplishments, leads to heightened social status. In a culture in which the ascription pattern is prevalent, social standing is acquired by virtue of heritage or social circumstances such as gender, age, title and belonging to the upper echelons of society.

People-Nature Orientation. In man's relation to nature, Trompenaars differentiates between cultures that try to subjugate nature and those that try to live in harmony with nature. In the first case, nature is seen as a sort of power in its own right, independent of human interference that requires constant confrontation. Man's duty therefore involves "wresting" inherent secrets from nature and "taming" its forces with the help of technology. In contrast, man sees himself as part of nature instead of its opponent, whose mission is to adapt to nature in order to co-exist in harmony.

Temporal Orientation. Trompenaars differentiates between three orientation forms with regard to time: In cultures that have past orientations, the past is the most important time form. Efforts are made to preserve the past, to pass it on over generations and to make its presence felt in the present. In cultures with future orientations, on the other hand, the past is considered "over and done with". The emphasis here is on reaching future goals, which, once achieved, lead on to higher goals. In contrast, systems with present orientations, neither the past nor the future play an important role. The focus here is on living for the moment as time is of relatively little importance in relation to other aspects of life.

What academic and practical value do these models have? Apparently, internationally active individuals who experience intercultural encounters daily in their work environment can draw upon the concepts and categories offered by such models for support. In addition, the overlaps and interrelated aspects between the individual models mentioned support the notion that despite different theories and concepts, they at least describe the same phenomena. So, how do these models contribute to the understanding of cultural differences? To answer this question, let's turn back to Hofstede's research, where results are reflected in interviews about work-related values conducted with employees of a multinational computer firm. The following questions arise: Can the results actually be transferred to other individuals who are not employees of this particular computer firm? Can the results also be ascribed to areas of life that exist apart from the interviewees' immediate work environment? Do the results represented outlast cultural patterns or is it a historical snapshot taken at the time the study was conducted? This excerpt from a multitude of critical questions, asked in relation to even such an encompassing study as Hofstede's, shows just how dangerous it can be to infer conclusions about national cultures based on the momentary observation of behavioral patterns.

The French researcher Jacques Demorgon (1989) developed a model that also includes cultural dimensions and which he imbedded in differentiated cultural theories suitable for dealing with some of the risks mentioned above. For those who are internationally active, this offers a grid that helps them to reflect upon and categorize unfamiliar actions more accurately.

Similar to Hall, Demorgon determines his cultural dimensions by attempting to cover the entire spectrum of possible human action. Consequently, this can only be a dimension that is characterized by two opposing poles. The example of the *action mode* – that is, the form that action takes – illustrates this: One can only act extremely *quickly* or extremely *informed*. Both occurring simultaneously is not possible. In this respect, all theoretical action modi can be exemplified between these two extremes. Thus, the action mode represents the first of a long list of dimensions defined by Demorgon. The most important of these are mentioned below:

Action orientation. This cultural dimension extends between the two poles labeled *simultaneity* and *consecutivity* and is related to Hall's differentiation between monochronic and polychronic patterns of time: According to consecutive action orientation, the focus is on one task at a time. Once completed, the focus shifts to the next step. In simultaneous action orientation, several tasks are tackled at the same time and thus can tolerate gaps in a given action process.

Attention. Demorgon sees a close connection between action organization and directing attention, which he defines as a separate cultural dimension. Its opposite poles are *centered* and *diffuse* attention. When concentration is centered, the focus is on a few things only, albeit with utmost intensity and precision. Accordingly, diffuse attention occurs when an observer perceives any number of aspects of a situation, however, with relatively little precision.

Communication mode. Demorgon differentiates between the two extremes *explicit* and *implicit* communication as it applies to communication in particular. At one extreme, every effort is made to explain all relevant information as precisely as possible. In contrast, at the other extreme, much remains unspoken and must be deduced from the context of the conversation, which, of course, depends on the nature of the relationship between the conversation partners.

Communication content. Demorgon describes this second dimension in communication as *objective* and *subjective* speech. In objective speech, the speaker detracts from himself by referring to statements about facts and tasks at hand, which he tries to present as precisely as possible. In subjective speech, on the other hand, the speaker himself is at the center of the communication process, while imparting personal views and emotions as descriptively as possible.

Motivation. According to Demorgon, this cultural dimension describes what motivates a person to act. At the *task-related* extreme, the tasks themselves motivate to action. This corresponds to Thomas' cultural standard of task orientation. In *relationship orientation,* action is dependent on completing a task involving important individuals. For example, a person wants to do another a favor or because a person has the authority to demand completion of a task.

Authority. This cultural dimension establishes a relation between motivation to act and a person's authority. Demorgon distinguishes between *external* and *internalized* authority. In the case of external authority, task completion depends on individuals higher up in the external hierarchy, who are in a position to order completion of the task, to supervise and to evaluate it. In the case of internalized authority, tasks are completed even when there is no assigned outside authority to ensure that the task has actually been completed. On the contrary, individuals who are higher up in the hierarchy are not welcome to "interfere" where they are not needed.

Responsibility. Authority is concerned with responsibility. Demorgon distinguishes between the extremes *determination* and *co-determination.* In the first case, authoritative persons do not tolerate interferences. Instead, they assert personal opinions or form them if they do not happen to have any explicit ones. Responsibility is thus concentrated on one person who must also carry the consequences. In the case of co-determination, those bearing responsibility encourage others to contribute their views and opinions to the decision-making process. In this way, the responsibility is evenly distributed.

Decisions. As is evident in the different approaches to responsibility, this subject relates directly to the issue of decision-making behavior. Here Demorgon differentiates between the extremes *dissent* and *consensus.* Dissent refers to opposing decision-making behavior, which can be a reaction to a person in charge in a higher position in the hierarchy. Much emphasis is placed on opposing opinions and suggestions to avoid a focus on one predominant view. During consensus-oriented decision-making behavior, only those thoughts are voiced that are not only realistic and feasible from the outset, but also bound to achieve a consensus. The idea here is to piece all ideas together in a sort of mosaic with the resulting compromise being accepted by all as the best solution.

Attitude toward Organizations. In organizations' decision-making behavior, responsibility, authority, communication mode and many more aspects we have discussed here are institutionalized. Thus, according to Demorgon, the relationship between individual and organization present a further important cultural dimension. Here, he distinguishes between the extremes *degradation* and *appreciation* in relation to institutions. In the case of degradation, all organizations are regarded with skepticism and are rejected or resisted with a feeling that they do not serve the individual. The opposite is true for the other extreme where institutions and organizations are seen as positive, providing the individual with identity, sense and security.

The manner in which Demorgan incorporates these cultural dimensions into a general cultural theory is just as important as the individual cultural dimensions or their description. On the basis of this general theory, Demorgan develops a grid that helps the practitioner to understand and consider unfamiliar forms of behavior from various angles. This approach prevents the viewer from regarding other-culture individuals as "cultural machines", who behave according to well-defined cultural dimensions.

If unusual forms of action are repeatedly observed, one might ask on which *level* the behavior is observed: Is it the behavior shown by an individual (individual level), a small group of individuals (group level) or that of a specific social class (subculture level) or is it a phenomenon that can be observed throughout all groups and subcultures of a nation (national-culture level)? Does one actually have enough contacts to answer this question? A business manager who spends some months on an international assignment within the scope of short-term project work hardly has the time to come in contact with local nationals outside of his immediate work environment. His business partners, on the other hand, represent a small section of the given population. Even Trompenaars narrows his scope when he refers specifically to cultural differences in the "business world". Considering the specific framework within which Hofstede surveyed his candidates, one might come to the conclusion that similar constraints would be more to the point. According to Demorgon, the issue of levels constitutes an initial filter through which observations should pass, before drawing conclusions about national-culture idiosyncrasies.

A second filter asks what specific modes of behavior can be observed in different *areas of life.* The manager who experiences his foreign business partners exclusively within a work-related context might be surprised to see the way these same people behave at a private party or a religious ceremony. Everyone knows, from personal experience, how many different types of behavior are displayed depending on the social context. Therefore, before jumping to conclusions, it is extremely important to ascertain if one is dealing with behavior that is related to particular areas of life and are only shown there, or if they overlap into other areas of life.

A third filter should be in place, according to Demorgon, when attributing national-cultural characteristics. Here, he refers to *history*.

Even if specific modes of behavior can be observed in all areas of life and social groups, they can still be, in a historical sense, situational snapshots taken under conditions of force or necessity, for example in connection with war or the collapse of the economy. If a country is suffering from inflation and stores are looted, then one will hardly conclude that this is a national-culture pattern. Not until particular modes of behavior reoccur throughout history can categories pertaining to national-culture characteristics be applied.

The cautiousness with which Demorgon treats the cultural dimensions that he himself developed should also be an example of how to treat the models developed by Hofstede, Hall, Trompenaars and others (considering the authors themselves do not do it). Aside from the previously mentioned questions, the determination of cultural dimensions poses two more fundamental problems, which Demorgon also faces and which, in concluding, we would like to explore further. Questions of this sort tend to arise when the described models are used as research tools. They can be useful where they provide practical orientation in reflecting on unfamiliar forms of action.

The Issue of One-dimensionality. Those who, like Hofstede, set up an axis with the extremes, "low power distance" and "high power distance" at either pole and line up all countries along this axis, implicitly imply that hierarchical constellations all over the world differ only in relation to the degree to which the existing power distances are accepted. The manager from our example, who has had experience with Japanese, French and Danish colleagues, would most likely report that this hardly appeared to be the only difference between the respective hierarchical systems. Rather, that each one of the three hierarchical systems takes on a different form. In some areas of authoritative style, he might find that the Japanese and the French are most similar, while he might get the impression that in issues of caregiving within hierarchical systems, the French are entirely different from the Japanese and, in fact, have more in common with the Danes. Most of the axes defined within the cultural dimensions do not represent one-dimensional characteristics, although this is suggested when, for example,

Denmark has a "power distance index" of 19, Japan an index of 52 and France an index of 70.

The Problem of Perspective. Let us stick to our example: Our manager finds the Japanese authoritarian because the leadership style practiced by his Japanese colleagues would be called "authoritarian" in Germany if he assumed a similar style. The French colleagues might not regard the Japanese as authoritarian at all and the Japanese might associate the behavioral style under discussion with entirely different definitions and concepts. This means that many of the cultural dimension models do not refer to an absolute designation of culture, but rather a description from a specific cultural perspective. Accordingly, the dimensions and concepts are used because they make sense to oneself. It is not at all clear if dimension concepts like "power distance", "uncertainty avoidance" or "individualism" are meaningful to a Mexican, for example. We can only say that a certain behavior displayed by Mexicans strikes *us* in a certain way and that we see much similarity or dissimilarity to persons from other countries. The issue of perspective becomes especially evident when concepts within the cultural dimension suggest certain valuation: In speaking about "diffuse", "affective" or "particular" cultures, then, from a German perspective, one is glad to find oneself at the other end of the scale. In spite of authors' efforts to keep valuation out of their models, any description of other cultures is always effected from the personal perspective.

Considering the many questions and problems related to the concepts used in the cultural dimension models, should the cultural dimension models be used at all? If they are used carefully, the answer is: yes. No doubt the concepts are handy and useful tools for structuring thoughts about unusual forms of behavior. However, it is important to remember that one is dealing with a temporary structure created from one's own-culture perspective and which must remain open to more precise differentiation once the other culture becomes more familiar. Without the finer differentiation, the practical aspect may quickly become an intellectual trap. In this case, the concepts turn into sophisticated-sounding academic labels that cling to empty clichés. People who are continually in contact with only a relatively homogeneous group of individuals in a foreign country should be aware of this risk at all times.

References

Chinese Culture Connection (1987): Chinese values and the search for culture-free dimensions of culture. Journal of Cross-Cultural Psychology 18: 143–164.

Demorgon, J. (1989): L'exploration interculturelle. Pour une pédagogie internationale. Paris.

Demorgon, J.; Molz, M. (1996): Bedingungen und Auswirkungen der Analyse von Kultur(en) und interkulturellen Interaktionen. In: Thomas, A. (Ed.), Psychologie interkulturellen Handelns. Göttingen, pp. 43–86.

Hall, E. T. (1985): Hidden Differences: Studies in International Communication. Hamburg.

Hall, E. T. (1990): Understanding Cultural Differences. Yarmouth, ME.

Hofstede, G. (1980): Culture's Consequences. International Differences in Work-Related Values. Beverly Hills.

Trompenaars, F. (1993): Handbuch Globales Managen. Wie man kulturelle Unterschiede im Geschäftsleben versteht. München.

Evelyne Glaser

1.5 Foreign Language Competence in Intercultural Cooperation

1.5.1 Language and Cultural Identity

Language has two contradictory characteristics. On the one hand, it can create misunderstanding and on the other, it can clarify misunderstanding. In this sense, language plays a key role in human communication not only within one's native culture, but also between cultures. Ting-Toomey (1999, p. 85) differentiates between three outstanding features of language: its arbitrariness, its complex rules and its language community. Here she defines human language as an arbitrary, symbolic system that specifies ideas, feelings, experiences, events, people and other phenomena and is regulated by a set of complex rules developed by the members of a specific language community.

The arbitrary nature of a language results from its phonemic and graphic illustration. The sounds and written symbols are part of an individual's cultural and ethnic identity and can elicit strong emotional attachment and convey the feeling of familiarity and security in a foreign environment. Since we acquire language effortlessly in the early phases of childhood, we are unaware of its strong influence on our identity. Until we encounter the linguistic systems of other cultures, we are likely to be unaware of the extent to which our identity is linked to the naming of objects, relationships and feelings. Perhaps this is what led the linguistic anthropologists Edward Sapir (1921, 1929) and Benjamin Lee Whorf (1950, 1952) to establish the hypothesis that language is a guide to cultural reality (Sapir 1921). Sapir goes on to claim:

"The fact of the matter is that the 'real world' is to a large extent unconsciously built up on the language habits of the group. No two languages are ever sufficiently similar to be considered as representing the same social reality. The world in which societies live are distinct worlds, not merely the same world with different labels. Even comparatively simple acts of perception are very much more at the mercy of the social patterns called words than we might suppose ... We see and hear and otherwise experience very largely as we do because the language habits of our community predispose certain choices of interpretation" (Sapir 1929, p. 209 f.).

Following his mentor, Sapir, Whorf concludes that language is not merely a tool with which to express ideas, but language is "the shaper of ideas" (Whorf 1952, p. 5). Whorf claims that grammatical structures shape our thought processes and grammatical structures are culture specific. Thus, language, thought and culture are integral components of our system of thought and determine the basic parameters of our experience. Hence, when we speak in another language, we enter another reality. However, since we view this new reality according to our own thought pattern that is formed by language, we tend to interpret this reality differently. Steinfatt (1989) extenuated Sapir and Whorf's relativity hypothesis somewhat by claiming that language *forms* our thought patterns but does not *determine* them.

In "Communicating Across Cultures" (1999), Ting-Toomey cites examples, illustrating the way in which the sentence structure used by an individual from another culture can lead to interpretations and reactions that were not intended by the speaker. In Chinese, for example, a description of causal connection is stated before the agent (person performing the action) appears on the scene. Thus, a Chinese sentence might be constructed in the following manner: "Since it was pouring with rain and the streets were flooded and since, in addition, I had to wait for a long time for my turn at the counter at the post office and since the counter closed before it was my turn, I wasn't able to mail the package." An English native speaker might get the impression that the person is conjuring up excuses, is trying to be evasive or maybe even that he is trying to mislead. The English version of the same statement, "I couldn't mail the package because the counter at the post office closed before it was my turn", would sound impolite to a Chinese person and evoke the impression that the person wants to make himself the center of attention. Thus, both speakers are formed by the structure of their own language, which inevitably influences the interpretation of what the other person is saying. Consequently, it is extremely important to be aware of structural differences in the language and to intentionally refrain from spontaneous judgment and assessment of one's counterpart until a more complete picture can be formed.

The Western world frequently considers concepts of "shame" and "loss of face" as the dominant characteristic of Southeast Asian cultures. Intercultural communication, in particular, requires members of Western cultures to choose language selectively in order not to risk a loss of face to both their Asian and Western partners. A loss of face inevitably leads to a termination of the relationship. Gesteland (1999) points out that the concept of "face" is also found in Western cultures and that it is actually universal. He demonstrates this by citing the concept of *onore* in Italian, *dignitad* in Spanish and *self-respect* in English. The concept of *honneur*, so significant in French society and extremely well characterized by Philippe d'Iribarne (1989), deserves further mention. Why are concepts of "shame" and "face" still seen as culture-specific for Asia? Frank et al. (2000) concluded in a study that Bedford's (1994 quoted from Frank et al. 2000) five different basic forms of "shame" are emotional experiences in Chinese culture, which incidentally Americans experience as well. In holding with Sapir and Whorf, they cite the hypothesis that the emotions are not as pronounced among Americans because English/American language does not have the nuances to differentiate between the concepts, that is, lacks definite and separate lexical expressions to describe nuances. This would substantiate the conclusion that the lexical scope of a language determines the importance and function of a specific concept in a given culture.

1.5.2 English as the *lingua franca*

Since the fundamental characteristic of language is not only to clarify misunderstanding, but also to generate it within both the indigenous culture and especially between cultures, the idealistic idea of a single language was born a long time ago to serve all cultures as a means of communication. As early as the first century B. C., a desire for one universal language emerged in Ancient Greece. Even back then, people dreamed of a language free of ambiguity and in which all things and thoughts could be described *in a way they really are.* Descartes (1596–1650), too, recognized that the different world languages are basically illogical and ambiguous due to the complexity of their development (cf. Cherry 1980). Based on the dominant empirical conviction that people want to and will communicate with each other regardless of language barriers, several hundred artificial languages were created to enable communication beyond linguistic and cultural boundaries, and simultaneously to recreate the people's "state of innocence" prior to the construction of the Tower of Babel. The most well known was Esperanto, a language spoken by two million people worldwide. However, Esperanto was conceived of as a second language and not meant to replace the native tongue (cf. Bailey 2002). As we can see from experience, the idea of a universal language is still in the stars. Over the last decades, English has evolved into the lingua franca between cultures.

There are more than 6,000 languages worldwide, many of which have no written form (Mallick 1997/2001, p. 102). At the end of the second millennium, more than 235 million people spoke English as a native language or official second national language. Does that make English a global language? What makes a language a global language? According to David Crystal (1997), a language becomes global, firstly, if it is spoken as a native language by a large number of people in several countries. Secondly, it must be accepted as the official language in a number of countries, even though no or only a few native speakers live there (this is the case for English in over 70 countries). Thirdly, even if it is not declared the official language of the country, it can have the status of a first foreign language. For English, this is the case for over 100 countries. (In 1996, even Algeria, a former French colony, gave English priority over French as a foreign language in schools.)

English meets the criteria for the three conditions specified by Crystal (1997, p. 3 ff.), thus making it the most widely spoken language in the world. Almost a fourth of the world's population, that is between 1.2 and 1.5 billion people, speak English fluently or at least adequately. With its eight different forms of the spoken language and a common written language, 1.1 billion people in China speak Chinese. Consequently, English is the predominant global language both geographically and numerically.

The numerical dominance of a language does not automatically make it a global language. Past theories claiming that English is better suited as a global language because of its simpler grammatical structure, less complex verb conjugations, lack of articles of gender or, quite simply, due to the fact that English is "classless" and therefore the more democratic language could not hold water (Crystal 1997, p. 6).

A language does not acquire the status of a global language because of the high regard given to its literature. Most importantly, it requires the political, military and economic hegemony of a country in which the language is the mother tongue. Crystal emphasizes that England was the world leader in trade and commerce at the beginning of the 19th century and Britain's political imperialism spread the English language across the globe. In the 20th century, the United States took over the economic and military world leadership. "And the language behind the US dollar was English", emphasizes Crystal (1997, p. 8).

Translation plays a key role in the interaction between cultures. If too many languages exist in a society, individuals will seek out a common language, a lingua franca, in order to sustain communication among its members. The largest group of English speakers includes the nonnative speakers. These individuals use English as their lingua franca to do business, most commonly with other nonnative speakers. Despite this fact, very little research has been done on English as a lingua franca (Seidlhofer 2001, p. 141). Even the "International Corpus of English" (ICE), which considers itself to be the first comprehensive research project on the development of

English as a global language, includes only those countries and regions where English is spoken by the majority of the population as a first language or where it is the country's official language. Thus, the project excludes the largest group of English speakers, namely, those who have acquired language proficiency with the goal of communicating with other nonnative speakers (Seidlhofer, p. 139). Most textbooks also reflect this condition and abide by the standards of British or American customs and accordingly accept only these norms as the parameter for accurate language usage.

Consequently, there is very little research material on English as a lingua franca (ELF) in intercultural communication. According to repeated observation, a very consensus-oriented approach is the rule, in which speakers support each other and generally overlook the many mistakes made (in comparison to the rules set by native speakers) (Firth 1996). Comments that could create difficulties tend to be passed over, which, according to House (1999, quoted from Seidlhofer, p. 143), might lead to ELF users initiating statements in a dialog rather than being active recipients. This means that the interaction typically lacks the conversational exchange and ease of switching between topics of conversation that characterize the natural communication behavior of native speakers. Firth (1996) found that according to his analysis of conversations, ELF speakers maintain a "let it pass" stance, that is, overlook grammatical, idiomatic or phonetic flaws, only as long as the message can still be understood and doesn't lead to a serious disruption in the interaction. As soon as this occurs, the conversational partners make attempts to clarify the message. If one participant, for instance, spells a name, his counter repeats this to make sure he heard correctly. In lingua-franca interactions, the speakers resort to a number of different forms of behavior when dealing with inadequate language skills. Some begin by describing and others try code-switching, meaning that they fall back on their native language and then ask what the expression means in English. In general, universally understood patterns of behavior such as laughing, hesitation, silence etc. are used to express verbal uncertainty. However, ELF speakers are less likely to correct, circumscribe or end the other's formulation, as is often the case among native speakers during "active listening". Firth emphasizes the flexibility and sturdiness of a lingua franca and the frequency with which speakers grasp the message even if the language goes against all the rules.

There have been a number of attempts (cf. Ogden 1930 or Quirk 1982) to shift the focus of English as a native language on to users of ELF. There was a frequent tendency, however, to regard the lingua franca as a form of Pidgin English. This approach hardly seems justified considering the increasing number of English-speaking people in the global economy, politics, the media or the sciences whose native language is not English, but who, nevertheless, have a high level of language competence. On the other hand, studies of this kind could reveal that a one-sided approach to native-speaker norms by one of the conversational partners in an ELF interaction can lead to communication problems, which in turn might lead to mutual adaptation and perhaps a higher level of effectiveness than focusing on language norms, idiomatic expression or pronunciation. If the speakers agree on the context of the conversation, there is less chance of misunderstanding or conflict (Seidlhofer 2001, p. 149). According to Seidlhofer, then, the question asked by ELF learners and teachers should not be: "Can you say it like that in (native) English?" Rather, the question would have to be reformulated as: "Has it every been used that way in English (as a lingua franca) and was it understood?" (p. 150).

Verbal communication in business contexts hardly requires fine-tuning content and forms when speaking about purchasing and sales prices, costs and often standardized quality characteristics of products and services. In these cases "roughly hewn" and often subject-specific language suffices. Stylistic nuances and grammatical correctness are often secondary. Luhmann (2000) claims that simplifying language in this particular domain can reduce the complexity of human communication and enhance trust between (business) partners from different cultures.

A fundamental problem underlying both the use of a lingua franca and a foreign language in communication with a native speaker is dealing with "conversational implicature" (Grice 1975). In this instance, Grice is referring to the ability to draw conclusions from a statement in which a part is not specifically mentioned. For example: A family visits a foreign city and turn to a passerby with the question, "Excuse me, we would like to have lunch". The passerby answers, "Yeah, there's a nice restaurant just a little way down the road on the other side of the street". Although the question referring to the restaurant was not explicitly mentioned, the passerby could infer what the tourist's actual question was.

The logical conclusion at this level is, of course, also possible in the foreign language. It is more difficult with expressions of irony, indirect criticism or with so-called POPE-Q–answers[1] (Bouton 1999), which belong to the category of rhetorical questions. Even a longer sojourn abroad does not guarantee that a nonnative speaker will interpret these nonspecific conversational nuances correctly.

---

1 POPE-Q-answers are a peculiarity of the English language and mean as much as "yes, of course" or "no, of course not". The definition comes from the prototypical question, "Is the pope Catholic?", which is actually an answer to a question. For example, the question, "Do you think Pete will come home late tonight?" Answer: "Does the sun come up in the east?" Understanding the answer to this question presupposes that the conversational partner is able to deal with such rhetorical questions.

1.5.3 The Role of Translators and Interpreters

Formal differences in languages occur in syntax (sentence construction, grammar), morphology (word formation), lexis (vocabulary) and phonology (pronunciation). Anyone who has ever learned a foreign language knows the challenge of trying to master all these aspects simultaneously. A translator's and interpreter's task is to formulate the message in the target language in a way that approximates the original language as closely as possible. In this respect, there are three main difficulties: 1. ambiguity, 2. interference, 3. lack of an equivalent expression in the target language. Ambiguity in this sense refers to the inability to clearly grasp the meaning of the word from the text or message sent. Interferences occur when the same word exists in both languages but has different meanings. An example here is the English word, "actual", which is easily confused with the German word *aktuell* (meaning current). Another example is the English word "delay" and the French word *délai* (meaning deadline). If there is no adequate equivalent, the translator/interpreter faces a particular challenge because he/she has to circumscribe the definition in a way that still conveys an idea of the meaning, as in the five different definitions for "shame" in Chinese and the many terms for "sand" in Arabic.

The greatest challenge for the translator or interpreter is thus not merely to change the words from one language into those of another, in other words, to give definitions new labels. A competent translator or interpreter is able to convey the psychological and culture-specific intention behind the terms (Holden 2002). The English word "interpreter" points out that the transfer of a message from the source language to the target language calls for an *interpretation* of how it is interconnected. For this reason, interpreting a brief comment from one language to another can be a matter of several minutes. Gestland (1999) points out that this is mainly the case between members of "deal-focused cultures" (e.g., Germany) and "relationship-focused cultures" (e.g., China). In such cases, the interpreter has to circumscribe very direct statements with polite phrases to sustain the relationship between conversation partners (Gesteland 1999, p. 40). If the interpreter were not to do this, he may provide a perfect translation from a linguistic point of view but, at the same time, would be acting contrary to cultural norms. This might disrupt negotiations and lead to losing a potential contract. This once again underscores Sapir's (1956) claim that, "No two languages are ever sufficiently similar to be considered as representing the same social reality. The worlds in which societies live are distinct worlds, not merely the same world with different labels attached". Various aspects in dealing with the issue of translating as a medium for cultural understanding and social integration are treated at length by Renn, Straub and Shimada (2000).

The challenge of finding a common cognitive basis in translating and interpreting is all the more difficult if the cultural, psychological, economic, technological and political distance between language and culture is very obvious. It must be pointed out, however, that the gap is not constant but varies according to the individuals communicating with each other. Thus, the gap can narrow or increase during the course of an interaction.

Negotiation partners, particularly politicians, sometimes choose to detour via an interpreter although both parties speak each other's language. This way they can be sure of having understood their partner correctly in precarious situations. On the other hand, it can be a political or national statement to emphasize the importance of one's own language. Switching into the negotiation partner's language would be a further political signal to put him under moral pressure to reciprocate in an effort to demonstrate his willingness to cooperate.

In some cases, the corporate negotiation teams may speak the partner's language but are unwilling to admit it, preferring to use interpreters for this reason rather than to demonstrate national differences. Perhaps they are counting on the advantage of gleaning more insight into the partner's sideline conversations than they could gain from the information divulged during the official negotiation (Gallois and Callan 1997). The risk inherent in a strategy of this kind cannot be underestimated. Should the other negotiation partner suspect a breach of trust, business relations are likely to suffer or fail in the long term. One recommendation is to go ahead and speak the partner's language to the extent possible in an effort to establish a personal relationship (for example over a meal at a restaurant), laying the groundwork for a relationship based on trust. In general, any effort made to speak the negotiation partner's language is welcome and honored as it shows a fundamental interest in the culture. This in turn fosters understanding for the business partner's behavior and expresses esteem, a factor that is helpful in sustaining relations in many cultures in Southern Europe, Middle and Eastern Europe, Africa, Arab countries, Asia and Latin America.

1.5.4 Nonverbal Intercultural Communication

Although the spoken language is essentially the way people communicate, the last centuries have seen an increased interest in research on body language. While verbalization seeks to transmit the content of the message, nonverbal communication conveys information about identity, emotions and relationships. Nonverbal messages can be conveyed intentionally or accidentally. Since body language is more difficult to direct and control than verbal communication, it is presumed that it is also more honest and thus reveals more about thoughts and inner attitudes. On the one hand, it may confuse the receiver, and on the other, it is often required for making the necessary connections for interpreting or decoding the verbal message. Just like the spoken language, body language is culture specific. Its rules are acquired during the socialization process.

Ting-Toomey (1999, p. 116) differentiates between the following forms of nonverbal communication:

- Kinesics (facial and bodily expression)
- Oculesics (eye contact)
- Vocalics/Paralinguistics (voice pitch, volume, silence)
- Proxemics (spacial distance)
- Haptics (touch behavior)
- Environment (e.g., room layout, architecture)
- Chronemics (time)

The long list of forms of nonverbal communication points to the complexity of nonverbal behavior and explains why decoding information beyond one's own culture is so difficult. In addition, it is not easy to acquire these elements while learning a foreign language since one's own culture's nonverbal forms of expression are often more dominant. One can sometimes notice, however, that Germans who speak good Italian also gesticulate and use mimicry more than they do in their native language or some people's voice has a different pitch when they speak in a foreign language. Since these elements can be relatively well described, they are often found in the "do's and don'ts lists" used by managers to prepare for trips abroad. Gesteland (1999) emphasizes the significance of spatial distance, physical contact, eye contact and body language in dealing with other cultures. Moreover, familiarity with culture-specific information concerning interpersonal distance and touch behavior is likely to prevent offending the negotiation partner by backing off impolitely or misinterpreting friendly gestures.

1.5.5 Communication Styles in Different Cultures

When communicating verbally it is useful to be familiar with Western communication styles. Hall (1976) in particular differentiates between "low-context" and "high-context" communication. *Low-context communication* is characteristic for Germanic cultures, Anglophone countries and western

Scandinavia. These cultures are characterized by individualistic values, linear and logical thinking, a direct communication style that revolves predominantly around the speaker and, above all, where words are of primary importance. The speaker tries to make a good impression and strives to save face in his choice of wording. In his message he conveys personal opinions, thoughts and feelings verbally. The speaker is responsible for formulating the message explicitly enough for the receiver to understand it without interpretation.

High-context communication is found mainly in East Asia and Arab countries. Southern Europe, too, is more inclined toward this style of communication, which tends to focus primarily on the receiver of the message, who in turn, has the task of interpreting the message himself and reading between the lines. The speaker will stand back and, in addition to the verbal message, conveys numerous nonverbal messages intended to help the receiver in decoding it. High-context communication draws upon multi-layered contexts (e.g., historical background, social norms, roles, status, relationship between the speakers), which are not explicitly mentioned. The receiver can deduce the meaning from the context. The conversational style tends to be indirect and the message does not have to be clearly formulated ... the speaker "beats around the bush" without getting to the point. Members of Western cultures often feel frustrated by this, as they have not really learned how to read the signs of nonverbal messages and to grasp them as part of the bigger picture. They may perceive the conversational partner as dishonest and think he is trying to hide something. On the other hand, the Japanese are put off by an overly direct style, finding it pushy and simple-minded. The speaker assumes that the conversational partner is not able to filter out the essential information for himself. If one considers that the Finnish language manages with a fourth of the words that the English language has, it is easy to imagine that Finnish words and sentences carry a deeper meaning (Brock et al. 2000). The ability to express oneself in many ways and nuances is greatly appreciated and phases of silence carry more weight in the course of the communication.

1.5.6 Language in Multicultural Organizations

In the corporate world, language is seen as an essential tool for transferring knowledge, values, experience and corporate goals. Holden coined the term "management language", which he claims targets three different goals. In the first place, language serves to describe management tasks. Secondly, it is instrumental in creating networks to enhance organizational learning and thirdly, it serves to spread knowledge and the corporate vision throughout the organization (Holden 2002, p. 232). This poses tremendous challenges for managers in transnational organizations because the receiver of the message translates all expressions according to his respective frame of reference while communicating with the sender, thus continually mixing with other individuals' translations during the interaction. This alone can cause drastic changes to the message within the same culture. The problem is magnified when individuals from different cultures speaking different languages communicate with each other. Consequently, Holden emphasizes the importance of an interactive translation process, in which individuals should practice *participative competence.* According to Holden, this pertains to the ability to participate in discussions in a foreign language on equal footing during the course of team projects and to share knowledge and experience with the group in an effort to achieve the common goal. A prerequisite here is that all participants have an equally high level of social competence. They need to know how communication is structured and can differentiate between key and peripheral questions. This ability will allow them to intuit messages and read between the lines. They must realize that messages can be coded in different ways (not only in language) and are willing to learn these codes. These aspects are the key to the coveted synergy effects that distinguish a learning organization, in which knowledge sharing has evolved into a tradition (Holden 2002, p. 229, 243, 237).

Holden sees the least of the difficulties in the description of management tasks (including the designation of the corporate strategy and announcing decisions) since the field-specific terminology used is easy to translate and leaves little room for individual interpretation. Translation into Western European languages as well as into American English, Japanese and Korean does not pose a particular hindrance, since the American influence prevalent in international management training in business schools has left its mark on the global arena. Consequently, upper management is quite familiar with management concepts (and terminology) (Holden 2002, p. 233). This has a primary effect on competence in the area of expertise. Cultural differences play a lesser role although they may become an issue in the long term (Reber and Jago 1997). The task becomes more difficult when translating into languages of the former socialist countries in Central and Eastern Europe, where the vocabulary lacks the typical management terminology and managers were never acquainted with the fundamentals of Western management (Holden et al. 1998).

While communication between organizations causes relatively little difficulty and language-based misunderstandings can usually be clarified with some effort on both sides in the process of doing business ("market"), intercultural cooperation in global operations requires closer interaction and points of contact. Interfacing at this level requires more specific and culture-sensitive communication skills. "Market" poses other challenges for the chosen lingua franca than "hierarchy" in global organizations (Williamson 1975).

1.5.7 Communication in Multicultural Teams

Most transnational operations see the work done in multicultural teams as a chance to apply different working styles and approaches in an effort to find creative and innovative solutions for the company (Watson et al. 2002). These teams must display considerable cooperative ability when management tosses them together, barely allowing for any time to get acquainted during a team building process. Frequently, these teams have to communicate with each other virtually over great distances via state-of-the-art technology without ever meeting face to face. The importance of face-to-face contact for relationship building, the quality of cooperation and the outcome of group effort is repeatedly emphasized in academic literature (Glaser 1998, 2001, 2002; Kirkman et al. 2001; DiStefano and Maznevski 2000). However, companies shy away from the high costs incurred by bringing the team members together, and thus put psychological pressure on these teams to meet nearly insurmountable challenges.

Communication is influenced by the interplay of situational and sociocultural conditions (Gumperz 1992). It follows certain culture-specific rules (e.g., the choice of topics, communication style[2], the speaker's social or gender-specific role, etc.), with which members of a culture are familiar due to their socialization in that culture. When using a lingua franca for communication in a multicultural team, participants intuitively transfer their own culture-specific rules when communicating in a foreign language with other-culture individuals (Wierzbicka 1994). From the others' perspective, this continually leads to unintentional rule violations and in the worst case to a breakdown in communication. Therefore, even if team members have a sophisticated command of the chosen lingua franca, there is no guarantee that they will be able to communicate effectively. On the

2 According to Scheu-Lottgen and Hernandez-Campoy (1998), "communication style" comprises the following elements: "(i) when to talk, (ii) what to say, (iii) prosodic patterns, (iv) listenership, (v) politeness, (vii) organization of discourse, (viii) accent accommodation, and (ix) swearing, insults and irony" (p. 379).

contrary, excellent, near-native foreign language competence increases the risk of falsely interpreting the underlying cultural meaning of certain terms when using the common team language. For example, two speakers use the same expression, which each imbues with the values of his/her respective culture. However, since the conversation is not interrupted by the nonnative speaker's lack of vocabulary or stumbling over linguistic rules, the native speaker falsely assumes that his conversation partner is also familiar with the cultural implications of the expressions and therefore perceives the meaning in the same way. If the conversation continues in this vein, serious communication barriers may arise and lead to the team partners losing confidence in one another.

If a multicultural team consists of both native speakers and nonnative speakers, the native speakers, in particular, have a specific responsibility. On the one hand, they should practice self-discipline and avoid using idiomatic expressions, local accents and culturally nuanced innuendos; on the other, they need to give nonnative speakers enough time to think and to formulate their comments. During the process of active listening, native speakers with practice in intercultural team communication often assume the task of paraphrasing what nonnative speakers have said to ensure that everyone has understood correctly. This kind of proactive behavior encourages the nonnative speakers and precludes giving them the feeling that their position in the group is less influential or their contributions less valuable due to their language handicap (cf. Scheu-Lottgen and Hernandez-Campoy 1998).

The participants experience feelings of insecurity and anxiety if they feel unable to communicate effectively with their teammates. In his "Anxiety/Uncertainty Management Theory", Gudykunst (1993; Gudykunst and Nishida 2001) points out the importance of managing anxiety and uncertainty productively:

"When anxiety is very high, ... individuals rely on simplistic information processing (e.g., stereotypes) and, therefore, cannot communicate effectively. When *uncertainty* is very high, individuals do not have the confidence necessary to predict or explain others' attitudes, feelings, or behaviors. When *anxiety* is very *low*, individuals are not motivated to communicate, and when *uncertainty* is very *low*, individuals are overconfident in their predictions of others' behavior. *When anxiety and uncertainty are either very high or very low, they do not predict effectiveness of communication*" (Gudykunst and Nisida 2001, p. 56; italics by the author).

Fear and uncertainty must lie within the maximum and minimum thresholds to allow for effective communication in a multicultural team.

To ensure cooperation in multicultural teams, it is essential that the members are familiar with the cultural characteristics of the communication styles of other members in the group. They, and this includes virtual teams, must pay particular attention, and this includes virtual teams, to the rules of communication established within the team, and to apply them continuously as a matter of practice within the scope of team building exercises. Skipping these steps entails the risk that team members might feel offended by a different communication style resulting in their withdrawal from the interaction, their refusal to contribute or their display of disruptive behavior, all of which can hamper team efforts.

1.5.8 Language as a Power Factor in Multinational Companies

The significance of an official corporate language in multinational companies and the role it plays in integrating the local language in interactions between headquarters and subsidiaries worldwide has not yet been extensively researched. There are, however, a number of studies (Marshan-Piekkari et al. 1997, 1999; Ferner et al. 1995: Park et al. 1996; Chikudate 1995) that indicate that most companies underestimate the significant multi-faceted influence their employees' (lack of) language competence exerts. Less than ten years ago, only 19% of American executives considered speaking a foreign language in a business context as very important (Dowling et al. 1994, quoted from Park et al. 1996). The employees in the subsidiaries, on the other hand, are expected to speak the official corporate language. While upper management may meet this requirement, employees at the mid- or operative level are rarely able to follow. This group considers the lack of foreign language ability a significant hindrance to communication within the corporation. Written material compiled by headquarters in the corporate language and distributed to foreign subsidiaries are frequently not understood and have to be translated on site into the local language before notice is taken of it (Marshan-Piekkari et al. 1999).

Moreover, it turns out that a lack of language ability obstructs horizontal knowledge transfer between the individual departments of a company. As a result, subsidiaries often form separate entities that are disconnected from both informal control mechanisms and personal networks at the horizontal level (Ferner et al. 1995).

In their research on the key function of language mediation between headquarters and subsidiaries in multinational Finnish companies, Marschan-Pickkari et al. (1999) identified another significant aspect. They found that an employee at the middle management level assumed responsibilities within the organization that clearly lay above his area of responsibility because of his language ability. Due to his networking skills, he was privy to information that was not accessible to others and could also gather information, giving him more influence on company matters than his actual responsibilities entailed. According to this study, an employee who speaks the language of headquarters, the corporate language and the language spoken at the subsidiary is in an absolute position of power since he can communicate at all levels of the organization. Because of the key position he holds in the company, this employee can influence established communication processes or, seen from another perspective, pose a risk to the entire formal corporate structure.

Another interesting research finding concerns the discrepancy between the official structure of the multinational (Finnish) organization and the shadow structures that evolve from the language clusters (Marshan-Piekkari 1999). Management had structured the organization according to geographic areas, so that officially there were divisions for northern Europe, central Europe, southern Europe, North America and the Asia/Pacific Region. In reality, however, a shadow structure developed due to linguistic affiliations and the ensuing closer cooperation between the organizations whose native language was English, German, Spanish or one of the Scandinavian languages. These shadow structures tended to wield more influence than the organizational structure originally prescribed.

On the basis of their studies, Marschan-Piekkari et al. (1999) claim that global businesses must realize that it is not possible to lead a worldwide organization efficiently if managers at headquarters are not multilingual. Surprisingly enough, however, literature on international management rarely mentions the language factor.

1.5.9 Conclusion

Language holds a key position in intercultural communication. Foreign language competence, especially English as a lingua franca, is expected from individuals active in the fields of business, politics and cultural affairs. Language competency as a linguistic tool, in itself, however, is not enough for acquiring the increasingly important intercultural competence, which above all requires a familiarity with the culture-specific rules of interaction. Thus, it is not necessarily a relief to know that the foreign negotiation partner speaks the other's native language. Language ability does not automatically imply communicative competence with other cultures. English native speakers, in particular, might benefit from this "wake-up call". Native speakers often assume that because English is the language of business worldwide, it is up to the nonnative speakers to be proficient in English. The English speakers' initial advantage might well backfire and lead to a competitive disadvantage if foreign language requirements are not integrated into the curricula. Even though foreign language skills alone do not suffice for competent intercultural communication, acquiring a foreign language within the context of modern foreign language education is closely linked to concepts of cultural sensitivity. This factor constitutes a significant step in the direction of intercultural competence.

References

Bailey, M. (2002): So you want to speak Esperanto? http://www.micheloud.com/FXM/LA/LA/esperanto.htm (as of 28. April 2002).

Brock, D. M., Barry, D.; Thomas, D. (2000): »Your forward is our reverse, your right, our wrong«: rethinking multinational planning processes in light of national culture. International Business Review 9: 687–701.

Bouton, L. F. (1999): Developing non-native speaker skills in interpreting conversational implicatures in English. In: Hinkel, E. (Ed.), Culture in Second Language Teaching and Learning, Cambridge, pp. 47–70.

Cherry, C. (1980): On Human Communication: A Review, a Survey and a Criticism. Cambridge, MA.

Chikudate, N. (1995): Communication network liaisons as cultural interpreters for organizational adaptation in Japan-Europe business environments. Management International Business Review 35 (Sonderheft): 27–38.

Crystal, D. (1997): English as a Global Language. Cambridge.

d'Iribarne, Ph. (1989): La logique de l'honneur. Paris.

DiStefano, J. J.; Maznevski, M. L. (2000): Creating value with diverse teams in global management. Organizational Dynamics 29 (1): 45–63.

Ferner, A.; Edwards, P.; Sisson, K. (1995): Coming unstuck? In search of the ›corporate glue‹ in an international professional service firm. Human Resource Management 34: 343–361.

Firth, A. (1996): The discursive accomplishment of normality: On ›*lingua franca*‹ English and conversation analysis. Journal of Pragmatics 26: 237–259.

Frank, H.; Harvey, O. J.; Verdun, K. (2000): American responses to five categories of shame in Chinese culture: A preliminary cross-cultural construct validation. Personality and Individual Differences 28: 887–896.

Gallois, C.; Callan, V. J. (1997): Communication and Culture. A Guide for Practice. Chichester/New York/Weinheim u. a.

Gesteland, R. (1999): Cross-Cultural Business Behavior: Marketing, Negotiation and Managing Across Cultures. Kopenhagen.

Glaser, E. (2001): Learning how to work in multicultural teams. In: Cuk, A.; Del

Campo, F., One Community and Many Identities: On the Crossroads of a New Europe. Sietar Europa Congress Proceedings 1999. Triest, pp. 298–310.
Glaser, E. (2002): Cultural Divergence or Convergence: What is Better for the Individual, the Group, and the Organisation? In: Cormeraie, S.; Killick, P.; Parry, M., Revolutions in Consciousness: Local Identities, Global Concerns in ›Languages and Intercultural Communication‹, pp. 91–102.
Glaser, E. (1998): The language class as a training-ground for working in multicultural teams. In: Killick, D.; Parry, M., Cross-Cultural Capability. The Why, the Ways and the Means: New Theories and Methodologies in Language Education. Leeds, pp. 202–210.
Grice, H. P. (1975): Logic and conversational implicature. In: Cole, P. (Ed.), Syntax and Semantics. New York, pp. 411–458.
Gudykunst, W. B. (1993): Toward a theory of effective interpersonal and intergroup communication: An anxiety/uncertainty management perspective. In: Wiseman, R. L.; Koester, J. (Eds.), Intercultural Communication Competence. Newbury Park, CA, pp. 33–71.
Gudykunst, W. B.; Nishida, T. (2001): Anxiety, uncertainty, and perceived effectiveness of communication across relationships and cultures. International Journal of Intercultural Relations 25: 55–71.
Gumperz, J. (1992): Contextualization and Understanding. In: Duranti, A.; Goodwin, C. (Eds.), Rethinking Context: Language as a Phenomenon. Cambridge, pp. 229–252.
Hall, E. T. (1976): Beyond Culture. New York.
Holden, N. (2002): Cross-Cultural Management: A Knowledge Management Perspective. Harlow/England/London/New York u. a.
Holden, N.; Cooper, C. L.; Carr, J. (1998): Dealing with the New Russia: Management Cultures in Collision. Chichester, UK.
Kirkman, B. L.; Gibson, C. B.; Shapiro, D. L. (2001): »Exporting« teams: Enhancing the implementation and effectiveness of work teams in global affiliates. Organizational Dynamics 30 (1): 12–29.
Luhmann, N. (2000): Vertrauen. Ein Mechanismus der Reduktion sozialer Kompetenz. 4th ed. Stuttgart.
Mallick, K. (1997): Language diversity and intercultural education. In: Woodrow, D.; Verma, G. K.; Rocha-Trinidade, M. B.; Campani, G.; Bagley, C. Intercultural Education: Theories, Policies and Practice. Aldershot/Burlington USA/ Singapore/Sidney, 2001.
Marschan-Piekkari, R.; Welch, D.; Welch, L. (1997): Language: the forgotten factor in multinational management. European Management Journal 15 (5): 591–598.
Marschan-Piekkari, R.; Welch, D.; Welch, L. (1999): In the shadow: the impact of language on structure, power and communication in the multinational. International Business Review 8: 421–440.
Ogden, C. (1930): Basic English. A General Introduction with Rules and Grammar. London.
Park, H.; Hwang, S. D.; Harrison, J. K. (1996): Sources and consequences of communication problems in foreign subsidiaries: the case of United States firms in South Korea. International Business Review 5 (1): 79–98.
Quirk, R. (1982): International communication and the concept of Nuclear English. In: Brumfit, D., English for International Communication. Oxford, pp. 15–28.

Reber, G.; Jago, A. G. (1997): Festgemauert in der Erde ... Eine Studie zur Veränderung oder Stabilität des Führungsverhaltens von Managern in Deutschland, Frankreich, Österreich, Polen, Tschechien und der Schweiz zwischen 1989 und 1996. In: Klimecki, R.; Renner, A. (Eds.), Personal als Strategie. Bern, pp. 158–184.
Renn, J.; Straub, J.; Shimada, S. (Eds.) (2000): Übersetzung als Medium des Kulturverstehens und sozialer Integration. Frankfurt a. M./New York.
Sapir, E. (Ed.). (1921): Language: An Introduction to the Study of Speech. New York.
Sapir, E. (1929): The status of linguistics as science. Language 5: 209–210.
Sapir, E. (1956): Culture, Language and Personality. Berkeley, CA.
Scheu-Lottgen, U. D.; Hernández-Campoy, J. M. (1998): An analysis of sociocultural miscommunication: English, Spanish and German. International Journal of Intercultural Relations 22 (4): 375–394.
Seidlhofer, B. (2001): Closing a conceptual gap: the case for a description of English as a lingua franca. International Journal of Applied Linguistics 11 (2): 133–158.
Steinfatt, T. (1989): Linguistic relativity: A broader view. In: Ting-Toomey, S.; Korzenny, F. (Eds.), Language, Communication, and Culture: Current Directions. Newbury Park, CA.
Ting-Toomey, S. (1999): Communicating across Cultures. New York/London.
Watson, W. E., Johnson, L.; Zgourides, G. D. (2002): The influence of ethnic diversity on leadership, group process, and performance: an examination of learning teams. International Journal of Intercultural Relations 26: 1–16.
Wierzbicka, A. (1994): Cultural scripts: A new approach to the study of cross-cultural communication. In: Pütz, M. (Ed.), Language Contact, Contact Language. Amsterdam/Philadelphia.
Williamson, O. E. (1975): Markets and Hierarchies: Analysis and Antitrust Implications. A Study in the Economics of Internal Organization. New York.
Whorf, B. L. (1950): Four Articles on Metalinguistics. Washington, DC.
Whorf, B. L. (1952): Collected Papers on Metalinguistics. Washington, DC.

Alexander Thomas

1.6 Intercultural Perception, Communication and Cooperation

1.6.1 Phases of Intercultural Perception

When individuals leave their country of birth voluntarily or are forced to do so and settle in a country that is foreign to them for a shorter or longer time period, it can be assumed that such persons will experience considerable difficulties understanding and adapting to their new environment during the initial phase. Psychological and, to some degree, physical well-being are particularly affected during this phase. However, the longer the stay in the foreign environment and the more the individual adapts and acquires coping skills, the easier it gets to interact with people of the host country. Soon the psychological and physical pressures, too, will subside and the sense of well-being will gradually improve and stabilize (q.v. Ch. I, 1.8).

Reports on the emotional state of mind during preparations for departure to the host country, at the time of arrival and during the initial adaptation phase, including scientific studies conducted over the different phases, show an entirely different development. During the preparation phase, the feeling is generally one of excitement and anticipation prior to the move abroad, especially if the choice was made voluntarily and accompanied by positive expectations. The next phase is apprehension, particularly with regard to the many details that must be taken into consideration prior to departure. Upon arrival in the host country, the anxiety felt earlier about adaptation dissipates. In spite of the differences, things appear familiar enough. An initial elation sets in, together with a euphoric sense of well-being and a clear reduction of acculturation strain. In the process of settling in and experiencing the differences with local nationals and business partners first hand, a gnawing feeling of insecurity gradually sets in with the realization that expectations are not being met and things are not going according to plan. Unexpected reactions seem puzzling, make little sense or cause astonishment and helplessness. These are the more harmless cases. A worst-case scenario can end in frustration, anger and aggression, eventually leading to a termination of the cooperation and a return to the home country. In most cases, once the lowest point of the adaptation phase has been reached, the acclimatization phase begins and, with it, a process of re-adaptation at a higher level of intercultural understanding. This reduces the stress factor considerably and contributes to an increased sense of well-being. This condition may last until the time for departure moves closer and the individual now feels anxiety at the prospect of returning home. Back home, the initial return phase is experienced as exciting without being aware of the inevitable re-adaptation crisis that follows. Gradually the re-adaptation stress subsides and is replaced by the reintegration phase.

Common wisdom teaches that every beginning is difficult and with time and gradual adaptation life becomes easier. This does not necessarily hold true for the transition from one culture to another. The strain of acculturation and the felt sense of well-being based on the quality of life from the initial planning phase prior to departure, to readjustment to the familiar environment that may have become very "foreign" over time, include a highly complex process of phases.

The reason for this phenomenon is, among other things, the specific organization of human perception. The given stimulus is not merely registered. It is sorted out in a variety of ways and interpreted on the basis of previously existing hypotheses, expectations and intentions. This is also the case with intercultural perception. The initial euphoria at the beginning of a stay in a foreign country is not only due to positive experiences made in the host country, but also to a sense of relief after releasing pent-up insecurities about anticipated adaptation problems, coping in an unfamiliar environment and communicating in a language in which one is not fluent. Against the backdrop of all imagined situations of what could happen while in the host country, experiences during the first phase actually turn out to be less threatening than expected. No doubt this also has to do with the behavior of the locals, who are curious and look forward to the encounter, and are at first friendly and polite in an effort to create a pleasant and welcoming atmosphere for the new arrival. As soon as this "honeymoon" phase is over and the daily routine sets in, the newcomer finds out fairly quickly that what he experienced and had come to expect during the beginning phase is not necessarily the rule. Encounters and communication partners are continually in flux, many of them behaving contrary to expectation. This can lead to considerable orientation difficulties as both the newcomer's and the locals' perceptions are colored by their different culture-specific systems of orientation. Interpersonal perception, communication and cooperation come into action in the beginning overlap situation, that is, a situation in which the culture-specific imprint of each individual determines how an experience is perceived and what response can be expected. This is the exact point at which the intercultural aspect emerges in the structure of the interaction.

Perception, communication and cooperation are closely interrelated during most phases of the intercultural encounter since communication always presupposes the partner's perception and communication, perception being the indispensable basis for any form of cooperation. This interlacing creates even more specific forms of character imprint.

1.6.2 Intercultural Perception

This work of reference is based on the following definitions of culture (q.v. Ch. I, 1.1): Culture refers to the part of the environment that was created by human beings. Culture always manifests in a system of sense-giving/orientation characteristic to a nation, society, organization or group.

This system of organization consists of specific symbols, such as language, which any given society, organization and group passes on from generation to generation. The system of orientation influences the perception, thought, values, feelings and actions of all members of a society. Culture structures a population-specific domain, reaching all the way from man-made tools and other objects to a culture's institutions, ideas and values.

The specific definition of culture as a system of orientation is central, providing the members of a given culture with a sense-giving capacity. This system of orientation and its significant function are not inherent, but are acquired during the course of individual socialization. If socialization is defined in terms of acquired socially relevant values, convictions and rules of behavior within a given society, which become internalized to the point of being experienced as an inextricable part of the self, then it becomes clear that the core process of personal development functions culture specifically. The decisive factor is that the culture-specific system of orientation is internalized to the degree that it automatically guides our behavior without requiring our conscious awareness for each step of this process.

Individuals who have developed a high level of social competence while incorporating socially relevant norms, values, convictions and behavioral rules during the course of their life are able to function relatively conflict-free within their culture and have learned to interact productively. In this respect, the individual has mastered the signs and symbols of interpersonal communication, can get his message across, convey thoughts and feelings and influence others in a strategic and convincing manner while working towards mutual understanding. This includes being able to intuit the communication partner's emotional state within the overall context, recognize wishes, goals, aspirations and intentions and the ability to empathize with the other person, thus allowing him to react to the other's wishes and expectations appropriately.

Problems arise when the individual encounters others, whose inherent system of signs and signals deviate so considerably from his own that unexpected reactions on the part of the partner are almost inevitable, possibly causing a total lack of understanding or, even worse, misunderstanding. In such cases, misperception, misinterpretation, misunderstanding and even conflict are almost pre-programmed and often occur while observing, interpreting and attributing traits to the partner's behavior (Thomas 2000).

In such an interaction, a feeling of mutual discomfort may be present as neither partner's expectations are being met in terms of respective familiar behavioral patterns. As a rule, they do not have the means to reflect or, for that matter, recognize the causes of such misperceptions and misinterpretations. Both partners observe and interpret the situation from the perspective of their respective culture-specific orientation systems, which kicks in automatically without conscious awareness since its effectiveness and consequences have become part of the daily routine. Each partner takes for granted that his way of perceiving and interpreting the world and his behavior in a given situation is the right way (truth postulate), the appropriate way (fairness postulate) and the reasonable way (rational postulate). Moreover, the assumption is that all human beings act in this way (universal postulate). Each partner most likely assumes that the other will act in accordance with respective expectations. If this does not happen, it is assumed that the partner did not understand (an explanation is required) or that he made a mistake because he doesn't know the correct way (educational background/training is required) or something is purposely done in a way that does not correspond to the "right way" (supervision is required). Consequently, the cause for such contrary behavior is attributed to the partner (interpersonal causal attribution) and interpreted as ignorance, incompetence or unwillingness. Repeated encounters with behavioral patterns which do not correspond with one's own expectations lead to causal behavior on the one hand, and to solidifying preconceived attitudes and stereotyping on the other. The association goes even further to include the partner's in-groups, for example, the department, trade or professional affiliation and the national/cultural affiliation to which he belongs and which he represents.

A further important factor in the organization of intercultural perception is the particular reaction types that emerge as a result of the demands placed on people during an intercultural encounter. Individuals react to intercultural situations in surprisingly different ways as can be seen in the four different reaction types characterized below:

- *The Ignoramus:* For this type, anyone who thinks and acts contrary to his expectations is either stupid, unwilling or incompetent. Whoever continues to behave "inappropriately" after all conceivable efforts to "educate" him is a hopeless case and will not be considered a suitable partner. Culture-based behavioral differences are considered irrelevant.
- *The Universalist:* This type believes that human beings all over the world are basically the same. Cultural differences have little significance. He is convinced that all problems can be overcome by friendliness, tolerance and assertiveness, while all culture-based differences quickly disappear as a result of cultural convergence and the "global village" factor.
- *The Doer:* This type is not particularly interested in the influence that culture exerts on thinking or behavior. According to him, the important thing is that a person knows what he wants, can communicate clear goals and knows how to implement them. The individual, who is aware of his strengths and applies his expertise to maintain the competitive edge, is considered successful, regardless of the culture to which he belongs or in which he operates.
- *The Enabler:* This type believes that a culture develops its culture-specific forms of thought and action, which are learned, considered appropriate and accepted by a given culture. In international cooperation, the key is to recognize and acknowledge the potential inherent in different thought and action patterns. Cultural differences can be integrated and aligned to create synergies, which will ultimately prove advantageous to the parties involved.

The Enabler is actually the only one among these reaction types who considers cultural differences to be of importance and makes an effort to deal with them constructively. For the Ignoramus, the Universalist and the Doer, culture-based influence is marginalized.

Another four-level model relative to this subject is treated in literature and discusses different forms of designating intercultural divergence. This model assumes that cultural differences constitute a relevant variable in cultural overlap situations. Different forms of problem-solving strategies are applied depending on the individuals and the difficulties inherent in the overlap situation:

- *The dominance concept:* Own-culture values and norms are considered superior to those of the other culture. Own strategies for managing conflict, crisis and problem solving are considered to be more appropriate and sophisticated with a proven track record and are enforced over other forms of coping mechanisms. The other-culture partners are pres-

sured to acquire new skills and to adapt their behavior to own-cultural standards.
- *The assimilation concept:* The other-culture values and norms are willingly accepted and integrated into the own modus operandi. Tendencies to adapt to the other-culture values and norms can be so intense that the identification with one's own culture pales as the wish to merge with the other culture intensifies.
- *The divergency concept:* Own- and other-culture values and norms are considered significant and effective. Many aspects, however, are incompatible and often contradictory leading to permanent and continual shifts between cultures. This becomes particularly evident in the beginning phase of the collaboration, when uncertainty about one's own values, norms and behavior emerge, affecting both individual quality of life and productivity at work in the long term.
- *The synthesis concept:* Culture-specific differences are considered to be equally important and valuable in developing overall potential. Efforts are made to synergize the salient resources of both cultures to create a new norm for future cooperation.

Based on Layes' (2000) model, in which experiences with and processing of encounters with otherness in cultural overlap situations is treated, three basic modes of experiencing can be differentiated (q.v. Ch. I, 1.9):
- *Goal Orientation:* Here the focus is on learning about the partner's task-oriented goals.
- *Clarification Orientation:* Here the focus is on finding out why the partner acts the way he does (action-guiding principle).
- *Relationship Orientation:* Here the focus is on the partner's situation-specific thoughts, feelings and intentions.

It is not clear if these typologies correspond to person-specific reaction and processing patterns, which are activated as soon as the individual is compelled to deal with cultural overlap situations or if it pertains more to reaction patterns specific to a particular domain. It is quite possible that the same person favors reaction and processing forms in everyday cultural overlap situations that are different to those in a work-related situation of cultural overlap. In any case, perception sensitivity, perception guidance, selection and interpretation of perceived events are influenced by these factors.

It could be argued that the emphasis here is on other-culture perception with intercultural perception playing a lesser role. The main focus is on how the person perceives the other-culture individual. In other words, the discussion centers on the preconditions of an actual encounter with other-culture behavior. Intercultural perception must ideally be aware of, and take into consideration, both own-culture and other-culture idiosyncrasies. This ability can be nurtured and developed by sensitization to own-cultural idiosyncrasies and orientation systems. From this vantage point of self-knowledge, other-culture systems of orientation can be perceived as different yet equally valid in their respective cultural domain. Congruent own- and other-culture perception is a prerequisite for the third, new and very specific level of stimuli configuration.

1.6.3 Intercultural Communication

Communication is the most important form of social interaction and intercultural communication plays a key role in cultural encounters. Socio-psychological studies done on methods of communication (verbal and nonverbal), communication channels (acoustical, optical, tactile, interpersonal and media), the nature of the message (symmetrical or asymmetrical) and the objective (informative, self-presentation, influence, power and relationship oriented) are key factors in verifying cultural determinants that regulate the communicative process. Tactile communication channels, for instance, play a far greater role in South America, North Africa, and the Middle East than in German or Anglo-Saxon culture.

Intercultural communication implies communication (forms, means and disruptions) under conditions of cultural overlap while the communication partners' cultural differences strongly influence the communication episode in terms of process and outcomes.

During the process of intercultural communication, the following psychological perceptions are stimulated and amplified:

- Dealing with the contrast between familiarity and otherness.
- A feeling of personal involvement, the intensity of which depends on the impact of prior experience and future action in cultural overlap situations.
- Cognitive and emotional conditions required for restructuring perception and judgment of persons, events and symbols.
- A need for social support for orientation and identity security.
- A need for interpersonal consistency, found in the increased tendency to strengthen cultural identity, group security and space-time stability (cf. Thomas, 1989).

The psychologically significant consequences of intercultural communication become evident in the following processes:

- Borderline experiences with regard to language competency, behavior routines and habits, as well as judgment patterns and attribution.
- Experience with differentiation and variability gained through other-culture ways of dealing with communicative challenges.
- Experience with unfamiliar categorization and labeling on the part of the other-culture partner. For example, the first encounter is with own national and cultural identity through the eyes of other-culture partners and their judgments.
- Becoming aware of and involuntary dismantling own-culture habits of perception, thought and action in dealing with other-culture patterns in the host country.

Misunderstandings frequently arise when people communicate because of information deficits, incompatible goals and expectations, mood and situational interpretation. Most often the causes of such misunderstandings are clarified and resolved. There are also conversations during which a latent feeling of not-understanding-correctly persists, in spite of all efforts to create mutual understanding. The cause is then attributed to the partner and takes on a personal note, such as the other's fixed idiosyncrasies, personality traits and other quirks. The cause for the misunderstanding then becomes personal and is blamed on the person's weakness or idiosyncrasy. Consequently, one tries to tolerate the partner's particular approach, perhaps also to endure it. If the dissonance proves insurmountable, the relationship is be terminated.

Communicative misunderstanding and interactions of this nature occur more frequently in intercultural encounters where interdependency exists between individuals from different cultures. While such dissonances occur more frequently in intercultural encounters than under mono-cultural circumstances, the causal typology is more inconsistent. Individuals who differ considerably from each other exhibit consistently adverse, unfamiliar and puzzling reactions and behavior in their communication under similar conditions.

Individuals who have task-specific, other-culture encounters on a regular basis were interviewed with regard to their experience with adverse behavior. They tended to categorize their observations on a relatively high level of abstraction according to typical characteristics and criteria. Moreover, they appeared to have difficulty giving a detailed description of a series of events and actual interaction episodes and in expressing feelings and expectations. The interviewees experienced some difficulty in grasping the meaning of the partner's reactions and were uncertain about the consequences of the encounter. The collected communicative interactions with other-culture partners, which are very detailed in the actual encounter, are transformed into a summary of experienced knowledge, reminiscent of culture-typical characteristics so that the experience can be communicated. Careful interviewing is required in order to obtain an account of real-time intercultural interaction. This presented a problem for the interviewees as they were thrown off balance and became disoriented as a result of the partner's unexpected and unfamiliar behavior. They were not accustomed to operating within an interaction framework that did not correspond to familiar rules of communication.

The subject of fluency in the partner's native language and how it affects the intercultural communication process is often a topic of discussion (q.v. Ch. I, 1.5). Many believe that language fluency in a given foreign language is the prerequisite for intercultural understanding and fundamental for the success and appropriateness of an intercultural encounter. No doubt, fluency in the language of the host country is a prerequisite for intercultural communication at a higher level. Frequently, however, intercultural communication does not take place in the language of the host country, but in a third language native to neither one of the partners, such as English, for example. Even if both partners allegedly speak the third language fluently, one can assume that sophisticated communication is no longer possible since much of what one partner wants to communicate in the way of nuances gets lost in foreign language discourses due to the process of de- and encoding. In most cases, however, the partners do not have an equal level of language fluency. If one of the partners is more fluent in the third language, then an asymmetrical relationship structure develops, in which one of the partners is in a superior and the other in an inferior position. If, in addition, the more fluent partner tries to accommodate his counterpart by simplifying his language, then the asymmetrical relationship is further aggravated with serious consequences for a communication process based on parity. Under such circumstances, it becomes necessary to rely on an interpreter even if both parties speak the language well enough in everyday situations. This is particularly true for important communication processes involving negotiations, conflict management and discussions dealing with attitudes and personal advancement. This asymmetrical relationship construct intensifies in cases where a foreigner abroad has to communicate in the host's native language because the host cannot speak the guest's language. The tense situation is alleviated somewhat when the host apologizes for not speaking the guest's language and attributes this to a deficit on his part.

All of the cases described here deal exclusively with verbal communication. A further decisive factor in mindful and mutually satisfactory communication is a form of nonverbal communication that is appropriate and acceptable to both parties. Here, clear cultural differences become evident, which are not merely perceived as pleasant or unpleasant accoutrements of the communication process. Moreover, they can be perceived as stressful and interpreted as provocative. If an individual from a culture in which it is usual to emphasize verbal communication with particularly expressive gesticulation and mimicry encounters a partner from a culture in which only the content of the verbal communication has any value and who considers mimicry and gesticulation to be unnecessary and unimportant by-products, then this behavior may be perceived and interpreted as an attempt to suggestively influence opinion or cover up for incompetence. The use of paralinguistic communication features as, for example, pauses of a certain length are perceived and interpreted from a member of one culture as signaling a change of speaker and, in another, as a normal transition from one sentence to another. In such cases a misinterpretation of a pause between sentences causes one of the speakers to feel that he is being cut off and not allowed to finish what he has to say. He will react with resentment and will most likely remain silent and turn away from the encounter, thereby minimizing the chances for resolving the misunderstanding.

Verbally communicated information within the context of intercultural communication differs in status and importance depending on the interaction framework (q.v. Ch. I, 1.4). Asians, for example, will not speak openly about emotionally charged issues on the basis of their strong culturally specific need for harmony. Potential conflict situations that may impact the relationship are treated with utmost care to avoid further aggravating the already impaired sense of harmony. In contrast, in some European and North American cultures, it is not only considered appropriate, but also essential for all involved to engage in in-depth discussions of causes and effects of interpersonal conflict and how to resolve the differences.

It goes without saying that cultures differ in the form of communication modes they use. Some rely on verbal communication, others use this form sparingly and instead employ nonverbal language including a large variety of symbol-laden expressions or simply silence. Members of a culture in which language is of prime importance in dialogue will find it difficult to comprehend the content meaning expressed through silence during an interpersonal encounter. The same goes for nonverbal symbols such as gifts, invitation rituals and honoring people. Frequently, other-culture individuals are not sufficiently sensitized to the array of symbols and profundity of seemingly simple expressions inherent in such gestures. Due to the given situational conditions, a form of meta-communication on the basis of observations of events, which might help to clarify matters, is not possible, as politeness, caution and consideration take precedence.

Everything mentioned so far is generally not included in foreign language learning and it is false to assume that learning a foreign language is sufficient preparation for cultural understanding.

1.6.4 Intercultural Cooperation

Cooperation generally refers to specific behavior that aims to achieve set goals and ensure the well-being of a group or collective on a sophisticated level. Essentially, goals in terms of individual performance and well-being are more likely to be achieved if a number of individuals synchronize their resources in an effort to reach desired results. One can basically assume that individuals strive to optimize the effects their actions will have and ensure that these are of high quality. While they may have their own interests at heart, it can be assumed that they strive for a general high standard of equality, fairness and well-being, such as in communities that are socially significant for them. Kelley and Thibaut's (1978) interdependence theory highlights the importance of understanding the development and the course of cooperative action. The theory assumes that individual action is partially or even entirely determined by other persons or groups, as well as the way in which single individuals can change and interpret a given social situation. Thus the *interdependence theory* provides a clue as to which characteristics are significant for the alternating dependence of action between individuals and groups.

The *extent of the alternating dependence* is based on the individual's ability to achieve performance goals only through the coordinated action of other individuals. If the interdependency is too binding, it can lead to negative feelings of dependency and obligation. Feeling obligated is proactive and an effective prerequisite for positive social behavior in interpersonal and formal organizational relationships. In intercultural terms, it can be expected that persons from individualistic cultures appreciate a balanced relation between a certain amount of alternating dependency and social obligation. On the other hand, they strive for a certain degree of independence, self-sufficiency and the freedom to choose between a range of possible actions. In contrast, persons from more collectively oriented cultures are much more likely to accept and support interdependence and dependency within the primary social collective such as family, organization, division and work group on the basis of their specific cultural system of orientation. This also explains their long-term orientation with regard to feelings of obligation. The need for independence, self-sufficiency and individual choice is noticeably less here, at least where the primary social collective is concerned.

Alternating dependency refers to the extent to which two individuals are alternatively or singly dependent on each other in terms of achieving desired results in an interaction. This aspect is particularly important in connection with symmetrical and asymmetrical contingency and power constellations (Jones and Gerard 1967 in Thomas 1992). Within an intercultural context, individuals from different cultures either remain largely unaware of problems related to the cooperation due to alternating dependencies or they are exaggerated. If, for example, a German entrepreneur plans to outsource production to a developing country for cost reasons and does this because he is convinced that he is helping the developing country by investing "good money" and highly sophisticated know-how in the developing partner company, then any subsequent co-operational endeavors are bound to result in a fundamentally one-sided dependency and power constellation. In this case, the stability of the relationship is seriously threatened. On the one hand, there is an increased risk that the more powerful partner will exploit the one-sided relationship to his advantage, and on the other, the partner may feel that he is being taken advantage of, suppressed and treated unfairly, whether this is justified or not. Notwithstanding a fundamental willingness to cooperate and share different power and resource potential and the determination to create something together, the asymmetrical contingency factor poses a persistent risk to a long-term, sustainable and mutually satisfying cooperation.

Congruent action results refer to the extent to which the results of mutual effort are in compliance. If the parties are unanimously aware of the outcome, then partners are more motivated to cooperate, are more inclined to trust each other and are more likely to commit to a long-term cooperation. If the action results are incongruent, then competition-motivated reactions and feelings of mistrust are triggered, leading to noncooperative and competitive behavior. Usually extra effort in intercultural cooperation is required to evaluate the partners' feelings about the result of an action and the extent to which a satisfactory level of consensus has been achieved. It is inevitable that the evaluation of these results is subject to culture-specific influence. If, for instance, a German subsidiary in a foreign country declares a profit on net earnings as a result of employee cutbacks, then the German corporate board might consider this to be a successful move from a cost-effective standpoint. The heads of the foreign subsidiary, in turn, might see the move as very negative, as employee cutbacks in such numbers goes against the culture's fairness norms and rules for treating fellow human beings, especially when considering the older employees, who in many cultures enjoy the respect due their age and years with the company. Strong economies and state-of-the-art corporate leadership set global norms and standards of evaluation and exert enormous pressure on foreign subsidiaries, particularly in developing countries. Corporate leadership hardly takes note of different evaluation results, not to mention their actual impact on the cooperation.

The basis for the dependency refers to the extent to which the results of an action are influenced by one person alone or by the actions of others. An action can be influenced by the person acting himself, via another person or together with another person. One-sided influencing on the part of one partner appears in the modality of the so-called destiny control. On the other hand, a single individual can influence an action on his own or together with the influence exerted by a partner in a modality of action control.

Destiny control occurs subliminally when one of the partners does the other a great favor, such as by procuring an official building permit for a desirable building site for the subsidiary. Head office in Germany, assuming that this is part of a cooperative goal strategy, takes the "favor" for granted. The partner, however, feels that he has established a binding relationship based on the benevolence of the foreign partner with all the amenities involved that pertain to the prospective cooperation.

Within the context of intercultural cooperation, and particularly with regard to the aspects of intercultural perception and intercultural communication discussed earlier, it becomes evident that if short-term self-interest is the motivation, then cooperation cannot be successful (q.v. Ch. I, 1.10).

The key is to strive for mutually satisfying results in an effort to achieve an enduring cooperation that ensures against setbacks and resistance.

The interdependence theory (Kelley and Thibaut 1978) introduces the concept of transformation based on a typology of social value orientation in this context (see Figure 5).

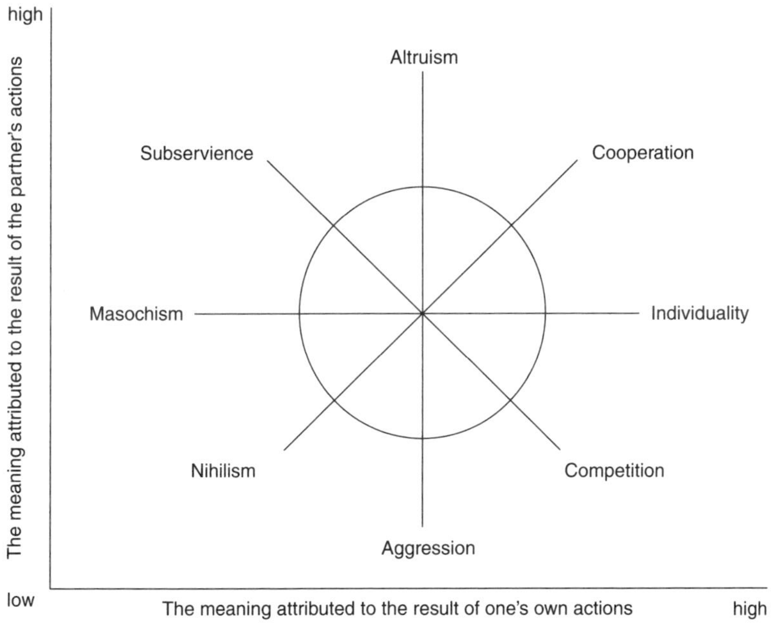

Figure 5: Typology of social values (according to McClintock 1972; from Stroebe et al. 2001, p. 392)

According to this model, cooperation stands in opposition to nihilism and represents the type of social value orientation that strives for positive action results for both oneself and the partner.

The driving force for the transformation process, e.g., a turning away from absolute self-interest toward including the partners in an orientation of positive action, includes the following:

- *Verification of the partner's behavior* based on prior information, expectations, observation of the partner's reactions to offers of cooperation, an agreement on expected goals for understanding the way in which verbal communication is to be conducted, an impression of the partner's personality and information about his group membership.
- *Relationship characteristics* based on personal satisfaction with the relationship, the extent of trust and willingness to commit to mutual responsibility.
- *Interpersonal disposition* based on individual value orientation (see Figure 5), including trust, honesty and responsibility for consequences.
- *Social norms* that are prevalent in a society/culture, such as equality of distribution, procedural justice, norms based on equal rights and norms of contribution and need.

The prerequisite for effective cooperation is the ability to deal with a large number of culture-based variables during the change processes. The efforts the acting partner must exert to identify his counterpart's intentions, willingness and likely reaction to decisions and behavior is far more complicated than in a mono-cultural cooperation. Intercultural cooperation not only involves individuals concerned with reaching common goals, but is also representative of a larger group. On this macro-level of society, the willingness to cooperate decreases with an increase in group size, due to more anonymity in larger groups, a feeling of incompetence at not seeing one's efforts rewarded and an increasing vagueness about "who does what". Strengthening norms, goal-oriented communication, commitment and reinforcing a feeling of "we are all in this together" can enhance cooperation in larger groups. These cooperative enhancement measures are difficult to implement in the process of intercultural communication and require stamina, repeated attempts at rapprochement and a high level of esteem for the other-culture partner. When individuals, as representatives of groups, interact with each other, e.g., where the focus is on inter-group relations, which is most often the case in intercultural relations as in all cooperative action, the discussion necessarily includes comparisons between own and other-culture issues. When this happens, a shift between interpersonal and inter-group behavior is probable (q.v. Ch. I, 1.7). This effect can be traced back to three different characteristics:

- There is less trust in inter-group relationships than in intra-group relationships due to the fear of being exploited by other groups.
- Within one's own group there is a higher level of mutual support if one's own-culture group is to be strengthened at the expense of the other-culture group.
- Compared to interpersonal relations, inter-group relationships have a higher tendency to attribute self-centered behavior, which results in a lower level of identification with the group (Pemberton et al. 1996).

In the case of intercultural cooperation at the group level, the socio-psychological influence emphasized in the theories of Tajfel and Turner (1986) become effective. For example, the own-culture group bias favors the own group over other groups by granting them more resources and competencies.

A decisive factor in effective intercultural cooperation is, without a doubt, mutual trust in both interpersonal cooperation and the cooperative inter-group relationship. Trust can gradually develop during the course of interaction in a relationship or it can be invested in advance in the relationship at the beginning and during the course of the interaction. The extent to which trust develops, is consolidated and strengthened is dependent on specific learning processes in each case. The most important factors for trust are, on the one hand, the reduction of complexity and, on the other, the simplification of the interaction. Moreover, the amount of trust developed leads to diminished fear, openness, psychological well-being, less inclination toward conflict, willingness to delegate, enhanced self-confidence and the likelihood that the trust granted will be reciprocated in turn. It may be assumed, however, that trust-building measures in terms of verbal and nonverbal communication, including signs and symbols, differ considerably from culture to culture. If, for example, one culture adheres to the motto, "trust is okay but control is better" and the other culture subscribes to "beware of the friend who seeks his own benefit" (Jesus Sirach 6.7), or still another culture believes that "trust is the key to establishing rapport", then this will probably determine the difference between success or failure in intercultural cooperation.

1.6.5 Performance Requirements

Intercultural perception develops once individuals become aware of their sense of cultural belonging, begin to take notice of each other and in some way become meaningful to one another. Such specific interpersonal interactions pose particular challenges to assimilating and processing information:

- Differentiating between personality-specific and culture-specific behavioral traits.
- Determining own- and other-culture specific cultural patterns of orientation regarding expectations.
- Verifying the extent to which one's own observable behavioral traits and those of the partner are determined independently or within the context of the intercultural nature of the encounter and if they are a result of the respective culture-specific system of orientation.
- Reflecting on the convergence and divergence between one's own self-concept, the image the partner has developed of me and what I think the partner's image of me is (self-concept, perception of others and presumed concept of others) and the pattern mirrored by the partner.
- Checking relevant attribution processes to avoid key attribution mistakes:
  - Fundamental attribution mistakes include judging the partner on the basis of behavioral characteristics without consideration of other outside influences and circumstances.
  - Actor-observer influence: As an observer the tendency is to attribute to the personality while the person acting tends to attribute to the situation.
  - Erroneous consensus effect: One's own behavior is seen as universal and norm-conforming. The partner's behavior, on the other hand, is considered unusual and inappropriate.
  - Erroneous attribution of self-confidence: The belief that success is attributable to one's own efforts. Lack of success, on the other hand, is attributed to outside circumstances.

Intercultural communication comprises all forms of communication between individuals from different cultures. Mutual understanding in communication is difficult enough to achieve within one culture, and yet the challenges multiply in intercultural communication due to the use of alternating and unfamiliar verbal and nonverbal symbols, such as foreign language and body language. Divergent attribution of own-culture meaning of familiar symbols such as the tradition of gift-giving, invitations and favor-granting increases the complexity. Considerable attention and sensitivity is required where unexpected behavior occurs, for instance, when a verbal reaction is expected from the partner in response to a verbal action to which he repeatedly does not respond. In this case, it could be assumed that he wishes to express a meaningful "action" by his unexpected silence but it confuses people who communicate verbally to solve problems, obtain information, to ask questions and to get to the heart of the subject matter. "Eloquence" and context-laden silence can be misleading, as blanks or so-called "black holes" in the communication make it difficult to understand the contextual meaning of the symbols and their impact on the communication process.

Problems and misunderstandings in intercultural communication cannot be solved by mere meta-communicative acts. Not all cultures consider it commonplace or appropriate to address problems verbally and publicly. In fact, it often goes against social norms and etiquette. An attempt to communicate on a metaphysical level might in fact unintentionally embarrass the partner and impart the impression that he made a mistake. Regardless of the level of foreign language performance, effective intercultural communication requires a high degree of basic communicative competence, open-mindedness on the social level, communicative agility and flexibility. Further prerequisites are versatility, expressiveness, sensitivity to nuances and empathy.

Anyone who tries not only to understand the partner's needs, but also to convey own goals, wishes and expectations convincingly enough for the partner to understand, accept and be prepared to adapt to them, is taking on a particular challenge in intercultural communication. Here the issue is not about any particular form of adaptation, but rather about achieving a specific balance between own- and other-culture needs during the communication process. This specifies requirements on at least four different levels that examine:

- to what extent own- and other-culture standards are similar to each other (cultural convergence), how far they deviate from each other (cultural divergence) and to what extent own- and other-culture aspects can co-exist (cultural compatibility).
- which own-culture aspects can be modified toward the other culture. The question here is: to what extent can and should one adapt to other-culture norms? Not adapting, or refusing to adapt in any way, usually leads to a direct confrontation with the other culture. Behavior of this sort may be perceived by the other-culture partner as arrogant, dominant or abrasive. On the other hand, the attempt to merge entirely with the unfamiliar culture risks bordering on the ridiculous, aside from the fact that this is unrealistic to begin with due to own-culture origin and socialization.
- to what extent other-culture elements can be modified toward own-culture standards and what chances there are of sensitizing the other-culture individual to own-culture goals and behavior in a way he can recognize, accept and perhaps even approach them. Frequently, the other-culture individual is forced to adapt to the host country or circumstances require him to adapt to the prevailing behavior.

- the productive and destructive effects such attempts at adaptation might have on both own- and other-culture aspects.

Forms of adaptation, on the one hand, and cultural independence, on the other, can certainly be emphasized differently according to different areas of life and working environment and can co-exist at the same time. An example would be the strict adherence to own-culture orientation and customs in private, and flexible adaptation to other-culture systems of orientation in the working environment.

This requires considerable knowledge and skill in dealing with an other-culture system of orientation.

Intercultural cooperation requires an excellent sense of perception for intercultural nuances and the ability to communicate interculturally. The main success factors consist of including both one's own goals and those of the partner in a plan of action in an effort to establish a long-term reliable relationship based on trust. The latter requires specific investments in the form of gifts, invitations, thank you notices, social support, honoring and acknowledging contribution and good will that must be regularly re-evaluated for appropriateness and effectiveness. Positioning this kind of social investment requires considerable intercultural sensitivity: On the one hand, they must be socially acceptable and on the other, they must not infringe on the partner's independence, ability and sense of self-worth. Intercultural competence cannot be mastered through learning by doing alone, that is, via a series of practical experiences, but rather in combination with training and the ability to reflect upon events.

References

Kelley, H. H.; Thibaut, J. W. (1978): Interpersonal Relations: A Theory of Interdependence. New York.

Krewer, B. (1996): Kulturstandards als Mittel der Selbst- und Fremdreflexion in interkulturellen Begegnungen. In: Thomas, A. (Ed.), Psychologie interkulturellen Handelns. Göttingen.

Layes, G. (2000): Grundformen des Fremderlebens – eine Analyse von Handlungsorientierungen in der interkulturellen Interaktion. Münster.

McClintock, C. G. (1972): Social motivation – a set of propositions. Behavioral Science 17: 438–454.

Pemberton, M. J. et al. (1996): Memory for and experience of differential distrust of individuals and groups. Journal of Personality and Social Psychology 71: 953–966.

Stroebe, W. et al. (2002): Sozialpsychologie. Berlin.

Tajfel, H.; Turner, J. (1986): The social identity theory of intergroup behaviour. In: Worchel, S.; Austin, W. G. (Eds.), Psychology of Intergroup Relations. Chicago, pp. 7–24.
Thomas, A. (1989): Kulturelle Bedingungen. In: Roth, E. (Ed.), Enzyklopädie der Psychologie, Band 3: Organisationspsychologie. Göttingen, pp. 186–201.
Thomas, A. (1992): Grundriss der Sozialpsychologie. Band 2: Individuum – Gruppe – Gesellschaft. Göttingen.
Thomas, A. (2000): Group Effectiveness: A Balance between Heterogeneity and Homogeneity. In: Stumpf, S.; Thomas, A. (Eds.), Diversity and Group Effectiveness. Lengerich.

Gabriel Layes

1.7 Intercultural Identity Management

The term "culture" as introduced in the preceding chapters refers to a group of individuals who think, feel and act in a similar way that sets them apart from other groups of individuals. As mentioned earlier, the size of such groups can differ. We have seen that it makes absolute sense to differentiate, for example between national and organizational cultures (q.v. Ch. I, 1). One could take this a step further and say that it would be reasonable to include even smaller entities, such as regional cultures and family cultures. Seen from this perspective, differentiating between cultures is, at the same time, differentiating between particular groups. In more complex societies, each person belongs to many such groups simultaneously. For instance, someone is "German", "a Wessi"[3], "a tax payer", "an automobile driver", "a local politician" and so on, at the same time, and can be identified via a number of very different social characteristics. For example, as the driver of an automobile, a person might be irritated by a radar trap in a strange city, yet as a local politician, the same person might advocate a 15 mph speed limit in his own town. In this way, the same person can present himself in a number of different ways depending on the circumstances, and manifests different or contradictory behavior. Seen from a psychological perspective, assimilating the diverse interests, roles and attitudes that make up an individual's personality into a consistent identity can be quite challenging. Since different attributes of *identity* are stimulated under a variety of circumstances, one must constantly mediate between the parts. This mediation process is referred to as *identity management*.

If culture is not specifically defined in terms of larger groups, such as nations and organizations, then different cultural attributes are reflected in the thought and action patterns of each individual and must be negotiated at this level. Successful identity management leads to the development of *self-perception*. Self-perception not only determines our view of the groups we belong to and the thought and action patterns that prevail in this domain, but also how we see ourselves as individuals in terms of wishes, val-

3 "Wessi" is a term applied to West Germans in unified Germany (i.e., "Wessis" are from former West Germany and "Ossis" are individuals from the former German Democratic Republic).

ues, goals, motives, abilities and attitudes. Naturally, the view we have of ourselves is not a fixed construct that provides specific information on demand. On the one hand, individual wishes, values and goals change dramatically during the course of one's life; on the other, it is difficult in any case to define one's values, the goals one pursues or the factors that motivate our actions because the development of self-perception does not consist of a sequence of fact-based functions, but rather of a unique design in which the individual course of action is interpreted and integrated into a greater sense-making context.

Seen from a psychological perspective, developing self-perception requires sophisticated feats of interpretation and integration and is continually re-evaluated during the course of one's life. Indeed, this uniquely individual development is not insulated against outside determinants. Instead, the surrounding cultural setting is responsible to a large extent for forming a sense of self-perception by suggesting a wide range of possible specific wishes, values, goals, etc.

This becomes particularly evident in the various phases of development that an individual goes through along the lines of a classic "Western" life history: From birth to starting school, the child is imbued with the cultural mindset prevalent within the family. Gradually, parental influence is replaced by the standards of a youth culture, which plays a major role in adolescent self-perception. A further example showing the strong influence certain cultural factors can have on the development of self-perception can be observed in the often dramatic changes in attitude and values of individuals who have spent a longer period of time abroad.

In a well-known article, the researchers Hazel Rose Markus and Shinobu Kitayama (1991) state that a fundamental difference between the self-perception of people in Western and non-Western cultures lies in the way each perceives themselves in relation to their social setting. According to Markus and Kitayama, Western individuals see themselves as autonomous, complete entities, equipped with specific characteristics that are distinctly separate from the social networks surrounding them. This self-perspective is closely related to what Geert Hofstede refers to as "individualism" in his cultural dimension model (q.v. Ch. I, 1.4). Markus and Kitayamma define the self-concept held by individualistic cultures as *independent self* and juxtapose it to the so-called *interdependent self*, which they attribute to the self-concept of individuals from collectivist cultures. Here, the interrelation between the self and the social network is more tightly knit than the independent self. This is illustrated in Figure 6 below.

The individual identity components pertaining to the independent self are marked with an × and are clearly distinct from the social context. In contrast, the interdependent self is perceived as an integral part of a closely-knit

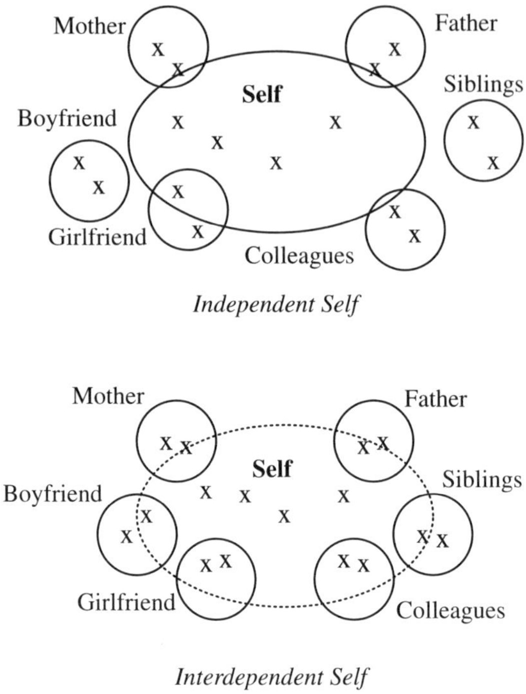

Figure 6: Concepts of self according to Markus and Kitayama (1991, p. 226)

social network. In this sense, the self is not perceived as a closed psychological unit that has "always" existed and is acted upon by the social setting. Instead, the self is seen as a construct that evolves out of interaction with the social network. A definition of the interrelatedness of self within the social network is described from a Japanese perspective by Sugitani (1996).

The development of a self-concept, and with it a sense of identity, always involves distancing oneself and one's in-group from strangers and unfamiliar groups. Correspondingly, each person holds a view of self and *otherness.* As a rule, the better you get to know a person, the more the perception of otherness subsides. In this sense, the view one holds of one's parents or loved ones is probably furthest removed from such a sense of otherness. Nevertheless, these concepts of otherness never correspond entirely with the other person's self-concept and will also never reach their level of differentiation.

It is difficult enough to form a perception of otherness to include the manifold levels of differentiation with persons who are close to us, not to mention how much more diffuse our perception of otherness is with individuals we do not know well or of whom we have only a very vague impression due to their different geographical, political, economic backgrounds and upbringing. Seen from this perspective, it is hardly surprising that en-

Table 2: Self-concept and perception of otherness

Self-concept of German soldiers	**Somali perception of otherness**
The United Nations, as representatives of the international community, sent us here on a humanitarian and peacekeeping assignment. We come here with financial and technical support and know-how. We are confronted with a number of political obstacles and make many material and other sacrifices. We will be able to achieve our peacekeeping goal.	These soldiers come from geographically advantageous regions of the world and have unlimited financial and material resources. We must be careful. This assignment surely involves some sort of benefit for them that they will not tell us about. Perhaps they want to exploit us again like they did in the past during colonial times or they want to persuade us to follow some kind of commandments from the bible that they ignore themselves.
German soldiers' perception of otherness	**Self-concept of Somalis**
The Somalis live in an economically and culturally backward country. Basically, they are to be pitied; especially now since they have become involved in a senseless conflict, the consequences of which they are unable to foresee. They are desperate and entirely dependent on our support.	We are a strong and civilized nation and in many respects superior to many other nations. We have succeeded in combining our traditional values with progressive cultural transformation.
Assumed perception of otherness: German soldiers	**Assumed perception of otherness: Somalis**
The Somalis realize that we come from a rich country and have a very high standard of technology and know that we are well equipped to secure peace. They will be very grateful for our willingness to provide support.	These soldiers probably think we are poor, uncultured and backward, just like the colonialists of the past. To them we are subjects that must be civilized and converted because they presume that our culture is inferior and we cannot manage on our own and thus continually create new problems.

counters between individuals who are very different from each other can lead to a clash between the respective self-concepts and perceptions of otherness, culminating in intercultural conflict. In addition, each party makes assumptions about how they are perceived by the other in such an encounter. In psychological terms this is referred to as an *assumed perception of otherness.* Within the scope of a research project evaluating intercultural episodes experienced by German military personnel on foreign assignments, Thomas, Kammhuber and Layes analyzed the self-concepts, perceptions of otherness and the assumed perception of otherness between German and Somali soldiers. An excerpt from this study highlights the rift between the respective assumptions (Thomas et al. 1997, p. 48, see Table 2).

The potential for intercultural conflict inherent in the different assumptions and expectations is evident. Moreover, this example reveals other characteristics of self-concept and perception of otherness, such as the astonishing revelation that one holds a perception of otherness even in cases where one has never met the dissimilar other or has formed only a vague idea through word-of-mouth descriptions. Although one might never have met the corresponding individuals, it is often assumed, for example, that Scotts are stingy, Japanese are friendly and South Americans are emotional. Perception of otherness like this, in which a population is collectively defined in terms of a few characteristics, is referred to as a *stereotype*.

Hardly anyone is free of such stereotypical assumptions about certain groups of individuals. Withholding judgment is called for here, as it is impossible to have a clear picture of every foreign country, collective or individual, much less be able to grasp the complexity of each individual's or group's corresponding concept of self. It is impossible to continually fine-tune perception to integrate every moment of the diversity that surrounds us without becoming entirely incapacitated. Consequently, the tendency to sort unfamiliar and multi-layered aspects into categories is a fundamental characteristic of human perception.

The situation becomes problematic when there is no longer an awareness of its temporary nature and stereotyping becomes indiscriminate. Under such circumstances, stereotypes can quite easily turn into *prejudices*. From a psychological perspective, prejudices belong to a particular form of social attitude that, like stereotypes, are characterized by simple assumptions based on very little personal experience, include negative overtones and can hardly be reversed even when new and very different information is added.

The psychologist Henri Tajfel (1982) showed that such negatively weighted stereotypes about others form very quickly. In his "Theory of Social Identities", he claims that people tend to attribute negative characteristics to strangers and unfamiliar groups in order to maintain their own positive social identity. In this case, the juxtaposition shown in Table 2 can, for instance, be understood as positive social identity management. The German soldiers perceive their own in-group as superior (selfless, competent etc.) while the dissimilar-other group is devalued (backward, needy etc.). The same thing happens on the Somali side, as they consider themselves competent and progressive while, at the same time, attributing negative characteristics, such as deceitfulness and bigotry, to the dissimilar others.

Individuals who are convinced of the correctness and appropriateness of their behavior during the course of their own identity management, also risk perceiving dissimilar behavior as inappropriate, fragmentary or simply wrong. This is the first step in the direction of prejudice and is continually reinforced by self-fulfilling prophecies. Someone who believes the stereotype that Americans are superficial, for example, may never try to initiate a more meaningful conversation and so never gives the other the chance to prove that he/she is indeed able to communicate on anything other than a "superficial" basis. In this way, the stereotype is confirmed and becomes entrenched. What was formerly an assumption now becomes a personal conviction and, as such, is difficult to change. Moreover, one can now say that one's judgment is based on personal experience.

This makes it clear why stereotypes and prejudices are so widespread and even more difficult to change. Stereotyping provides a range of advantages for one's own identity, such as: orientation in a complex social environment; protection from dissimilar others and groups and the threat to one's own sense of self-worth; a sense of belonging to "favorable" social groups; and it legitimizes subversive behavior against members of an out-group.

Individuals who interact with dissimilar others for professional reasons may have the impression that they are immune to prejudicing. Psychological research, however, has shown that, on the contrary, the mere contact with dissimilar others may even reinforce prejudices. The reason behind this phenomenon is that while observing others, individuals tend to focus on exactly those aspects of behavior that will confirm their preconceptions. If, upon contact with dissimilar others, their behavior actually conforms to their preconceptions, then they are reassured in their initial assessment of the person or situation according to the motto "I actually experienced it!" The person is often even more convinced than before the actual contact occurred.

It is not impossible, however, to break down prejudices. Research has identified specific conditions through which an atmosphere free of prejudices can be fostered or enabled:

- *Cooperation instead of competition.* Cooperation between two individuals on first contact decreases prejudice. Competition promotes prejudice. This is one of the main reasons why prejudices occur, namely the human tendency to segregate persons into own-group and other-group members. Such differentiation is further aggravated in competitive situations. Choosing individuals to join one's own group or the other group depends on subjective selection criteria. The nationality-based differentiation criteria are often based on outside factors such as skin color or other exterior attributes and members are chosen accordingly. If the partners are cooperative, however, similarities and common interests in other areas can emerge and overshadow differences in nationality. In this way, a stranger can become a member of the in-group.
- *Similar status.* Prejudices can be minimized if the partners share a similar economic and social status. Precisely this similarity in status is not given when Europeans or North Americans travel to economically challenged countries. A German diplomat, for example, advises his German colleagues: "When Germans travel to Indonesia, they should be aware

of the fact that they are likely to be bigger, louder, better educated and richer than their Indonesian counterparts. Moreover, they should be aware that these factors may lead Indonesians to perceive them as arrogant, an impression which is easily reinforced by corresponding behavior" (Thomas et al. 1998, p. 284).

- *Close versus superficial contact.* The more superficial the contact between the self and dissimilar others, the greater the danger that the apparent prejudices will be confirmed and consequently strengthened. The closer and more intensive the contact, the better the chances that the partner's perception will be unbiased and more differentiated.
- *Positive social climate.* Prejudices are less likely to arise if the encounters occur in an environment conducive to intercultural exchange and that promotes mutual interaction.
- *Role models.* Prejudices are further minimized if extroverted and socially competent individuals are present and are able to create a mutually satisfying intercultural setting to provide a learning model for others.
- *Overlapping categorization.* During an intercultural encounter, categorization in "we" (e.g., the Germans) and "you" (the others) can hardly be avoided and often occurs automatically. Thus, if possible, it is always a good idea to form a third category to which members of both groups belong, thus expanding beyond a one-sided national-culture collective. For example, in a German-French youth camp, the group of "tennis players" may evolve into an entity that members identify more with than with their common nationality.
- *Avoiding negative, extremist attitudes.* If different views on important subject areas are not overly negative, prejudices can be avoided. In contrast, prejudices prevail if extremely negative pre-existing prejudices are brought to the encounter, for example, when two extremists from enemy countries meet.

On the basis of such criteria, individuals who have a lot of contact with dissimilar others can gauge to what extent their intercultural encounters take place in an unbiased setting and can intuit the situations in which they are prone to becoming victims of their own prejudices. The themes presented here suggest different approaches that may be applied in intercultural situations to ensure a satisfactory outcome in terms of eliminating prejudices. Educators involved in the field of intercultural education can benefit from approaches like these, helping to eliminate stereotyping within the scope of their international youth programs, for example. Raising awareness of existing prejudices and the way they work is quite often a learning experience in itself and the first real step toward preventing prejudices in the first place.

References

Markus, H. R.; Kitayama, S. (1991): Culture and the self: Implications for cognition, emotion, and motivation. Psychological Review 98 (2): 224–253.

Sugitani, M. (1996): Kontextualismus als Verhaltensprinzip: »Kritisch« erlebte Interaktionssituationen in der japanisch-deutschen Begegnung. In: Thomas, A. (Ed.), Psychologie interkulturellen Handelns. Göttingen, pp. 227–245.

Tajfel, H. (1982): Gruppenkonflikt und Vorurteil. Entstehung und Funktion sozialer Stereotypen. Bern.

Thomas, A.; Kammhuber, S.; Layes, G. (1997): Interkulturelle Kompetenz. Ein Handbuch für internationale Einsätze der Bundeswehr. Untersuchungen des Psychologischen Dienstes der Bundeswehr 32: 1–190.

Thomas, A.; Layes, G.; Kammhuber, S. (1998): Sensibilisierungs- und Orientierungstraining für die kulturallgemeine und die kulturspezifische Vorbereitung von Soldaten auf internationale Einsätze. Untersuchungen des Psychologischen Dienstes der Bundeswehr, 33: 1–289.

Gabriel Layes

1.8 Intercultural Learning and Acculturation

This reference book offers an in-depth description of cultural differences and their substantial conflict potential in many areas. However, it would be a mistake to limit the work to a diagnosis of cultural differences and related problem areas. Practical, hands-on professionals who frequently interact with other-culture individuals in private and work-related situations can reap particular benefit from knowing how to preempt problems arising in intercultural situations and to constructively negotiate intercultural issues. Obviously, this knowledge cannot be acquired without a specific, step-by-step learning process. Accordingly, intercultural research differentiates between forms of intercultural learning and develops criteria for both successful and unsuccessful methods of intercultural learning and analyses the conditions under which successful and unsuccessful intercultural learning take place. The definition "intercultural learning" may be understood in terms of intercultural training programs that target intercultural learning initiatives within the scope of a three-day workshop. This deliberate initiative and organized approach is in fact central to intercultural learning and merits further discussion in a separate chapter (q.v. Ch. I, 2.2). The structured approach to intercultural learning within the scope of intercultural training is by no means the only solution. Intercultural learning takes place the moment an individual enters an other-culture setting and begins coping as best he can. In time, this kind of experience is bound to lead to what Stefan Kammhuber refers to as "experience of dissonance between own- and other-culture elements" (2000, p. 51). Intercultural trainings do not usually prepare individuals for dealing with experiences of dissonance, considering the many different global constellations that can lead to intercultural conflict. The scope ranges from the voluntary tourist on a short-term visit in the host country to the involuntary and open-ended sojourn of a refugee struggling to cope in a foreign environment. Individuals are often unaware of the spontaneous intercultural learning and adaptation processes that are mobilized and which are summarized in the concept of *acculturation.*

The Canadian psychologist John W. Berry researched processes of acculturation in depth and differentiates between five types of acculturating groups on the basis of their mobility and willingness to interact with dissimilar others (Berry 1997). One of these five types, the so-called "sojourner", is characterized by his voluntary contact with an unfamiliar culture but who does not intend to stay in the culture. Managers and exchange students in the Western world, for instance, are good examples of this acculturation type. All of the acculturation types studied by Berry have the following characteristics in common: their intercultural contact takes place on other-culture territory and they are in the minority. According to Berry, the form of acculturation depends on the visitors' cultural-based perception of self and otherness (q.v. Ch. I, 1.7). Different forms of acculturation manifest depending on whether or not different cultural characteristics are honored and appreciated. If own-culture values are considered acceptable and appropriate but other-culture values are rejected (*separation*), then the visitor is likely to avoid social interaction with local inhabitants in the host country. In such cases, same-culture individuals group together and interact as they would "at home", avoiding all contact will locals.

In the reverse case, the other culture might be valued to the point where one's own culture, together with its intrinsic orientation system, is rejected (*assimilation*) in favor of other-culture norms, values and behavioral patterns. The idea behind this phenomenon is that of a "cultural melting pot", in which differences merge and develop into an entity.

Where both cultures are equally honored (*integration*), an attempt is made to merge compatible elements of both cultures into an integrated whole. This is the idea behind the cultural mosaic that includes disparity within the entity.

If both one's own culture and the other culture are rejected (*marginalization*), an individual may tend to distance himself from local and social interaction. Fear, a sense of isolation and identity loss often develop alongside of the acculturation process and can lead to sustained personality disorders.

Immigrants are, of course, not always free to choose an acculturation strategy. Rather, they are often required to adhere to specific acculturation strategies imposed by a given society. While open, multi-cultural societies honor the immigrant as an individual and offer him integration and assimilation possibilities, closed and xenophobic societies tend to marginalize immigrants. In some cases, these approaches may become dependent on the host culture's behavioral characteristics and create a discrepancy between the intention to acculturate and the ability to do so, increasing the chances of experiencing "culture shock" in the process. The extent to which possible acculturation stress may be perceived depends on how the acculturation experience is processed and the individual's acculturation stress threshold. According to Berry, the success or failure of dealing with acculturation stress depends on the answers to the following questions:

- What acculturation strategies are used in contact with unfamiliar cultures?
- To what extent can the desired acculturation strategy be implemented with respect to the other-cultural characteristics?
- What status does one's in-group have?
- To what extent does intercultural competence exist at the individual level?
- What phase of the acculturation process is the person going through at the moment?

Aside from these factors, it can be assumed that anyone who regularly interacts with individuals from another culture has had at least a few irritating or stressful experiences. The way in which acculturating individuals deal with such experiences has lead to a number of theoretical models that can be roughly divided into models consisting of steps and phases. The step model focuses in particular on the learning and development opportunities offered by the acculturation experience and distinguishes between different features of intercultural learning. Table 3 by Hoopes (1981) provides a good example of the classic step model.

In contrast to the step models, the phase models attempt to identify prototypical phases and processes during the acculturation process. According to Thomas (1993), a prototypical acculturation process develops according to the diagram in Figure 7.

At the time of departure, certain fears about leaving home arise and are replaced shortly after arrival by initial euphoria triggered by the many exciting new experiences. The novelty of the situation is perceived as positive. However, as the novelty fades, the unfamiliar, often negatively perceived aspects of the culture become more apparent. Eventually this condition leads to an adaptation crisis or culture shock, at which point acculturation stress is highest and the wish to return home at a peak. If this adaptation crisis is mastered successfully, the individual begins to accept and honor the unfamiliar culture and downplay the virtues of the own culture. Now anxiety about returning home sets in. Upon returning, the anxiety subsides initially, only to re-emerge once the initial return euphoria has passed. Frequently, the process leads to a reintegration crisis or heightened acculturation stress in the indigenous culture.

Two phases within this prototypical acculturation process merit particular mention: the experience of culture shock upon entering a dissimilar culture and its counterpart re-entry shock upon returning to the indigenous culture. "Culture shock" has become the generic definition for all negatively experienced phenomena on the part of persons encountering an unfamiliar culture. The concept is misleading as it suggests the kind of

Table 3: Step-by-step model of intercultural learning according to Hoopes (1981)

Step/Level	**Characteristic**
Selective adoption	Partial integration of the foreign world view into one's own world view
Conscious value judgment	Comparison of own and other world views with the help of culturally overlapping and fair standards
Acceptance	Acceptance of other world view without value judgment
Understanding	Honoring the rationale of a foreign world view
Awareness of otherness	Recognizing other world views
Ethnocentricity	One's own world view as the only possible one

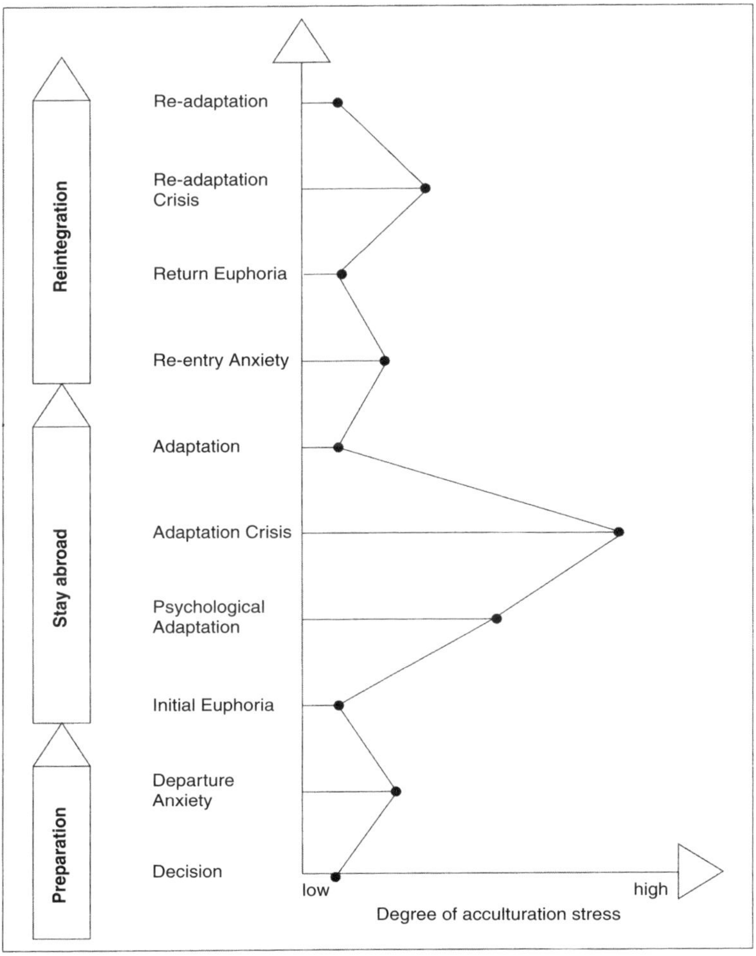

Figure 7: Prototypical acculturation process according to Thomas (1993)

massive shock episodes that are experienced in conjunction with trauma after serious accidents. The definition of culture shock, however, can also be applied to milder forms of irritation and confusion when experiencing foreignness in another culture as well as lead to its rejection. According to Ward et al. (2001), a total of six factors contribute to culture shock. The four "push-factors" lead to rejection of the other culture and the two "pull-factors" attract to the other culture.

"Push" factors (cause rejection of the other culture):
- *Effort:* Dealing with unfamiliar circumstances is difficult. Familiar coping strategies are, for the most part, no longer effective. The process requires concentration as well as trial and error approaches. Things take considerably longer than at home and still do not guarantee success.
- *Helplessness:* Repeated failure can lead to self-doubt and general doubt about the possibility of being able to adapt at all, all of which leads to feelings of helplessness.
- *Role confusion:* There is uncertainty about one's own role from the perspective of the dissimilar other and what role the dissimilar other plays in the grand scheme of things. Consequently, expectations on either side are unclear.
- *Perception of divergence:* It becomes increasingly clear that the other culture adheres to different norms and values, much of which is perceived as irritating, unpleasant or even repulsive. This can lead to racism and discriminating behavior on the one hand, and to increased self-reflection (especially after intercultural trainings) on the other, accentuating feelings of guilt as one feels increasingly incapable of respecting other-culture norms and values.

"Pull" factors (attract one towards the indigenous culture):
- *Homesickness:* One begins missing family and friends and familiar leisure activities. In addition, one begins to worry about things falling apart at home during one's absence.
- *Loss of status:* Occasionally individuals enjoyed a higher social status at home than in the host culture. This is particularly true for individuals who live in a relatively stable social environment within which they are liked and respected. The feeling that one is insignificant in the foreign culture contributes to a feeling of disappointment and a desire to return to the familiar environment.

According to Ward et al. (2001), the intensity of the culture shock depends on the following five factors:

- *Cultural distance:* The less similarities and common interests that exist between the indigenous and other culture, the stronger the effects of culture shock are felt.
- *Task discrepancy:* The more disparate the task that must be accomplished in the indigenous and the other culture, the stronger the effects of culture shock are experienced.
- *Social support:* The less support an individual receives in the other culture, the stronger the effects of culture shock are likely to be felt.
- *Duration and temporal clarity:* There is a tendency to experience culture shock more intensely, the longer the stay in the foreign culture lasts. However, chances of overcoming the initial effects of culture shock increase with the length of the stay. Consequently, a key factor is to be clear on the expected duration of the stay abroad. The clearer an individual is about the prospective stay, the milder the effects of culture shock are likely to be.
- *Choice:* Culture shock is likely to be experienced more intensely if an individual feels that he has been coerced directly or indirectly into an international assignment.

While many individuals with extensive experience abroad are familiar first-hand with the culture shock phenomenon or can, at least, emphasize with it, the return to the indigenous culture is considered by most to be a relatively unimportant event. From a psychological perspective, reintegration shock, e.g., the stress-inducing effects of re-habituating to the indigenous culture is nothing short of culture shock in reverse, as the process of acculturation in the foreign environment caused a certain amount of estrangement from one's own culture. Gerhard Winter (1996) calls this a "return to unfamiliar territory". Most returnees do not expect this seemingly paradoxical phenomenon and consequently are not prepared for it. The following symptoms of reintegration can be observed in individuals returning from an extended stay abroad:

- *A shift in value orientation and outlook on life:* A shift in value orientation and outlook on life is particularly likely to occur if the stay was in an economically challenged country, resulting in negative feelings about the native country (in this case Germany). The main points of contention include excessive consumerism in all areas of life, materialism, bureaucracy and the corresponding inflexible approach to problem solving. The wasteful handling of resources and the environmental damage it causes is a further source of contention.
- *Estrangement from friends and family:* Feelings of estrangement may develop in cases where an individual spends an extended period of time abroad during which he/she was separated from family and friends. The

shift in value orientation and outlook on life are likely to have shifted to a point where spouses, children and friends no longer share the same views.
- *Loss of professional and private spheres of influence:* Some individuals assume tasks that exceed their original job description at home base. Returning to business as usual back home usually involves some downscaling. Strict hierarchical and bureaucratic systems replace decision-making privileges and specific fields of specialization. Spouses and children may have been managing quite well at home on their own during the extended absence and have assumed roles that the absent family member previously had.

According to Winter (1996), the intensity of reintegration shock depends on the following factors:
- *Experience in living abroad:* Individuals who have repeatedly lived abroad for an extended period of time generally experience milder reintegration shock than a person who lives abroad for the first time.
- *Personality factors:* Certain personal prerequisites have an ameliorating effect on reintegration shock, such as younger age, an outgoing personality, fearlessness and self-confidence.
- *Contact to the home culture:* Individuals who remain in regular contact with their relatives and make an effort to keep informed about political, economic and social change in their home country usually suffer less reintegration shock.
- *Preparing for return:* Individuals who prepare for their return, are aware of the changes they have undergone and have kept abreast of developments at home are less affected by reintegration shock than individuals who assume that everything will be as it was before their departure.
- *Planning:* Individuals who plan for reintegration in advance, without taking on too much at once, are likely to experience less reintegration shock than those who have unrealistic expectations upon their return.

Similar to the initial culture shock described above, the cultural dissonance experienced between one's own culture and that of the other culture has an effect on the intensity of reintegration shock. Of course, not every person experiencing acculturation goes through each phase of the acculturation process and certainly not everyone experiences the process in the same way. A prototypical acculturation process as described here is, in fact, quite uncommon, which may be a reason why the phase model is occasionally accused of oversimplification. This is due to the fact that the evaluation of parallel learning and adaptation processes is limited to vague criteria regarding the general state of well-being. Accordingly, efforts are being made

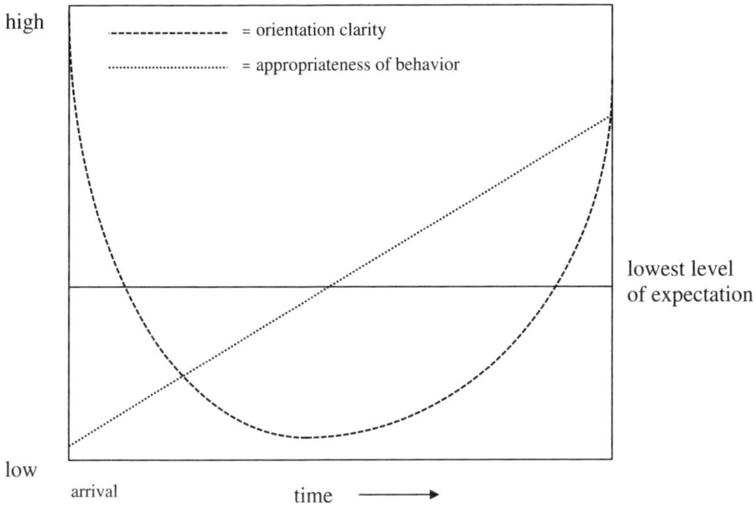

Figure 8: Prototypical acculturation process according to Grove and Torbiörn (1985, p. 212)

within the scope of process-based acculturation to fine-tune the differentiation between acculturation experiences. A well-known model of this type was created by Grove and Torbiörn (1985). The authors highlight the acculturation process not in terms of a one-dimensional, global process, but rather divide it up into three components: appropriateness of behavior, clarity of orientation and the level of minimum expectation (Kühlmann 1995, p. 8). *Appropriateness of behavior* can be interpreted as the degree of overlap between one's own behavior and other-culture behavioral patterns within an other-culture environment. *Clarity of orientation* may be interpreted as the degree to which particular and unambiguous forms of behavior can be traced back to an individual's inherent, socially relevant knowledge. The *level of minimum expectation* refers to the degree to which an individual experiences his/her own behavior as appropriate and his/her orientation clarity as adequate. Grove and Torbiörn summarize the interaction of these components in the above model (Figure 8).

As illustrated in Figure 8, appropriateness of behavior and clarity of orientation undergo very different phases and in some instances even contrary developments. Initially, a person arriving in a foreign culture might realize quite quickly that many of his/her behavioral patterns are not the norm. He/she will initially not doubt the appropriateness of his/her behavior in terms of familiar cultural norms. Such doubts evolve over time and tend to lead to a loss of orientation clarity, reaching its lowest point when appropriate behavior stabilizes at a satisfactory level.

Grove and Torbiörn's model shows that an acculturation process poses several learning challenges and the way in which they are mastered differ from one individual to the next. This can elicit very individual intercultural learning experiences: For one person, the main intercultural learning challenge may consist of understanding how to interact with other-culture individuals in order to achieve specific goals; another person might try different approaches to establishing a personal relationship with other-culture individuals; and a third person is interested in understanding more about other-culture thought patterns.

A further consideration is that the acculturation process follows different patterns in different areas of life at different rates. This means that living in the other-culture environment may be experienced as extremely difficult and unsatisfactory, while at the same time doing business in an other-culture environment may proceed without the effects of culture shock and with a high level of orientation clarity. In this case, appropriate behavior is likely to fall in step with events.

The factors underlying such intercultural learning challenges are not randomly selected, but rather represent the levels that most researchers consider to be instrumental criteria in the success of intercultural learning and adaptation processes. Most researchers consider the following criteria significant:

- "Subjective satisfaction with work and living conditions in the foreign country.
- The quality of the relationship with representatives of the host country.
- The extents to which tasks are accomplished" (Kühlmann 1995, p. 12).

Although the focus here is on so-called balance sheet criteria, or such criteria that can only be accurately evaluated at the end of a stay abroad, the levels in question nevertheless reflect key criteria for successful intercultural learning. One of these criteria is the extent to which *perspectives* can be *adopted* and defined as "the ability to *understand* the psychological conditions and processes taking place in the other person. These include thinking, feeling and wishing to *understand* the other person in his/her action within the context of the situation (i.e., from their perspective), recognizing their needs and what conclusions are drawn as a result" (Silbereisen 1998, p. 831; emphasis by the author). Research shows that this is not a one-dimensional concept. Many different adopted perspectives can be differentiated, within which the three levels already mentioned are also reflected (Layes 2000). An object-based perspective tries to adopt the partner's perspective in an interaction with regard to the *interaction object* – or the subject of the interaction; while an emotional perspective transfer is an attempt to understand the partner's perspective in an *interpersonal rela-*

tionship. In contrast, a conceptual perspective transfer attempts to understand the partner's perspective from the *socio-cultural context* within which the interaction is imbedded.

Challenges in intercultural learning are found in three areas: in an objective domain dealing with tasks and observable behavior; in a social domain including relationships and emotions; in a subjective domain, in which individual thinking patterns flow into the interaction. This means that during the course of intercultural learning it helps to be open to different situation scenarios than one is accustomed to focusing on. Secondly, one must learn to conceptualize the new situations differently and thirdly, the new understanding must be translated into goal-oriented action. Thomas, Layes and Kammhuber (1998) illustrate this in an example of a critical interaction situation.

A lieutenant colonel in the German army who is on assignment within the scope of a UN peacekeeping mission in Croatia reports:

"My responsibility included dealing with personnel matters concerning Croatian employees. I was accompanied by an interpreter, who I got along with quite well. Let me tell you, she was really surprised the way I reacted to certain things. For instance, one day she asked me to hire a woman she knew whose husband was killed in the war. She was left alone with five kids etc. I told her I would have to look into it to see if there was an opening in the hiring plan. I mentioned that the woman must have certain qualifications, such as speaking and writing fluent German. I noticed that she seemed puzzled, apparently not understanding the logic of my thinking. I actually believe that she was quite upset with me" (quote according to Thomas et al. 1998, p. 29).

The critical incident above evidently occurred as a result of the German officer's goal-oriented approach with a focus on the task implied in the conversation, while the translator focuses on the relationship factor implied in the context of this interaction. The German officer illustrates intercultural learning in several ways: Firstly, he needs to be aware of and sensitive to the diverse interpersonal aspects of the relationship within the specific social interaction. Secondly, he interprets these aspects in a way to which he is accustomed and considers the interpersonal factor an "irrelevant addition". He might, instead, stop to consider how such factors impact the relationship and are meaningful within the context of the interaction, and on a larger scale within the framework of the Croatian translator's life experience. On the basis of his new awareness, he might be able to react to similar situations in the future with more sensitivity to avoid future misunderstandings. This brief example illustrates the highly complex nature of intercultural learning that entails being able to shift perspectives on a number of levels in order to be successful. This is one reason why contemporary intercultural learning concepts, such of the one designed by Kammhuber (2000), emphasize the simultaneous interaction between perception, cognition and action, and stresses the importance of assuming multiple perspectives as a core criterion in the design of intercultural training programs.

References

Berry, J. W. (1997): Immigration, acculturation, and adaptation. Applied Psychology: An International Review 46 (1): 5–34.

Grove, C. L.; Torbiörn, I. (1985): A new conceptualization of intercultural adjustment and the goals of training. International Journal of Intercultural Relations 9: 205–233.

Hoopes, D. S. (1981): Intercultural communication concepts and the psychology of intercultural experience. In: Pusch, M. D. (Ed.), Multicultural Education. A Cross-Cultural Training Approach. Chicago, pp. 9–38.

Kammhuber, S. (2000): Interkulturelles Lernen und Lehren. Wiesbaden.

Kühlmann, T. M. (Ed.), (1995): Mitarbeiterentsendung ins Ausland. Auswahl, Vorbereitung, Betreuung und Wiedereingliederung. Göttingen.

Layes, G. (2000): Grundformen des Fremderlebens. Eine Analyse von Handlungsorientierungen in der interkulturellen Interaktion. Münster.

Silbereisen, R. K. (1998): Soziale Kognition: Entwicklung von sozialem Wissen und Verstehen. In: Oerter, R.; Montada, L. (Eds.), Entwicklungspsychologie. Ein Lehrbuch. Weinheim, pp. 823–861.

Thomas, A. (1993): Psychologie interkulturellen Lernens und Handelns. In: Thomas, A. (Ed.), Kulturvergleichende Psychologie. Eine Einführung. Göttingen, pp. 377–424.

Thomas, A.; Layes, G.; Kammhuber, S. (1998): Sensibilisierungs- und Orientierungstraining für die kulturallgemeine und die kulturspezifische Vorbereitung von Soldaten auf internationale Einsätze. Untersuchungen des Psychologischen Dienstes der Bundeswehr, 33: 1–289.

Ward, C.; Bochner, S.; Furnham, A. (2001): The Psychology of Culture Shock. 2nd ed. London.

Winter, G. (1996): Reintegrationsproblematik: Vom Heimkehren in die Fremde und vom Wiedererlernen des Vertrauten. In: Thomas, A. (Ed.), Kulturvergleichende Psychologie. Eine Einführung. Göttingen, pp. 365–381.

Barbara Hatzer/Gabriel Layes

1.9 Applied Intercultural Competence

1.9.1 Foreword

General consensus throughout the Western world holds that over the last decades, individuals have been steadily confronted with the consequences of globalization, mobilization and technology, all of which have been demanding a range of new competencies from individuals. More and more, Western mindsets within pluralistic societies are confronted with unfamiliar experiences. This is true for both adolescents participating in exchange programs and managers working for international corporations or soldiers chosen for a posting abroad. Accordingly, large corporations nearly always list "applied intercultural competence" as a requirement when recruiting up-and-coming talent. The younger generation, having grown up with regular trips abroad and student exchange programs, school friends, other-culture neighbors, satellite television and the internet are actually, albeit somewhat prematurely, expected to be interculturally competent. Nevertheless, all agree that applied intercultural competence is a necessity. What this means in reality and how it can be achieved is often vague and, unfortunately, also approached quite naïvely.

"Applied intercultural competence" is of interest to politicians and the corporate world in as far as it addresses the questions: How can one tell if a top executive is able to meet the demands of an international assignment in Asia? What sort of individual is suited to working in culturally diverse teams? What characteristics are required for negotiating in international conflicts?

The definition of "competence" in this case refers to a specific *ability*; in other words, the ability to interact in a sensitive, reflective and productive manner in situations with other-culture individuals. At this point, psychologists speak intentionally of *action* instead of "behavior" in order to emphasize the interplay of thoughts and feelings during observation, which precede, accompany and retrospectively judge manifested behavior over behavior observed objectively from a distance. While "behavior patterns" can proceed according to reaction, reflex or automatically, an action enables us, at least potentially, to make conscious choices, can be randomly influenced and reflected, and consequently brought to light in discussion.

Jürgen Straub notes: "Every action is a form of behavior, but not every form of behavior can be defined as action" (Straub 1999, p. 12).

The number of studies conducted in the field of intercultural research are numerous and draw upon an extensive research tradition, ranging from attempts at theoretical definition and empirically supported concepts all the way to concrete training programs to enhance applied intercultural competence. These efforts have shown that the best way to approach the definition of "applied intercultural competence" lies in the attempt to closely describe the successful outcome of an intercultural encounter. A very pragmatic definition coined by Richard W. Brislin (1993) made its mark in this context stating that the individual whose actions are successful in an intercultural encounter:

- has extensive contact to other-culture individuals.
- is someone who other-culture individuals enjoy being in contact with.
- successfully accomplishes his assignments in an other-culture environment.
- does not perceive interacting with other-culture individuals or accomplishing tasks as stressful.

If one were to continue along these lines or specify attributes, then the following list of criteria for successful intercultural competence could be established against the backdrop of current research standards:

- Accomplishing tasks effectively and job satisfaction
- Family well-being
- Personal satisfaction and adaptation
- Ability to communicate effectively (quality of language knowledge)
- Quality of intercultural interaction:
  - Satisfactory social relations between guest and host from the perspective of the other-culture partner
  - Satisfactory social relations between the guest and members of the host culture from the perspective of the host culture
- Ability to cope with psychological stress:
  - Absence of stress-related symptoms (psychosomatic disorders)
- Identification with the foreign subsidiary and headquarters

Accordingly, Kealey and Ruben define the qualities of an interculturally successful person as follows: "The resulting profile is of an individual who is truly open to and interested in other people and their ideas, capable of building relationships of trust among people. He or she is sensitive to the feelings and thoughts of another, expresses respect and positive regard for others, and is nonjudgmental. Finally, he or she tends to be self-confident, is able to take initiative, is calm in situations of frustration or ambiguity, and is not rigid" (Kealey and Ruben 1983, p. 165f.).

The mere description of such ability profiles may give the impression that only a few, individual "supermen and women" are successful at interacting interculturally. As Thomas (2003) notes, this pertains in particular to a list of strengths and abilities which are derived from scientific economic analyses of interculturality and often sound like "a personality profile of a modern human being with exaggerated, sought after and unattainable performance features. Leadership skills, dominance and assertiveness stand side by side with empathy, composure and tolerance of otherness with little regard for the incompatibility of required competencies, let alone brought up for discussion". How, for example, can the intercultural competence of a manager be determined who has fulfilled the tasks assigned to him from headquarters, but is extremely unpopular with the employees of a foreign subsidiary because of his management style? Or can a worker in the service of developmental aid be described as interculturally successful if, despite his selfless commitment to the task and his understanding of the locals' interests and wishes, his psychosomatic afflictions are disrupting his marriage?

Research approached features of applied intercultural competence from three perspectives: On the one hand, attempts were made to identify specific *personalist factors* that support the development of intercultural competence. On the other, attempts were made to identify *situational factors* that either promote or hinder interculturally competent action. Obviously, both factors play a role and are therefore under study in current conceptual designs with regard to the interactive dependency between person- and situation-based factors and how they influence the development of applied intercultural competence.

1.9.2 The Personalist Approach

From time to time, concepts were represented which stated that there were certain personality types, in the sense of a "universal communicator" (Gardner 1962), whose character traits enabled them to interact especially successfully in intercultural situations. These traits include an unusual degree of integration skill and personal stability, extroversion, believing in a universal set of values, culturally universal socialization or intuitive sensitivity. However, lists of character traits of this kind pose a range of questions and concerns: aside from the more philosophical questions pertaining to what a "universal set of values" might consists of, such personalistic approaches overlook the fact that specific personality traits can only unfold their positive character in relevant situational contexts. This becomes particularly evident in the character trait "extroversion", for example: it is doubtful whether cultures that place a high value on personal restraint consider extroverted behavior in general as interculturally competent. Possibly such lists of character traits are a result of research conducted within a North American framework, leading to the assumption that there is some cultural distortion.

The absence or presence of applied intercultural competence can therefore not be traced back to solely personal factors. On the other hand, personal factors are not irrelevant for the development of applied intercultural competence. Pertinent personal influence factors discussed in literature are compiled in Table 4 below.

Table 4: Personality traits for applied intercultural competence

Makes contact easily
Optimism
Openness and nonethnocentricity
Tolerance
Ability to adopt perspectives
Empathy
Frustration tolerance
Ambiguity tolerance
Role flexibility
Patience
Preparedness to question own perceptions
Positive self-concept
Social problem-solving ability
Goal orientation
Willingness to change
Ability to learn

One of the main factors, the ability to adopt another perspective, is discussed in more detail in the chapter on intercultural learning (q.v. Ch. I, 1.8). This concept deals with the ability to adapt so-called multiple perspectives to particular forms of action and to be aware of them in one's own actions. To illustrate the principle of "seeing the world through another's eyes", the experiences and thought processes of a German exchange student in the U. S. serve as an example here (Hatzer 2000): "On his way across the university campus, a German student meets an American student with whom he had had an engaging conversation and heated discussion about the university system and the basketball league the evening before. The German student is happy to see him again and stops to exchange a few words. The American acquaintance, however, returns his greeting with a friendly 'Hello, how are you doing?' but then continues on his way without hesitation. The German exchange student is speechless".

Possible interpretations that take an American perspective into account could be:

- Perhaps all Americans make a distinction between personal and work-related issues?
- Perhaps an agreeable party acquaintance represents a pleasant interlude without involving any kind of commitment?
- Perhaps the German student was too German in his discussion about the university system and put the American off with his heady, direct way?

As it turns out, the German student believes it is possible that his American acquaintance separates work-related and social matters and views the importance of a party acquaintance or the appropriate manner of discourse differently than he does. The German student recognizes that there are different perspectives on the same experience at work here and decides to go over the actual encounter once more.

Applied intercultural competence is not limited to a mere retrieval of stored knowledge about culture, as in the form of learned cultural standards, for instance, but includes the ability to "translate" the awareness of an unfamiliar perspective into corresponding behavior. The authors Adrian Furnham and Stephan Bochner (1986) differentiate between *perceptual sensitivity* and *behavioral sensitivity*. Perceptual sensitivity refers not only to the awareness of an interaction partner's reactions, but also to an inherent sensitivity toward the complete psychological episode in an interaction. Behavioral flexibility is an extension of the ability to retrieve observed behavioral traits that appear to have been appropriate.

Another personal feature that is frequently under discussion is *ambiguity tolerance*. This is the ability to deal with new and seemingly unstructured situations, and incomprehensible information including unpredictable actions and communication on the part of the interaction partner. Individuals with a high degree of ambiguity tolerance are able to remain calm and capable of action even in unclear or difficult situations. In fact, some experience such ambiguous and unstructured situations as a particular challenge to their problem-solving savvy. Such individuals are not easily thrown off track by ambivalent messages and are less likely to experience deviations from familiar norms, unexpected reactions and actions as threatening.

In contrast, individuals with low ambiguity tolerance experience unclear situations as unpleasant and feel stressed when people, messages or working environments appear unpredictable, unstructured or uncontrollable. They tend to install either new or assigned regulatory systems in an effort to bring order and structure to their surroundings, and in so doing, tend to resort to either black or white solutions. Reis (1997) developed a test to document ambiguity tolerance.

1.9.3 The Situational Approach

Situational factors can either complicate or facilitate the ability to act appropriately. Here, situational factors refer to the possible combinations of persons, places and events with which an individual is likely to be confronted during a sojourn in a foreign country. According to Brislin (1981), the following situational factors impact the development of applied intercultural competence (see Table 5).

All pertinent studies show that the *form and intensity of contact with the local population* is generally considered an important indicator of success, which is, however, weighted differently according to the phases of the stay abroad. It is important to note the effect these factors have during the stay abroad. While intensive contact with the local population is initially experienced as an additional stress factor, the proportion tends to change over time.

In the long run, studies show that individuals "who have a well-developed sense of intuition, seek contact with locals and are open to new experiences turn out to be more successful" (Stahl 1998, p. 64). Apparently, contacts to locals seem to provide a lasting social network that can be helpful during difficult and stressful times. Stahl comments further that "it is not so much outside conditions that are decisive factors, but rather the individual processing of information input" (Stahl 1998, p. 63). Thus, it certainly makes sense to confront the specific situational factors inherent in

Table 5: Situational Factors of Intercultural Action (according to Brislin 1981)

1. Climatic conditions
2. Number of persons present in a given situation
3. Personal or impersonal interaction
4. The counterpart's status
5. The counterpart's behavior
6. Familiarity vs. anonymity
7. Structured vs. unstructured situation
8. Time framework
9. Over-challenged vs. under-challenged
10. Existence of personal space
11. Presence or nonpresence of a role model
12. Power dynamics
13. Consequences for self and others
14. Supervisor-employee relations
15. Level of familiarity

an unfamiliar environment early on, such as within the framework of an intercultural training, in order to become familiar with the many relevant influence factors. In fact, applied intercultural competence consists of a certain amount of self-knowledge and being aware of the situational demands one can handle and those that are bound to cause difficulties. Seen from this perspective, the simultaneous consideration of both personalist and situational factors make the most sense.

1.9.4 The Interactionist Approach

Intercultural action should be considered a process in which personal and situational factors *interact*. Extroversion in approaching individuals of another culture, for example, will only be considered successful in cultures where this behavior is not perceived as lacking the appropriate respect for personal space. The person's intercultural competence is judged according to whether or not he is able to recognize pertinent signals and modify his behavior accordingly. Thomas emphasizes the need for "a sense of perception for people and situations, the ability to adequately interpret behavior and intuit the way in which a situation is experienced from the perspective of the other-culture system of orientation" (1996, p. 115) as a prerequisite to culturally appropriate action. An appropriate atmosphere can only be achieved if the situation itself is adequately interpreted. However, no one is able to interpret each new intercultural situation adequately without context. Consequently, applied intercultural competence means the ability to admit to this fact, and to start by asking the appropriate *questions* with regard to a new situation before attempting to recall pat answers. Müller and Thomas (1995) suggest keeping several key questions in mind when facing an interpretation of a new interaction:

- What is important to my other-culture counterpart in this situation?
- What is his focus?
- What must I do to make sure my intension is understood?
- What behavior is expected of me?

Applied intercultural competence does or does not merely exist as a given competency profile of an intercultural "apparition" which one will hardly find in real life, rather applied intercultural competence develops with, and as a result of, experience in the course of the highly sensitive and learning-intensive process involved in each intercultural encounter. Key requirements are learning to recognize and take advantage of learning opportunities and experiences and the focused application of reflection and communication regarding the planning, implementation, documentation and evaluation of results of situation- and goal-specific behavior (Thomas 2003).

Thomas (2003) elaborated on the key factors of the role played by learning processes in the development of applied intercultural competence within the conceptual framework of complex application and theoretical learning. As a result he arrived at the definition of intercultural competence as: "... the ability to perceive, judge, feel and act according to cultural conditions and influence factors as they pertain to self and others, to respect, honor and apply them productively in an effort to achieve mutual adaptation, tolerance of incompatibilities and a development toward synergetic forms of cooperation, co-habitation and effective orientation patterns as regards world view and an individual's unique place in it."

Foreignness and otherness must be perceived in terms of their underlying cultural conditions (intercultural perception) and understood that this is meaningful within the interactive context. It is necessary to acquire an understanding of the other-culture system of orientation and the way in which it affects action (intercultural learning). The person engaged in an action must understand and be able to reconstruct the person's different way of perceiving, judging, feeling and acting. In addition, he must be prepared to respect these thought and behavioral patterns and to honor them within the context of other-culture cultural development (intercultural esteem).

Furthermore, he must be aware of, reflect and be able to relate to his own cultural system of orientation, understand how it directs his own thinking and, what effect the confrontation of own- and other-culture specific system of orientation has on interactive and mutual understanding (intercultural understanding). The actor must be sensitive to the intercultural situation, be able to react to his partner on the basis of his understanding of both his own and the other-culture system of orientation and to partially adopt the other's culture-specific perspective (intercultural sensitivity). Theoretical knowledge about effective characteristics of one's own and culturally other specific orientation patterns require an understanding of the procedure involved in dealing appropriately and effectively with culture-specific differences. This is a prerequisite for creating a basis for the interactive process with the goal of avoiding or clarifying misunderstandings and engaging in mutual problem-solving efforts which are accepted and productively implemented by all involved (intercultural competence).

A further example of a modern, interactive approach to the idea of applied intercultural competence is provided by Stahl (1998), who sees in applied intercultural competence the ability to cope with difficult issues while under stress. Within the scope of his study with executives in upper management in international corporations, Stahl attempted to distinguish between different stress-resistant character types, approaches to problem-solving and problem-solving resources in his examination of how these factors interact. The resulting model lists the above-mentioned personal characteristics, which, together with environmental conditions, create the coping mechanisms that support successful interaction in intercultural situations. As seen here, interculturally competent action depends on specific types of stress and can, in fact, manifest in different forms of behavior. In this sense, *confrontation* in the form of aggression, self-assertion and control over others can represent competent coping mechanisms in the same way as *conflict mitigation* (conflict prevention, de-escalation, compromise) or *change of perspective* (assuming a different perspective, empathy) can.

Furthermore, applied intercultural competence is not a trait that stands for a unique ability that must first be acquired from scratch. Psychological literature points to many attempts that have been made to expose and analyze the close relationship between general social competence and applied intercultural competence (e.g., Eder 1996). The interrelatedness between these two constructs is already evidenced in the fact that every intercultural interaction is at the same time a social interaction depending on how narrowly the definition of culture is defined. Already existing social skills add certain other perspectives to an intercultural situation and can be seen as partial competencies of a more encompassing ability, which could be defined as "applied social competence in intercultural contexts" (Layes 2000). The analogy to the definition of applied social competence describes the ability to perceive an intercultural interaction from a general problem-solving, relationship and clarification perspective and to act appropriately and effectively in an interaction in accordance with the partner's perspective. Layes sees the difference between general social interaction skills and specific intercultural interaction ability in the latter's emphasis on a need for transparency. This difference becomes more significant the more the partners' action-guiding concepts differ.

References

Brislin, R. W. (1981): Cross-cultural Encounters: Face-to-face Interaction. New York.
Brislin, R. W. (1993): Understanding Culture's Influence on Behavior. Forth Worth.
Eder, G. (1996): »Soziale Handlungskompetenz« als Bedingung und Wirkung interkultureller Begegnung. In: Thomas, A. (Ed.), Psychologie interkulturellen Handelns. Göttingen, pp. 411–422.
Furnham, A.; Bochner, S. (1986): Culture Shock. Psychological Reactions to Unfamiliar Environments. London.

Gardner, G. H. (1962): Cross-cultural communication. The Journal of Social Psychology 58: 241–256.

Hatzer, B. (2000): Erfassung interkultureller Handlungskompetenz unter Berücksichtigung der lernpsychologischen Basisannahmen des Situated Learning. (Unveröff. Dipl.-Arbeit, Universität Regensburg)

Kealey, D. J.; Ruben, B. D. (1983): Cross-cultural personnel selection, criteria, issues, and methods. In: Landis, D.; Brislin, R. W. (Eds.), Handbook of Intercultural Training, Vol. I: Issues in Theory and Design. New York, pp. 155–175.

Layes, G. (2000): Grundformen des Fremderlebens. Eine Analyse von Handlungsorientierungen in der interkulturellen Interaktion. Münster.

Müller, A.; Thomas, A. (1995): Studienhalber in den USA: Interkulturelles Orientierungstraining für deutsche Studenten, Schüler und Praktikanten. Heidelberg.

Reis, J. (1997): Inventar zur Messung der Ambiguitätstoleranz. Bern.

Stahl, G. K. (1998): Internationaler Einsatz von Führungskräften. München.

Straub, J. (1999): Handlung, Interpretation, Kritik. Grundzüge einer textwissenschaftlichen Handlungs- und Kulturpsychologie. Berlin.

Thomas, A. (Ed.) (1996): Psychologie interkulturellen Handelns. Göttingen.

Thomas, A. (2003): Interkulturelle Kompetenz. Grundlagen, Probleme und Konzepte. 2nd ed. Erwägen – Wissen – Ethik 14(1). Stuttgart.

Gerhard Winter

1.10 Ethical Guidelines for Intercultural Action

1.10.1 Preface

Ethics in economic, political and social interaction has developed into a key issue over the past years, emphasizing the importance of economically and socially responsible action. Gone are the days when ethical behavior was considered an irrelevant and overly emotional side attraction. A number of economic and political scandals together with scientific and technological developments in the field of medicine, biology, energy generation and environmental research have raised questions about ethical behavior and accelerated the search for viable solutions.

Today the development of ethical values in business and society in general is a necessary prerequisite for operating globally; for maintaining one's competitive edge and striving for economic performance in a post-industrial world. According to Kleinfeld (1999), there are at least three reasons for the increase in ethically oriented thinking in business:

1. "The realization that the person in 'his entire personality' is an important factor in the success of ongoing change processes and is indispensable for sustaining business success.
2. A lack of mutually binding and globally valid (ethical) value orientation at both a national and international level as a basis for viable corporate cultures and successful intercultural management.
3. An ethical mindset replaces a socio-political and economic framework with international standards by voluntary commitment to ethical behavior in an effort to protect corporate self-determination and avoid overly stringent regulation" (p. 363).

The case of a Bavarian company with 1200 German and 120 Czech employees located near the German-Czech border illustrates an example of ethical behavior:

A company located in the German-Czech border district benefits from the wage differentials among its employees, while the Czech employees also gain advantages. How is this possible? The German company offers each employee at the Czech subsidiary the opportunity to work in Bavaria within the scope of German law if there is an open position (which is usually the case unless the work can be completed by overtime hours). This offer includes a salary according to wages paid in Bavaria. From the Czech perspective, this is a rare opportunity for the employees to boost their earnings. At the Czech subsidiary, everyone from blue-collar workers to engineers apply for the positions and are hired to work in Bavaria in compliance with in-company "fairness proceedings" (e.g., each employee is hired for an equal duration and time interval). The German manager had to explain the reason for the German employees' deduction of overtime hours caused by this procedure in a works council meeting. He found himself having to repeatedly justify the decision in various meetings with the employees. Any envious or discriminatory behavior is followed by a personal reprimand from above. It works! Things have not only calmed down at the company, but in fact an actual collegiality has sprung up between the Czechs and the Germans. This is of key importance and is, in the meantime, integral to official status-quo discussions. The manager has declared equality and fairness a company priority. Those who refuse to adapt are welcome to resign. The procedure is reciprocal: if the Czech subsidiary needs support, German employees are sent to assist, albeit at their regular German salaries.

1.10.2 Ethically Relevant Problem Areas in International/Intercultural Communication

Business ethics spokespersons expect that as long as there is no globally valid frame of reference for business and socio-political issues, multinational organizations should be responsible for assuming the moral responsibility of promoting social and environmental standards worldwide. There is a direct correlation between power and responsibility and the entrepreneurial license represents an obligation to fulfill this responsibility in a socio-ethical sense. "Where corporate license is abused, the call for control and supervision becomes attractive" (Leisinger 1997). Once the large multinational corporations understand this connection, they can act in accordance with the fundamental conditions upon which their livelihood depends.

Bribery, race discrimination, child labor and investment in countries accused of human rights abuse (Kleinfeld 1999, p. 367) constitute the most common examples of ethical dilemmas faced by transnational operations. Another frequently mentioned issue is the exploitation of wage difference due to political and economic factors caused by relocating production facilities to low-cost countries. A natural outcome is the higher unemployment rate, resulting in higher costs for social security at home. The ethical dimension of this process does not adhere to any kind of legal stipulation. Rather, it constitutes an act of voluntary commitment and, as such, approximates ethical action in its true sense (Kant 1785). Personal responsibility and vision form and strengthen the international corporation's *corporate identity*. In this sense, organizations are not the moral and ethical authority. Only individuals can act ethically and responsibly. If leaders are part of an organization that is not founded on the ethical values embodied by the corporate identity, they may be caught in a conflict of goals between their own values and the organization's predominant economic interests. Where market demand sets the course, an individual may experience a deep and involuntary rift between personal integrity on the one hand, and his/her commitment to his/her profession on the other. Genuine moral and ethical action in a corporate setting can only flourish if corporate policy embodies ethical personal responsibility as a part of company-specific commitment and honors this accordingly.

The more an individual is wholeheartedly involved, particularly when faced with stiff international competition, and the more is required of him/her in terms of innovation, commitment, creativity, performance, teamwork and intercultural competence, the more specific dimensions of personal responsibility are involved. The integrity and dignity of each employee of the corporation, regardless of hierarchical level, is a key success factor for the corporation. Full potential can only develop in a supportive corporate climate with responsible leadership.

"A top priority here is the commitment to the fundamental ethical requirement of mutual respect for human dignity. The company's emphasis on soft skills play a key role in sustaining values such as a healthy corporate climate, collegiality and a commitment to cooperation instead of competition and confrontation, an atmosphere of trust, an openness and transparency within the scope of an appropriate structure of communication" (Kleinfeld 1999, p. 368).

From the perspective of occupational and organizational psychology, the ethical norms in intercultural relations that specialists and executives on international assignment are expected to negotiate are categorized under socio-psychological themes such as "prejudice, polarization of self and others, and racism. In a more positive light, the terms ambiguity tolerance, cultural sensitivity, openness to and appreciation for otherness and behavioral flexibility are mentioned" (Eckensberger 1993; Kühlmann and Stahl 2001). These ethno-friendly characteristics play a key role in the selection of candidates for international assignments. The criteria lists for potential "successful" candidates read like a collection of ethical guidelines. In fact, they resemble the criteria for overall communication skills and can be applied to interdisciplinary situations and interactions (Stahl 1995; Spieß and Winterstein 1999). Selection criteria for international assignments include a few additional features, such as openness to other cultures, acceptance of behavior different from one's own, physical and psychological stress-tolerance under unfamiliar conditions and the ability to tolerate conflicting interests (Thomas 1995; Großschädl 1995). It is worth considering, however, that the selection processes for international managers differ from one country to the next (not to mention the significant cultural differences already existing within the Western cultural hemisphere) in terms of content, preferences and selection methods (Smith et al. 2001).

In addition, research into issues related to the international assignment focuses on bridging intercultural differences in the workplace, motivation, problem solving, negotiation styles, perception of time, dealing with personal space, concepts of fairness and the willingness to relocate (Eckensberger 1993; Korff et al. 2001). Other significant comparative parameters include rules for coding and decoding news, goal expectations, cooperation in international teams and commitment to headquarters at home (Smith et al. 2001). In preparation for an encounter with intercultural differences, especially between the West and Asia, actual situations are chosen to simulate realistic conditions (e.g., role plays, case studies, culture assimilator trainings) and can be adapted to the participants' learning styles and needs. The goal is to achieve an effective modus of communication, consisting of an ethical correlate designed to prevent an infraction of collective rules while respecting the other-culture partner's personal sensibilities. The responsibilities of an international manager can be summarized in terms of organizational, social, religious and civic responsibility while sustaining a satisfying relationship with the business partner (Dülfer 1991).

Ethical questions regarding the modus operandi among culturally diverse work teams deserve further mention. Should goods and social rewards be distributed on the basis of equality, need or performance? Should procedural rules be based on neutral criteria, cultural competition between subgroups, altruism, solidarity, integrity or fair sportsmanship (Organ 1990)? In most cases, the preferred procedure is to overcome, transcend and synthesize cultural divergence in an effort to harness synergetic potential creatively as well as enhance motivation. Research results on the subject of distribution and procedural justice are currently very inconsistent. Further differentiation between countries and corporate affiliation is required. Discussions and questions related to fairness, for instance, tend to unfold when the cultural and political circumstances in the partners' countries of origin differ considerably. This is evident, for instance, with participants from countries with individualistic or collectivist, high or low power distance, and modern or traditional mindsets. In addition, it is not clear whether participants perceive themselves as individuals in terms of such cultural dimensions or if they include their social peer and in-group as well as their families and relatives (Volkmann 2001).

Meanwhile, guidelines for managing culturally diverse work groups are standard for managers on international assignment. Behavioral dimensions include positive feedback and criticism, dissemination and withholding of information, conflict resolution, problem solving, negotiation, quality control, performance expectations and means of communicating these factors to the group. Thomas (1992), for example, differentiates between models of dominance, compromise and synergy. In this context, Heenan and Perlmutter (1979) defined four management strategies in multinational corporations including a basis for orientation defined as ethnocentric, polycentric, region-centric and bio-centric. According to Müller (1992), family, social harmony, humanistic and in-group principles guide Japanese management, depending on the task and the situation in which decisions are made.

The typical characteristics of international managers and related guidelines for successful international communication can be gauged according to performance requirements. Among these are: leading complex and sophisticated discussions; recognizing tension in terms of development potential instead of something threatening; the ability to observe one's self and one's own cultural mindset from a reflective distance; embracing lifelong learning as a prerequisite for reaching global horizons together with the ability to adapt, persevere under duress and knowing when a compromise is called for. In addition, traits such as independent thinking, being a team player and identification with the corporation are emphasized (Tichy and Devanna 1986).

Understanding, accepting and honoring other-culture values, norms and rules of behavior, modus operandi and specific systems of orientation take on another, more challenging dimension in intercultural communication and cooperation. Intercultural communication requires a comprehensive repertoire of personal, social, emotional and intuitive intelligence. Underlying any interaction is the most basic act of ethical behavior, namely, conveying esteem and acceptance of the individual. This requires a shift from an egocentric perspective, in order to become aware of the communication partner's perspective, and adopting an attitude of goodwill and tolerance as well as a willingness to be open to the completely unknown and foreign. It is precisely this ability to put oneself in the other person's position both cognitively and emotionally that leads to the kind of empathy that is integral to the intercultural network. Dealing with intercultural conflict requires an understanding of the participants' underlying values, moral standards and the extent to which they differ and influence everyday work situations. To do this, one must be able to reflect on one's own socio-cultural conditioning, including one's attitudes. Smooth-flowing and successful cooperation in multinational and interdisciplinary teams requires not only a common basis for linguistic and conceptual understanding, but also a common normative level of understanding and a shared sense of ethos. Being able to reflect on values of this nature and agree on how to communicate according to mutually acceptable norms of behavior and moral standards are the essence of ethics. *Corporate ethics* plays an integral, identity-giving role on both the national and international level. Once the corporation has agreed upon and designated its own corporate ethic, it is less susceptible to diverse forms of ethical conduct. Most importantly, members of the organization commit to common values in all areas and at all levels of the organization, providing them with a sense of meaning and reliable orientation. In summary, ethics and an ethical value orientation are key success factors in change and intercultural management (Kleinfeld 1999, p. 369).

Bribery, corruption, supplier quality, wage dumping, ethnic discrimination or ignoring minimum standards for working conditions are the kind of ethical questions that arise with regard to a company's operating procedures. Typical examples include environmental transgressions and protection, reasonable working hours and regular breaks. Preventative measures, such as the legality principle, noncompetitiveness and self-governance, safeguard against ethically questionable developments. In addition, ethics audits (Wieland 2001; Schroll-Machl 1996) ensure that ethical responsibility is honored and oppose the exploitation of ethical principles for image purposes, as an alibi function or as a cover-up for the absence of so-called civil conduct. Ethical guidelines emphasize the responsibility of capable leaders and their function as role models for living the continuity, sustainability and commitment embodied in corporate ethics. The latter conveys identity and strengthens internal social and international corporate credibility.

1.10.3 The Role of Ethics in the Field of Intercultural Communication

Proponents of ethical business conduct and responsibility are often accused of moralizing without getting actively involved in the change process, their message often coming across like Sunday school lectures. Indeed, debating ethical issues in times when the company is doing well and business is booming does not strike very close to home. In times of stiff competition, impending bankruptcy, insolvency and other economic crises, ethics take a back seat until more urgent problems are solved. This negative image can only be confronted if the fundamental function of ethical behavior has been determined. Ethical behavior in this connection should be discussed within the context of an accepted concept of ethics in contemporary psychological theory that includes intercultural aspects in business environments.

A suitable premise is offered by the key concept of *responsibility* in applied psychology. Theories on interaction including attribution relative to work and organization processes are quite common and frequently used in intercultural communication processes (Volpert 1983; Lenk and Maring 1992). Normative aspects of the action theory are included in such buzzwords and concepts as actual-theoretical comparison and regulation-supervision approach in the form of a permanent "ethical memory" (Kaminski 1970). Regulation and supervision act as constitutive moments in action planning, implementation and evaluation and are not explicitly intended to impede anti-social impulses detrimental to relationships and the community as a whole, nor can it prevent egocentric profit mongering. Instead, regulation and supervision serve the development of orientation and internal self-check mechanisms that are activated during interpersonal conflict and decision making.

When applying psychological models to communication processes, it is recommended to keep dialogues face-to-face under the auspices of nonviolent and peaceful interaction, mutual understanding and fair agreements that go hand-in-hand with clearly understood, mutual interests. Prototypical situations of this form of intercultural communication include negotiations in which participants act out the role of managers, corporations and experts. They simulate situations with a strong potential for differences, conflict or even crises and work toward an agreement. There is no pat answer to the question of a fundamental concept of moral and ethical behavior within the context of international business, nor can it be answered from a culture-free perspective. One possible approach lies in perceiving each given situation in relation to its culture-specific characteristics. The author himself bases his discourse on a Western perspective against the backdrop of unmitigated perception and interpretation. In his discussion, he assumes the perspective of a German expert and manager who is inevitably influenced by a Western mindset, was socialized within the context of Western symbols and meaning, was imbued with its particular moral code and was essentially formed by a Western way of life and its institutions. Core values of Western civilization generally include: human dignity and personal freedom, striving for personal happiness and individuality, social justice, solidarity, equal rights and a Christian world view (Hunold et al. 2000).

An intercultural, or for that matter, trans-cultural ethics in the form of general human rights and a universally accepted standard for the evaluation and design of international and intercultural relations currently does not exist and will perhaps never exist. The global community and its religions have not yet been able to agree on a form of global ethics although a start has been made (Küng 1990). Consequently, it is more realistic to focus on individual aspects of business ethics minus the core values and focus on manners, guidelines for decision making and agreement modalities for negotiating international contracts within a task-related negotiation framework. This scenario speaks more for a certain formalization of procedures and a rational, ethically nuanced approach to the situation in contrast to interpersonal and culturally diverse interaction and ethical requirements. Needless to say, the concept of reason, in principle, includes culturally and temporally independent demands and thus approximates the idea of Kantian ethics (Höffe 1997, p. 46).

It appears as if the definition of responsibility applied here lends itself to the skillful adoption of doctrines on obligation, commodities and virtue (Kerner 1990). The disadvantage, of course, is the extensive contextual uncertainty that directs action and principles. In the first place, ethical responsibility refers to the consequences of an action and then interconnects these with ethically meaningful, collectivist values such as general well-being, pleasure, benefit or happiness.

In an intercultural overlap situation, responsibility must be assumed not only for oneself, but also for the other-culture interaction partner. The key term, *cultural standards*, addresses important cultural differences and potential conflict areas in work motivation, leadership and negotiation styles, conflict-resolution procedures, team communication and expectations of fairness (Smith et al. 2000). In view of the empirically proven, fundamental differences in the above-mentioned dimensions between German, American, Chinese and Indonesian managers, for example, it is difficult to envision or, for that matter, administer a general, interculturally valid canon for negotiation etiquette that can apply, other than in a specifically designated situation. On the other hand, one can conceive of extraneous solutions and agreements through compromise or innovation (Thomas 2000; Thomas et al. 1997). There are, however, country-specific conciliatory strategies that follow a sequential pattern, such as communication that is based on previously established trust, and allow for an open, honest and more direct approach. Another form of communication takes place through the third-party mediation of a high-ranking individual who is considered particularly trustworthy and responsible.

In closing and in transition to the next section is the following example of an actual episode of ethical behavior:

A German general manager of a medium-sized textile company that outsourced its production sites to Hungary is faced with the prospect of closing half the operation due to decreasing revenue. He discusses the potential consequences of this decision with headquarters in Munich but there is no alternative. He returns to Hungary, calls many meetings and chairs the works council meeting in which he officially announces that half of the employees will be laid off at the end of the month. The decision is deeply troubling, for he knows what this means in this particular area of Hungary: Condemning them to unemployment, poverty and ... famine! The men have been out of work for years and the women had been able to keep the family afloat with their work. He stands up at the podium and speaks without hiding his distress. There is no choice but to admit that there is no alternative and that he understands if everyone were now to hate both him and the company. He expresses his sincere regrets for what has happened. The only positive thing he can come up with is to promise the women their jobs back, provided that is what they wish, as soon as business recovers. The meeting is unpleasant for everyone and is accompanied by much complaining and commotion ...

The laid-off employees, however, maintain contact. They visit the general manager and their colleagues regularly and even pay visits to his wife at their home (he had built a small house in the area) to talk about their problems and the positive aspects of the company. The general manager is surprised and very pleased about this development. Apparently, the employees did not blame him personally for the lay-offs. The company, too, is spared hate tirades although there is a lot of complaining.

Today, two years later, fortune has changed. Production is increasing and the women praise their boss effusively, proclaiming that they will work for him again. He stood by them through difficult times, an act that affected them personally and that they honored.

1.10.4 Ethical Responsibility in Intercultural Communication

The main emphasis here is on a humanistic approach to ethical responsibility in the sense of the European cultural tradition. The key moral aspects of this ethic lie in the autonomy and freedom of the subject, personal responsibility, a binding, moral and legal standard for particular action in situations subject to sanctions and personal liability (Kaufmann 2000; Höffe 1997).

In a philosophy based on ethics, God is replaced by the individual, an autonomous conscience and the future in itself (Körtner 1999). The key values at risk in a global community are, in effect, nonnegotiable, require commitment and are considered pillars of Western civilization. Among these are a sense of identity and well-being, synergy and community, reason as a regulatory factor, the protection and maintenance of creation, supervision of high-risk technical innovations and ... an ethical process legitimized through democratic discourse. Ethics in this sense manifests through conciliatory participation in complex human decisions instead of through prescribed finality (Hockel 1994).

Ethics based on responsibility, on the other hand, is comparatively open, diverse and includes basic human rights as well as the protestant social ethic (Blickle 1998). It differentiates between business-related tasks between supervisors, colleagues and business partners according to the forms of interpersonal relations within relevant socio-political frameworks. Guidelines for managing cooperation and conflict go beyond a purely descriptive designation of ethical behavior. Ethics based on responsibility draws conclusions from personal action or nonaction and suggests strategies for mediation in both social and intercultural situations.

The strategic premise advocated here progresses within a field of tension between a stable, basic principle of normative ethics as exemplified by the protestant social ethic and a normative-critical ethic of reason (Immanuel Kant), on the one hand, and a comparatively flexible and informal procedural fairness on the other. The normative position, which is nonnegotiable in its core properties, is located at one end of the scale, and a pragmatic position consisting of negotiated fairness inherent in the communication process at the other end. The communication process itself continually adapts and readapts to any given situation in which individuals interact with the express purpose of creating a common ground for discourse (Meran 1992). Normative-critical ethics is characterized by the basic belief that argumentation based on reason and moral assessment of human action is possible. The intended message about the acceptable or questionable acts of those directly involved in the contract demands not only intersubjective validation, but also an objective commitment under the auspices of rational argument. The expectations here involve the highest possible degree of social approval that goes beyond the actual situation and the participating individuals. Three main problem areas can be identified with regard to reflecting ethical issues in intercultural contact.

The Effect of Unfamiliar Experience on the Self

Ethical self-reflection in intercultural contact impacts self-perception, self-respect and self-control of individuals involved in intercultural cooperation and communication. The perception of personal responsibility and its identity-giving values are key factors, ranging from egocentric repudiation, discrimination and outright rejection (xenophobia and ethnocentricity) to uncritical, nonconditional admiration, adaptation to and perceived superiority of everything foreign at the expense of one's own identity and way of life (xenophilia).

A middle path can be found between these two extremes through an objective and critical distance toward both extremes (Layes 2000). This ability requires a relatively high degree of openness, flexibility, willingness to adapt and emotional tolerance. This in turn allows for a wider range of more nuanced categories on the behavioral level, making it possible for individuals to resonate with the multifaceted stimulus. In the process of intercultural communication, formerly detached and unconscious aspects of personality re-emerge and become accessible to cognitive adaptation so this development can, to an extent, be perceived in terms of development due to other-culture impulses (Sundermeier 1996, Epstein 1991; Krewer 1992).

One's own personality is enriched by gradually opening up to new experiences, incorporating new awareness into one's value system and developing many diverse sources for comparisons and decoding symbolism. Instead of launching into preconceived notions, judgments and expectations, observing the intercultural situation from a more objective distance is more likely to settle the initially confusing mosaic-like impressions into a sense of order so that they can be integrated into the personality (Straub 1999).

The Communicative Perspective and the Relationship Aspect

To describe an encounter with otherness from an interactive and communicative perspective means defining partners as communicators and recipients of messages. This refers to the message itself, messages about and intended for the other, for external constituents and their interests, and messages containing open or hidden messages regarding goal setting, attitudes and feelings. During the communicative process, and through the continual interchange of roles as observer and active participant, the partners develop impressions of each other, revise original expectations, tune in to learning and adaptation modes and quite possibly reach mutually satisfying solutions either subliminally or in open discourse.

The following dimensions for negotiation serve as a basis for the communicative process:

- *Responsibility* for the clarity of one's own communication as perceived by the partner's internalized, hypothetical perspective.
- *Authenticity* of expression in the sense of sincerity, honesty and truthfulness. The partner perceives cues signaling that the communicated intentions, plans, needs and state of mind are free of deception and subterfuge. Here the ideal is inspired by ethical business standards.
- *Reserve* in the decoding of messages and observation of nonverbal behavior and frequent, real-time feedback on interpretations by applying new information and different evaluation methods for the message conveyed.
- *Social and partner-based responsibility* with regard to the possible effects one's own message has on the other-culture partner's vulnerability. For example, when the partner's key value concepts, fears and taboos are violated by unmindful and arbitrary communication.
- *Binding rules to which both parties commit* in the sense that rules that have been either previously agreed upon or which are agreed upon in the course of the contact, such as reciprocity, agenda, speaking time and the scheduling of breaks, are in fact adhered to.
- *Responsibility and loyalty* toward one's own group, company policy or corporate philosophy, in the name of which business negotiations are led and intercultural contacts are established. In a larger sense, negotiation partners are representatives of their economic systems, of their countries and nations and are bound by their established ties and obligations in an international context. Individual negotiation partners use the higher resources available to them by participating social systems and, in turn, are obligated to provide goal-oriented and conscientious service (Mieg 1994).

Rationality and Fairness, Cooperation and Ethics

The appropriate relation between rationality and fairness plays a role in the issues discussed here and becomes relevant in view of the difference between cooperative and noncooperative strategies according to socio-psychological research. According to research, the dilemma lies in short-term, profit-maximizing self-interest and long-term, mutually profitable and cooperative strategies. When both parties act out of egotistical, profit-oriented motives, they inevitably create an atmosphere that undermines any kind of trust-based relationship and forego a more mutually advantageous and cooperative problem-solving culture. The chances that one of the partners gains the upper hand is greatest when one has self-serving motives and is able to exploit the other, who plays the good-natured and cooperative-minded partner. The assumption is that this "unethical" strategy is the more rational and clearly the better option to any arbitrary strategy the other partner may choose. The key question in this interaction is: under what circumstances should a self-serving partner act "irrationally", that is, playact cooperative behavior while knowing that in the end he risks being left out in the rain? There is actually only one "rational" answer to this rather pointedly polemic question: the cooperative play actor can count on his partner playing a similarly cooperative role that may not be evident immediately until after a few more cooperative moves on the part of a valiantly good-natured, optimistic and gullible counterpart. Trust, in this form, need not be based on the secure knowledge of a person's reliable, ethical disposition, such as in the case of a trusted partner, brother or good friend. Rather, this form of trust can develop in the process of logical reasoning during the interaction itself, as in negotiations. During the process of give-and-take beyond all interpersonal and intercultural boundaries, the partners realize that the greatest mutual advantage can be achieved by attributing corresponding and rational advantage strategies. In the course of the interchange between cooperative and uncooperative strategies, the relationship settles into a sort of secondary, procedural ethic that offers a midway level of satisfaction that has proven to be the more rational alternative strategy. Ethics and business are reconcilable even under conditions of self-interest and egocentricity as they evolve qualitatively during a competitive interaction and move toward a common goal.

These strategies relate to interculturality in that the rational and egotistical competitors can still hope for a mutually acceptable solution under conditions of alternating dependency. In fact, this might prove even more effective than a premeditated approach (Lenk and Maring 1992). Rational egotism is defined by some researchers as "intelligence", however, one could also refer to the term as "universal reason". In business, as in everyday interaction, ethical behavior is most likely to come into play when, after realistically assessing the ways of human nature including egotism, power aspirations, desires and suffering, it resorts to common sense in spite of these interruptions. According to McIntyre (1995), the most effective form of social and intercultural ethics is likely to be found in programs designed to enhance common sense.

According to this rationale, business ethics is not merely an even give-and-take, but rather an opportunity to enhance common-sense thinking and personality development (Höffe 1992).

By recycling the concept of ethics and applying it to "rational decision-making under suboptimal and relatively futile circumstances", the idea of ethics in an economic context is plausible. However, it surely does not meet the standards of the official designation of ethics. Above and beyond its place in the business world, a much wider scope opens up to embrace other forms of interpersonal relationships, empathy, friendship and love. This constitutes another form of ethics, namely one that reaches beyond the conventional modus operandi for dealing purposefully and rationally with a minimum amount of information. Friendship means living up to a partner's expectations as far as possible even when at risk and with no guarantee of reciprocity in a rational sense in the foreseeable future. Cooperating on principle, relating joyfully and experiencing self-improvement in the process comprise a natural communicative strategy and an alternative to "sensible" and "honorable" behavior within the framework of national and international business cooperation.

1.10.5 Conclusion

Difficult ethical dilemmas involving profit-oriented interests and obligations are often aligned with a long-term perspective. Behavior linked to short-term profit loss is not only unacceptable in view of predictable changes but may, in the end, also be perceived as a rational economic alternative. Responsible and ethical business behavior is well worth the effort and is likely to prove the more sensible and wiser alternative:

- Individuals will not submit to exploitation over the long term in a cooperative relationship. Their resistance will inevitably undermine performance and corporate loyalty.
- Ethical behavior shows character and reflects reputable standing, is appreciated externally by customers and internally by employees who express their loyalty to the company. It is a prerequisite for keeping and recruiting personnel. Motivated employees contribute to the company's overall performance and step up efforts during hard times. Trying to compensate for a damaged reputation is costly in all respects.
- A clear corporate ethic together with sustained ethical behavior is likely to develop into a corporate tradition and contribute to the company's prosperity.

Intercultural conflict requires open, optimistic and proactive individuals with social, emotional and intuitive intelligence. It is all about esteem, the ability to change perspectives, giving up a fixed, egotistical mindset and becoming involved with dissimilar others. This requires not merely tolerance but also a willingness to open up to otherness.

References

Blickle, G. (1998): Ethik in Organisationen – eine Standortbestimmung. In: Blickle, G. (Ed.), Ethik in Organisationen. Göttingen, pp. 3–15.

Dülfer, E. (1991): Internationales Management. München/Wien.

Eckensberger, L. H. (1993): Kulturvergleichende Psychologie. Göttingen.

Epstein, I. (1991): Chinese Education. Problems, Policies and Prospects. New York.

Großschädl, A. (1995): Die Auswahl von Mitarbeitern für den Auslandseinsatz: Aus der Praxis des Bereichs Öffentliche Kommunikationsnetze der Siemens AG. In: Kühlmann, T. M. (Ed.), Mitarbeiterentsendung ins Ausland. Göttingen, pp. 73–84.

Heenan, D. A.; Perlmutter, H. V. (1979): Multinational Organization Development. Wesley.

Hockel, C. M. (1994): Gesellschaftlicher Rahmen der Angewandten Psychologie. In: Rosenstiel, L. v.; Hockel, C. M.; Molt, W. (Eds.), Handbuch der Angewandten Psychologie. Landsberg/Lech, II-O: 1–2.

Höffe, O. (1992): Gerechtigkeit als Tausch? Ein ökonomisches Prinzip für die Ethik. In: Lenk, H.; Maring, M. (Eds.), Wirtschaft und Ethik. Stuttgart, pp. 119–133.

Höffe, O. (1997): Lexikon der Ethik. München.

Hunold, G. W.; Laubach, T.; Greis, A. (Eds.) (2000): Theologische Ethik. Ein Werkbuch. Tübingen/Basel.

Kaminski, G. (1970): Verhaltenstheorie und Verhaltensmodifikation. Stuttgart.

Kant, I. (1785): Grundlegung der Metaphysik der Sitten. Gesammelte Schriften, Band IV. Berlin 1911.

Kaufmann, S. (2000): Blick in die Zukunft. Regensburg.

Kerner, M. (1990): Politische und ökonomische Aspekte des gegenwärtigen Systemwandels in den sozialistischen Ländern Osteuropas. Berlin.

Kleinfeld, A. (1999): Identität durch moralische Integrität: Die Rolle der corporate ethics. In: Bickmann, R., Chance: Identität. Berlin.

Körtner, U. H. J. (1999): Evangelische Sozialethik. Göttingen.

Korff, M.; Gureje, O.; Simon, G. E. (2001): A Cross-National Study of the Course of Persistent Pain in Primary Care. Ibadan/Nigeria.

Krewer, B. (1992): Kulturelle Identität und menschliche Selbsterforschung. Saarbrücken.

Kühlmann, T. M.; Stahl, G. K. (2001): Problemfelder des internationalen Personaleinsatzes. In: Schuler, H. (Ed.), Lehrbuch der Personalpsychologie. Göttingen, pp. 534–554.

Küng, H. (1990): Projekt Weltethos. München.

Layes, G. (2000): Grundformen des Fremderlebens. Münster/New York.

Leisinger, K. M. (1997): Unternehmensethik. Globale Verantwortung und modernes Management. München, p. 182.

Lenk, H.; Maring, M. (1992): Wirtschaftsethik – ein Widerspruch in sich selbst? In: Lenk, H.; Maring, M. (Eds.), Wirtschaft und Ethik. Stuttgart, pp. 7–30.

McIntyre, A. (1995): Geschichte der Ethik im Überblick. Weinheim.

Meran, J. (1992): Wirtschaftsethik. Über den Stand der Wiederentdeckung einer philosophischen Disziplin. In: Lenk, H.; Maring, M. (Eds.), Wirtschaft und Ethik. Stuttgart, pp. 45–81.

Mieg, H. A. (1994): Verantwortung. Opladen.

Müller, S. (1992): Entscheidungsfindung: Eine interkulturelle Betrachtung am Beispiel Japan. In: Bergemann, N. J.; Sourisseaux, A. L. J. (Eds.), Interkulturelles Management. Heidelberg.

Organ, D. W. (1990): The motivational basis of organizational citizenship behavior. In: Staw, B.; Cummings, L. L. (Eds.), Research in Organizational Behavior. Greenwich, pp. 43–72.

Schroll-Machl, S. (1996): Kulturbedingte Unterschiede im Problemlöseprozess bei deutsch-amerikanischen Arbeitsgruppen. In: Thomas, A. (Ed.), Psychologie interkulturellen Handelns. Göttingen, pp. 383–409.

Smith, P. B.; Fischer, R.; Sale, N. (2001): Cross-cultural industrial/organizational psychology. In: Cooper, C. L.; Robertson, T. (Eds.). International Review of Industrial and Organizational Psychology. Chichester, S 147–193.

Spieß, E.; Winterstein, H. (1999): Verhalten in Organisationen. Weinheim.

Stahl, G. K. (1995): Die Auswahl von Mitarbeitern für den Auslandseinsatz: Wissenschaftliche Grundlagen. In: Kühlmann, T. M. (Ed.), Mitarbeiterentsendung ins Ausland. Göttingen, pp. 31–72.

Straub, J. (1999): Handlung, Interpretation, Kritik. Berlin/New York.

Sundermeier, T. (1996): Den Fremden verstehen. Göttingen.

Thomas, A. (1991/1992): Grundriss der Sozialpsychologie. Band 1, Band 2. Göttingen.

Thomas, A. (1995): Die Vorbereitung von Mitarbeitern für den Auslandseinsatz: Wissenschaftliche Grundlagen. In: Kühlmann, T. M. (Ed.), Mitarbeiterentsendung ins Ausland. Göttingen.

Thomas, A. (2000): Globalisierung und interkulturelle Managementkompetenz. In: Fahrenhorst, B.; Musto, St. A. (Eds.), Grenzenlos. SID-Berlin-Berichte Nr. 13. Berlin, pp. 162–174.

Thomas, A.; Kammhuber, S.; Layes, G. (1997): Interkulturelle Kompetenz. Bonn.

Tichy, N. M.; Devanna, M. A. (1986): The Transformational Leader. New York.

Volkmann, R. (2001): Beschäftigungspolitik! Opladen.

Volpert, W. (1983): An den Grenzen des Modells der hierarchisch-sequentiellen Handlungsorganisation. Berlin.

Wieland, J. (2001): Eine Theorie der Goveranceethik. Zeitschrift für Wirtschafts- und Unternehmensethik 2 (1): 8–33.

2. Diagnosis – Training – Evaluation – Coaching

Eva-Ulrike Kinast

2.1 Diagnosing Applied Intercultural Competence

The globalization of markets places increasing demand on people everywhere to internationalize. Ever more individuals live and work abroad under unfamiliar circumstances in the economic and political arena and within the scope of science, education, developmental aid, tourism and migration. Consequently, these individuals, and those who choose to stay at home, are increasingly faced with the specific challenges of dealing with people from other countries and cultural backgrounds in both their places of work and their daily lives. Coping constructively with such cultural diversity requires applied intercultural competence. Methods of *intercultural diagnosis* can determine whether a person is interculturally competent. The following sections offer a practical overview of various methods of intercultural diagnosis.

2.1.1 The Current Situation

There is a growing need for diagnosing applied intercultural competence. New areas of research and occupational choices are opening up for intercultural psychologists and other professional groups. Literature on the subject is proliferating. Corporations and other organizations continue to implement measures to evaluate the intercultural competence of their executives and specialists. In Germany, external consultants specialized in intercultural diagnosis are also growing in number.

The *intercultural assessment center,* here referred to as culture assimilator training, is considered to be the most important instrument for diagnosing applied intercultural competence among the methods discussed, due to its high prognostic validity (precision of the prognosis) and objectivity (how autonomous the observer's assessment is). Well-known authors working in this field in Germany are Bolton (2001), Deller (2000), Kühlmann and Stahl (1998). Culture assimilator trainings were developed on the basis of research conducted since the 1920's in *intra-cultural assessment centers* mainly in Germany and the U. S. (Jeserich 1981: Kitzmann 1990; Obermann 1992; Schuler and Stehle 1992). Awareness gained from intercultural research (Thomas 1993b; Thomas 1996) and comparative culture studies (Thomas 1993a) have contributed to further development of culture assimilator trainings.

2.1.2 The Intercultural Assessment Center

Definition

The term assessment center was first mentioned at a round-table discussion during the Weimar Republic, referring to the selection of officers for service in the *Reichswehr*. Today the term is generally accepted although it is misleading: Center connotes a facility or institute where something takes place. It would be more appropriate to refer to an assessment-center method or assessment-center technique and therefore is also frequently referred to as culture assimilator training. A distinction is made between international culture assimilator training and intra-cultural assimilator training, which has a mono-cultural and national character.

Concept

In a culture assimilator training, participants are observed and evaluated by several observers over a longer period of time according to a set of defined criteria of intercultural competence and programmed sequences in multiple game situations (cf. Sarges 2001, p. VII). Culture assimilator trainings assess the proactive character of applied intercultural competence. Candidates are introduced to a simulated intercultural situation such as a roleplay or a group discussion with one or more other-culture individuals. Together they must master tasks on the merit of their personal characteristics, such as openness, ability to empathize and ambiguity tolerance, which are manifested in their behavior. Their behavior is observed and evaluated.

Function

Culture assimilator trainings take place predominantly in corporations in order to:

- select the most qualified candidates for an international assignment. In this sense, they are instrumental in the *selection* of qualified candidates.
- select those candidates most qualified to explore the markets of specific cultural regions (e.g., Asia, Europe). Here, they support candidate *placement.*
- determine the level of executives' and managers' applied intercultural competence. Although this professional group may operate from home base, they are internationally active. Narrowly defined, the culture assimilator training is instrumental in *diagnosing* applied intercultural competence.
- determine the potential in terms of applied intercultural competence of young executives with international career ambitions. Here, culture assimilator training facilitates the *prognosis* of applied intercultural competence.
- compile a strengths-weaknesses profile following a diagnosis or prognosis, on the basis of which coaching and training programs can be adapted to specific needs with a focus on applied intercultural competence. Here, culture assimilator trainings serve *needs-assessment* measures.
- follow up and promote a needs assessment with coaching and training measures for applied intercultural competence. Here, they encourage the *development and support of applied intercultural competence.*
- evaluate the participants' learning success following intercultural trainings and coaching. Here, they enhance methods of *evaluation.*

Even if assessment centers do not specifically target personal development, participants profit from the experience and can continue to develop their intercultural competence. The same applies to observers of the evaluation process.

Requirement Profile and Evaluation Criteria

Depending on the requirement profile and observation criteria, there are basically two types of culture assimilator trainings.

The *culture-general assimilator training* uses the characteristics of intercultural competence for profiling and then applies them to the observation criteria (e.g., openness, ambiguity tolerance, ability to adapt one's perspective).

The *culture-specific assimilator training* uses the key cultural standards of a specific culture as prerequisites and applies them as observation criteria (e.g., interpersonal distance and social harmony).

Depending on the purpose of the culture assimilator training, it can be designed according to culture-general (i.e., *diagnosis*) or culture-specific criteria (i.e., *placement*). Because of their complexity, culture assimilator trainings rarely operate independently. Culture assimilator trainings serve to identify qualified candidates within corporations and other organizations not only on the basis of their intercultural competence, but also on their general management skills including their practical expertise and social, individual and strategic competence (cf. Bolton 2001). Culture assimilator trainings of this nature are instrumental in assessing international management competency of promising young candidates and upper management. They are often referred to as *international culture assimilator trainings*. Should a specific position be filled in a corporation or other organization in a particular country (*selection*), then the specific requirement profile for the position must be considered separately from the characteristics of intercultural competence and the individual culture.

Management Simulation Scenarios

Ideally management simulation in the culture assimilation trainings should reflect real-life scenarios. For this reason, it is important to simulate the candidate's actual work situation as it might occur within the company in a national/international context as closely as possible. Aside from the usual scenarios used in the culture assimilator trainings, such as group discussion, presentations, case studies and other exercises (cf. Jeserich 1981), candidates use *critical incidents* simulating interactions with other-culture individuals as material for *role plays* and *interaction exercises*. Empirically tested critical incidents based on real-life situations are described in culture assimilator trainings and are available in most larger bookstores. The candidates could, for example, hold a meeting before a group of sleeping Chinese within the scope of a culture-specific assimilation training on China (cf. Thomas and Schenk 2001, p. 124 f.) or handle a conflict situation with a Chinese contractor who failed to install an air conditioner in a new building on time (cf. Thomas and Schenk 2001, p. 92 f.). Alternatively, they could simulate a typical workday scenario abroad in their particular company. Naturally, setting up situations like these costs considerably more and takes more time.

Another approach is to show a *video sequence*, illustrating a critical incident that reflects an ethical dilemma. Candidates are then asked to analyze (one-on-one or in a group) the situation. For example, a film made at the University of Regensburg entitled "Father's Veto" describes the situation of a Somali father refusing to let German doctors amputate his son's diseased leg even though this will mean the boy's certain death. The physician experiences an ethical conflict because of his adherence to the Hippocratic oath.

Creativity is limitless in designing these scenarios. The decisive factor in a culture assimilator training lies in observing behavior along the lines of the observation criteria, on the one hand, and a feedback session with each candidate following the exercise on the other. The purpose is to reflect on both the other-culture individuals' and the candidates' own feelings, thoughts, expectations, interpretations etc. in response to the critical incident.

Ideally other-culture individuals who are privy to the "rules of the game" and can play along with them take part in the scenarios. This makes the simulated intercultural situation more authentic. It is, however, costly and difficult to implement. Alternatively, individuals from the same culture who have a high level of intercultural competence as well as culture-specific background knowledge can be substituted as participants. Psychology students, for example, or those with a background in business, who have already worked abroad and are familiar with different working conditions are a good alternative. Other options include students who have acquired a more in-depth knowledge about the theories and concepts behind intercultural learning and interacting during the course of their studies.

One interesting approach combines individual scenarios in a culture assimilator training to simulate a typical workday in the life of an international executive or that of a typical project in an international corporation thus creating an entire *management simulation game.* These approaches are referred to as *systemic culture assimilator trainings* as compared to *selective culture assimilator trainings* (cf. Bolton 2001) and are becoming more popular.

The person or persons who design the scenario are, of course, influenced by their own cultural mindsets. Therefore it is recommended to include culturally diverse individuals. Another criterion for scenario selection depends on the culture a person belongs to. American candidates, for example, are much more likely than Germans to respond positively to role plays because of their intrinsic, key cultural standard of "action orientation". It can therefore be assumed that Americans will tend to participate more actively in role plays that the Germans ever will.

The question as to whether to conduct culture assimilator trainings in a foreign language (q.v. Ch. I, 1.5) remains open. It is advisable, in this case, to play through several scenes in the native language of the specific country or in English. It is not a good idea, however, to conduct *all* simulations in a foreign language. On occasion, participants found it difficult to act naturally (e.g., contact behavior) because they felt unsure of their language ability. An "In-tray" exercise might be more suitable for exercises conducted in a foreign language. Another option is to administer a written or oral language competency test to measure realistic language ability in a neutral situation.

In closing, it is important to mention that the selection of upper management candidates and experts for a specific position abroad, aside from the diagnosis of intercultural and general management competence, necessarily includes factors such as mobility, the family situation and other relevant issues and must be considered in the final evaluation. Here, biographical questionnaires or structured selection interviews can be very helpful (cf. Kühlmann and Stahl 1998).

Drawing Conclusions

Assessing an individual's intercultural competence involves objectively *observing* and *describing* the behavior of participants in the game situation. The second step involves correlating behavior descriptions with the observation criteria. Finally, the results are measured against the profile criteria and *evaluated* according to a predetermined scale. The timeframe between observation and evaluation is very important. The separate observations and evaluations are compared and discussed in an observer conference until a common decision has been reached. A *strengths-weaknesses profile* of each participant is developed on the basis of the findings.

Procedure

The intercultural assessment is sequenced in three phases (cf. Jeserich 1981, p. 35):

The preparation phase for culture assimilator trainings involves identifying goals and target groups as well as selecting observers. The requirement profile is defined, if necessary, with observers in order to ensure transparency. The exercises are selected or created according to previously defined criteria. When preparations are complete, the participants are initiated and organization can begin.

During the implementation phase of the culture assimilator training, the observers are informed about the content and how to proceed. They are instructed in the difference between observation and evaluation and introduced to the many different angles of observation. When the participants arrive, the content and procedure, including the observation criteria of the culture assimilator training is explained. Next, participants enact the situation and the observers monitor and evaluate the behavior. Following each game sequence, each observer's observations and assessments are analyzed.

In the final round, there is a *conclusion with feedback* where the final evaluations are fine-tuned by the group of observers (observer conference), and a final verdict is returned. The evaluations and referrals are compiled into a report, recommending enhancement and personal development measures. Once a candidate has been selected and placed, he goes into a last round for the final decision. Upon completion, the candidates are given their results. Results of the in-house culture assimilator trainings determine the enhancement and development measures that are agreed upon with the candidates.

A culture assimilator training should last at least three days. Because of the costs involved, however, they are often shortened to one day. Consequently, the precision factor is also likely to be reduced.

Observers

As a rule, from three to six observers and six to twelve candidates participate in a culture assimilator training. The ratio should be 1:2.

The demands made on the observer during a culture assimilator training are even higher than those for intra-cultural assimilator trainings. The observers should have different cultural backgrounds and yet be able to speak and understand the language spoken during the assessment in order to avoid misunderstandings. They should be in higher management, at least two levels above but not the direct supervisors of the participating candidates. They should be active internationally and have much experience in intercultural overlap situations.

Prior to culture assimilator training, the observers take part in an observation training, where they are familiarized with the observation process, possible mistakes and theories of intercultural action and learning.

Precision increases when psychologists participate as observers as they are already professionally trained to observe and evaluate behavior. Where culture assimilator trainings are concerned, it is advantageous if the psychologists have specialized in intercultural psychology.

Expectations placed on the observers, as described here, are very high and are rarely met. The trainings are very cost-intensive and consequently not commonplace. Alternatively, an observer group can be assembled consisting of at least two executives from two foreign countries and two local executives for a total of twelve participants including two psychologists who specialize in intercultural psychology. All of them should have completed the observer training. Language problems can, if need requires, be solved by employing the services of a simultaneous interpreter. Whichever alternative a company chooses and the amount it is willing to spend depend entirely on their priorities and understanding of the need for diagnosing applied intercultural competence.

Validity

To date hardly any research findings are available to validate the reliability and precision of culture assimilator training measures. In light of results obtained from research conducted on intra-cultural assimilator trainings (cf. Sarges 2001), this method can be clearly recommended over others (e.g., interview) as long as specific quality standards are applied and adhered to and competent staff are responsible for organizing and implementing the culture assimilator training.

There is some thought on how to validate intra-cultural assimilator trainings. The two most important factors for supervising the trainings are *reliability* and *validity.* Reliability is measured according to the degree of precision with which the culture assimilator training is evaluated. This is not limited to factors it is intended to measure or those that it claims to measure. Here, two forms of reliability can be differentiated: the inter-rate reliability (objectivity) and parallel-test/re-test reliability (Obermann 1992).

The *inter-rate reliability* measures the extent to which the observers agree on the evaluation. The key question is to what degree a candidate's overall assessment is influenced by an observer's perspective. From a systematic standpoint, each observer's evaluations are correlated. Research among intra-cultural assessment centers shows that, overall, the inter-rate reliability suffices. Its reliability is, however, affected: by an exchange of information among observers prior to submitting the evaluation by participation in an observer training prior to the culture assimilator training (they will be more familiar with the procedure and able to avoid observation errors); by particular game situations (e.g., "In-tray" exercises, nondirected group discussions); when particular training characteristics (e.g., organization, planning) are observed; if the observer group is homogeneously assembled. It is important to note that, from a mathematical perspective, the degree of reliability influences the rate of validity.

A question with respect to culture assimilator trainings remains unanswered: can a high degree of inter-rate reliability be achieved considering the observers' diverse cultural backgrounds and their different perceptions, thought patterns and actions? If this is the case, then the validity of a culture assimilator training can hardly reach the degree of validity of the intra-cultural assessment center.

The parallel-test reliability is the result of one and the same culture assimilator training. Creating a parallel equivalent is precluded due to cost and time factors. To conduct the same intercultural assessment after a time interval also seems unrealistic from a methodological perspective since personality characteristics are not static and hence can be observed as behavioral traits that are modifiable even as learning increases as a result of the training. Such learning effects make it nearly impossible to calculate re-test reliability. For this reason, claims can actually only be made relevant to inter-rate reliability.

The validity criterion, meaning the degree of precision against which the culture assimilator training is measured according to the available data, is the second most important criteria in the evaluation of culture assimilator trainings. There are many forms of validity. Prognostic validity is a frequent topic of discussion as it relates to intercultural assimilator training.

Prognostic validity is the extent of precision accorded the predictability of observation criteria. It is the most important evaluation tool for gauging the validity of trainings because it gives an indication of a candidate's likely chances of success. A culture assimilator training is instrumental in predicting a candidate's applied intercultural competence and his effectiveness on an international assignment. From a methodological perspective, the prognostic validity is determined by measuring training results against quantifiable outside criteria. In many cases, the salary serves as an outside criterion. This means that success is linked to salary. If a candidate is chosen on the basis of excellent intercultural assimilator training results and if his salary has increased considerably since this time, then the person has proven himself in the field and the assimilator training can be considered valid from a prognostic point of view. Other outside criteria include the amount of points received on the supervisor appraisal and the promotions the candidate has received. Outside criteria are misleading and pose a number of problems. Salary increases are not merely a reflection of a manager's performance, but also depend on such things as his negotiation skills, his standing with his supervisors or the company's current economic situation. The supervisor's point-for-point evaluation may well be affected by inaccurate observation and promotions largely depend on the time spent with the company, age, the presence of mentors and protégés in addition to overall performance. Factors that elicited criticism in the intra-cultural assessment center are bound to intensify in intercultural assimilator trainings. The salaries received by specialist and executives on assignment in China for three to five years in the 1980's and1990's exceeded that of equally successful managers at home. Interestingly, these higher amounts were attributed to their assignments to "hardship posts", which was meant to compensate for the difficult situation faced by Europeans in China at that time. This is still standard today, although living conditions are becoming increasingly Westernized. Today Western products are available in almost all industrialized countries, or at least in the major cities, at reasonable prices. Hence, the salary can only be used to a certain extent as an outside criterion for the evaluation of prognostic validity. The idea behind this is to use criteria for *applied intercultural competence* as it refers to accomplishing a task successfully, for example, or establishing good rapport with locals, knowing how to care for personal well-being and being able to quantify and live according to these maxims. Claims made by participants of cultural assessment trainings, should be exchanged with the notes of local observers and the evaluators on site.

Culture assimilator trainings are very cost-intensive in terms of organization and implementation and are therefore only cost-efficient if trainings are held on a regular basis. On the other hand, a training can only be organized if candidates are available who meet the requirement profile for interculturally competent specialist and executives. Currently, the candidate pool is quite meager with further development in sight. The exorbitant costs incurred by prematurely terminated international assignments are very likely to offset the investment in culture assimilator trainings.

Culture assimilator training has two drawbacks, which must be mentioned:

Firstly, despite increasing globalization and internationalization, the *mobility* of specialists and executives is steadily decreasing. Consequently, not many candidates at this level are available who, on the one hand, are able to accomplish the task and, on the other, are willing to work abroad. Often a company cannot afford to include intercultural competence in their selection criteria for fear of not having enough candidates available who could qualify for an international position or operate in an international arena. To date, companies often avoid diagnosing candidates for intercultural competence in their selection and placement procedures with the result that unsuitable candidates are chosen for international assignments.

Secondly, culture assimilator training is a method originally developed in Germany, exported to the U. S. and then re-imported to Germany after WWII. Consequently, it is a method developed in the Western cultural hemisphere. Its *transferability* to other cultural groups is limited. In China's case, for example, it is difficult to simulate conflict situations in role plays in culture assimilator trainings on the basis of their cultural standard "social harmony". The feedback discussions at the end of the training may also prove complicated because exposing strengths and weaknesses clash with the cultural standard of "saving face".

2.1.3 Final Statement

Considering how many possibilities there are for diagnosing applied intercultural competence in an assessment center, it is startling to see how many interculturally incompetent managers are active internationally. Frequently the high cost of diagnosing intercultural competence and the organization and implementation involved in the process are cited, and that the results do not necessarily guarantee the desired success. Compared to the costs incurred by failed international assignments, however, the investment in diagnosing intercultural competence is clearly insubstantial.

If specialists and executives do not have the necessary intercultural competence, then international endeavors and projects are destined to fail. Applied intercultural competence can be enhanced and further developed in intercultural trainings. The next chapter will explore this topic in more depth.

References

Bolten, J. (2001): Interkulturelles Assessment-Center. In: Sarges, W. (Ed.), Weiterentwicklungen der Assessment-Center-Methode. 2nd ed. Göttingen/Bern u. a., pp. 213–218.

Deller, J. (2000): Interkulturelle Eignungsdiagnostik. Zur Verwendbarkeit von Persönlichkeitsskalen. Waldsteinberg.

Jeserich, W. (1981): Mitarbeiter auswählen und fördern: Assessment-Center-Verfahren. Handbuch der Weiterbildung für die Praxis in Wirtschaft und Verwaltung Band 1 (Hg. von W. Jeserich; G. Comelli; O. Daniel; H. Karus; J. Krahnen; H. Rühle; K. Vollmer). München/Wien.

Kitzmann, A. (1990): Assessment-Center. Personalförderung und Personalauswahl. 3rd ed. Bamberg.

Kühlmann, T. M.; Stahl, G. K. (1998): Diagnose interkultureller Kompetenz. Entwicklung und Evaluierung eines Assessment-Centers. In: Barmeyer, C. I.; Bolten, J. (Eds.), Interkulturelle Personalorganisation. Berlin, pp. 213–224.

Obermann, C. (1992): Assessment-Center. Entwicklung, Durchführung, Trends. Wiesbaden.

Sarges, W. (Ed.) (2001): Weiterentwicklungen der Assessment-Center-Methode. 2nd ed. Göttingen/Bern/Toronto u. a.

Schuler, H.; Stehle, W. (1992): Assessment-Center Methode als Methode der Personalentwicklung. Beiträge zur Organisationspsychologie, Band 3. 2nd ed. Göttingen/Stuttgart.

Thomas, A. (1993a): Kulturvergleichende Psychologie. Eine Einführung. Göttingen.

Thomas, A. (1993b): Psychologie interkulturellen Lernens und Handelns. In: Thomas, A. (Ed.), Kulturvergleichende Psychologie. Eine Einführung. Göttingen, pp. 377–424.

Thomas, A. (1996): Psychologie interkulturellen Handelns. Göttingen.

Thomas, A.; Schenk, E. (2001): Beruflich in China. Trainingsprogramm für Manager, Fach- und Führungskräfte. Göttingen.

Eva-Ulrike Kinast

2.2 Intercultural Training

2.2.1 Foreword

Intercultural diagnosis can rapidly identify the basic level of applied intercultural competence a person has. However, how is one to proceed if there is a lack of cultural sensitivity, little experience in dealing with dissimilar others and only marginal intercultural competence? And if, as a result, it can be expected that the specialist or executive will not meet the performance requirements demanded of him in an international setting? Intercultural competence, after all, is not a birthright, but must be developed. This is the purpose of intercultural training.

2.2.2 Present Situation

The first intercultural trainings were developed in the U. S. during the 60's. Since then, many types of intercultural trainings have been developed. Bhawuk and Brislin (2000) provide a general overview of the subject. The importance of intercultural training is steadily increasing. In fact, in the last few years, psychologists and professionals from other disciplines, including intercultural diagnostics, have explored interesting research possibilities, which in turn have opened up new career opportunities in the field. Research papers and publications related to intercultural competence are proliferating. The standard work in the U. S. is still the "Handbook of Intercultural Training" in three volumes by Landis and Brislin (1983). The work was published again by Landis and Bhagat in 1996 in a much revised and extended edition. Many research findings relative to intercultural training are published in English in the "Journal of Intercultural Relations".

Companies and organizations in Germany and other countries have long since recognized the need for intercultural training. Intercultural trainings have become a standard feature there over the last few years, in particular to prepare specialists and executives for longer-term international assignments. Currently, this situation is changing as managers who live in their home countries and work internationally participate in the trainings. They are in contact with other-culture individuals via e-mail, telephone, video-conferencing, fax or during business trips. In addition, many self-employed intercultural trainers offer their services, an aspect that probably requires more caution than for other trainings. Qualified trainers have, for instance, specialized in the theory and concepts of intercultural interaction and aspects of intercultural psychology within the scope of their studies in psychology and have spent many years studying the characteristics of different cultures. This qualifies them as intercultural experts. If, in addition, they have trainer qualifications and spent time abroad working for international organizations, then they meet the high standards required of intercultural trainers. It is not sufficient, after having lived in a foreign country for a number of years, to offer training on that particular country and its culture. In this case, many personal experiences with other-culture individuals have, no doubt, accumulated over the years. However, it is not enough to pass on experiences in a foreign country without trained reflection and didactic expertise. It is much easier to compensate for a lack of experience abroad by working with a co-trainer who is native to the country in question than to proceed with little formal training in the field. The chamber of commerce (IHK) in Lübeck (1999) and Tschöcke and Kölling (2000) offer an overview of trainers and their services – albeit not reviewed. The "Society of Intercultural Training and Research" (SIETAR), the largest association of researchers, trainers and other professional groups involved in the subject of intercultural learning in Europe provide further information (www.sietar.de).

Intercultural trainings differ in scope, methodology, including the didactic approach, their goals and how they are rated on evaluations.

2.2.3 Concept and Design of Intercultural Trainings

Definition

Intercultural training takes measures to enhance intercultural learning and promote applied intercultural competence (Thomas 1990). The conceptual design and content of intercultural trainings are based on the findings of general training research (Thomas 1993b; Thomas 1996a), in particular research on trainings for intercultural training conducted by Landis and Brislin (1983), and Landis and Bhagat (1996), and the research findings on comparative culture (Thomas 1993a).

Training Goal

The overall goal of intercultural training is to develop and enhance applied intercultural competence to enable individuals to apply their intercultural competence. Depending on the specific training goal, intercultural trainings should provide the means for developing and promoting the affective, cognitive or behavioral components of applied intercultural competence. For instance, intercultural trainings can enhance emotional self-control in interactions with dissimilar others (affective training goal); can provide background knowledge about other-culture systems of orientation (cognitive training goal) or train participants to adopt behavioral patterns that are similar to those in the foreign culture (behavioral training goal). Hence, one differentiates between *affective, cognitive and behavioral intercultural trainings.*

Training Content

Depending on the training curriculum, culture-specific trainings differ from culture-general trainings (Gudykunst and Hammer 1983). Culture-specific trainings, as suggested by the title, prepare participants for a specific culture (e.g., USA, China) and the curriculum includes the specific culture's key cultural standards. General intercultural trainings stimulate an awareness of culture-specific differences in the thought patterns and actions of dissimilar others. For the most part, these trainings treat subjects that play a role in every culture, the difference being that they manifest differently in every culture. Typical examples are aspects of work, time, space, language, gender differences and group orientation instead of dealing with individuals. Furthermore, it is advisable to design the trainings according to the needs of a *specific target group* (e.g., upper management, soldier, student) and *task-specific* needs. (e.g., sales, marketing, lectures, medical services).

Training Methods

Knowledge-based intercultural trainings differ from experienced-based intercultural trainings depending on the training goal (Gudykunst and Hammer 1983). In *knowledge-based training methods* the assumption is that merely providing content knowledge about the other-culture orientation system will render participants capable of successfully negotiating cultural overlap situations. The largely cognitive training approach attempts to reach training participants through lectures, books or films. In contrast, *experienced-based training methods* are based on the assumption that providing content knowledge about the other-culture system of orientation, in fact, does not provide the necessary know-how to deal successfully with cultural overlap situations. Here, for instance, intercultural games, role plays or case studies are used as training components to simulate a situation that the participant may encounter in a foreign country. This approach implies that in order to be successful internationally, a training participant must first be confronted with affective experiences within the scope of an intercultural training and practice behavior in a sort of laboratory situation. A collection of training components can be found in Pederson (1988), Rademacher (1991) and Losche (2000).

Every training solution and each component have their pros and cons. Meanwhile, there are hardly any intercultural trainings on the market that are based on a single training method. It is always advisable to incorporate a well thought-out combination of different methods and tools while taking the participants' culture into consideration. North Americans, for instance, are very motivated by role plays because, as a rule, they enjoy the interaction. The Chinese on the other hand, tend to react negatively to the extensive feedback following such role plays due to the deep-seated cultural standard of "saving face".

Scope of Training

Depending on duration, intercultural trainings are divided into *education, training* (in the narrower sense), *orientation* and *briefing.*

"Education is well-suited for (sic) relating large bodies of content knowledge and developing in-depth mastery of one or more subjects whereas training usually focuses on "process" and/or on developing competency in performing specific skills or meeting specified objectives in a cost-effective manner. Orientation prepares a person to understand and function effectively in a new or radically different environment, and to achieve this shift in the least traumatic manner. Briefing provides a broad overview, or it can focus on a particular part of a larger program, in the most time-effective way" (Kohls 1987, p. 91).

The length of an intercultural training most likely has an effect on its effectiveness. Literature on the topic suggests that trainings last three days. A single day is very little. Experience has shown that participant motivation drops considerably after two days. Consequently, the recommended optimal training duration is two days.

Point of Training

Another point of interest is at what phase of the international assignment an intercultural training should take place. Thomas (1996b) differentiates between: *orientation training*, prior to the international assignment to prepare for the foreign culture and the unfamiliar working and living conditions in the host country; *in-process training*, during the international assignment to work through critical interaction situations with or for other-culture partners; and *reintegration training*, shortly before or after termination of the international assignment with a view to facilitating reintegration into the home culture and work environment, which may have become "foreign" in the mean time. Orientation trainings are most common while in-process trainings and reintegration trainings are catching up rapidly.

At what point a person participates in an intercultural training most probably impacts the effectiveness of the training. If the orientation training takes place shortly before departure, the participant will be too focused on departure formalities, packing, saying goodbyes to family and friends etc. to concentrate on the training (given that he even shows up for the training due to his busy schedule). If the training takes place too early, that is, too far in advance of the departure date, the training participant may not have a sense of immediacy about the impending change and is not ready to think about culture-specific differences and the problems they may pose. Based on past experience, intercultural orientation trainings should take place six to eight weeks before departure. It is interesting to note, that individuals with prior experience in a particular country tend to be more motivated with regard to the training and consequently profit from it more. Therefore, it makes sense to schedule the training at a time after the participants have had the chance to visit the target country for a week or two.

Experience has shown that in-process trainings are more effective after eight to twelve weeks in the target country, after the first critical interactions have occurred and to refresh cultural standards basics that were treated during the orientation training. Reintegration trainings should be scheduled four weeks after return to home base at the latest in order to buffer the re-entry-shock and integrate experiences into the participants' repertoire of intercultural competence.

Didactic Approach

According to Thomas (1995), the most important differences between intercultural trainings lie in their didactical approach.

Information-Based Training

provides important dates and facts about the economic, political and social conditions in the host country and information about what to expect in terms of living and working conditions. Frequently, colleagues who have lived and worked in the particular country are invited to speak and give practical insider tips and information on the climate, living conditions, leisure activities and how to build relationships with locals. Personal experience can be worked into case studies so the audience can begin relating to the cultural differences in specific areas. Information-based trainings use a content-oriented approach and a combination of methods consisting of lectures, films, written material, graphics, stories based on experience and case studies. The advantage of an information-based training is that it satisfies the participants' need for concrete information. In general, participants are more eager for information the closer they are to the date of departure. Anxiety about what to expect is reduced when more information is forthcoming. The disadvantages of the information-based approach is, firstly, that information-based trainings rely predominantly on cognitive teaching and learning methods while leaving other channels of perception unused. Secondly, too much information can be counter-productive and thirdly, there is a risk involved in presenting rules of behavior in the trainings, especially when former expatriate colleagues simplify business etiquette to the level of a cookbook recipe, which can actually reinforce stereotypical thinking. Discussions and reflection help to understand behavior in its cultural perspective and avoid preconceptions.

Culture-Based Training

sharpens participants' awareness of the influence that one's own culture has on feeling, thinking and acting and sensitizes them to the culture-based differences inherent in thinking and behavioral patterns of individuals with different cultural origins. Training methods listed in U. S. literature as cultural (self)-awareness trainings and experiential learning can be classified under this term. In contrast to the information-based trainings, this approach is experiential. Preferred training tools include intercultural games such as the well-known BAFA BAFA (Shirts 1973) and ALBATROSS (Gochenour 1977) and the later simulations, self-awareness exercises, role plays and case studies created on the basis of these ideas. The training content is of culture-general nature. The advantage of culture-based trainings lies in the participants' tendency to involve all senses when their own cultural patterns are reflected on and, in contrast to the information-based trainings, they are not only involved cognitively but, above all, can treat the subject from an emotional perspective. Furthermore, in this form of intercultural training the emphasis is more on applied intercultural competence than on culture-specific information, so that culture-based trainings can also be used to prepare participants for international assignments within the scope of trainee programs. The question arises, however, as to what extent the acquired material is applicable to the target country.

Interaction-Based Training
also aims to raise awareness of the influence of culture on thinking and action on other-culture individuals, albeit through direct contact with individuals from the target country or so-called *resource people.* In contrast to culture-based trainings, interaction-based training curricula emphasize culture-specific content. Here too, personal experience and working through culture-based differences are conducted interactively. As in the culture-based trainings, experiential methods are used together with selected training tools consisting of role plays and communication exercises. During the first weeks of an international assignment or during a field trip prior to departure, actual critical interactions between participants and the resource people are simulated. The critical interactions are then measured against the cultural standards, whereby misunderstandings and misinterpretations are brought to light. Another version of intercultural trainings is *bi-cultural training* in which participants from the relevant target countries interact and learn from each other. However, this approach is not suited for all cultures. Chinese participants, for example, might react negatively to discussions about cultural standards that may lead to disagreement because of their key cultural standard of "social harmony". In the presence of resource people, an important success factor for this type of intercultural training is proactive communication with dissimilar others. Foreign language skills are a prerequisite for this activity. Another alternative is to integrate interaction-based trainings into a *foreign language workshop.*

The challenge is finding suitable resource people. Ideally, they will be in tune with their own cultural makeup as well as knowledgeable about the culture of the other participants. In this case, it is recommended to *train in tandem* with a trainer from the target culture. The same-culture trainer can then design an intercultural training curriculum and procedure according to participant needs and the other-culture trainer can provide more in-depth insight into culture-specific content. This approach contributes to the authenticity of intercultural trainings.

Compared to other training forms, the interaction-based training is more expensive and complex than other forms of training because more personnel is required and groups have to be smaller. The advantage of this method is that the participants have to deal directly and interactively with the foreign culture, thus prompting them to respond spontaneously to a situation.

Training Based on Understanding
assumes that cognition determines action. The training goal, therefore, is to provide knowledge about a specific culture. According to Thomas (1995), the participant should be familiar with the following aspects after the intercultural training:

- The partners will behave differently in certain situations than he/she may be used to (knowledge of other-culture patterns of action),
- Why they behave in a certain manner (culturally isomorphic attribution),
- The behavior, attitudes, judgments, patterns and scripts expected including the reactions elicited in the partner as a result (intercultural anticipation) and
- The advantage gained from the divergent cultural systems of orientation, situational rules of behavior and interpretations with a view to reaching a common goal (intercultural acknowledgment) (p. 109).

Hence, the training content is based on the key cultural standards of a particular country. The preferred approach here is a knowledge-based methodology. A typical training tool to evaluate cultural understanding is the *culture assimilator*. Culture assimilator training is the most evaluated form of training to date and thus merits a unique position. The following chapter will discuss this subject in more detail.

Culture Assimilator Training

Culture assimilator training was developed in the U. S. in the 1960's and is described in depth by Albert (1983) and Lange (1994).

The goal of culture assimilator training is to develop *cognitive characteristics of applied intercultural competence.* The key competence here is *isomorphic attribution* as it applies to other-culture behavior (q.v. Ch. I, 1.7). This does not mean that training participants should give up their own cultural identity, as the term culture assimilator may suggest, rather own and other-culture systems of orientation are integrated and made accessible to participants, assuming that this will enhance their cognitive facilities, contributing to both *emotional and behavioral characteristics of intercultural competence.*

Culture assimilator training can be either culture specific or culture general. In the U. S., culture-specific culture assimilator trainings for specific target

Table 6: Published culture-specific culture assimilator training

Culture	Target Group	Authors
China	German upper management and specialists	Thomas and Schenk (2001)
Germany	Chinese upper management and specialists (in Chinese)	Thomas et al .
Germany	Chinese upper management (in German)	Thomas et al.
Indonesia	German upper management and specialists	Martin and Thomas (2002)
South Korea	German upper management and specialists	Brüch and Thomas (1995)
Argentina	German upper management and specialists	Foellbach et al. (2002)
Great Britain	German upper management and specialists	Schmid and Thomas (2003)
Germany	British (in German)	Bock und Thomas
Russian	German upper management and specialists	Yoosefi and Thomas (2003)
Czech Republic	German upper management and specialists	Schroll-Machl und Nový
Kenya and Tanzania	German upper management and specialists	Mayer and Boness (2003)
USA	German university and high school students and trainees	Müller and Thomas (1995)
Germany	American university and high school students and trainees	Markowsky and Thomas (1995)
China	German trainers and facilitators	Lindner et al. (2001)
China	German students and trainees	Schenk et al.
Germany	International upper management (in German and English)	Schroll-Machl (2002)

countries and specific target groups, occupational fields and tasks are meanwhile widespread. Over the past few years, they have also appeared in greater numbers in Germany. An overview of this topic can be found in Table 6.

Culture-general assimilator training was developed in the U. S. during the seventies for training on how to interact with ethnic minorities. Meanwhile Germany, too, has culture-general assimilator trainings that prepare German military personnel for international missions (Thomas et al. 1998).

Culture assimilator trainings consist of written material and are knowledge based. They can be administered individually or as training components in a comprehensive intercultural training. Culture assimilator trainings are divided into separate training modules, each one treating a specific, key cultural standard. Each module contains case studies *(situations)* that describe critical interactions between visitors and members of a foreign culture. Each case study suggests a number of different *interpretations* for the other-culture partner's motives and behavioral patterns. One presents a culturally acceptable interpretation as seen from the perspective of members of the host country, and the others contain misinterpretations typical of members of one's own country that reflect a lack of insight into cultural influences, an ethnocentric mindset and prejudice. The participants' task is to choose a culturally adequate explanation for the dissimilar other's behavior from the case study provided. First, the participant reads through the options and assesses them for their appropriateness. Feedback is provided a few pages on in the training manual regarding the appropriateness of the options including the reasoning behind them from a foreign culture perspective, e.g., why the interpretation is culturally appropriate, plausible or culturally inappropriate. The explanatory statements contain the essential characteristics of a given key cultural standard and point to significant cultural differences based on the interaction partners' different cultural conditioning. Following the case study in each training module, participants are informed about the underlying key cultural standards on a more abstract level. The key cultural standards are explained including how they apply within the context of the country's cultural history *(cultural anchoring)*. The goal here is to provide an in-depth understanding of how key cultural standards affect behavior and to enable participants to accept cultural differences. The more recent culture assimilator trainings contain *solution strategies* for critical interaction situations that are presented prior to dealing in-depth with the key cultural standards (Thomas 2000).

Thomas and Schenk (2001, pp. 92–97 and 102) cite the case study, "Air Conditioner", taken from a culture assimilator training to prepare German managers and field specialists for an international assignment in China. It illustrates the content and methodology used in culture assimilator training.

■ Example 11: Air Conditioner

■ Situation

Things always go wrong during construction, be it in Germany, China or wherever. Mr. Praunges believes he has strong nerves. During the recently completed restructuring of the offices for the company he represented, however, he was close to losing his mind.

"Renovations on the office buildings had almost been completed but I couldn't find an air conditioner in my room. I asked an employee of the firm why an air conditioner hadn't been installed and how this could have happened. He began explaining in a very friendly way that the faucet in the bathroom was dripping but that tomorrow, yes, tomorrow for sure they would fix it. I thought he was joking! I nodded and asked him again about installing the air conditioner. This time he didn't expound on the dripping faucet, but launched into an explanation about painting the staircase, and that it would be done next week so that this would no longer be a problem. I repeated that I was not interested in the staircase but rather in the air conditioning and that a painted stair railing would not cool my office! He noticed that I was not about to be put off by his attempts at changing the subject. It was quite clear. They had simply forgotten about the air conditioner! Instead of apologizing or promising to take care of matters immediately, he came up with all kinds of excuses and wouldn't stop smiling. Then they literally fled, promising to 'take care of it' tomorrow. They did come back the next day and install the air conditioner ... but how!?"

Why doesn't the Chinese construction manager respond to Mr. Praunge's question?

- Now read through the possible answers consecutively.
- Determine the value of each explanation for the situation above and indicate it on the scale below. There may be the same value for more than one alternative.

■ Interpretation

a) The construction manager tries to detract from the question with excuses because the air conditioner had indeed been forgotten. He had noticed this oversight himself and intends to take care of it. That is no reason, however, for the German to expose him in such a way!

fully applicable	highly applicable	not very applicable	not applicable

b) The Chinese construction manager didn't understand Mr. Praunges and tried to answer him by explaining the work that still had to be completed.

fully applicable	highly applicable	not very applicable	not applicable

c) The Chinese manager thinks the German is an arrogant know-it-all getting all worked up about a trifle like the air conditioner and making rude jokes. He tries to brush him off with stubborn ignorance.

fully applicable	highly applicable	not very applicable	not applicable

d) The Chinese manager tries to avoid conflict in order to maintain harmony and "save face".

fully applicable	highly applicable	not very applicable	not applicable

- Try to justify your evaluation for each option. Note down your answers in point form.
- Now read the explanations for each option and compare them to your own reasons.

■ Reasons

Explanation for a):
In Germany this answer would be right to the point. From the Chinese perspective, however, a decisive factor is missing that explains why the Chinese makes excuses instead of answering the question. It is not about avoiding an embarrassing situation, for this has already happened (smiling is intended to soften the embarrassment). The risk of losing face is worse than being exposed by repetition of the question. The insistence on an answer goes against all the fundamental principles of communication among the Chinese. The irony inherent in the "joke" about the noncooling stair railing is a blatant insult. From the Chinese perspective this has nothing to do with humor. The construction manager has indeed understood the problem and tries to signal this by adroitly redirecting the conversation to the water faucet that he promises to repair the following day. The second hint that things would be taken care of the next day was wasted on Mr. Praunges. The answers are actually intended as such and not merely stupid excuses. They just have to be decoded, something Mr. Praunges is incapable of doing.

Explanation for b):
One can assume that in all likelihood this has nothing to do with not understanding. Someone who can communicate the status of work on the stair railing and dripping water faucet will certainly be able to understand the term "air conditioner".

Explanation for c):
No, this is certainly incorrect even if, according to our rules of communication, it is a perfect example of leaving someone stranded or just plain stubbornness. The Chinese will occasionally tend to see Westerners as know-it-alls, and some even act that way, like Mr. Praunges with his continual questioning and misplaced sarcasm. In this case, however, the cause of the disagreement is the missing air conditioner, which is by no means a trifle and does not justify such behavior.

Explanation for d):
Disagreements, arguments and argumentative banter, clarifications, and corrections are communication modes that are not exactly popular in China, nor do they reflect good manners. The German word *sich auseinandersetzen* (literally "to set oneself apart" or to altercate) sounds paradoxical to the Chinese. It is precisely when things get difficult that it is important to "come together". Mr. Praunges demonstrates very insensitive behavior. He simply does not hear the answer that he has been given long since (cf. a), and hears only excuses. Naturally, his insensitive behavior causes him to lose face, from the Chinese perspective. His attempts to intentionally cause the Chinese construction manager to lose face, by insisting that the Chinese manager admit that he is in the right and the Chinese in the wrong by having committed a stupid mistake, is a far more serious encroachment. And making him admit his mistake wouldn't change the fact that the air conditioner still isn't installed.
- Answer the following question: How would you react in a comparable situation?
- What is your response to this situation (in key words)?

■ Solution Strategy
According to Chinese hierarchy, a subservient person may not contradict his super-

visor. One step over this invisible line is enough to disrupt hierarchical order and the principles of etiquette. Evading questions and distracting by changing the subject signal a potential face-losing situation and a threat to harmony. If the person criticizing is interested in maintaining the relationship, he/she should try to avoid excessive, senseless questioning and resolve problems harmoniously.

In Chinese discourse, arguments are exchanged only if they are related, overlap or are actually based on mutual points of view. If someone does not agree, the subject is changed. Both the goal and highest priority in an interaction is preserving harmony. Harmony in this sense differs from the concept in the West, where harmony pertains more to maintaining order.

While strategies designed to avoid conflict have top priority in Chinese context, it would be a mistake to assume that every controversy is evaded or politely skirted. If subjects are considered "important" and bring decisive material advantages, then voices will certainly be raised while airing unambiguous demands and opinions. This may surprise Europeans who have been led to believe that differences are always dealt with in a polite and factual manner. The challenge is to recognize what is actually important. It is not always the controversial issues that are the most important. Depending on the situation, there may be demonstrative shows for purely tactical reasons. Any kind of "useless" argumentation or those that bring no advantage, however, will be avoided. The Chinese, unable to relate to such an approach, will avoid every form of self-aggrandizement, such as presenting elaborate, diverse and very personal opinions intended to garner attention or prestige.

Instead of criticizing and blaming, it makes more sense to find out where the mistakes were made and how they can be resolved. One suggestion is to try this approach from the start with one colleague who is in charge, instead of running through a checklist of mistakes, possible mistakes and tasks. It is important to show him that you honor his competence and commitment and trust fully that he will complete the task required of him. Try to become acquainted with the fact that things that you might find puzzling or strange are not necessarily so for your Chinese partner. Create a common language through exploring, identifying and analyzing the problem together.

Criticism should be sandwiched between praise and the emphasis on achievements. Problematic issues, provided they cannot be avoided altogether, should be addressed at the end of a conversation instead of at the beginning as is commonly done in Germany. Criticism can almost always be encoded and hidden between the lines.

■ Culturally Based Concepts of "Social Harmony"

The concept of "social harmony" is based on the Chinese understanding that social order, like the law of nature, functions according to an innate sense of harmony instead of adhering to a logical framework of cause and effect. Similarly, social order consisting of etiquette and rather arbitrarily constructed codes of conduct sustain social harmony. The thought behind this lies in correlative thinking, linking and attributing universal truths to social conduct instead of logical explanations. Material substances such as wood, steel and water are in alignment with the seasons, the points of the compass and color, which in all is considered a harmonious state. This interdependency also affects political decisions and rules of behavior in keeping with the harmony in nature. From the opposite perspective, the heavens and earth respond to human action. Hence, maintaining social harmony is directly linked to

sustaining the natural, cosmic order. Disrupting social harmony or "Iuan", creates the greatest threat to political authority.
From a political perspective, chaos in society, as illustrated by numerous peasant revolts and revolutions, is caused by a transgression on the part of the emperor, who represents the key link between cosmic "authority" and "authority" on earth. Social unrest is interpreted as a sign of the heavens, indicating that the current "illustrious one" is not fulfilling his mandate. Hence, he must step down, which actually means that there is a change of dynasty. This, for all practical purposes, legitimizes an insurrection as the people are authorized by the heavens to reinstate the social and cosmic order.
Many dynasties have replaced each other in this way throughout the course of Chinese history and the phenomenon is referred to as the dynastic cycle. The key factor is that insurrection and disempowering the emperor is not designed to usher in a new order, but rather to rebuild and restore order to its previous, harmonious condition. The philosophical foundation underlying this concept was laid down by Mengzi as early as the 3rd century B. C.

The written part of the training takes up the most time depending on the number of case studies. Some culture assimilator trainings include five case studies that must be completed in approximately 50 minutes. Others have 100 case studies that must be completed in approximately 10 hours. In order to optimize the learning effect without asking too much of the participants, culture assimilator trainings should contain between 20 and 30 case studies that last a total of five hours.

Set Up

It takes a considerable amount of time, effort, background knowledge, skill and financial resources to set up culture assimilator trainings. The complexity is often underestimated. I will illustrate the procedure in more detail in the following pages for specialists in HR development interested in developing company, target-group, task- and culture-specific culture assimilator trainings. However, readers who prefer leaving the work to the experts but are nevertheless interested in the step-by-step process of developing this complex training tool are invited to join in.

1. The first step in the procedure involves the "The Critical Incident Technique" developed by Flanagan (1954) in *Sammlung von kritischen Interaktionssituationen (Collection of Critical Incident Situations).* "An incident would be any activity that was sufficiently complete to permit inferences and predictions to be made about the person performing it. The act would need to have definite consequences and its purpose would need to be fairly clear to an observer" (Albert 1983, p. 190). In order to qualify as a critical incident in a culture assimilator training, an interaction situation must, according to Fiedler et al., fulfill the following criteria: 1) The critical incident must be an everyday interactive encounter between visitors to

and members of a given host country. 2) The situation must be experienced by the visitor as conflict prone and confusing. 3) The cultural aspects inherent in the encounter will probably be misinterpreted by visitors to the host country. 4) With sufficient background knowledge about the host culture, the encounter should lend itself to a culturally appropriate interpretation. 5) The critical incident should be relevant to visitors' actual tasks and requirements. Critical incidents can be obtained by interviewing persons who have lived in the target country for a longer period of time.

2. The second step involves the *identification of key cultural standards.* This requires formulating both culturally appropriate and inappropriate explanations from the perspective of host country members for the visitor's behavior. The idea here is that the explanation deemed appropriate by members of the host country is reflected in the behavioral norms that are typical to members of the host country and illustrate its key cultural standards. To this end, members of the host culture are invited to join group discussions to mediate if members of the discussion panel cannot agree on certain typical behavioral characteristics of the host country. This way, critical incidents can be screened for their appropriateness (e.g., typical, atypical) and those not suited can be removed from the data bank. The culturally appropriate explanation for each critical incident is reviewed by the panel to make sure members agree on the attribution of causes. Individuals with little or no experience in interactions with members of the host country are shown the rest of the critical incidents and asked to give their interpretation of the behavior of members of the host country in order to obtain alternative samples of plausible culturally inappropriate explanations. The chosen critical incidents are then successively categorized into group processes and search systems. The next step involves identifying the key cultural standards underlying the critical incidents. The final version of the categorization system matches up with the identified key cultural standards. The system's validity can be increased by comparing and, if need be, modifying the categories, e.g., the key cultural standards that were obtained empirically to host country characteristics frequently referred to in reference literature.
3. In the third step, former visitors and members of the host country review the collected data and are asked to select what they feel to be the most appropriate explanation. This serves to *validate* and *select* the most applicable critical incidents to be included in the final training material. Members of the host country indicate on the scale how typical, that is how likely and exemplary, the host country member's demonstrated behavior is. The former visitors to the host country indicate to what extent they feel the demonstrated behavior is relative to future visitors. The critical incidents undergo statistical analysis according to: the distribution of the answer criteria among members of the host country; selectivity between random samples provided by visitors and members; general answer distribution; evaluation of how probable and typical the situation is from the host country member's perspective; the relevance of the situation from the perspective of former visitors to the host country. Again, the selected critical incidences are included in the final training materials.
4. The fourth step involves *creating training materials.* The critical incidences (case studies) are matched according to their underlying key cultural standards and sorted according to difficulty. The explanation alternatives for each specific response are formulated and written next to the note stating whether or not the

chosen answer was correct or incorrect and gives a reason why. In this way, the training participants can check the key cultural standards. Suggested answers are provided for each case study, if need be. As a rule, background information based on the literary sources mentioned earlier is compiled for each key cultural standard, including a number of specific descriptions conveying historical origin and the respective consequences.

Training Procedure

The prototype of a typical intercultural training is the orientation training offered to prepare for a specific culture. The elements of the curricula can be treated alternatively or added as needed depending on the time factor involved. In addition, the choice of appropriate material and methodology must be considered with a view to the didactic preferences in culturally diverse groups. The target group and the time factor determine which modules will be emphasized in the training.

First Module: *Introduction*

- Greeting and introduction of the trainer or trainer team
- Introductions including a question-answer session on the subject
- Expectations and goal statements (participants' expectations and goals; training overview presented by the trainer; suggestions and special wishes; clarification of what training does not offer; organizational questions)
- Exploring/sharing key experiences with the target country (culture specific) or intercultural issues (culture general).
  1) Key phrases (stereotypes, attribution, prejudices "proven" by experience, etc.),
  2) Sharing own experiences (on the basis of lead questions)

Second Module: *Key cultural standards of the target culture and one's own culture (culture specific) or key cultural dimensions (culture general)*

- Definitions: What is culture? How is culture related to business?
- Cultural standards/cultural dimensions:
  1) Prepared to serve as input (information based),
  2) Role plays based on own experiences and analysis (interaction based; understanding based)
  3) Culture assimilator (understanding based)
- Contrasting simulations/role plays depicting cultural encounters based on particularly significant cultural standards/cultural dimensions (interaction based/culture based).

Third Module: *Cultural Scripts for important business situations*

- e.g., teamwork, meetings, negotiations, leadership, presentations
- Case studies (understanding based)
- Input (information based)
- Culture assimilator training including subject-related critical incidents (understanding based)
- Reflection on own experiences (understanding based)

- Role plays or simulations for specific tasks with detailed instructions (culture based; interaction based)

Fourth Module: *Successful intercultural cooperation*
- Input: Models and conditions of intercultural competence (information based)
- Reflection on and discussion of other-culture experience according to guidelines (understanding based)
- Case stories from key areas of operation (understanding based)
- Culture assimilator training – critical interaction including its successful outcome (understanding based)
- Reflection of own "success stories" and analysis of success factors (culture based; understanding based)
- Exercises to practice modifying behavior based on very typical key cultural standards or aspects of the script (interaction based)
- Feedback exercises (interaction based)

Additional examples for training programs can be found in Clement and Clement (2000, p. 221 f.) and Kinast (1998, p. 392 f.).

2.2.4 Conclusion

This chapter introduced intercultural trainings with a view to developing applied intercultural competence. In closing, the different terms are summarized in an overview in Table 7.

Table 7: Classification and designation of intercultural trainings

Criteria	Designation
Training goal	Affective intercultural training Cognitive intercultural training Behavioral intercultural training
Training content	Culture-specific intercultural training Culture-general intercultural training
Training method	Knowledge-based intercultural training Experience-based intercultural training
Scope of training	Education Training Orientation Introductory
Point of training	Orientation training In-process training Reintegration training
Didactic approach	Information-based training Culture-based training Interaction-based training Understanding-based training Culture Assimilator Training

Considering that intercultural trainings are becoming popular, it is still surprising that they are not implemented more extensively. Among the reasons cited here are cost factors on the one hand, and the uncertainty about the effectiveness of intercultural trainings on the other. Compared to the cost of training, however, a failed international assignment clearly amounts to more. The effectiveness of intercultural trainings and their evaluation will be further explored in the following chapter.

References

Albert, R. D. (1983): The intercultural sensitizer or culture assimilator. In: Landis, D.; Brislin, R. W. (Eds.), Handbook of Intercultural Training. Volume II: Issues in Training Methodology. New York, pp. 186–217.

Bhawuk, D. P. S.; Brislin, R. W. (2000): Cross-cultural training: a review. Applied Psychology: An International Review 49 (1): 162–191.

Bock, D.; Thomas, A. (2001): Zusammenarbeit mit Deutschen. Vorbereitungsmaterial für Engländer. Köln. (in deutscher Sprache)

Brüch, A.; Thomas, A. (1995): Beruflich in Südkorea. Interkulturelles Orientierungstraining für Manager, Fach- und Führungskräfte. Heidelberg.

Clement, U.; Clement, U. (2000): Interkulturelles Training. In: Regnet, E.; Hofmann, L. M. (Eds.), Personalmanagement in Europa. Schriftenreihe Wirtschaftspsychologie. Hg. v. H. Schuler. Göttingen/Bern u. a., pp. 212–22.

Fiedler, F. E.; Mitchell, T.; Triandis, H. C. (1971): The culture assimilator: An approach to cross-cultural training. Journal of Applied Psychology 55 (2): 95–102.

Flanagan, J. C. (1954): The critical incident technique. Psychological Bulletin 54 (4): 327–358.

Foellbach, S.; Rottenaicher, K.; Thomas, A. (2002): Beruflich in Argentinien. Trainingsprogramm für Manager, Fach- und Führungskräfte. Göttingen.

Frey, D.; Hoyos, C. Graf; Stahlberg, D. (1992): Angewandte Psychologie. Ein Lehrbuch. Weinheim.

Gochenour, T. (1977): The Own and the Albatross. In: Batchelder, D.; Warner, E. G. (Eds.), Beyond Experience. Brattleboro, VT, pp. 47–53.

Gudykunst, W. B.; Hammer, M. R. (1983): Basic training design: Approaches to intercultural training. In: Landis, D.; Brislin, R. W. (Eds.), Handbook of Intercultural Training, Volume I: Issues in Theory and Design. New York, pp. 118–154.

Industrie- und Handelskammer zu Lübeck (Ed.) (1999): Auslandsknigge. Verhaltensregeln, Geschäftssitten, Etikette. Eine Auswahlbibliographie sowie Anbieter Interkultureller Beratungs- und Trainingsleistungen in Deutschland. Lübeck.

Kinast, E.-U. (1998): Evaluation interkultureller Trainings. Lengerich.

Kohls, R. L. (1987): Four traditional approaches to developing cross-cultural preparedness in adults: education, training, orientation, and briefing. International Journal of Intercultural Relations 11 (1): 89–106.

Landis, D.; Brislin, R. W. (Eds.) (1983): Handbook of Intercultural Training. Volume I–III. New York.

Landis, D.; Bhagat, R. S. (1996): Handbook of Intercultural Training. 2nd ed. Thousand Oaks, CA.
Lange, C. (1994): Interkulturelle Orientierung am Beispiel der Trainingsmethode »Cultural Assimilator«. Beiträge zur interkulturellen Didaktik, Band 3. Göttingen.
Lindner, W.; Schenk, E.; Thomas, A. (in Vorb.): Unterricht in China. Übungsmaterial zur Vorbereitung deutscher Dozenten und Ausbildungsleiter auf den Chinaaufenthalt. Regensburg.
Losche, H. (2000): Interkulturelle Kommunikation. Sammlung praktischer Spiele und Übungen. 2nd ed. Augsburg.
Markowsky, R.; Thomas, A. (1995): Studienhalber in Deutschland. Interkulturelles Orientierungstraining für amerikanische Studenten, Schüler und Praktikanten. Heidelberg (Fassung in englischer Sprache; unveröffentlicht).
Martin, M.; Thomas, A. (2002): Beruflich in Indonesien. Interkulturelles Orientierungstraining für Manager, Fach- und Führungskräfte. Regensburg.
Mayer, C. H.; Boness, C. (2003): Beruflich in Kenia und Tansania. Trainingsprogramm für Manager, Fach- und Führungskräfte. Göttingen.
Müller, A.; Thomas, A. (1995): Studienhalber in den USA. Interkulturelles Orientierungstraining für deutsche Studenten, Schüler und Praktikanten. Heidelberg.
Pedersen, P. B. (1988): A Handbook for Developing Multicultural Awareness. Alexandria.
Rademacher, H. (1991): Spiele und Übungen zum interkulturellen Lernen. Berlin.
Schenk, E.; Bauer, S.; Schnabel, R.; Thomas, A. (in Vorb.). China Study and Culture Assimilator. Übungsmaterial zur Vorbereitung deutscher Studenten und Praktikanten auf den Chinaaufenthalt. Regensburg.
Schmid, S.; Thomas, A. (2003): Beruflich in Großbritannien. Trainingsprogramm für Manager, Fach- und Führungskräfte. Göttingen.
Schroll-Machl, S. (2002): Die Deutschen – Wir Deutsche. Fremdwahrnehmung und Selbstsicht im Berufsleben. Göttingen.
Schroll-Machl, S.; Nový, I. (2003): Beruflich in Tschechien. Trainingsprogramm für Manager, Fach- und Führungskräfte. Göttingen.
Shirts, G. (1973): BAFA-BAFA: A Cross-Cultural Simulation. Del Mar, CA.
Thomas, A. (1990): Interkulturelles Handlungstraining als Personalentwicklungsmaßnahme. Zeitschrift für Arbeits- und Organisationspsychologie 34 (3): 149–154.
Thomas, A. (1993a): Kulturvergleichende Psychologie. Eine Einführung. Göttingen.
Thomas, A. (1993b): Psychologie interkulturellen Lernens und Handelns. In: Thomas, A. (Ed.), Kulturvergleichende Psychologie. Eine Einführung. Göttingen, pp. 377–424.
Thomas, A. (1995): Die Vorbereitung von Mitarbeitern für den Auslandseinsatz. Wissenschaftliche Grundlagen. In: Kühlmann, T. M. (Ed.), Mitarbeiterentsendung ins Ausland. Auswahl, Vorbereitung, Betreuung und Wiedereingliederung. Göttingen, pp. 85–118.
Thomas, A. (1996a): Psychologie interkulturellen Handelns. Göttingen.
Thomas, A. (1996b): Psychologische Bedingungen und Wirkungen internationalen Managements – analysiert am Beispiel deutsch-chinesischer Zusammenarbeit. In: Engelhard, J. (Ed.), Interkulturelles Management. Theoretische Fundierung und funktionsspezifische Konzepte. Wiesbaden, pp. 111–134.

Thomas, A. (2000): Forschungen zur Handlungswirksamkeit von Kulturstandards. Handlung, Kultur und Interpretation. Zeitschrift für Sozial- und Kulturwissenschaften 9(2): 231–279.

Thomas, A.; Schenk, E. (2001): Beruflich in China. Trainingsprogramm für Manager, Fach- und Führungskräfte. Göttingen.

Thomas, A.; Schenk, E.; Lindner, W. (in Vorb.): Interkulturelles Training für chinesische Fach- und Führungskräfte zum Umgang mit deutschen Partnern (in chinesischer Sprache). Regensburg.

Thomas, A.; Schenk, E.; Lindner, W. (in Vorb.): German Business and Culture Assimilator. Übungsmaterial zur Vorbereitung chinesischer Manager auf den Deutschlandaufenthalt. Regensburg.

Thomas, A.; Layes, G.; Kammhuber, S. (1998): Sensibilisierungs- und Orientierungstraining für die kulturallgemeine und kulturspezifische Vorbereitung von Soldaten auf internationale Einsätze. Untersuchungen des psychologischen Dienstes der Bundeswehr 1998. München.

Tschöcke, K.; Kölling, M. (2000): Asien lernen. Interkulturelles Training: Ziele, Konzepte, Anbieter. Hamburg.

Yoosefi, T.; Thomas, A. (2003): Beruflich in Russland. Trainingsprogramm für Manager, Fach- und Führungskräfte. Göttingen.

Eva-Ulrike Kinast

2.3 Evaluation of Intercultural Trainings

Intercultural trainings are becoming an important source of intercultural learning and acquiring applied intercultural competence. Do intercultural trainings, in fact, bring about the desired results? Are they capable of bringing about a shift in terms of feeling, thought patterns and behavior? The following chapter will explore these questions with the help of evaluations for measuring their effectiveness.

2.3.1 Present Situation

A total of 50 research studies have meanwhile been conducted worldwide to evaluate and confirm the effectiveness of intercultural trainings. Research results (e.g., Wottawa and Thierau 1990), particularly evaluation results conducted within the scope of management trainings (e.g., Nork 1989) and managerial behavioral trainings (e.g., Gülpen 1996; Kirkpatrick 1979), as well as results from methodology research (e.g., Lamnek 1988; 1989) provide the basis for the development of specific evaluation methods for intercultural trainings. The most comprehensive overview of studies and methods of evaluation of intercultural trainings are provided by Kinast (1998) in her book "Evaluation of Intercultural Trainings".

In companies and other organizations, intercultural trainings are rarely evaluated due to:

- a lack of competence on the part of personnel responsible for training evaluation,
- not enough employee capacity in training and development,
- time constraints on the part of managers and specialists,
- resistance to evaluation projects due to these time constraints.

It is essential, however, that intercultural trainings be evaluated, especially since they represent a considerable cost factor. If they do not deliver the anticipated results, then a closer look needs to be taken at the reasons why. The intercultural trainings can then be modified and ineffective elements can be removed (e.g., method, content, trainer) in order to obtain optimal results. The results must be evaluated to obtain reliable data and to determine what elements of the training are effective.

2.3.2 Methods of Evaluation

Definition, Goals, Functions

Evaluations, also described in literature as performance reviews, efficiency studies, effectiveness control and quality control, among other terms, strive to determine what effect intercultural trainings have on performance and what benefit they bring to both the company and the training participants. Evaluations serve the following four purposes:

- *Legitimization and enforcement:* Once the effectiveness of intercultural trainings has been ascertained by means of an evaluation, training measures are easier to enforce and costs can be justified.
- *Decision:* Evaluating trainings help in making informed decisions regarding new developments, modifications or deciding between alternative training methods.
- *Supervision and optimization:* Evaluations can reliably determine the training components that are acceptable and unacceptable to participants and can then be either improved upon or left out entirely.
- *Insights:* Evaluation provides professional intercultural trainers with the reliable theoretical knowledge as well as an idea of what constitutes an effective intercultural training concept and how it can be implemented effectively.

There are always several people involved in the evaluation of intercultural trainings, which often makes the process quite difficult. The sponsor, for example the head of training and development, has a vested interest in convincing top management of the quality and advantage of an intercultural training in order to fulfill his mandate as a "learning architect". The evaluator, on the other hand, unwilling to jeopardize his reputation as an expert in matters of evaluation, is reluctant to tailor his interpretation of the results to please members of the training and development department. The training participants are, above all, interested in learning how to get along and cooperate with their foreign partners abroad. They are generally not interested in the cost of the training or its evaluation. Training participants tend to fill out the questionnaires to please the training facilitator and the decision makers in training and development.

Evaluation processes are divided into phases. First, costs are calculated followed by planning. Then the evaluation is conducted and assessed. The results of the evaluation become a part of the new plan and are implemented in the intercultural training.

The evaluation focuses on an object, such as an intercultural training in this case. Training participants, too, are evaluation objects, although here one is better advised to speak of *evaluation subjects.*

Evaluation is description *and* assessment. Results of an evaluation are only valid if the intercultural training, its goals, content and methods have been carefully described and documented and the effectiveness and benefit of the intercultural training were evaluated on this basis.

The evaluation process should be interdisciplinary. Psychologists, educators, economists, engineers and others contribute important input to the evaluation. In addition, evaluation uses up-to-date scientific methods and takes place between the poles of field research and practical application.

Procedure and Methods

Literature cites many models and methods for evaluations (Wottawa and Thierau 1990), all of which help to structure and design an evaluation project, to classify and describe it. "Evaluation of Intercultural Trainings" by Eva Kinast (1998) provides a comprehensive overview of models and methods and their significance for evaluations of intercultural trainings. One of these, the Level Evaluation Model by Kirkpatrick (1979), has recently influenced research on intercultural trainings to a great extent (e.g., B. Bhawuk 1998; Bhawuk and Brislin 2000).

Generally, training participants complete a questionnaire to evaluate the intercultural training to determine their satisfaction with the training and what they learned from it. This indicates the participants' level of satisfaction and lets them assess the learning benefit subjectively. Kirkpatrick (1979) calls this level of evaluation "reaction". A questionnaire of this nature is available from Thomas and Lulay (1999) and Bhawuk (1998).

This form of evaluation is important and uncontested. The evaluation in itself lets the training participants know that their opinions are heard and respected. Moreover, participants take responsibility for their own learning progress. However, following this kind of intercultural training evaluation, provided it proved beneficial, participants are automatically expected to be successful in their interactions with dissimilar others abroad, at home, per telephone, e-mail, fax or similar modes of communication. This is often misleading! There is not necessarily a correlation between the general satisfaction with an intercultural training and its actual effect on interaction with dissimilar others following the intercultural training. In the past, training participants were satisfied if the trainer made a competent impression, the training seemed well structured and the content well founded, the training itself was experienced as motivating, the materials were well prepared and the training itself was well organized. It is conducive to the training atmosphere if the seminar hotel is pleasant and offers at least a 3-course lunch menu. An extra point is added if the restaurant serves specialties from the target country under discussion. Despite the efforts taken, there is no guarantee that an intercultural training will prove effective when the chips are down, that is, when the training participant encounters an other-culture individual in "real life", outside of the intercultural training setting. It may in fact occur but it is not necessarily a given. There is much evidence that all the above-mentioned conditions influence the acceptance of the training, and there is enough evidence that even a very mediocre intercultural training can prove to be effective in later encounters with other-culture individuals. Hence, there does not seem to be a linear correlation between acceptance and later effect.

In addition, it is not enough to measure only the learning effect offered by intercultural trainings according to the second level mentioned by Kirkpatrick (1979). This approach is reminiscent of testing procedures used in schools to test what information has been retained. The B-version of a culture assimilator training, for instance, consisting of case studies and multiple choice answers (without feedback to the answer options and background information), illustrates to what extent the training participants actually have acquired culturally-appropriate background knowledge about a specific culture upon completion. Another option is to measure intercultural sensitivity by means of a test (e.g., "Intercultural Sensitivity Inventory" by Bhawuk and Brislin 1992). However, here too there is no guarantee that the training participants will actually apply their acquired sensitivity and knowledge in their interactions with other-culture individuals, provided, of course, that they have indeed acquired the necessary knowledge and been sensitized to the differences in thinking and action of their other-culture partner as a result of an intercultural training.

In order to be sure, the level of behavior mentioned by Kirkpatrick (1979) must be evaluated. This method provides an answer to the question of whether intercultural competence is acquired as a result of the intercultural training and if it actually determines behavior. If, in fact, it does, then is the participant actually able to apply this acquired knowledge by translating it into appropriate behavior and interact satisfactorily with dissimilar others? It is unlikely that simulated intercultural encounters can evaluate the behavior level adequately, as suggested by Harrison (1992). One method, consisting of an interview and an evaluation procedure (Kinast 1998), which is used when a training participant returns from abroad, is functional despite the disadvantage that everything the interviewee discloses is very subjective. In this case it is difficult to verify the information objectively. For these reasons, a combination of different methods is surely the best choice, albeit the more complex.

Once it has become clear that the training participant enjoyed the training (reaction), if in fact learning took place (learning) and if he was able to apply what was learned (behavior), the question is to what extent the participant actually benefited from the training process: For instance, did the intercultural training improve their sense of well-being in the foreign country? Were they able to establish satisfying relationships with locals? Did the training improve performance? – just to mention some of the key aspects of intercultural adaptation. Other questions include the advantages of the intercultural training for the company (or other organization): Has the company become more internationalized as a result of the training and its effects? Has turnover increased? Have costs been cut as a result of fewer failed international assignments? Kirkpatrick (1979) calls this level of evaluation "results". Unfortunately, here is where evaluation reaches its limit in many cases. It is extremely difficult to deal with this level in a methodically correct manner, as the effect of the intercultural training on the parameters of success criteria like these is nearly impossible to determine. How can you prove without a doubt that someone feels at ease in a foreign country or has performed successfully just because he participated in an intercultural training prior to departure? An international assignment or extended stay abroad is far too complex without taking other influencing factors into consideration. Methodological approaches to dealing with the "results" level are available from Blake and Heslin (1983), Layes (1995) and Thomas and Lulay (1999).

2.3.3 Evaluation Research Findings

Describing the Studies

The most evaluated intercultural training is the culture assimilator training (q.v. Ch. I, 2.2). Among these are culture-general, culture-specific, task-specific and nonspecific task culture assimilator trainings. In addition, there are culture assimilator trainings designed as preparation for international assignments and working with ethnic minorities. Some intercultural trainings combine different training methods and others borrow elements from psychotherapy and are evaluated accordingly. Other studies are evaluated on their separate training components (e.g., video sequence, role plays). Many trainings are orientation trainings: however, none of the studies have evaluated in-progress or reintegration trainings.

Training participants come from upper management or are junior executives, members of the military, teachers, pupils, students, physicians and nurses, consultants and developmental aid workers. The number of individuals whose evaluation data is available varies between N = 1 for qualitative single cases and N = 1500 in quantitative evaluation design. The individuals come from 20 different countries including 95% from the U. S. Evaluees are of Caucasian and African origin. Most of the candidates are male. Only one random sample study is made up entirely of women.

A number of different aspects of applied intercultural competence are considered as criteria and each component is defined differently. According to Kirkpatrick, they are located on different levels. Often participants are simply asked if they thought the intercultural training was good. In contrast, the majority of the studies mentioned here attempt to evaluate the actual learning effect. Some studies even evaluate the "behavior" level or "results" level. It is, however, not entirely clear which level the criteria targets. A laboratory experiment, for instance, is hardly suited to evaluating "behavior" or, for that matter, the "results" at first glance. It may be assumed that there is a difference between the training participant applying the knowledge he acquired through interacting with members of the target country immediately after the intercultural training in a familiar environment in a twenty minute simulated interaction, and doing this six months later in an actual encounter with several other-culture interaction partners in the host country and under unfamiliar conditions. If, for instance, a culture assimilator training with the purpose of enhancing interaction between Caucasian Americans and African-Americans were held, then an evaluation of this training, conducted laboratory style, could very well touch upon the level of "behavior" or even that of "results". One factor here is that both groups interact under similar conditions in an environment that is familiar to both.

Many common research methods and designs are used to evaluate intercultural trainings (e.g., Lamnek 1988; 1989). Data sources for most of the studies consist of the training participants' self-evaluation, which often does not bring the desired objective results. There are, however, studies that include objective observation and evaluation by others. Studies involving observation of behavior in a host country have not been conducted, presumably for reasons of time and expense.

The studies include laboratory experiments and field studies. Field studies are particular popular in an intercultural context because of the more authentic conditions. The data is collected at home base, in the host country and upon returning home. The time period between the intercultural training and the evaluation of data varies considerably, ranging from immediately after the intercultural training to a maximum of one year later. Long-term effects of intercultural trainings have yet to be assessed.

While qualitative studies rely almost exclusively on a qualitative interview form for collecting data, quantitative studies use custom-designed questionnaires for the most part. Standardized tests, such as the "Intercultural Sensitivity Inventory" by Bhawuk and Brislin (1992) to assess intercultural sensitivity, are rarely used although it would be preferable from a methodological standpoint. Simulated interaction tasks with interaction partners from the given target culture are widely used to screen appropriate behavior. Some studies use the diary technique. The data material is evaluated according to methods common in research, such as the Qualitative Content Analysis method developed by Mayring (1993).

Impact of Intercultural Training

Results of evaluation studies attest to the effectiveness of intercultural training. The evaluation results relative to the effect intercultural training has on the training participants' cognitive processes is largely consistent (cf. Albert 1983; Kinast 1998). The difference between trained individuals and those who have not undergone training is that the former perceive that something is "not right", or deviates from the norm, in an encounter with dissimilar others and are able to categorize the situation as well as the other's behavior as culturally divergent. That, in itself, is a great feat considering that if a person does not even realize he has just "put his foot in it", he will not feel moved to reflect on his behavior and modify it accordingly (q.v. Ch. I, 1.6). In situations like these, individuals who have participated in intercultural trainings have a clear advantage over those who have not, since they benefit from the knowledge acquired in the intercultural training. Frequently, intercultural training "graduates" can refer an experience or situation back to particular training components such as a culture assimilator case study or exercises on cultural standards. In interviews, expatriates often claim that certain situations reminded them of incidences covered in the training and that, as a result, they were able to understand why a person acted in a certain way. Compared to individuals who have not been trained, training participants are more knowledgeable about the foreign culture and use this information to negotiate critical situations with dissimilar others because they are more adept at interpreting behavior isomorphically, i.e., from the perspective of other-culture individuals. As a result, they are better able to reflect on the situation and anticipate the consequences.

Evaluation studies show that the effect of intercultural trainings on emotion and behavior are inconsistent (cf. Albert 1983; Kinast 1998). Emotions may not necessarily be involved even if the training participants recognize a critical situation in time, categorize it as culturally divergent, recognize training components, understand what is going on in the situation, can orient and anticipate consequences. The following situation, for example, is not uncommon. A German student studying in the U. S. is annoyed and frustrated by an American student, who, after a brief meeting, immediately suggests exchanging phone numbers and promises to call up the German student, which he never does. This is no different at the executive level. Although the German student may know, on the basis of his intercultural training, that many Americans deal with interpersonal distance differently due to their different cultural conditioning, the German student nevertheless feels offended. Intercultural trainings may also have the opposite effect on a person. Instead of feeling hurt or rejected, he simply smiles and shrugs off the incident. This is precisely the way that intercultural training can influence behavior. In many cases intercultural training leads to behavior that corresponded to that of the foreign culture. Without the benefit of insight gleaned from the training, a person may have behaved quite differently.

Seen from an overall perspective, it can be concluded that intercultural training very definitely has an impact on successful intercultural interaction in a foreign country, including a heightened sense of personal well-being in the host country, the ability to create rapport with locals and to master work-related tasks, despite the fact that this could not be consistently verified in all of the studies.

So, how effective is intercultural training? Participants have a heightened sensitivity for culture-based influences on behavior, even after years of living abroad while perceiving and experiencing critical encounters. In an intercultural training, participants are familiarized with other-culture orientation principles, which help in navigating difficult situations. The principles of orientation are like walking aids that, after a time, become superfluous, becoming internalized to the point where applying them is automatic *(transposition effect)*. The training "graduate" is culture-specifically competent. In addition, intercultural training progressively increases *process knowledge* in a unique way. Consequently, the participant is able to function in any foreign culture by determining which rules the particular culture plays by and incorporating them into his own system of orientation, adapting or adhering to them when necessary. This is the highest level of applied intercultural competence.

In the *first type*, the intercultural training takes effect immediately in a critical interaction. The training participant gains insight into key cultural

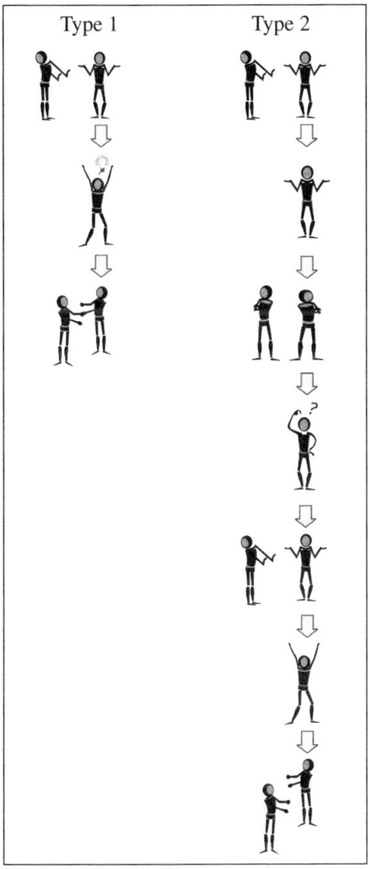

Figure 9: Types of effect patterns of intercultural trainings (cf. Kinast 1998).

standards in an intercultural training. During the course of his assignment abroad, he is involved in a critical interaction with locals, in which this particular key cultural standard plays a role. The training participant is aware of his partner's behavior and categorizes it as culturally divergent, an aspect he recognizes from the intercultural training, and remembers the part in the training that dealt specifically with the role of cultural standards in a critical incident. Due to the intercultural training, the training participant is familiar with culturally appropriate behavior and is therefore able to attribute the foreign partner's behavior isomorphically. Hence, he maintains his orientation in the situation and can intuit its consequences. This, in turn, affects feelings that guide him in his actions, rendering his behavior appropriate. In this example, the critical interaction was negotiated successfully, giving credence to the benefit of intercultural trainings.

The effect of intercultural training on the *second type* takes a little longer to develop. The training participant learns about a key cultural standard in the intercultural training. During his assignment abroad he becomes involved in a critical incident with locals in which the key cultural standards become evident. While the training participant is aware of the situation, he does not categorize it as culturally divergent. He does not recognize any of the elements from the intercultural training nor is he able to access the knowledge acquired in the intercultural training and his response is not in line with culturally appropriate behavior. He feels disoriented, is unable to anticipate the consequences of the situation and feels increasingly ill at ease. The situation is bound to be unpleasant for both parties and the critical interaction is not resolved. Later the same evening, relaxing comfortably at home, the training participant might reflect upon the day's events and what went wrong. Suddenly he remembers a case study from the cultural assimilator training within the scope of the intercultural training. In a stroke of insight, the training participant suddenly realizes why his interaction partners acted the way they did. In retrospect, he is able to attribute their behavior isomorphically. At this point, he can see the situation in perspective and vows to remember the cultural standard the next time he becomes involved in a critical interaction of this nature. Sure enough, when a similar interaction took place, he knew what to do and was able to react appropriately.

2.3.4 Conclusion

In this chapter, we have attempted to ascertain the validity of intercultural training and how it affects the way a person acts from a psychological perspective.

One result is especially noteworthy. Following a critical interaction, the training participant suddenly remembers the intercultural training and recognizes the parallels to the situation he actually experienced, realizing that the next time he has a similar encounter he will know how to react. Other examples include situations in which the training participants are made aware of their culturally unacceptable behaviour by a local and think back to the intercultural training as soon as they realize the *faux pas*. At precisely this moment, they become aware of the way they could have behaved. In summary, this means that orientation trainings prior to the international assignment impart knowledge about the foreign culture that is then reinforced by in-process training. Participants are able to tap into their intercultural knowledge in their interactions with other-culture individuals. However, there are situations in which this knowledge does not come into play, causing the participant to act inappropriately. If he repeatedly experiences such situations, the participant is likely to become frustrated to the point where he must force himself to face each new day. The knowledge acquired during the training can, however, be activated through self-reflection or by being made aware of a situation by others. The problem of *transferring* the knowledge acquired in a training to an actual situation can be solved by intercultural coaching. The training participant can work through and reflect on the critical interaction scenarios with the help of a competent intercultural coach within the scope of intercultural coaching at home or abroad. On the whole, this offers an excellent opportunity for intercultural learning.

References

Albert, R. D. (1983): The intercultural sensitizer or culture assimilator. In: Landis, D.; Brislin, R. W. (Eds.), Handbook of Intercultural Training. Volume II: Issues in Training Methodology. New York, pp. 186–217.

Bhawuk, D. P. S. (1998): The role of culture theory in cross-cultural training: a multimethod study of culture-specific, culture-general and culture theory-based assimilators. Journal of Cross-Cultural Psychology 29 (5): 630–655.

Bhawuk, D. P. S.; Brislin, R. W. (1992): The measurement of intercultural sensitivity using the concepts of individualism and collectivism. International Journal of Intercultural Relations 16: 413–436.

Bhawuk, D. P. S.; Brislin, R. W. (2000): Cross-cultural training: a review. Applied Psychology: An International Review 49 (1): 162–191.

Blake, B. F.; Heslin, R. (1983): Evaluating cross-cultural training. In: Landis, D.; Brislin, R. W. (Eds.), Handbook of Intercultural Training. Volume I: Issues in Theory and Design. New York, pp. 203–22.

Gülpen, B. (1996): Evaluation betrieblicher Verhaltenstrainings. München.

Harrison, J. K. (1992): Individual and combined effects of behavior modeling and the culture assimilator in cross-cultural management training. Journal of Applied Psychology 77: 952–962.

Kinast, E.-U. (1998): Evaluation interkultureller Trainings. Lengerich.

Kirkpatrick, D. L. (1979): Techniques for evaluating training programs. Training and Development Journal 33 (6): 78–92.

Lamnek, S. (1988): Qualitative Sozialforschung. Band 1: Methodologie. München.

Lamnek, S. (1989): Qualitative Sozialforschung. Band 2: Methoden und Techniken. München.

Layes, G. (1995): Quantitative Evaluation eines interkulturellen Managementtrainings für deutsche Manager zur Vorbereitung auf die Kooperation mit Chinesen. Unveröffentlichte Diplomarbeit. Universität Regensburg.

Mayring, P. (1993): Qualitative Inhaltsanalyse. Grundlagen und Techniken. 4th ed. Neuausgabe. Weinheim.

Nork, M. E. (1989): Management-Training. Evaluation, Probleme, Lösungsansätze. München.
Thomas, A.; Lulay, G. (1999): Evaluation interkultureller Trainings zur Vorbereitung von Bundeswehrsoldaten auf internationale Einsätze. Untersuchungen des psychologischen Dienstes der Bundeswehr 1999. München.
Wottawa, H.; Thierau, H. (1990): Lehrbuch Evaluation. Bern.

Eva-Ulrike Kinast

2.4 Intercultural Coaching

Intercultural coaching is frequently referred to as a one-on-one training for managers and specialists within companies and other organizations who are preparing for an international assignment or deal with dissimilar others on a regular basis at home and need to acquire intercultural competence in a minimum of time. This, of course, is accurate. However, intercultural coaching goes a step further by emphasizing *the personality factor.*

2.4.1 The Present Situation

To date, very few research studies have been conducted on intercultural coaching and very little has been published on the subject (Barmeyer 2002; Clement and Clement 1999; Peuker et al. 2002).

In companies and other organizations, the importance of intercultural coaching is increasing significantly, as seen from the growing number of intercultural coaches on the market. Consequently, it is of the utmost importance when choosing a professional coach that he or she has had professional training in the field and is a certified coach. The individual may have studied psychology and specialized in aspects of intercultural psychology in addition to a certification as coach. In order to communicate at the same level with corporate managers, the international coach should be familiar with the corporate world and have lived abroad for an extended period of time. He should have excellent soft skills including the ability to sincerely acknowledge the dignity and integrity of each individual, be discreet and always maintain a neutral bearing in the presence of his clients. Ideally, his training will have honed his self-perception and he should ask a colleague or coaching expert to evaluate his work on a regular basis. A professional coach can be recognized by his unique coaching approach and the human aspect he brings to the profession as well as by the diversity and quality of the methodology, and, of course, by the success of his work.

2.4.2 Concept and Definition

The concept of coaching was developed in the Anglo-Saxon realm in the 1970's by Singer (1974) and made its way to Germany in the early 80's. By definition, intercultural coaching focuses on the intercultural content and context of this form of coaching.

Intercultural coaching is a new and comprehensive measure consisting of a variety of methods for developing people interculturally. It was designed with internationally active specialists and managers in mind, as a supplement to intercultural trainings. Approached professionally, intercultural coaching draws upon research findings from: coaching (Rauen 2002; Schreyögg 2001); general psychology (Zimbardo and Gerrig 1999); clinical psychology (Davison and Neale 1998); findings from intercultural research (Thomas 1993b; Thomas 1996); research on comparative culture (Thomas 1993a).

Like intercultural training, intercultural coaching opens the door for intercultural learning and develops both applied intercultural competence and individual, social and strategic (management) competence (q.v. Ch. I, 1.9). Intercultural coaching, however, considers the whole spectrum of the coachee's personality. Undoubtedly, we are constantly confronted by opposing forces, telling us to do or not to do something (Satir 1988; 1989). Some people tend to make things difficult for themselves by not being able to change their behavioral patterns to comply with other cultural contexts in a foreign country. For example, a specialist or manager embodies a strong "dictator" tendency, is power driven and seizes every opportunity to demonstrate his control, giving orders on how to do things and how to behave. This type of individual expends a lot of energy in trying to change and dominate people. In so doing, they are constantly implying that the person is not okay the way they are. This type of individual will inevitably encounter resistance and rejection in Asia, for example, due to the prevailing key cultural standard "social harmony".

Intercultural coaching encourages this clientele to "hold up a mirror" and develop an awareness of the motivating force within them. If this procedure is repeated often enough, they eventually learn to harness and redirect the force: In a critical encounter, the person feels the "dictator" force, for instance, and can then make a conscious decision whether or not to accept the force or keep it in check according to the motto "if you are aware of what you are doing, then you can choose your actions".

Intercultural coaching is not psychotherapy, even if some approaches have been borrowed from psychotherapy.

"Coaching does not have the depth that psychotherapy does, focusing more on competencies instead of on correcting misguided development, which manifests in dysfunctional behavior and perception of experience.

Coaching deals primarily with the context-related problems arising in work situations" (Roth et al. 1995, p. 212).

Intercultural coaching is different in that the coach relates to the client from the adult perspective rather than offering the coachee standardized answers or how-to recipes for success. The coach acts as a *catalyst*, encouraging individuals to discover and develop solutions to their problems on their own so that, in time, they learn to explore information in culturally unfamiliar situations and implement their own problem-solving strategies without the help of an intercultural coach.

The difference to intercultural trainings is the emphasis on the coachee's *momentary state of mind* while working on assigned tasks. Specialists or managers who have recently been sent abroad often feel sandwiched between the demands of headquarters at home and those of the subsidiary abroad. Once problems with colleagues, co-workers and customers arise due to culture-based differences in accomplishing tasks, the expatriate is likely to feel overwhelmed and experience feelings of exasperation that can lead to physical and psychological stress.

2.4.3 Target Groups

The target group for intercultural coaching consists primarily of individuals in responsible positions, particularly specialists and senior executives in corporations and other organizations, who work internationally or pass on knowledge as multiplicators. It makes no difference if they communicate with other-cultural individuals from home, during a brief business trip or are actually sent on an international assignment. Expatriates are, of course, most in need of intercultural coaching. Managers' expressed wish to be coached is an important prerequisite for the success of intercultural coaching. Intercultural coaching always brings about change, including a change of a personal nature and should always be voluntary. If coaching is prescribed from above, there is little willingness to accept new ideas and the effort is usually in vain.

2.4.4 Methods and Approaches

Methods of coaching described in literature are generally also applicable to intercultural coaching. Rauen (2002) and Roth et al. (1995) provide an overview of the subject. Regardless of which method is used, it is important to take the whole person into consideration, which includes feelings, emotions and bodily sensations. The preferred approach is a combination of experience-based and knowledge-based methods.

A method of intercultural coaching that has so far shown excellent results in an intercultural context will be introduced within the scope of this handbook. The method is *body-oriented* and based on Vermeulen's (1998) analysis model, a method that was developed in a national context and has been successfully implemented by the author in an international context.

The method relies on reflection, exploring and processing critical encounters with other-culture individuals, symptoms of culture shock, low energy levels and motivation, and dealing with conflict.

The basic idea is that all information that an individual accumulates during a lifetime is stored like a hard drive on a computer. This information has been passed down to us by our genes and influenced by our environment. Information about the culture in which we grew up is also stored there. We are not necessarily aware of the information stored on our hard drive, yet it may well express itself cognitively in our behavior in the form of thought, emotions, feelings and bodily sensations. In order to bring about change, we must become aware of the information stored within us in order to reprogram it. In unfamiliar situations a person will behave according to his own-culture information stored on the hard drive. For instance, if a German wishes to behave more "Chinese" in an encounter with a Chinese person, then he must first become aware of the German information stored on his hard drive in order to incline his behavior toward a more "Chinese way". The coaching method introduced here draws upon methods from different schools of psychology such as transactional analysis (Berne), Bioenergetics (Lown, Heysen), breath therapy (Middendorf), progressive muscle relaxation (Jacobsen), Gestalt Therapy (Perls) and other combined approaches (for the methods mentioned see Kriz 2001). The key component of the approach is the *analysis of a critical relationship*. A critical relationship exists when someone leads an inner dialogue with another person (or even an issue) that is, if in his mind he is in dialogue with the person or his concern, or if he accuses, perhaps even condemns, the person or situation. Experience has shown that individuals get stuck in an inner dialogue in which a thought pattern is constantly repeated in the same sequence. A German manager caught in a critical interaction with his Chinese construction manager, as in the case study "Air Conditioner" (Thomas and Schenk 2001, pp. 92–97 and 102–103), will most likely spend plenty of time wondering what actually went wrong in the situation. This is a cognitive response to the situation. In the case of the German manager, the repetitive inner dialogue can become unbearable, taking over much of the capacity for conscious thought and withdrawing energy from the tasks he must accomplish. Quite often a slump can be observed in a manager's performance while on an international assignment, a condition which can be traced back to channeling energy into managing culture-based differences in thinking, feeling and behavior. The energy expended on dealing with these differences is then no longer available for the actual work. Repetitive thought patterns revolving around the same issue can be interrupted by reducing the space the problematic issue occupies in a person's consciousness. This is achieved by shifting from the purely cognitive level to a sensory or kinesthetic level. In this way the coachee changes perspectives and sees the issue at hand from another angle. The problem itself may not necessarily disappear, but makes room for alternative problem-solving options.

Let's consider the case study "Air Conditioner" used in the culture assimilator training (q.v. Ch. I, 2.2). The critical incident between the German manager and the Chinese construction manager is based on an actual situation. Mr. Praunges admits to questioning his own sanity during the recent renovation of his company offices. He was utterly perplexed when the Chinese construction manager responded to his inquiry about the air conditioner by launching into the issue of the dripping water faucet and the banister that had not been painted yet. Mr. Praunges was thrown off track and disoriented. We can assume that he felt that he had been made a fool of, especially in view of the Chinese manager smiling at him throughout the interaction. He must certainly have mulled over this behavior and, because of a lack of clarifying information, begun running around in circles over the issue. We can also assume that Mr. Praunges gave the Chinese construction manager clear instructions and told him what he thought. Hence, Mr. Praunges and the construction manager are experiencing an unresolved critical interaction.

The critical incident was dealt with on the basis of Vermeulen's analysis model (1998). After instructions on the *method of writing seven letters* (author unknown), the German manager is asked to write letters to the Chinese construction manager ("I resent that you ...", "I regret that ...", "I wish that ..." etc.). The manager writes these letters and then brings them to the first coaching session.

During the session the manager proceeds to draw a picture of himself and the Chinese partner. The picture is given a title and the persons in the drawing are each given a physical, an emotional and an intellectual characteristic. This approach of drawing a picture brings negative feelings and thoughts about the critical partner in the incident to the surface and allows the coachee to vent his anger.

The process continues with a series of dyads. According to Vermeulen, dyads are "structured communication exercises done in pairs. The structures and rules allow the partners to access the depths of their own subconscious and to confront blocks and resistance to others" (1998, p. 23). In the case of the illustrated critical interaction, a so-called *negative round*, a dyad dealing with expectations, more precisely, the unfulfilled expectation on the part of the German manager, could be included. Mr. Praunges, for instance, had expected an apology ("but instead of apologizing, this person ...") and a guarantee to rectify the situation immediately ("... or had promised to take care of the situation by tomorrow ..."). A sensible approach here would be to go over the situation again in a dyad, to find out what irritated the German manager about the Chinese construction manager or what characteristics he simply did not like. A *positive round* could follow in the form of a relationship dyad to allow the German manager to become aware of the aspects of the Chinese construction manager's behavior that he does like, aspects they can agree upon, and what the Chinese construction manager is permitted to know about Mr. Praunges. This may appear to have nothing to do with the critical incidence in question and the critical interaction between the two of them.

In the next step, the manager is asked to read the letters he wrote to the Chinese construction manager out loud. The coach is present and listens. A relaxation exercise can be included within the scope of reading the letters. A number of exercises can be found in Brooks (1997).

Toward the end of the coaching session, the manager is asked to draw another picture of himself and the Chinese construction manager, giving it a title and the characteristics of each. Following a feedback session after the coaching, he is given homework, for example, to write a report on the analysis of the critical interaction or to observe any differences in further encounters with the Chinese partner in comparison to prior encounters and what has remained unchanged.

In line with past experience, many personal assumptions are revealed in the letters, which can be traced back to own-culture conditioning. In the case study, the manager accuses the Chinese construction manager of trying to mislead him by directing his attention to the dripping water faucet and the unpainted banister. In this context, the general theme "personal assumptions" and its impact on feelings, thoughts and behavior can be picked up in a second coaching session. Here the coachee can explore the basis of his assumptions with the help of a dyad. If, for instance, the issue is "interpersonal distance", the dyad's topic could be "tell me something about yourself and proximity (or distance)". If the subject is "intercultural leadership" (q.v. Ch. II, 2.5) then the dyad might begin with "tell me something about yourself and leadership". The response is likely to include personal assumptions. In the course of the dyad, light is shed on the significant role that one's own-culture mindset plays. Consequently, the perspective can be widened to include other-culture behavioral patterns (in this case the Chinese culture). By referring back to the specific key cultural standards, the coachee can make the connection to the actual critical incident. This is followed by a body-focused exercise focused on the topic under consideration. If the issue is interpersonal distance, then an exercise can follow in which the coach and the coachee sit across from each other, place the palms of their hands together and then move their arms and hands in a circular pattern. The coachee undergoes a sensory experience indicating how much proximity or distance he can tolerate or even experience as pleasant. If the issue is intercultural leadership, an exercise called blindman's walk can be initiated, whereby the coach and coachee take turns leading each other through the room, allowing each other to explore. The person being lead keeps his eyes closed. In this example, the coachee experiences himself kinesthetically, an aspect which is designed to strengthen his leadership ability on the home front. This exercise is followed by another dyad. A third coaching session may be indicated for problem-solving strategies. By shifting to the sensory or kinesthetic level, the coachee experiences a shift of perspective and gradually creates more room for alternative approaches to problem solving.

2.4.5 Critical Acclaim and Conclusion

A coaching session generally lasts between three to four hours and is cost-intensive (fee, flight, accommodation). The benefits, however, tend to compensate for the cost. To date, there are no evaluation results on intercultural coaching. It seems, however, that this method is effective. Specialists and senior executives repeatedly report that two weeks after having completed their coaching, their relationship with the critical partner was no longer critical and they began to perceive their former critical partner in a new light. They returned to work with renewed gratification and energy, all of which can be attributed to a shift in perspective brought about by the coaching.

Research conducted into the evaluation of intercultural trainings has shown that background knowledge can often be acquired in intercultural trainings. However, it is not necessarily activated during an intercultural encounter. Individuals tend to behave inappropriately during critical interactions and then feel bad about it later. With the help of intercultural coaching, clients learn to assume responsibility for their feelings, thoughts and behavior. They learn that they create their own feelings, thoughts and behavior and are consequently responsible for them. The automated process of interconnecting perception, thought, interpretation (assumption), feeling and behavior is interrupted through intercultural coaching. The client becomes aware of a perception which, as a rule, he instantaneously interprets and assumes something about. On the basis of this assumption, he creates specific feelings, which in turn affect his behavior. Once this process has been understood, a conscious decision can be made, either to interpret perceptions negatively in a critical interaction, conjure up negative feelings (e.g., anger, exasperation, sadness) and behave accordingly, or simply let it be.

The great advantage of the Vermeulen (1998) approach to intercultural coaching compared to other methods (e.g., team development), is that the individual clarifies the critical relationship for himself and not in cooperation with the critical partner. Open conflict resolution in the presence of both partners is not possible in all cultures (e.g., China). However, a German, for instance, may need to clarify his critical relationship to the Chinese. It is precisely the fact that the Chinese partner in question need not be involved that makes this method so advantageous.

Intercultural coaching is capable of expanding consciousness. Clients extricate themselves from obsessive thought patterns revolving around the critical partner. Relaxation exercises play an important role in this process. According to experience, the method is not effective without the body-oriented exercises. Hence, it is the combination of methods that achieve the overall effect of expanding consciousness. This condition is a prerequisite for opening up to more in-depth learning about another culture and key cultural standards, and for acquiring culturally appropriate behavior in role-play situations. Moreover, the formerly bound energy becomes available for the coachee to invest in reaching his work-related objectives.

References

Barmeyer, C. I. (2002): Interkulturelles Coaching. In: Rauen, C. (Ed.), Handbuch Coaching. 2nd ed. Göttingen/Bern u. a., pp. 199–231.

Brooks, C. V. W. (1997): Erleben durch die Sinne (Sensory Awareness, in der deutschen Bearbeitung von C. Selver). 9th ed. Paderborn.

Clement, U.; Clement, U. (1999): Interkulturelles Coaching. In: Götz, K. (Ed.), Interkulturelles Lernen/Interkulturelles Training. Reihe Managementkonzepte, Band 8. Hg. von K. Götz. München/Mering, pp. 157–168.

Davison, G. C.; Neale, J. M. (1998): Klinische Psychologie. 5th ed. Weinheim.

Kriz, J. (2001): Grundkonzepte der Psychotherapie. 5th ed. München/Weinheim.

Peuker, L.; Schmal, A.; Götz, K. (2002): Interkulturelles Coaching für Expatriates im Ausland. Ein neues Betreuungskonzept soll Fach- und Führungskräfte direkt vor Ort bei ihrem Auslandseinsatz unterstützen. Personalführung 11/2002.

Rauen, C. (2002): Handbuch Coaching. 2nd ed. Göttingen.

Roth, W. L.; Brüning, M.; Edler, J. (1995): Coaching – Reflexionen und empirische Daten zu einem neuen Personalentwicklungsinstrument. In: Wilker, F.-H. (Ed.), Supervision und Coaching. Aus der Praxis für die Praxis. Bonn, pp. 201–224.

Satir, V. (1988): Meine vielen Gesichter. Wer bin ich wirklich? München.

Satir, V. (1989): Mein Weg zu dir. Kontakt finden und Vertrauen gewinnen. München.

Schreyögg, A. (2001): Coaching. Eine Einführung für Praxis und Ausbildung. 5th ed. Frankfurt a. M./New York.

Singer, E. J. (1974): Effective Management Coaching. London.

Thomas, A. (1993a): Kulturvergleichende Psychologie. Eine Einführung. Göttingen.

Thomas, A. (1993b): Psychologie interkulturellen Lernens und Handelns. In: Thomas, A. (Ed.), Kulturvergleichende Psychologie. Eine Einführung. Göttingen, pp. 377–424.

Thomas, A. (1996): Psychologie interkulturellen Handelns. Göttingen.

Thomas, A.; Schenk, E. (2001): Beruflich in China. Trainingsprogramm für Manager, Fach- und Führungskräfte. Göttingen.

Vermeulen, B. (1998). Analysemodell. Unveröffentlichtes Manuskript. München.

Zimbardo, P. G.; Gerrig, R. J. (1999). Psychologie. 7th ed. Berlin/Heidelberg/New York.

II. Areas of Application

1. Intercultural Competence and Cooperation in Corporations

Siegfried Stumpf

1.1 Intercultural Management

1.1.1 Areas of Application in Intercultural Management

A manager's scope of activity is multifaceted. Managers must assume a variety of different roles in an organization. According to Mintzberg (1991), the range of roles taken on by a manager is made up of the aspects shown in Table 8.

Managerial positions differ depending on the different roles the manager is required to assume and the extent to which he is challenged by his

Table 8: Range of roles assumed by managers according to Mintzberg (1991)

Role	Brief Description
1. Representative	Observes ceremonial obligations, e.g., at receptions, celebrations, visits
2. Leadership	Maintains direct contact with employees: support, encouragement, acknowledgment
3. Liaison	Responsible for multi-level networking
4. Observer	Seeks and gathers information
5. Information dissemination	Passes on information
6. Speaker	Represents the organizational unit's point of view to the public
7. Entrepreneur	Initiates and supervises measures to safeguard and develop the organization
8. Mediator	Deals with disagreement and manages conflict
9. Allocation of resources	Determines who receives what in a particular organizational unit (tools, supplies, budgets . . .)
10. Negotiator	Negotiates deals in the organization's interest

social surroundings. Based on his own and others' expectations of the position he holds, every manager defines himself in terms of specific role expectations, some of which are emphasized over others.

Empirical studies conducted on the average workday of managers offer the following picture (cf. Neuberger 1990): A manager's average workday is comprised of many brief episodes. A manager must be prepared for frequent interruptions and unpredictable changes in circumstances. Managing is synonymous with communicating. Oral communication takes up the majority of the daily workload.

Based on these studies, the impression of managers as proactive and visionary leaders seems justified given that they are continually subjected to quickly changing and unpredictable events and circumstances, which call for agility and improvisation skill. Depicting management leadership in the form of a symphony orchestra conductor is a popular metaphor:

"The manager is like the conductor of a symphony orchestra, who is dedicated to maintaining the melodic quality contributed by each instrument, coordinating and sequencing the flow into a pattern that will coalesce into a rhythmically balanced performance while the orchestra members are each dealing with their personal issues. The stagehands move the music stands, alternating bouts of hot and cold temperatures are hard on the audience as well as the instruments, and the concert sponsors insist on irrational program changes" (Leonard Saylor, quote according to Mintzberg 1991, p. 33 f.).

This illustrates a manager's challenging scope of responsibility. Not only are they required to meet a number of different expectations and demands, in the process of which they not only actively set the course, but often must also deal with external influences and factors beyond their control. All of this can lead to feelings of uncertainty (cf. Neuberger 1990) and extreme psychological duress.

Intercultural requirements are an additional challenge. If each interaction partner proceeds from the standpoint of a different cultural orientation, then this must be taken into consideration within the scope of each of the management roles described by Mintzberg (1991). If this aspect is disregarded, misunderstandings and unproductive interactions are the inevitable result. This handbook illustrates the many different roles managers play (e.g., representative, negotiator, and conflict mediator).

The following groups of individuals and areas of application are involved:

- Specialists and executive staff who have been working abroad for several years, such as expatriates and developmental aid workers;
- Specialists and executive staff who represent global organizations responsible for initiating international contact and networking;

- Specialists and executive staff who work in culturally diverse project teams within the framework of international project teams;
- Specialists and executive staff at headquarters who supervise foreign subsidiaries or partner organizations (e.g., joint ventures) or who have customers abroad;
- Specialists and executive staff in organizations who employ culturally diverse staff.

1.1.2 Requirements for Intercultural Management

Demands on intercultural management change according to the intercultural task involved: an international assignment over several years as an expatriate working for the company's subsidiary abroad involves a different set of challenges and burdens than leading a culturally diverse work group at home (q.v. Ch. II, 2.4 and 2.6). International assignments in particular place high demands on individuals in management positions.

Studies conducted on managers sent on international assignments came up with rather dismal findings: Black and Gregersen (1999) report that between 10 to 20 percent of managers sent abroad terminate the assignment prematurely, dissatisfied with their new tasks or their new surroundings; nearly a third of the managers do not meet expectations; and a quarter of them resign shortly after returning, which translates into a considerable loss of know-how for the company. According to Stahl (1998, p. 2), estimates of the number of international assignments terminated prematurely fluctuate between 10 and 40 percent. In the case of specialists and executive staff sent on assignment to developing countries, the number of staff terminating their assignment even reaches 70 percent. The percentage of staff that neither fulfills their commitment to the company, nor feels at ease in the host country, nor meets the expected performance requirements is estimated much higher.

In interviews with 116 German managers sent on an international assignment by their companies for a period of several years to either Japan or the U. S., Stahl identified the problem areas with which the managers were confronted during their stay. The results are illustrated in Table 9 below.

Most of these problems are chronic, that is, continual or reoccurring stress factors (cf. Stahl 1998, p. 156). Forty-eight percent of the managers report problems with personnel and leadership (e.g., different leadership preferences, accustomed leadership techniques do not apply) (q.v. Ch. II, 2.5). Eighty percent of this group rank these particular problems from serious to extreme (intensity ranking: 1). Forty-seven percent of the group,

Table 9: Problem areas associated with the international assignment (cf. Stahl 1998, p. 157) based on the duration of the assignment to date. The more intense the problem is, the lower the ranking.

Problem areas (examples)	Frequency in% (N = 116)	< 2 years (N = 24)	2–6 years (N = 54)	6 years (N = 38)	Intensity ranking
Reintegration/future (work-related, personal fear of returning, fear of the future)	65%	46%	76%	61%	5
Relations with headquarters (autonomy, lack of support ...)	60%	50%	61%	63%	8
Staff/leadership (personnel management, development and recruitment)	48%	50%	48%	47%	1
Language/communication (problems with understanding and orientation ...)	47%	58%	54%	32%	4
Contacts in the host country (lack of or unsatisfactory contact ...)	44%	46%	50%	34%	9
Working hours/workload (long working hours, deadlines, business trips ...)	43%	25%	56%	37%	10
Role as representative (conflict of interest and loyalties, mediator role ...)	39%	29%	35%	50%	2
Spouse (lack of employment opportunity, isolation ...)	38%	58%	44%	16%	3
Quality of life (leisure, accommodation, climate ...)	35%	3%	37%	34%	7
Job description/processes (novelty of tasks, excessive demands, internal processes ...)	29%	33%	30%	26%	6
Business practices (relationship building, different business etiquette ...)	23%	22%	22%	26%	11

in particular those whose assignment was in Japan, reported language and communication-oriented problems (e.g., information deficits due to a lack of language ability, misunderstandings due to different communication styles). A further rating concerns problems with relationship building in the host country (44%), data that is not available in sufficient quantity or quality. According to manager reports, 38% cite problems experienced by spouses as having a substantial impact (e.g., adaptation difficulties, communication and orientation difficulties, lack of social contact) (q.v. Ch. II, 2.9). In preparing managers for problems likely to be encountered during an international assignment, Stahl found that: "In accordance with surveys on the practice of sending managers abroad in German companies, study findings indicate that only in exceptional cases is the staff systematically prepared for life and work in the host country . . . one can hardly speak of a thorough preparation in the majority of cases where managers are sent abroad" (1998, p. 247).

The frequency of problematic situations depends on the duration of the assignment: Problems related to the roles assumed during the assignment seem to increase over time; language and communication problems, as well as problems related to the spouse's well-being, decrease over time. Other factors, such as personnel and leadership issues, tend to remain constant.

Working and living abroad is not a continuum of living and working at home. An extended stay abroad, such as an international assignment over a longer period of time, is typically accompanied by specific acculturation stress that results from the contact with a foreign and unfamiliar environment. These stress factors impact psychological well-being in the form of depression, fear, feelings of estrangement and identity issues. A number of different models illustrate the process of acculturation stress and successful adaptation during the stay abroad. According to Berry (1985), the adaptation crisis occurs during the course of the stay abroad rather than at the beginning. A second crisis can be expected upon returning home (q.v. Ch. I, 1.8, q.v. Ch. II, 2.9): the individual must first get re-acquainted with the formerly familiar culture.

These findings show that the shift from one system of cultural orientation to another results in specific acculturation stress and demands placed on the person involved, which must be effectively overcome.

In his research, Stahl (1998) could further illustrate that successful and unsuccessful delegates differ in their approach to dealing with these problems. Successful delegates display the following problem-solving strategies:

- *Proactive problem-solving:* careful planning on how to proceed, comparing the pros and cons, informing themselves, step-by-step problem solving;
- *Learning about the culture:* learning through observation, acquiring knowledge, asking specific questions to clarify problems, modifying one's own behavior;
- *Assimilation:* honoring the host culture, representing local interests, integrating host country norms, distancing from the home country;
- *Relationship building and care:* signalizing a willingness to make contact, common leisure activities, visits, maintaining contact to headquarters at home;

- *Providing instrumental support:* passing on know-how, feedback and support when problems arise, acting as information mediator to headquarters;
- *Conflict resolution:* reaching agreement on decisions, de-fusing conflict, reaching compromises, avoiding "loss of face";
- *Maintaining identity-giving activities:* maintaining enjoyable leisure activities, habits, rituals and contacts to home;
- *Substitution:* focused search for new hobbies, gradual shift to local leisure activities;
- *Future-orientation:* making plans for the future, remaining aware of the limited timeframe of an international assignment, optimism.

In contrast, unsuccessful delegates often display these problem-solving strategies:
- *Avoidance/retreat:* avoiding difficult situations, retreat to the expatriate community, inactivity, escape from the host country;
- *Tolerance/acceptance:* giving up quickly when confronted with resistance, ignoring own needs, accepting aversive conditions, fatalism;
- *Identity maintenance:* distancing from locals, devaluing and criticizing the host country, asserting headquarters' interests;
- *Self-preservation:* placing blame on individuals of the host country, self-serving cause attribution, justifying own deficits;
- *Negative comparison:* envy of others, idealizing German virtues, nostalgia, attribution of negative host country characteristics.

The problem areas identified by Stahl are not necessarily applicable to all managers who work abroad. It is possible that specialists and executive staff who represent globally operating organizations as well as initiate and keep in contact with business contacts worldwide are confronted with other-culture influences to a lesser degree. Within an industry sector, or in the case of specific business activities, for example, transnational conventions have emerged which business partners from countries all over the world are familiar with. More in-depth and possibly irritating contacts with foreign cultures can be largely avoided, for instance, if managers limit contact to a narrowly defined business area. Even in these cases, however, cultural influences cannot be entirely eliminated due to the fact that country-specific orientation patterns have been inculcated since earliest childhood and the socialization process is deeply rooted in extensive areas of their lives, both privately and in the workplace.

Intercultural management is not only indispensable for both overseas deployment and international assignments, but also indicated in many other related areas. Managing cultural differences and diversity, for instance, is required in the case of international mergers (q.v. Ch. II, 2.7), running overseas operations via headquarters or leading culturally diverse work groups (q.v. Ch. II, 2.4 and 2.6). Generally, a number of different reactions are possible when encountering own- and other-culture differences (Adler 1997):

- *Cultural dominance:* action concurs with own-culture parameters;
- *Cultural accommodation:* action adapts to other-culture parameters;
- *Cultural avoidance:* cultural differences are ignored or covered up;
- *Cultural compromise:* a compromise is achieved between own- and other-culture parameters. Each side moves away from their respective views and approaches the other's viewpoint;
- *Cultural synergy:* new, innovative and productive solutions and parameters are developed that are neither derived from one's own nor the other culture.

Studies conducted with culturally diverse work groups (q.v. Ch. II, 2.6) show that cultural differences in teams are often approached by means of domination or adaptation strategies (Schroll-Machl 1996; Zeutschel 1999). Frictional loss and inadequate processes are typical for culturally diverse teams in the beginning phase. In the course of group development and with adequate encouragement and support for the group process (e.g., through process and performance feedback), team performance potential can be tapped (Watson et al. 1993).

Individual attempts to deal with cultural diversity in international organizations always take place against the backdrop of explicit or implicit organizational internationalization strategies. Ethnocentric strategies (cf. Adler, 1997), which are characterized by headquarters' attempts to transfer their own values and norms as well as decision-making and action patterns to the overseas subsidiary, bear considerable conflict potential. This strategy of cultural dominance can lead to the foreign subsidiary's open or hidden resistance to rigorous and culturally oblivious strategies. A personnel evaluation and development tool such as the 360 ° feedback measure, in which an employee is evaluated not only by his direct supervisor, but also by his subordinates and colleagues, is common in many Western organizations. Here, the socio-cultural context is characterized by relatively low power distance (q.v. Ch. I, 1.4 f.) between supervisors and subordinates. The export of such a system to Indonesia, China or South America, for instance, is not experienced as compatible with the respective cultural system of orientation and is likely to elicit defensive behavior. The forced implementation of these systems is likely to prove ineffective (cf. Fletcher and Perry, 2001).

1.1.3 Developing Intercultural Management

The success of intercultural management depends on a number of factors. Stahl (1998) suggests the following success factors for intercultural management within the scope of international assignments:

- *Characteristics:* knowledge of headquarters' modus operandi and contacts, loyalty and the ability to balance opposing interests, language skills, intercultural competence and personality characteristics, such as ambiguity tolerance or openness to other cultures;
- *Family:* adaptable and willing spouse/partner, work or other meaningful activity for the partner;
- *Position and organization:* unambiguous and conflict-free role, clear field of competence, independent decision-making and freedom to influence situations, qualified local employees, background knowledge of the host country at headquarters;
- *Structuring an international assignment:* uniform and transparent assignment guidelines, careful screening of candidates, culture-relevant preparation, continual support, long-term planning for reintegration;
- *Host country conditions:* cultural distance to home, language difficulties, legal and bureaucratic obstacles, quality of lifestyle and leisure time, supportive expatriate network.

This itemization shows that the interplay of a number of factors is responsible for the success of an international assignment. Characteristics, personal attributes or field and intercultural expertise are only a few of the factors that influence the success of the assignment. Seen against this backdrop, it becomes evident why studies conducted to determine the connection between personal characteristics and assignment success have led to rather inconsistent results (cf. Deller 2000). A personal characteristic, such as high ambiguity tolerance, is unlikely to contribute substantially to the success of the assignment if structural factors such as an incomplete job description or poor dispatching measures are in place. If an organization wishes to improve the chances for a successful assignment, then they have to consider different approaches simultaneously. Systematic personnel selection and development must be a priority, the candidates' social environments must be included in the measures, and suitable personnel policies and organizational strategies must be developed and implemented (dispatch procedures, job descriptions in the sense of delineating tasks, rights and responsibilities . . .).

Intercultural management involves specific challenges for the staff of an organization. A key factor here is the diagnosis and promotion of applied intercultural competence. According to Thomas, Kammhuber and Layes

(1997, p. 67f.), applied intercultural competence is the ability to understand cultural conditions and influencing factors in terms of perception, judgment, feeling and action, and how it affects oneself and others. Once this ability becomes second nature, learning to honor, respect and employ these aspects while striving to achieve mutual adaptation, incompatibility tolerance and synergetic forms of co-existence and orientation in the world will come naturally. Applied intercultural competence is a decisive factor in the selection and development of candidates. The following discussion emphasizes this point:

Defining Management Requirements

There are plenty of lists of character traits in literature describing what requirements suffice for intercultural managers. According to studies by Black and Gregerson (1999), the main character traits for candidates considered for international assignments include individuals who enjoy the exchange of ideas and opinions, are extroverts, open-minded and win-win negotiators. Other frequently mentioned characteristics include politeness, tact, integrity, sensitivity, intellectual curiosity, empathy, reliability, tolerance, self-confidence, discipline, punctuality, orderliness, openness to new experiences, awareness of the mission, enthusiasm, organizational skills, ability to tolerate uncertainty and social competence.

Relevant character and competence criteria are too general for a specific diagnosis and development of managers. Qualification criteria that adhere closely to given specific requirements for international management are more to the point. For this to be the case, the requirements for applied intercultural competence must be clearly defined. This means that the specific set of conditions in which the intercultural interaction takes place, and which differs from organization to organization and task to task, must each be analyzed from a different angle. In order to understand and record this set of conditions, the existing data on intercultural experiences should be systematically put to use. Hence, managers with overseas experience could be interviewed to obtain real-time insight into the specific, key interaction components required in intercultural encounters. Qualitative surveys based on the method of critical incidences (Flanagan 1954) provide a variety of intercultural data. Key criteria dimensions for intercultural interaction can be derived from the quality material and can be compiled in a comprehensive pool of case descriptions that can be translated into training material. Organization-specific intercultural criteria won in this way provide an excellent point of departure for target-oriented selection and development of candidates. An overall candidate profile description, which can be used for a number of positions within the company, as well as a more specific criteria profile for particular positions, is served by this method. The former, for instance, can be used for junior staff development projects while the latter lends itself to the targeted selection and preparation of candidates for an existing position.

Identifying Intercultural Management Potential

On the basis of the established intercultural criteria, a systematic approach can be launched to evaluate employee potential in terms of their ability to meet the requirements. It can be assumed that not every employee has the necessary ability or can be developed to meet the necessary requirements without feeling overburdened. Rather than leave the identification of potential to chance, corporations should use reliable and conclusive procedures. Cultural assimilator training, which tests for intercultural criteria in real-life scenarios, offers one such alternative for identifying potential (Study Group Assessment Center 1992; Kühlmann and Stahl 1996; Neubauer 1980).

Developing Intercultural Competence

There are a number of different methods of developing applied intercultural competence. The spectrum ranges from nontheoretical learning-by-doing, as is apparently preferred in the practical approach, all the way to seminar-oriented learning, which often lacks a background of real-life experience. As so often, the truth lies somewhere in between: the different approaches can complement each other quite well. The following approaches, in particular, are worth mentioning:

On-the-job development: In applied intercultural competence, too, one can assume that experience is an important teacher (cf. McCall et al. 1995; Yeung and Ready 1995). If a person wishes to strengthen his intercultural competence, it is advisable that he join a culturally diverse group, which he will eventually lead (cf. Gregerson et al. 1998, p. 30). The competencies required here can only be learned superficially in courses or seminars. In this case, learning-by-doing is a must. Practical experience sensitizes to cultural differences and one can learn to adapt one's behavior accordingly; one can explore the extent to which one communicates in a culturally adequate manner and attempt to integrate the different culture-based styles and begin to resolve conflict in a way congruent with the interaction partner's cultural mindset (cf. Ayman et al. 1994). This learning-by-doing approach should be flanked by consultation and training activities that prepare for experiences of this kind, and provide feedback for evaluation and reflection (cf. Boud et al. 1985; Kolb 1984).

Consultation: The persons involved will hardly be able to understand and solve all problems arising from an intercultural encounter on their own. Consultants from in or outside the company can support in the process of reflecting and interpreting experiences, problem solving, and the development and experimentation with alternative behavioral modes. A trust-based and supportive relationship with a coach or mentor can be very helpful in this situation (e.g., Mendenhall and Oddou 1988).

Training: A plethora of training approaches are available to prepare managers for their future tasks in the intercultural arena and to assist them in dealing with these challenges (q.v. Ch. I, 2.2). These approaches can be categorized according to the two dimensions of "culture-general vs. culture-specific" and "didactic/meditative" vs. "experience and exploration oriented" (Gudykunst and Hammer 1983). A detailed survey of training needs should precede an intercultural training. Research findings regarding adequate and inadequate problem-solving strategies in intercultural management can be used within the scope of this training. An evaluation of the training effects should follow (cf. Thomas et al. 1999). Experience has shown that it is important to involve the family in training and preparation measures for the international assignment. The accompanying spouse in particular is subjected to stress factors. According to Mendenhall and Oddou (1988), one of the main reasons for terminating an assignment prematurely is the spouse's inability to adapt to unfamiliar circumstances abroad.

Systematic Care and Designation of Intercultural Competence

Intercultural experience and competencies acquired by managers are a valuable resource in the organization. It is important to maintain and update this useful information for use on future challenges posed by both intercultural leadership and management issues. Upon their return from an extended assignment abroad, managers often find there is little interest in their experiences and competencies within the organization. Managers should be given the opportunity to contribute their experiences, for instance, by using the experiences to review and update selection criteria and improve training measures. Managers with international experience should be encouraged to act as mentors to employees preparing for work in an intercultural context. A company can reduce both employee turnover and the significant loss of valuable knowledge caused by the frustration of returning expats by honoring and taking the intercultural experience of corporate employees seriously.

References

Adler, N. J. (1997): International dimensions of organizational behavior. 3rd ed. Cincinnati, Ohio.

Arbeitskreis Assessment Center (Ed.) (1992): Standards der Assessment Center Technik. München.

Ayman, R.; Kreiker, N. A.; Masztal, J. J. (1994): Defining global leaderships in business environments. Consulting Psychology Journal 46(1): 1061–1087.

Berry, J. W. (1985): Psychological adaptation of foreign students. In: Samuda, R. J.; Wolfgang, A. (Eds.), Intercultural Counselling and Assessment – Global Perspectives. Lewiston, NY, pp. 235–248.

Black, J. S.; Gregersen, H. B. (1999): Auslandseinsätze: Was sie erfolgreich macht. Harvard Business Manager 21(6): 103–111.

Boud, D.; Keogh, R.; Walker, D. (Eds.) (1985): Reflection: Turning Experience into Learning. London.

Deller, J. (2000): Interkulturelle Eignungsdiagnostik. Zur Verwendbarkeit von Persönlichkeitsskalen. Waldsteinberg.

Flanagan, J. C. (1954): The critical incident technique. Psychological Bulletin 51: 327–358.

Fletcher, C.; Perry, E. L. (2001): Performance appraisal and feedback: A consideration of national culture and a review of contemporary research and future trends. In: Anderson, N.; Ones, D. S.; Sinangil, H. K.; Viswesvaran, C. (Eds.), Handbook of Industrial, Work and Organizational Psychology, Volume I: Personnel Psychology. London/Thousand Oaks/New Delhi, pp. 127–144.

Gregersen, H. B.; Morrison, A. J.; Black, J. S. (1998): Developing leaders for the global frontier. Sloan Management Review 40(1): 21–32.

Gudykunst, W. B.; Hammer, M. R. (1983): Basic training design. In: Landis, D.; Brislin, R. W. (Eds.), Handbook of Intercultural Training, Vol. 1. Elmsford, NY, pp. 118–154.

Kolb, D. A. (1984): Experiential Learning. Englewood Cliffs.

Kühlmann, T. M.; Stahl, G. K. (1996): Fachkompetenz allein genügt nicht – Interkulturelle Assessment Center unterstützen die gezielte Personalauswahl. Personalführung Plus: '96: 22–24.

McCall, M. W. Jr.; Lombardo, M. M.; Morrison, A. M. (1995): Erfolg aus Erfahrung. Effiziente Lernstrategien für Manager. Stuttgart.

Mendenhall, M. E.; Oddou, G. (1988): The overseas assignment: A practical look. Business Horizons 31(5): 78–84.

Mintzberg, H. (1991): Mintzberg über Management. Wiesbaden.

Neubauer, R. (1980): Die Assessment Center Technik: Ein verhaltensorientierter Ansatz zur Führungskräfteauswahl. In: Neubauer, R.; Rosenstiel, L. v. (Eds.), Handbuch der angewandten Psychologie, Band 1: Arbeit und Organisation. München, pp. 122–158.

Neuberger, O. (1990): Führen und geführt werden. Stuttgart.

Schroll-Machl, S. (1996): Kulturbedingte Unterschiede im Problemlöseprozess bei deutsch-amerikanischen Arbeitsgruppen. In: Thomas, A. (Ed.), Psychologie interkulturellen Handelns. Göttingen, pp. 383–409.

Stahl, G. K. (1998): Internationaler Einsatz von Führungskräften. München/Wien.

Thomas, A.; Kammhuber, S.; Layes, G. (1997): Interkulturelle Kompetenz. Bonn: Bundesministerium für Verteidigung.

Thomas, A.; Kinast, E.-U.; Schroll-Machl, S. (1999): Entwicklung interkultureller Handlungskompetenz von international tätigen Fach- und Führungskräften durch interkulturelle Trainings. In: Götz, K. (Ed.), Interkulturelles Lernen / Interkulturelles Training. München/Mering, pp. 97–122.

Watson, W. E.; Kumar, K.; Michaelsen, L. K. (1993): Cultural diversity's impact on interaction process and performance: Comparing homogeneous and diverse task groups. Academy of Management Journal 36(3): 590–602.

Yeung, A. K.; Ready, D. A. (1995): Developing leadership capabilities of global cooperations: A comparative study in eight nations. Human Resource Management, 34(4): 529–547.

Zeutschel, U. (1999): Interkulturelle Synergie auf dem Weg: Erkenntnisse aus deutschen/U.S.-amerikanischen Problemlösegruppen. Gruppendynamik 30(2): 131–149.

Eva-Ulrike Kinast/Alexander Thomas

1.2 Intercultural Human Resource Development in International Organizations

1.2.1 Problem Statement and Present Situation

According to estimates in literature (e.g., Meckl 2001; Stahl 1998), 40 to 70% of all international projects fail and 10 to 40% of all specialists and senior executive staff terminate their international assignment prematurely. In developing countries, the failure rate can even reach up to 70%. The number of employees who fulfil their overseas assignment but are neither happy with the situation nor do they meet performance expectations is estimated to be even higher than employees who leave prematurely. The wrong choice in filling a senior executive position for an overseas assignment can cost the company three to four times the yearly salary, not to mention the financial loss incurred by "losing face" and, among other irritations, disrupting relations with local employees and customers (Stahl 1998).

It is considered very likely that the failure of international projects and assignments is caused by a lack of applied intercultural competence on the part of expert and executive staff. This is hard to prove based on the limited availability of systematic evaluation methods.

From this perspective, intercultural human resource development seems to be an absolute necessity if specialists and senior executive staff are to be interculturally competent in the long term. To meet this goal, intercultural personnel development strives for the development of a strategy compatible with the overall corporate game plan, including appropriate measures to diagnose and develop applied intercultural competence, for instance culture assimilator training and/or intercultural training and coaching. These measures are systematically evaluated to ensure quality.

The prerequisite for intercultural human resource development is the company's international business outlook. According to Drumm (2000), this includes collaborations with international partners, joint ventures, the founding of a new company with several overseas partners, founding or taking over overseas operations, or setting up an independent affiliate abroad in cooperation with a national operation. In addition, intercultural human resource development is essential for strengthening the import and export sector while internationalizing its business activities.

In smaller and medium-sized operations, this is generally the responsibility of HR. In large corporations, there is frequently an organizational unit within the central HR department in charge of international issues. The expectations for those responsible for intercultural staff development are very high. *Intercultural personnel developers* should have a university background with an emphasis on aspects of personnel development, such as psychology and business administration, and in-depth knowledge of the theories and concepts of intercultural interaction including their practical application. Preferably the candidates have spent several years abroad and are able to apply their intercultural competence with confidence. In addition, they have culture-specific knowledge of at least one country.

There are no statistics available on how many organizations actually maintain a separate and professional department for developing staff interculturally. In view of the shockingly high numbers of failed international projects and international assignments, however, it is not likely that there are many. This is unbelievable! On the one hand, research findings confirm the effectiveness of intercultural trainings and, on the other, the cost of developing staff interculturally is trifling compared to the cost of failed international projects or assignments.

The number of global mergers and international company acquisitions is steadily increasing. Systematic intercultural training and maintaining a resource pool of interculturally competent specialists and senior executives would expedite integration processes considerably.

1.2.2 The Human Resource Cycle

The goal of any human resource endeavour is to fill positions that will ensure the company's efficiency and effectiveness (Drumm 2000; Scherm 1999). In international organizations, intercultural human resource development contributes to securing interculturally competent individuals for international assignments.

Intercultural HR development often begins with *personnel marketing* and *recruitment* prior to the public announcement of an open international position and predeparture intercultural training. The idea is to attract young leadership potential with international career ambitions via customized marketing and recruiting strategies (cf. Wirth 1996). Multilingual advertising on the company's homepage, for instance, or close contact with international universities, trade fairs and international trainee programs are a way to reach the target group.

The process of candidate selection should include an evaluation of the person's intercultural competence in addition to his field of specialization and social, individual and strategic competence. Here, for instance, a culture assimilator training might be indicated (q.v. Ch. I, 2.1). In the case of individual candidates, the training can be tailored to specific needs. Otherwise, a group culture assimilator training can be organized. The bottom line, in any case, is to ascertain whether potential candidates are willing to work internationally and agree with assignment specifications.

After the selection process and contract stipulations to include indicated country-specific differences, the candidates' next career step involves *performance improvement coaching.* On the one hand, priorities are set to decide which goals should be reached when, what standards must be met and what criteria will be used to measure the extent to which the goal has been achieved. After an agreed-upon interval, performance will be reviewed and evaluated. Usually an incentive is involved here consisting of salary, bonuses, company car and more. Aside from measuring results and process-oriented goals, it is essential to include a standard of behavior required for intercultural competence within the scope of intercultural HR development. For instance, it could be agreed that an individual participates in a culture-general awareness training to improve his intercultural competence, followed by a performance evaluation as part of the agreement. Learning progress could be evaluated by means of a culture assimilator training tool. An incentive here could be to integrate a stint abroad into the training program, lasting for several weeks in a country of key importance to the company, if it agrees with company policy.

On the other hand, personnel development in the narrow sense (including the development of senior executive staff), whose evaluation tools range from in-placement, analysis of employee potential and development all the way to qualification, could be designed to include applied intercultural competence as a follow-up to performance improvement coaching. Within the framework of *in-placements,* a program comprising the first 12 months of an employees' time with the company, international welcome days or weeks for newly employed specialists and senior executive staff from around the world could be organized at one international site. Another possibility would be for the company to organize international entry programs for young leadership potential including a qualification program with integrated intercultural trainings and coaching, in addition to project work in culturally diverse teams.

An initial *appraisal of employee potential* should be administered at least six months after employment. A good time to do this might be within the scope of an annual performance review (cf. Wirth 1996). Another option is for HR to conduct a culture assimilator training. It is important that both of these options include criteria and evaluation for applied intercultural competence. Culture assimilator trainings, for now, offer the best solution for diagnosing intercultural competence. Intercultural competence criteria used for candidate evaluation should be identical to the criteria for intercultural competence used to assess potential. If this is not the case, then it can be assumed that intercultural competence is measured according to two different criteria. This makes it impossible to evaluate the development of intercultural competence later.

In talking about *development,* the emphasis is on defining specific developmental processes that clearly indicate a specialist's or senior executive's ability to master a particular position in the company based on his past experience. In international organizations, methods of developing staff should be designed for an international audience, as it is also a good opportunity for intercultural learning (provided the training methods are linked to intercultural qualification measures). The minimum requirement for an international career should include at least six months experience abroad. Methods of further development can, for instance, be agreed upon within the scope of yearly performance reviews.

Qualification is clearly the focus of intercultural human resource development. Intercultural trainings and coaching are instrumental in developing applied intercultural competence. Every specialist or senior executive who strives for an international position should have attended at least one culture-specific awareness training during his career. The content and design of needs-specific trainings and coaching are predominantly based on the data gleaned from employee potential appraisals. If the data was compiled within the framework of yearly performance reviews, it might be a good idea to undergo culture assimilator training in advance to ensure objectivity and validity in assessing needs. In any case, the learning progress needs to be monitored and evaluated.

Human resource management is reflected in the cycle beginning with the selection of a candidate all the way to his or her qualification. If the individual steps in the cycle are interconnected and implemented on a regular and systematic basis, then, in time, a resource pool of interculturally competent staff will be available for international assignments and can ensure succession. An integrated human resource cycle, as described here, with an emphasis on aspects of intercultural learning and interaction, allows the company to recruit interculturally qualified staff from within its own ranks, instead of hiring external candidates where, to date, there is a lack of interculturally qualified specialists and management. This situation is likely to worsen, at least in Europe, due to demographic developments.

The envisioned human resource cycle is illustrated in Figure 10.

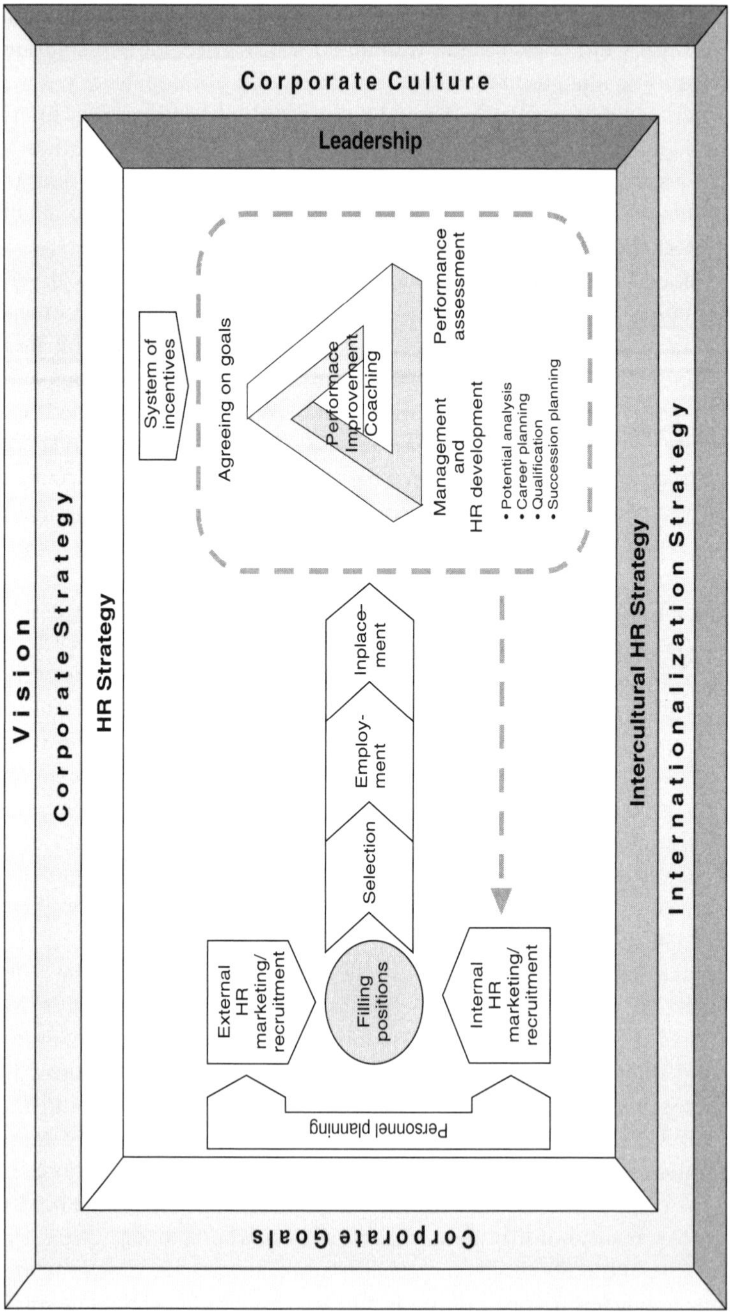

Figure 10: Human Resource Cycle

The success of intercultural human resource development depends on three main factors:

- Firstly, prior to the conceptual design of a program for intercultural HR development, a *strategic qualification diagnosis* must be conducted. To achieve this, the board of directors and top management must develop a common vision indicating the direction of the company's strategic development (as far as planning this far in advance is possible today). Based on this diagnosis, the competencies required by specialists and senior executives can be determined, and also how many in this group need these skills. If, for instance, a German company wants to establish a large-scale sales operation in the U. S. and offer its products on the U. S. market, then one can assume that at least one senior executive at the CEO level will be required who is either a native of the U. S. or a German national with a thorough knowledge of the American mindset. Either way, both must have the relevant expertise and social, individual and strategic skills, have culture-specific knowledge of both the U. S. and Germany, and have general intercultural competence.
- Secondly, the success of intercultural HR development depends largely on the company's *leadership model.* Honoring and productively exploiting employee interculturality should be a key component of corporate philosophy. In addition, the leadership model should postulate that the company promotes its employees' international interests and expects each of its employees to nurture an international outlook. If this is not yet the case, then a revision or an amendment to the leadership model is highly recommended.
- Thirdly, the company should instate a clear *basic international strategy* that sets a premise for the employees' interculturality. The basic international strategy determines who maintains the upper hand in the case of conflict.

Human resource development, in this sense, is more than a mere standardized catalogue for continuing education, offering the occasional routine intercultural training. Rather, this form of HR development assumes the responsibility for maintaining a readily accessible pool of specialists and senior executive staff who, aside from being highly competent interculturally, also have the necessary expertise and social, individual and strategic skills. This factor contributes substantially to a company's efforts to internationalize HR responsibilities.

The pool of interculturally competent specialists and senior executives can be accessed whenever:

- an overseas position opens up, requiring a specialist or senior executive

from another country to relocate as an expatriate (together with his family).
- international projects are in place, for example, in the case of the introduction of standard software for the purpose of production planning and installing company regulatory systems.
- specialists and senior executive staff are involved in international projects and frequently communicate electronically with employees, colleagues and clients from other cultures.

Up until now, the main focus in intercultural HR has been on expatriates and their families.

1.2.3. Intercultural Human Resources Development for the International Assignment

Intercultural HR development is, as a rule, separated into seven phases based on international assignment requirements (cf. Thomas et al. 1999).

1. Should an overseas position open up, a candidate can be selected from a pool of interculturally competent specialists and senior executives whose qualifications also include the required expertise and social, individual and strategic skills. This is the best-case scenario. Unfortunately, the case in many international companies is that intercultural development is not integrated into the human resources cycle. As a result, when an international assignment becomes imminent, there are only a few specialists and senior executive staff to chose from who are, on the one hand, both interested in an international assignment and prepared to relocate and, on the other, have the necessary expertise and social, individual and strategic skills, as well as adequate intercultural competence and comprehensive culture-specific knowledge. So, the question arises as to what should be done with the few available specialists and senior executives who may be experts in their fields, fulfil the requirements and are prepared to relocate, yet whose intercultural competence, however, is not up to par. In many cases, they are simply sent on the overseas assignment without further ado. This is corporate practice to date. It is hardly surprising then, that so many international projects and collaboration plans fail! If intercultural HR development has not managed to pool interculturally competent candidates in its resource bank, then at least they should make sure that the available candidates are suited to working and living internationally. One possibility would be to conduct interviews during the selection phase or suggest a culture assimilator training. An international assignment is demanding of specialists and senior executives. Not only are

they expected to function adequately in the typical fields of management, such as presentation, negotiation, conflict situations, project work and leadership, etc., but their families, too, are affected by a range of social, sociocultural and work-related stress factors. For this reason, it is highly recommended that the selected candidate visit the target country before he makes a final decision.

2. Following the decision phase and after the candidate has been selected and has agreed to accept the assignment, he would be well advised to attend a culture-specific intercultural orientation training to enhance his intercultural learning and competence and to provide him with knowledge about the target country's key cultural standards. The intercultural training should be tailored to both the expatriate's specific needs as well as to the specific company. If the expatriate is trained externally, he will learn about interculturality. However, the approach is likely to be standardized without considering the company's particular needs. This is, of course, preferable to no preparation at all! In any case, the customized approach is advisable as it addresses specific needs. A problem here is that often only one expatriate has been selected and an intercultural training lasting two to three days for one person is simply too cost intensive. The expatriate can then either be trained externally or within the company with a focus on both the expatriate's and the company's needs without the extra overhead. This type of training is usually referred to as "intercultural coaching" (q.v. Ch. I, 2.4) and can last an entire day. It is often assumed that coaching of this nature is more intensive. Individuals who have observed intercultural trainings note that learning and interacting with other training participants heightens the learning effect due to the ensuing group dynamic. Hence, it is recommendable to offer an in-company training and invite expatriates, other specialists and senior executives who have frequent contact with other-culture individuals to attend. The training can then be tailored to meet the needs of both the expatriate and the company, encompass the complexity of the subject and not exceed costs, since participating executive staff will also profit from the training. Moreover, this kind of in-company intercultural training can be outsourced to other companies, although it will then no longer be company or needs specific.
3. Due to the particular difficulties faced by accompanying spouses, it is highly recommended to include the spouse in preparatory trainings. A couple may, of course, attend the training together. However, it has often been observed that one of the spouses gets bored if training focuses too heavily on typical management themes. An alternative to this could be that the expatriate attend an in-company training that meets his and the company's needs and focuses on typical areas of management while the

spouse attends another, external training that focuses more on individual needs. A few intercultural training institutes (IHK Lübeck 1999) have even specialized in preparing children from the age of six on for life abroad.

4. During the departure phase and shortly after arrival in the target country, an on-the-job intercultural training should take place to monitor effects of culture shock and to accompany the expatriate through the acculturation process while enhancing intercultural learning and practical skills.
5. After departure, intercultural progress training should take place in the target country to strengthen intercultural reflection and attribution skills, as well as job-specific learning and practical skills. The appropriate time frame for this depends on the progress of acculturation. The initial progress training or coaching, however, should take place no later than twelve weeks after arrival. Expatriates and their spouses should have the option throughout their entire stay abroad to attend intercultural coaching sessions to assist them in working through critical encounters with culturally dissimilar individuals. In this way, the physical and psychological stress caused by an entirely new work environment and living conditions can be ameliorated. Intercultural team coaching is another option for dealing with conflict situations among culturally dissimilar employees and colleagues.
6. During the return phase, expatriates should be prepared for the "new" work situation at headquarters back home within the scope of a reintegration training. Frequently, there is no guarantee that the expatriate can fill a particular position upon his return. The same goes for an expatriate's loss of status as the uniqueness of his experience abroad is overlooked in the process of reintegration into the daily work routine at headquarters. Assurances of moving up in the company all too often turn out to be empty promises. It is important that the expatriate be prepared for such a possibility upon his return to take the edge off any likely disappointments. In addition, the appointment of a replacement to the host country should take place during this phase.
7. The re-entry shock phenomenon should be addressed in reintegration training during the reintegration phase. The returnee is then gradually reintroduced to corporate life and national culture at home, allowing him to reflect and process his intercultural experiences.
8. During the distribution phase, the expatriate's experiences are passed on to his successor as well as new, internationally active employees and fed into the expert pool. Upon their return, expatriates are often disappointed by the lack of interest in their experience abroad. By recycling the expatriate's experiences, disappointment and bruised feelings can be

kept to a minimum. It is crucial that typical, critical intercultural incidences are compiled in the expert pool to provide the raw material for culture assimilator training and intercultural training curricula.

The phases of intercultural human resource development are illustrated in Figure 11.

Phases of the international assignment	Selection, consultation and training measures
Preparation phase: • HR development for senior executive staff • Anticipating an international assignment • Interest in a foreign assignment	**Culture-general awareness training**
Personnel selection	**Selection process** • Interview • Culture assimilator training • Trial visit to the target country
Final decision and acceptance of the international assignment to a particular country	**Culture-specific orientation training** • enhancing intercultural learning ability and skill • training process: information-based training – culture-based training – interaction-based training – culture assimilator training
Departure phase	**Getting acquainted training** • dealing with culture shock • acculturation assistance • strengthening intercultural learning and experiencing skills
International assignment	**Assistance training:** • intercultural reflection and attribution capacity • task-specific learning and interaction skills (assessment) • individual/team-based intercultural coaching
Return phase	**Reintegration training I:** • preparing for the "new" work situation at home headquarters • handing over responsibilities to a replacement in the host country
Reintegration phase	**Reintegration training II:** • dealing with culture shock • getting reacquainted with corporate and national culture • reflecting on intercultural work and life experience
Distribution phase	**Recycling experience and value** • handing over responsibilities to the new expatriate replacement • feeding intercultural experience into an information pool

Figure 11: Phase model of intercultural HR development in preparation for international assignments

Expatriates and their families can be supported during all the phases mentioned where intercultural personnel development is integrated as a function, or even separate department, within the company. It is essential to recognize early on where assistance is indicated and when to step back to allow the expatriate to experience on his own. It is more often the case that expatriates feel left in the lurch by the company, than supported. Or in another scenario, as described in the words of a German expatriate of a large international corporation based in Germany: "... in my experience, I've found that expatriates not only expect to have their coffee served, they also expect the intercultural HR development department to stir in the sugar". Certainly this is not the responsibility of a company's intercultural HR development division. The individual steps and existing options are described in detail by Bittner and Reisch (1994).

In the past, expatriates and their families were the focus of intercultural human resource development. Over the years, another development has become evident involving a stronger interest in specialists and senior executives who live in their home countries but whose work has taken on international dimensions. A main issue here is to ensure that intercultural experiences of staff on international assignments are fed back into the intercultural HR development cycle to provide the raw material for the design of diagnostic tools and trainings. This in turn provides the basis for preparing specialists and senior executives in culture- and company-specific trainings for international assignments. The only way to prepare staff adequately for the challenges of an international assignment is to instate an intercultural HR development policy that will compile the intercultural knowledge gained from those individuals who actually work in the international arena and are experiencing working and living conditions abroad first hand.

1.2.4 Summary and Forecast

Intercultural HR development is necessary in international operations in order to have a sufficient number of specialists and senior executives available at precisely the time an overseas position becomes available, and who have the required expertise, social, individual and strategic competencies in addition to applied intercultural competence. The purpose of international HR development is not merely to offer a single intercultural training, which is then listed in the continuing education program. Intercultural HR development is a cycle composed of interconnected individual steps and components which build upon each other.

Today the emphasis in intercultural HR development is no longer on preparing, assisting and reintegrating expatriates and their families. Increasingly, other target groups, in particular, specialists and senior executive staff who live in their native country but work internationally, are gaining in importance. This trend lends intercultural HR development an entirely new dimension. A company must make sure that their entire HR staff is internationalized. Intercultural HR development plays a strategic role in this process.

One limitation remains: The HR cycle can indeed impact aspects of specialists' and senior executives' intercultural learning and interaction in the steps and methodology described here. Cultural influences on the cycle and the design of individual components are not considered here. The approach illustrated pertains to HR management procedures in Germany and is not necessarily applicable worldwide (cf. Regnet and Hofmann 2000).

References

Bittner, A.; Reisch, B. (1994): Interkulturelles Personalmanagement: internationale Personalentwicklung, Auslandsentsendungen, interkulturelles Training. Wiesbaden.

Drumm, H. J. (2000): Personalwirtschaftslehre. 4th ed. Berlin/Heidelberg u. a.

Industrie- und Handelskammer zu Lübeck (Ed.) (1999): Auslandsknigge. Verhaltensregeln, Geschäftssitten, Etikette. Eine Auswahlbibliographie sowie Anbieter Interkultureller Beratungs- und Trainingsleistungen in Deutschland. Lübeck.

Meckl, R. (2001): Der M&A-Prozeß. In: Bolten, J.; Schröter, D. (Eds.), Interkulturelle Wirtschaftskommunikation. Forschungsstand und Perspektiven. Sternenfels.

Regnet, E.; Hofmann, L. M. (Eds.) (2000): Personalmanagement in Europa. Schriftenreihe Wirtschaftspsychologie (Hg. v. H. Schuler). Göttingen/Bern u. a.

Scherm, E. (1999): Internationales Personalmanagement. 2nd ed. München/ Wien.

Stahl, G. K. (1998): Internationaler Einsatz von Führungskräften. München/Wien.

Thomas, A.; Kinast, E.-U.; Schroll-Machl, S. (1999): Entwicklung interkultureller Handlungskompetenz von international tätigen Fach- und Führungskräften durch interkulturelle Trainings. In: Götz, K. (Ed.), Interkulturelles Lernen/Interkulturelles Training. München/Mering, pp. 97–122.

Wirth, E. (1996): International orientierte Personalentwicklung. In: Bergemann, N.; Sourisseaux, A. L. J. (Eds.), Interkulturelles Management. 2nd ed. Heidelberg, pp. 201–228.

Georg Felser

1.3 Intercultural Marketing

Everyone wants to have "Billy". That's why the Swedish furniture manufacturer IKEA embarked on the long journey to the "Middle Kingdom" and opened its 150th branch in Beijing (Wenderoth and Schmitz 2002). The step onto the Chinese market is entirely in tune with the spirit of globalization – assuming that practically anything can be sold anywhere in the global marketplace. Hence, the 5000 items in the Beijing branch are identical to the ones in Hamburg or Stockholm (Wenderoth and Schmitz 2002).

As convincing as IKEA's sales strategy may be, the limits of globalization become evident again and again where culture-specific aspects are involved. The following examples appear both amusing and bizarre: Chinese children don't wear diapers. Instead a hole is left in the crotch of their pants to allow the contents of the diaper free access to nature. This situation causes concern for those responsible for childcare on the ground floor as they wonder if it's advisable to "fill the basin with thousands of red plastic balls" (Wenderoth and Schmitz 2002, p. 172).

Western observers find the way Chinese customers settle down matter-of-factly for a nap in one of the comfortable exhibition beds or sofas equally odd. Toward noontime, when things begin to slow down, the sales floor turns into a regular dormitory (Wenderoth and Schmitz 2002, p. 169).

Examples like these do not yet pose serious problems for marketing. They do indicate, however, that consumer behavior is far from reflecting global behavior – just one of the cultural characteristics that marketing must be aware of. Considerations of this kind will be discussed here. The emphasis in this contribution will be on the psychological aspects of marketing, in particular on the conformity of market participants and less on the logistics required in implementing the marketing mix.

1.3.1 Standardization and Differentiation

A key question in international marketing is often: Can the marketing strategy be the same for all targeted countries? Can the advertising be the same? Does product design or labeling need to be changed depending on a new market? A readapted strategy would be much too cost intensive and, on the other hand, country-specific differentiation would minimize the effect of a clear international label.

If advertising for a product worldwide could be achieved with one spot, then millions of euros could be saved. Even the process of settling on a product label, provided it is professionally done, is very complex (Kohli et al. 2001). In this respect, in particular, international applicability should be considered in advance and tested in other linguistic and cultural environments.

Up to a point, it can be predicted if a label will prove effective in translation. Classic examples here are the Chevy Nova, which gave rise to derisive associations in the Spanish-speaking world even before the first mishap: "*Chevy no va* – the Chevy doesn't work". The Toyota MR2 two-seater sounded like *merde* to the French, which suggest as much sophistication as the label for the Rolls Royce model "Silver Mist" (silver manure) does for the Germans (cf. Kohli et al. 2001; Müller and Kornmeier 1995).

In contrast, Coca-Cola stands as the all-time positive example for worldwide success. Even where the most obstinate adherence to uniform marketing policies would have come up against obstacles, the organization was blessed with a fortuitous stroke of luck. When Coca-Cola was launched on the Chinese market, the problem arose of how to translate the label into the foreign characters. There are two options in this case: For one, the phonetic integrity can be maintained, which generally translates into meaningless nonsense words. Secondly, one can try incorporating particular product characteristics in the new label or stick to the label's original meaning.

Coca-Cola succeeded in bridging the gap between the two options. The Chinese word sounds phonetically similar to the original and has a message to boot:

"*Kekou kelè* is the phonetic translation of *Coca-Cola*. ... Everyone in China knows the Chinese translation. The sound is similar enough to *Coca-Cola* so that the consumer thinks immediately of a foreign product. In addition, the Chinese sound sequencing takes the imagination in a specific direction. Literally the word means: "It tastes good and one drinks it with relish". From a consumer and commercial perspective, this appealing translation can be considered an excellent example of using a foreign product label" (Jinlong 1994, p. 19).

IKEA was similarly successful. The Chinese translation *Yi Jia*, too, is phonetically similar to the original and means "suited to the family". Certainly, the furniture magnate can live with that translation (cf. Wenderoth and Schmitz 2002, p. 168).

The Chinese translation of the word *Riesling*, on the other hand, fares less well. *Léi Silìng* may sound similar to the original but translated it means "Commander Thunder" (Jinlong 1994).

If it were possible to do without the complex measures required to adapt marketing strategies to other countries, then the ensuing cost savings would be clearly reflected in more centralized organizational structures in corporations. The next step offers possibilities for passing cost and price benefits on to the consumer while strengthening a market position. A strong market position essentially means that a large number of people buy one's products, which in turn is a sign for the homogenization of markets. This completes a theory-based cycle (quoted from Müller and Kornmeier 1995, p. 341 f.):

- *Homogenization* of consumer needs makes
- *standardization* of marketing means possible. This facilitates the
- *centralization* of organizational structures resulting in
- *cost and price advantages*, which in turn strengthens the home market position and leads to a homogenization of consumer needs. And so on.

This idea is valid in theory. Practical application looks different. This cycle is not without a range of obstacles that require interculturally differentiated marketing strategies as opposed to standardized versions.

1.3.2 Why Intercultural Marketing?

Frequent travelers are generally more attuned to cultural differences and variety. Deducing from this assumption, Müller and Kornmeier (1995, p. 346) have arrived at the theory that ever-increasing foreign travel is evolving toward a general need to preserve cultural singularity. The motives here certainly differ. For one, the otherness of the target country is a tourist's main motive for traveling. For business travelers this same otherness can be a handicap. On the other hand, perhaps the target country feels threatened by too many visitors and fears a loss of identity. Müller and Kornmeier's argument do point to one aspect: it is precisely characteristics of globalization such as increasing contact between different cultures that speak against the complete homogenization of living conditions.

This aspect is also evident on the level of consumer goods marketing. Often products are marketed as "foreign" or "exotic" and appeal to other cultures exactly for this reason. Too much adaptation to the foreign market would be contraindicated here as long as such adaptation impacts the other-culture character. Seen from this perspective, Coca-Cola does not represent a universal product, but rather it is an ambassador for the American way of life. IKEA too, makes an effort to maintain its Swedish character in

China. In fact, with the help of a picture gallery, the Chinese are invited to gain an impression of the Swedish landscape and lifestyle (Wenderoth and Schmitz 2002, p. 168).

It may even be that a number of differences between cultures will be preserved or even strengthened by increasing globalization rather than diluted. For the midterm, there is probably no other choice but to adapt marketing efforts to the culture under consideration and be aware of the differences involved. The following discussion aims to substantiate this assumption on the basis of a range of examples. Please keep in mind that the cultural differences mentioned also differ in their flexibility.

1.3.3 Political and Legal Frames of Reference

One of the first obstacles for intercultural marketing is dealing with authorities in the target country to obtain the necessary authorization. IKEA, thanks to its Chinese joint-venture partner, was fortunate enough to be granted authorization after a relatively brief waiting period of six months. On the other hand, hygiene inspections conducted without prior notice covering the cafeteria, toilets and then on to sofas, curtains and carpets were, in fact, quite unexpected. The sudden decision of the city council to insist on replacing all European plugs, although compatible with Chinese sockets, with official Chinese plugs was another unforeseen development (Wenderoth und Schmitz 2002, p. 171 f.).

Market strategies must adapt to local attitudes and opinions in terms of market development. The American market, for instance, is much more liberal than its European counterpart. In Europe, particularly in pre-WWII Germany, it was not unusual for companies to form syndicates. It was similar in Japan. Against this historical backdrop, attitudes regarding the danger of monopolies still differ from country to country (cf. Usunier and Walliser 1993).

Government and state intervention in the development of individual companies, such as the German chancellor's intervention to save the construction company Holzmann in 1999, is accepted in a form that would be unthinkable in the U.S.

In February 2002, "Time" magazine commentator Josef Joffe expressed his dismay about the German government's reticence regarding foreign investment plans. Joffe cited the example of Australian media mogul Rupert Murdoch, who expressed an interest in Leo Kirch's disintegrating media empire, or the American telecommunications company Liberty Media, run by John Malone. In the latter case, foreign investment would have meant considerably more comfort for private internet users. The rate of transmission for internet data is at least six times higher in the U. S. than what the German Telekom can offer its customers. Joffe adds: "Again the basic mercantilist motto is: 'Don't help the consumer, protect the producer' – by keeping out foreign competition" (Time, 2.25.2002, p. 25).

This type of behavior forms the expectations of foreign investors and provides the basis for intercultural marketing decisions.

Further limitations are set by legal frameworks for market behavior. Here, too, cultural differences are reflected and whoever ignores the regulations, risks not only the failure of his venture but also future sanctions. Intercultural differences that affect regulations, for example, are found in:

- illustration of taboo subject matter (nakedness, sex, death) in advertising,
- advertising with and in front of children,
- closing time for shops,
- consumer protection measures, for example, through specific sales promotion gimmicks that pressure the customer (freebies, discounts).

The latter was, for instance, regulated in Germany by the discount law, according to which it was not permitted to grant discounts or distribute freebies that amounted to more than 3% of the product price. This rule dates back to 1933 and was meant to protect consumers from exaggerated pressure exerted by sales people in the form of favors and privileges. The thought behind such a prohibition can hardly deny the psychological premise – the expectation that it is easy for any responsible consumer to extricate himself from the situational pressure of such a sales strategy. It is difficult, however, to prove this empirically (Cialdini 2001; Felser 2001).

The protection measures enforced against pirating or imitating market labels also differ from one country to the next. China is extremely tolerant in this respect. Each year market labels worth 15 billion euros are copied. Visitors to the Beijing branch of IKEA, for example, are regularly greeted by: "We wish you a pleasant time at IKEA – but please refrain from taking photographs!" (Wenderoth and Schmitz 2002, p. 170).

1.3.4 Cultural and Economic Frames of Reference

Some products are so closely associated with cultural customs that without their cultural background they make no sense at all. Take, for instance, carnival costumes, Halloween masks but also wedding attire. Other products are more subtly associated with cultural preferences but are dependent on these conditions all the same. Marketability of convenience foods is dependent on the social function that meals have in the particular culture: When, how, in what company and how much time is spent for meals? What role does preparation of the meal play? How do the types of food have to be combined?

According to the culture, it makes sense to indicate the time factor, the steps involved in preparation, availability of exotic ingredients or other product characteristics. It is easy to find cultures where convenience foods have no chance on the market whatsoever.

Economic limitations are especially disruptive. One of IKEA's biggest challenges in Beijing is the constricted living space available to the Chinese population. Built-in kitchens or closets are difficult to sell as "the average Chinese kitchen is the size of a wardrobe from our perspective" (Wenderoth and Schmitz 2002, p. 170). This condition impacts turnover in China to a great extent. Everything that "saves space, can be affixed to the wall and is collapsible" sells well. Cups and tea candles are also popular; spacious furniture, on the other hand, sells poorly. In addition, IKEA's prices, in relation to the Chinese income, are much too high. Although IKEA is considerably more reasonable in China than in Europe or North America, the furniture company is still considered expensive. Further price cuts are in the works (Wenderoth and Schmitz 2002, p. 170).

The importance of certain consumer goods in the overall budget is affected by the general economic conditions of a culture as well. A country in which the average citizen spends 10% of his income on clothing and shoes is bound to be more partial to this product category than the individual consumer who spends at most 5% on items like these. Interestingly enough, it is precisely this structural characteristic in Europe that points to increasing differentiation between cultures. From 1985 to 1990 the differences in spending patterns in European countries increased in almost all larger product categories (findings cited according to Müller and Kornmeier 1995, p. 344). Energy spending, alone, leveled off in European countries over the five years of study. In other areas, such as body hygiene products, clothing, telecommunications or household spending, the differences between European Union members increased. The strongest divergent development was in spending for food and luxury foodstuffs with a contingent of 20%, which represents the largest product category in European private households.

1.3.5 Socio-Psychological Frames of Reference

If one asks employees in different nations about the kind of behavior they prefer a supervisor to exhibit, the answers differ considerably. Now, if employees in international work groups are asked, that is, individuals who already work in a multicultural environment, then these differences do not decrease, as one might expect, but are even more emphasized (cf. Usunier and Walliser 1993, p. 53ff.). These findings underline the presumption that cultural differences in attitude and value systems continue to exist in multicultural societies and probably become even more pronounced.

From a socio-psychological perspective, this result is not necessarily surprising. Many studies (e.g., Taijfel 1981) have shown that individuals have a strong tendency to form a group identity and to communicate this to the outside, even if the group to which they belong is disadvantaged. Accordingly, it is not plausible, for example, that all individuals want to be and live like Western Europeans or Americans, even if members of other groups admit that a number of elements of these cultures are in fact meaningful and worth striving for.

From the psychological perspective mentioned, it does appear plausible that a people and culture have a stronger need for differentiation and individuality the closer they are to the other culture. As a result, it could be expected that different cultures encountering each other in the same company or the same nation state contrast more strongly than cultures that coexist within a certain distance from each other.

The indicated differentiation has been proven within the scope of smaller groups. Transferring these findings to cultural spheres encompassing several states is likely, albeit largely speculative. In the same vein, the question arises as to what extent the globalization trend, which is based primarily on Western values, fuels the need of non-Western cultures to communicate their own values or even to defend themselves by resorting to belligerent isolation.

The tendency to communicate identity via group belonging can be considered a psychological constant. The variable in this case is the group-defined criteria. Social strata, nationality or religion form sub-groups in different ways. The emphasis on elements of group criteria may shift according to which criteria dominates and is particularly conspicuous.

A typical member bonus also becomes evident in market behavior. Indigenous products are generally preferred. This predominant tendency, however, is re-moderated according to the given culture: Guerhan-Canli and Maheswaran (2000) were able to show that members of collectivist cultures (Japan) preferred Japanese-made products to all others, even if the indigenous products were qualitatively inferior. U. S. consumers preferred American-made products only if they were of superior quality.

1.3.6 Dimensions of Dissimilarity

Usunier and Walliser (1993, p. 38 ff.) have compiled research findings from different sources and have developed a system of cultural differences. The main dimensions of differentiation are described in the following characteristics:

- The significance of individuals vs. the group
- The importance of time
- Attitudes toward taking action
- Concepts of self vs. concept of otherness

The following section will explore the above dimensions in more detail with a view to market-relevant psychology.

Individual and Group

The first dimension emphasizes group belonging, for instance, the consequences of group belonging or the conditions for becoming a group member. Group membership rules are important to intercultural marketing for a number of reasons. Products that could serve to improve status in a group can do this only if group membership rules permit the sought-after improvement of status through such means. In past centuries in Europe, for instance, citizens could not aspire to nobility status on the basis of wealth. Advertising for excellent economic performance was limited by stipulations that forbid suggestions of "status improvement" in its message ...

In addition, it is a question of trust to what extent trust is granted. A merchant who belongs to the "out-group" is therefore more dependent on trust-building measures than a member from the "in-group". European IKEA customers trust blindly that a carton will contain the product of the color indicated on the packaging. In the Chinese subsidiary, on the other hand, "all kinds of half-opened packages lay around because customers did not trust the labeling on the package". IKEA-Bejing, therefore, "switched to installing view windows" on their packaging (Wenderoth and Schmitz 2002, p. 172). Whether this mistrust goes back to the assumption that members of the "out-group" are generally less trusted, is open to speculation. Other cultural differences, too, could offer an explanation. Hence,

Chinese customers tend to ask for information even if they see it in print directly in front of them. "'The Chinese don't like to read', complains a Chinese merchant. Besides, they mistrust anything in print. 'You ask for directions not with your eyes, but with your mouth', as the Chinese proverb goes" (Wenderoth and Schmitz 2002, p. 173).

Concept of Time

The concept of time in terms of a limited resource is perceived differently. Cultures that do not see time as a scarce resource are less influenced by advertising promoting time effectiveness. Furthermore, the role played by the past or the future impacts perception differently depending on the culture. Our tendency to document the past as a matter of course is not common practice in every culture. The same holds for detailed planning for the future. Products such as photographic equipment, photo albums or building loan contracts are based on a particular concept of time that is not necessarily universally valid.

Attitudes toward Taking Action

Future orientation also reflects the third dimension concerning attitudes to taking action. The belief that change can be brought about and nature can be dominated is very Western. Many Eastern countries, on the other hand, have a fatalistic view in this respect. If the priority is being proactive, then the former will be inclined to intervene where, objectively seen, there is little chance of influencing the situation. For instance, in Western cultures many measures are taken to avoid getting sick. This tendency extends to afflictions upon which outside factors have little influence, allowing a large market to develop for presumed and actual health enhancing products.

Concept of Self and Concept of Otherness

One particularly striking dimension in which cultures differ is the extent to which each adheres to an individualist or collectivist mindset (q.v. Ch. 1.4). European cultures generally are considered individualistic, while Asian cultures are viewed as collectivist.

The relationship of the Chinese consumer to family ties (e.g., Usunier and Walliser 1993, p. 9f.), for example, illustrates the concept of collectivism. For a Chinese person, living in a collectivist environment means:

- *The community has access to or insight into things that the West considers to be of private concern.* In some cases, this may mean more freedom for advertising in matters concerning the consumer's private and intimate issues – provided there are no limitations posed by cultural taboos. This does mean, however, that the desire for privacy, the demarcation of a private sphere from the general public, is not taken for granted in China; hence it is unlikely that a case can be made for a successful advertising campaign.
- *The actions of an individual are not necessarily an indication of their needs and motives.* In influencing consumers it is therefore neither necessary nor effective to influence the motives of individual consumers. Exposing sub-conscious motives or implied attitudes within the scope of market research would provide even less feedback about market behavior than in Europe.
- *The goal of an action is not individual satisfaction but communal harmony.* The improvement of co-existence is, indeed, a realistic motive. Products that cater to this need have a relatively good chance of succeeding. Accordingly, the Chinese respond less to products that are geared toward the individual in contrast to products meant for others. The risk aspect, too, is involved in purchasing products in this respect: While occidental consumers would probably consider a flawed product to be the main problem and would be likely to have no qualms about complaining to the salesperson, a Chinese person would tend to be more reserved in his approach to voicing a complaint. A particular issue for the Chinese is the risk of "losing face". In the case of complaints, both persons involved take this risk (cf. Usunier and Walliser 1993, p. 11).
- *The goal of preserving harmony often takes precedence over task-oriented goals.* This Asian characteristic often poses an obstacle in collaborations. A Swedish representative for IKEA in Beijing, for instance, complains: "So you reach an agreement with a Chinese negotiation partner . . . only to find that the next day he presents you with the very same demands as before – as if the agreement had never been closed" (Wenderoth and Schmitz 2002, p. 269). The agreement of the day before was possibly a gesture toward achieving harmonious cooperation in order to end the day in mutual understanding.
- *Community is quite naturally given and is taken for granted. Thus, there is no need for gestures of reassurance or gifts.* The European mindset distinguishes between many forms of community that need to be defined and cultivated. Products and services exist in this area that would hardly be marketable in the Chinese sphere of cultural influence.
- *The group looks after the individual and the individual is expected to remain loyal to the group.* Thus, it is not as demanding for the individual

of a collectivist society to be concerned for his own welfare only, or for that matter, for his own future. Because of this, people are less inclined to amass capital or have insurance. It may be assumed that group loyalty is also reflected in product and market loyalty, making it more difficult to crack specific consumer habits in collectivist cultures (cf. Usunier and Walliser 1993, p. 48).

– *The appropriate behavior is conformity, emphasis on the individual is considered inappropriate.* This characteristic is probably the most striking difference to Western cultures. The discrepancy between the mindsets is already evident on the level of colloquial speech. While in Western cultures the saying goes: "The squeaky wheel gets the grease", a Chinese proverb says: "The nail that stands out gets pounded down" (quoted from Baumeister 1995, p. 56). This cultural difference manifests in the differently weighted emphasis on appearing socially acceptable. The need to feel socially accepted regularly distorts market research data. Keillor, Owens and Pettijohn (2001) can show that these distortions are due to intercultural differences.

  In Western cultures it is easy to find a market for products that give the consumer a feeling of being unique or of owning something that is unusual (e.g., Lynn and Harris 1997). In China, this sales approach is far less successful as a remarkable flop on the part of IKEA showed when they advertised their Christmas special: IKEA added blown glass sparkling wine glasses to their assortment at short notice. Unfortunately, the Chinese are not particularly fond of sparkling wine. However, the learning effect gained from the reaction of Chinese customers to the valuable handmade items was even more beneficial: The customized glasses inevitably had small flaws that indicate to the connoisseur that the product is indeed unique. The Chinese consumers, however, interpreted these characteristics as an entirely unnecessary perfection deficit (Wenderoth and Schmitz 2002).

In this pointed illustration, the contrast between collectivist and individualistic cultures are not found in the respective nations and not even in the usual overt style of television advertising. Cho et al. (1999) compared Korean and American advertising spots and found definite individualistic and collectivist traits in both. They differed only in the relative emphasis placed on content.

1.3.7 Intercultural Validity of Consumer Psychology: General Psychological Effects

The psychological rules of consumer behavior can be viewed as generally valid, albeit according to different parameters.

Traditionally, so-called general psychology assumes that the universal laws it treats in its discussions pertain to all individuals. Accordingly, general psychological effects should be easily transferable to intercultural marketing as well.

However, culture functions as an important moderator of a variety of postulates considered valid by general psychology. Here, for instance, Africans are said to be less susceptible to particular types of optical illusions than Europeans (Segall et al. 1990). The set way in which habits of perception manifest play an important role here. Conditioned patterns of information processing may also be responsible for culture-dependent, intellectual performance. Such differences do indeed exist. Usually, the differences are "factored out" by determining different testing norms for different cultures.

Using advertising as an essential marketing instrument requires that the general validity of specific rules of information processing address the entire target population. If the rule stipulates that the first and last elements in a linear presentation are easier to remember than the middle section, then one should be able to assume that this is similar all over the world. This known effect recommends placing the most important message, such as the name of the product and the manufacturer, at the end of the advertising spot (for an overview see Felser 2001).

Tavassoli, however, was able to show that in the case of a purely spoken presentation, the memory channels of Chinese and American individuals differed considerably depending on the serial position of the information presented. While for the Americans, the placement of words was relatively closely related to the channels of longer-term memory, for the Chinese, the semantic connection between concepts was important for retaining the message.

Ad design, in contrast to advertising spots, recommends placing information that is usually perceived early on in the upper left-hand side (e.g., Meyer-Hentschel Management Consulting 1993). This recommendation, however, is based on an effect that is likely to stem from cultural conditioning. According to theoretic speculation, the viewer tends to fix his sight on objects placed in the upper left-hand side as a matter of habit. Should the "eye-catcher", a picture perhaps, appear in another spot of the ad, then the eye is automatically drawn to it and then, generally, does not return to the habitual spot, so that the content of the message on the upper left-hand side disappears from view.

This rule should, of course, not apply in cultures where the reading order does not begin on the upper left side. Empirical findings for this assumption exist for Japan, where readers might be more inclined to begin viewing from the upper right-hand side in keeping with their reading habits.

Mind you: Here, findings based on general psychology mingle with culture-specific ones. A picture in an ad is, however, bound to draw attention in all cultures. In order to call attention to other elements in the ad, the picture will be placed on the left-hand side in our cultural sphere of influence, whereas it is more likely to be placed on the right-hand side in Japan.

Another perception characteristic that is important for advertising design concerns the emotional effect of color. Here too, there are intercultural differences, aside from a range of similarities: Adams and Osgood (1973) report from a study conducted in 23 different cultures that there is a largely unanimous preference for lighter as opposed to darker colors. Most countries unanimously evaluated black as negative. Still there were exceptions (Hindus from Delhi).

1.3.8 Social Cognition

A number of socio-psychological techniques of influencing consumers have been checked for intercultural effect. Here too, it can be assumed that the basic principles are universally valid. The validity of persistence mechanisms, (cognitive dissonance, foot-in-the-door approach), consensus heuristic (e.g., the tendency to like something simply because others do) or the law of reciprocity (Cialdini 2001), for instance, is well established.

At the same time, the respective culture, too, constitutes a significant moderator variable. The fact that negotiation partners can be put under pressure according to the law of reciprocity by granting favors and making concessions is universal. The amount of pressure felt, however, differs from one culture to the next. In a comparison between Poland and the U. S., Cialdini et al. (2001) were able to show that consensus heuristic and principles of persistence have an influencing effect in both countries. Here too, however, the moderating effect of culture was evident. The willingness in Poland to adhere to a prior commitment was greater than in the U. S.

The mechanisms of influencing are mainly effective in social relationships, such as between salespeople and customers. The relationship factor plays a significant role for the success of market trade in all cultures. In Asian cultures, such as China, the relationship is more important than the product that is being negotiated. The relationship itself, on the other hand, is defined according to own, culture-specific rules that are considerably more coherent than is usually the case in Western cultures. According to findings by Merrilees and Miller (1999), the salesperson-customer relationship in Western cultures is impacted by largely independent factors such as: "reciprocity, trust, friendliness and good rapport". In contrast, Asian cultures differentiate less between types of relationships.

1.3.9 Forecast

In general, one could say that the conditions for the equalization of markets are improving steadily and that we are well on our way to homogenization. Hence, it is less a question of the markets adapting, but rather of what factors stand in the way of total homogenization and make intercultural marketing necessary. These factors create the "field of work" for intercultural marketing.

For large corporations like Nestlé, the home market has long since accounted for only a small portion of total turnover. In Germany, for instance, at least a third of the GNP is derived from the export of products and services (Müller and Kornmeier 1995). In the case of IKEA, the proportion that the Chinese market contributes to global turnover amounts to only one percent. If, however, 20% of the world population could be convinced of the advantages of Swedish-Western home décor, then huge profits could be expected, even if below average turnover were attributed to the individual buyer.

References

Adams, F. M.; Osgood, C. E. (1973): A cross-cultural study of the affective meanings of color. Journal of Cross-Cultural Psychology 4: 135–156.

Baumeister, R. F. (1995): Self and identity: An introduction. In: Tesser, A. (Ed.), Advanced Social Psychology. New York, pp. 51–97.

Cho, B.; Kwon, U.; Gentry, J. W.; Jun, S.; Kropp, F. (1999): Cultural values reflected in theme and execution: A comparative study of U.S. and Korean television commercials. Journal of Advertising 28: 59–73.

Cialdini, R. B. (2001): Influence – Science and Practice. 4th ed. Needham Heights, MA.

Cialdini, R. B.; Wosinska, W.; Butner, J.; Gornik-Durose, M. (2001): The differential impact of two social influence principles on individualists and collectivists in

Poland and the United States. In: Wosinska, W. et al. (Eds.), The Practice of Social Influence in Multiple Cultures. Mahwah, NJ, pp. 33–50.
Felser, G. (2001): Werbe- und Konsumentenpsychologie. 2nd ed. Heidelberg/ Stuttgart.
Guerhan-Canli, Z.; Maheswaran, D. (2000): Cultural variations in country of origin effects. Journal of Marketing Research 37: 309–317.
Jinlong, X. (1994): Coca-Cola, Minirock und Toffee. Die Bedeutung der Übersetzung von internationalen Warenbezeichnungen für den Markterfolg in China. Unijournal – Zeitschrift der Universität Trier 3: 18–20.
Keillor, B.; Owens, D.; Pettijohn, C. (2001): A cross-cultural/cross-national study of influencing factors and socially desirable response biases. International Journal of Market Research 43: 63–84.
Kohli, C.; LaBahn, D. W.; Thakor, M. (2001): Prozeß der Namensgebung. In Esch, F.-R. (Ed.), Moderne Markenführung: Grundlagen – innovative Ansätze – praktische Umsetzungen. 3rd ed. Wiesbaden, pp. 451–474.
Lynn, M.; Harris, J. (1997): The desire for unique consumer products: A new individual differences scale. Psychology and Marketing 14: 601–616.
Merrilees, B.; Miller, D. (1999): Direct selling in the West and East: The relative roles of product and relationship (Guanxi) drivers. Journal of Business Research 45: 267–273.
Meyer-Hentschel Management Consulting (1993): Erfolgreiche Anzeigen: Kriterien und Beispiele zur Beurteilung und Gestaltung. Wiesbaden.
Müller, S.; Kornmeier, M. (1995): Internationales Konsumgütermarketing. In: Hermanns, A.; Wissmeier, U. K. (Eds.), Internationales Marketing Management. München, pp. 339–386.
Segall, M. H.; Dasen, P. R.; Berry, J. W.; Poortinga, Y. H. (1990): Human Behavior in Global Perspective. New York.
Tajfel, H. (1981): Human Groups and Social Categories. Studies in Social Psychology. Cambridge.
Tavassoli, N. T. (1999): Temporal and associative memory in Chinese and English. Journal of Consumer Research 26: 170–181.
Usunier, J.-C.; Walliser, B. (1993): Interkulturelles Marketing. Mehr Erfolg im internationalen Geschäft. Wiesbaden.
Wenderoth, A.; Schmitz, W. (2002): Der lange Marsch zu »Billy«. Wohnkultur in China. Geo Jan. 2000: 162–174.
Yamanake, J. (1962): The prediction of ad readership scores. Journal of Advertising Research 2: 18–23.

2. Central Areas of Management from an Intercultural Perspective

Stefan Kammhuber

2.1 Intercultural Rhetoric

Your presentation should convince the audience? Then you might want to take a look at the following basic rules:
- Keep a low profile!
- Praise the listeners!
- Apologize for the incompleteness of your presentation!
- Don't speak up!
- Keep gestures to a minimum!

Is this what you learned in seminars on presentation techniques? Perhaps you were told not to dampen the participants' expectations from the outset (e.g., Allhoff and Allhoff 2000)? The reason for the confusion caused here could be that the basic rules were laid down with a Chinese audience in mind, who expect particularly modest and polite behavior from an important speaker. A presenter who launches into a dynamic opening, interspersed with reference to personal performance and ability, is considered to be neither competent nor likable from the Chinese perspective. The first impression is the most lasting, impacting perception and assessment of a person. In this case, the speaker would have missed his target entirely and would have little chance of convincing his audience in the future.

"Rhetoric is the ability to find something possibly worth believing in, in every object". This is how Aristoteles (1995) defined the character and goal of rhetoric in the first systematic work on the subject. Aristotelian rhetoric is based on three ways of convincing an audience and manifest in
- the speaker's character: How convincing is he or she as a person to the audience?
- the audience: What are the expectations, what is the mood and what previous knowledge do they have?

– in the speech itself: How persuasive are content and sequence of the arguments presented?

However, the situational and cultural context determine which arguments are convincing, the expectations preceding the interaction, the speaker's manner and whether it is appropriate to both content and situation, and how rapport is created between the speaker and his audience. This, in turn, comprises the intention and the reason for verbal interaction: the social role assumed by the speaker in relation to his audience, for example, if he is a colleague or supervisor; at which point the speech takes place, for example, a first contact; the location, for example, in a ballroom, in a production facility or at a conference center. Different forms of presentation and behavior are indicated according to the way the situation unfolds. The elements involved in a verbal interaction are illustrated in the communication model developed by Geissner (1981) (Figure 12):

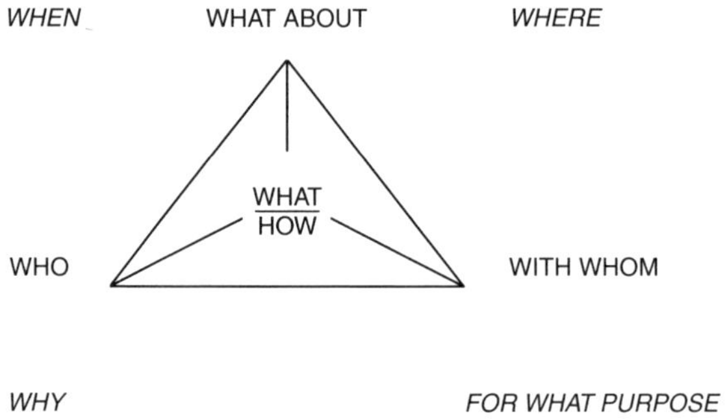

Figure 12: Communication model according to Geissner (1981)

The model can be used to analyze intercultural communication situations and to prepare for a presentation. During the preparation phase, each element should be tested for its cultural sensitivity, such as which patterns of behavior correspond to speaking in the supervisor or employee role in a specific country.

2.1.1 The Speaker

The Speaker in the Eyes of the Audience

Psychological studies conducted to find out what convinces people have shown that the audience is more likely to be convinced if they perceive the speaker as credible, similar to themselves or as demonstrating power (Hovland and Weiss 1951). In a classic experiment, American test persons were divided into two experimental groups. They were given texts about different current controversial themes, for example, about the possibility of building atomically powered submarines. The text was identical, only the authors were different. While one text was passed off as an article from "Prawda", the other group believed they were reading a text from the famous atomic physicist, R. J. Oppenheimer. When asked if they agreed with the opinion in the text, 77.8% of the subjects agreed with the Oppenheimer text while only 50% agreed with the "Prawda" text. In a previous test, the researchers assessed the credibility of specific sources of information in the U. S. and found that 93.7% believed Oppenheimer to be credible in contrast to "Prawda", which only 1.7% found to be a serious source of information at the beginning of the Cold War.

These results clearly indicate that the audience's predisposition toward the speaker plays a significant role in the rhetorical effect. In an intercultural situation, it is necessary to take the audience's preexisting concept of otherness regarding the speaker into consideration. An Indonesian senior executive gave his German colleagues the following advice:

"When Germans come to Indonesia they should be aware of the fact that they are normally taller, louder, better educated and wealthier than a comparable Indonesian. Therefore they should be aware that these factors in themselves might be construed as arrogance. Such feelings are readily enforced by corresponding behavior" (Thomas et al. 1998, p. 284).

These statements attest to the fact that a multitude of verbal and especially nonverbal indicative stimuli generate or reinforce the audience's impression and are interpreted according to own-culture socialization, forming the basis of the person's behavior.

Verbal and Nonverbal Signals

In Germany an individual is perceived as more convincing the less he uses belittling additions such as "maybe", "about", or "probably" in his argumentation. In contrast, the Japanese use such expressions consciously in order to avoid premature commitment that could lead to opposition and harmony-threatening conflict (Okabe 1983). It has nothing to do with less certainty.

To reinforce statements ("I swear by God") is important in Arab countries, for example, in order not to create the impression that one actually disagrees. To Germans this kind of behavior seems exaggerated and thus less credible. From the Arab perspective, however, the speaker is perceived as emotionally uninvolved, distant and difficult to interpret (Gudykunst 1994).

Nonverbal and paralinguistic indicative stimuli, in particular, such as gestures, mimicry, eye contact, proxemics, voice pitch, volume and speed, cause the audience to make a judgment about the personality and competence of the speaker within seconds. In a psychological experiment, American test persons were asked to judge politicians from different countries, who they had never seen before and who were presented to them in short, muted video clips. The speaker's nationality was not revealed in the clip. The evaluation turned up surprising similarities: the American politicians were judged as "intelligent", "competent" and "powerful" by the American test persons, the French as "compassionate", "energetic" and "cheerful" while the Germans had frequent hits on adjectives such a "boring", "ugly" and "cold" (Frey 1999).

Nonverbal signals accompany speech (gestures, mimicry, proxemics), emphasize or minimize the meaning of what is being said or even replace speech altogether (nodding for "yes"). Different cultures have developed specific rules for how to behave in social situations for members of a common system of orientation to facilitate interpretation of perceived behavior (Ekman and Friesen 1978). Signals that replace language, in particular, can lead to misunderstanding. In Indonesia and other Asian cultures the palm of the hand faces the ground and the fingers are contracted inward to motion someone to approach. The Western style of beckoning with an open palm is seen as extremely impolite and arrogant. To express "no" in Greece, the head is raised accompanied by a click of the tongue as opposed to Germany, where declination is expressed by a side-to-side movement of the head. Even more disastrous is the German gesture for "well done", which connotes an obscenity (Italy). For this reason, it is extremely important for a speaker to know and respect different gestures, including the taboos, of the various countries (Axtell 1994).

Fundamentally, cultures can be differentiated according to the extent to which individuals are either expressive or neutral in expressing their sentiments (Trompenaars 1993). Within the German sphere of cultural influence a speaker tends to be more convincing if he seeks out and maintains eye contact with his audience, uses natural and authentic gestures, displays mimicry that corresponds with what he is saying, has a deeper voice, modulates and increases the volume of his voice in argumentative situations and lowers the volume at the end to emphasize statements that carry significant meaning. Excessive eye contact might be construed as presumptuous and, as in the case of Japan, the volume or voice pitch might signal aggression. It is particularly important in intercultural verbal interaction to keep in mind that the intended message does not always correspond with the impression it evokes in the receiver.

However, it would hardly make sense to imitate the other culture's nonverbal behavior because of these differences. The outcome would, no doubt, be the famous Japanese in *Lederhosen* or the bowing German in a Kimono, a scenario that is taken in stride, but hardly considered serious. A better idea might be to become aware of one's own presentation style, for example, by using video feedback and knowing how an other-culture audience expects a convincing speaker to behave, and finally, to be able to direct behavior through moderate gesturing and volume while speaking. A study conducted with French and Spanish language learners showed that even with fluent foreign language skills, one's own culture-typical non-verbal communication patterns persist (Frey et al. 1993).

2.1.2 Presenting Content

Clear Speaking

Intercultural rhetorical situations are particularly difficult when communication is in a foreign language or mediated by an interpreter. To "smooth the way", it is a good idea to be aware of the four most important signals for understanding when speaking and prepare accordingly: simple expression, structure and sequencing, brevity and clarity, as well as the interesting presentation of content (Langer et al. 1990). This means that a presentation needs to be checked in advance for expressions to make sure that the expressions used have the same connotation for the other-culture audience. The more abstract the concepts are, such as "democracy" or "justice", the more important it is to clarify connotation.

Presenting the subject matter in visuals, particularly in intercultural settings, is a good way to achieve maximum understanding. In using visuals, however, it is important to be aware of the audience's culture-specific conditioning when, for instance, inserting cartoons. Cartoons are culture-specific products and may be perceived as insulting by an audience instead of an exaggeration intended as irony. Jokes and humor of any kind require special attention, as humor is a cultural commodity and if misunderstood, or not understood at all, may well be the cause of intense embarrassment.

Argumentative Reasoning

In order to be convincing, the object under discussion must stand up to a line of reasoning. Argumentation in theory and practice constitutes the pil-

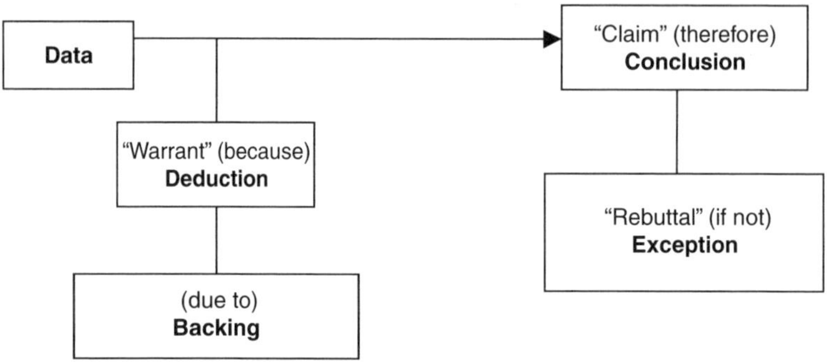

Figure 13: Argumentation pattern

lar of rhetoric. Toulmin (1996) analyzed everyday patterns of argumentative reasoning and found the following basic pattern (Figure 13).

Argumentative reasoning always contains a given (data) and a conclusion, which is more or less drawn from the diverse exceptions to the rule. The persuasiveness of an argument depends on how compelling the connection is between the data and the conclusion. This deduction, which is usually unspoken in everyday conversation, is a result of culture-specific agreement. It is upheld by collective norms and value patterns, which defy generalization. These supportive deductions are called "topoi" and represent the ground for argumentation. "Topoi" catalogues were assembled to portray the rhetorical common sense of a given society as early as Hellenistic and Roman times (Ueding and Steinbrink 1994).

Let us consider the sentence uttered by an annoyed German manager to his colleague while watching a member of the board drive by: "Hey, take a look at Mr. XY. He just fouled up the million dollar project in Mexico and now he's driving around in a posh company car . . ."

Data: Mr. XY fouled up a project.
Conclusion: So he should not get a company car.
Deduction: Only someone who completes a project successfully should be rewarded.
Backing: Privileges must be legitimized according to performance.
Exception: The deduction in only valid if Mr. XY has not been of service or merit to the company earlier.

It is precisely this "topos" underlying deduction that is culturally specific and the result of a protestant work ethic according to which a place in heaven must be earned by the sweat of one's brow. In cultures with a high power distance, in which hierarchical differences are natural and one's status in society is symbolized by privileges and aligns with group rules according to family, religious or other membership affiliations, this kind of argumentation finds little resonance. In presentations or speeches that take a particular stance, it is therefore important to make sure the underlying "topoi" can also be used in the other culture. Marketing campaigns, in particular, represent cumulative sequences of argumentation instances and therefore it is necessary to check the culture-specific elements underlying their "topoi". In international politics too, ethnocentric argumentation can cause irritation: The initial cover name for the military action against the Al-Qaida organization in Afghanistan in 2001 was called "Infinite Justice". The conclusion underlying this reasoning is: The U. S. and its allies stand for justice. They ensure all-encompassing justice and whoever is on their side is equally just. This description, however, provoked vehement protest, particularly in the Islamic world because, according to their belief, only Allah can offer and guarantee unlimited justice. In response, the military operation was renamed.

A style of reasoning becomes evident in the process of a presentation and follows culture-specific thought patterns. According to Galtung (1983) there are four different cultural traditions that convey specific thought and reasoning styles:

- Anglo-Saxon style, e.g., the U. S. and England
- Gallic style, e.g., France
- Nipponese style, e.g., Japan, China
- Teutonic style, e.g., Germany

The Anglo-Saxon style of reasoning is dominant in England and the U. S. It has a strong empirical orientation, i.e., statements of reality must be backed by relevant data and facts. The development of far-reaching theories and models of thought are subordinated to detached and detailed questioning, which can hold up under investigation. In a figurative analogy, the individual who thinks according to the Anglo-Saxon style aligns many separate little theory pyramids.

The Gallic style, typical for the French, is characterized as a vast, far-reaching and above all linguistically aesthetic structure of theory that, instead of resolving contradiction or opposition, tries to elegantly circumscribe or keep things in balance.

The Nipponese style of reasoning and thought pattern can be found in many Asian cultures and tends to assume a more holistic approach, avoiding the separation of facts into individual entities. Reasoning tends toward ambiguity, as a direct statement about how the world functions would appear immodest and presumptuous to individuals with this thought pattern. Learning proceeds according to a specific school, which means that persuasive power of reasoning depends on the school one attended or which famous master one has followed up to now.

In contrast, the Teutonic thought pattern, particularly in German-speaking countries, tends to concentrate on constructing clearly structured, logically persuasive frameworks. If, in spite of sound theory, assumptions cannot be backed empirically, then, in the case of doubt, theory is given priority over data that is influenced by the multitude of uncertainties of everyday life. The theory pyramid that develops from this has a peak, a well-structured foundation and is very large and solidly built. As Galtung describes it quite accurately:

"There is so much at risk! Should something prove to be invalid, this would not be a great catastrophe for the other three styles. For the Anglo-Saxon intellectual, just one pyramid would be destroyed, and he could immediately set about constructing another little pyramid from the ruins. The Nipponese intellectual, at the very least, has a very flexible wheel that turns through all sorts of facts. The Gallic intellectual will generally be able to disguise any difficulties he is having in additional, very elegant formulations that are ambiguous and flamboyant enough to be acknowledged as *votre presentation magistrale*. Therefore, it is not surprising that the Teutonic individual approaches his work with a certain inner nervousness, which manifests in muscle tension, distancing and a face absent of the last remnants of humor. No amount of analogy, euphemism nor playful juggling with definitions – nothing can veil the disaster that may tumble the Teutonic pyramid" (Galtung 1983, p. 24).

In a nutshell, the individuals to whom the four styles pertain ask themselves the following questions:

- Anglo-Saxon style: "How can that be orchestrated?" (U.S. version);"How can that be evidenced?" (UK version);
- Teutonic style: "How did you arrive at that?"
- Gallic style: "Can this be formulated so that the French can understand it?"
- Nipponese style: "Who is your master/teacher?"

These different patterns of thought and reasoning emerge and become problematic where intercultural encounters are involved, for instance in formal speeches, meetings or presentations. In a worst-case scenario, the Anglo-Saxon is perceived by the Teutonic listener as not interested in the long-term, and vice-versa, the Teutonic speaker comes across as an "overdose of humorless intellectuality". The Gallic speaker is perceived as full of hot air by the Teutonic listener while the Teutonic speaker comes across as simply boring. The Nipponese speaker is perceived as illogical and unstructured while the Teutonic speaker is considered unpleasantly presumptuous and arrogant.

In order to avoid such misjudgments, it might be a good idea to review one's line of reasoning with the audience in mind. Is there enough data and statistical backup in the academic presentation to meet the expectations of an Anglo-Saxon audience? Or can a presentation to a French audience be designed with more versatility than the standard "I have divided my speech into three main parts. Firstly . . ."?

2.1.3 The Audience

Rhetorical success lies not in the speaker's eloquence but in how the message is perceived by the audience. A presentation hits its mark only if its message has struck a cord with the audience; in other words, they understand the message fully and can relate to it. In order for an exchange to take place at all, the audience must be willing to follow the speaker, which cannot be automatically assumed, as the following critical incident experienced by a German manager in the People's Republic of China illustrates:

"After having gotten acquainted with my department here in China, I couldn't help noticing how curious my approximately 300 Chinese employees were about me and my responsibilities. So, I decided to call a meeting on a Saturday afternoon to introduce myself and my work. That Saturday we were sitting in our large conference room where the employees were assembled. My Chinese deputy read his speech very meticulously from sheets of paper, which had been prepared well in advance and actually contained all pertinent information. This approach reminded me of a Sunday school litany. To my horror, I noticed that the faces in the audience were gradually going blank. Heads sank further forward and some simply laid their heads down on the table and slept. I tried to think of something I might possibly add to my deputy's speech. Meanwhile, half the team was asleep. Suddenly, it was my turn. Deliberately, I stood up rather boisterously, looked around the room and said nothing. There was absolute silence. All of those who were not yet asleep looked up in expectation. I waited to see what would happen next, but nothing happened. Finally, I started in: 'I am here of my own volition this afternoon . . . it is my day off. I realize, of course, that you have a difficult week behind you and the last two hours weren't the easiest either, however, I would like to ask you for your patience to listen to what I have to say. I would ask those of you who do not want to listen any longer to leave the room'. My interpreter's eyes widened in amazement, whereupon I asked him to translate exactly what I had said. Gradually some of the people woke up while others snoozed on unperturbed. I took the next step and pointed to some of the people and said, 'If you think you can take the liberty to sleep here, then please leave the room immediately!' To my amazement everyone remained seated and began laughing" (Thomas and Schenk 2001, p. 124 ff.).

The behavior of the Chinese audience can be explained by looking at China's history where, in the past, but more specifically during the communist regime, regular meetings or gatherings for civil servants and high-ranking officials was the rule in order to introduce new regulations. This tradition has carried over into state-owned enterprises. The audience knows that presentations of this nature deal mostly with superfluous and uninteresting propaganda. The "sleepy" reaction is therefore quite understandable. The German manager is totally off track, he thinks that his audience can decide on their own whether or not to leave the room. Such behavior would be absolutely impolite and the laughter in response may be seen as an attempt to deal with an embarrassing situation (cf. Thomas and Schenk 2001).

The length of a speech or presentation depends on the culture-specific attention span. Thus, according to Lewis (2000), an American or Australian audience is accustomed to shorter presentations than a German audience.

Questioning or discussions following a presentation often confront the speaker with a difficult and uncertain task since he is obliged to take a position ad hoc without prior preparation. During this phase in intercultural discourse, culture-specific characteristics may arise, which the speaker should be aware of in order to respond appropriately to comments from the audience. A French or German audience, for instance, will not hesitate to point out discrepancies or voice counter arguments directly, which the speaker must respond to. On the other hand, an American or British audience will tend to praise aspects of the presentation before following up with criticism where they feel it is necessary and a Japanese speaker is likely to hear very few questions and still less criticism following his presentation. Here too, contrary to American custom, the audience is less inclined to express enthusiasm und uncritical acceptance about what has been heard, but rather, politeness toward the speaker is considered a matter of higher order in an effort not to embarrass him publicly.

2.1.4 Preparing for the Intercultural Presentation

Thorough preparation is required for maintaining individual style and persuasiveness in the context of an intercultural presentation, which the following key questions offer advice to:

1. In what role do I speak to whom, why and when? What culture-specific

behavioral patterns are expected of me? Can I, and more specifically, do I want to meet such expectations with the behavioral repertoire I have at my disposal?
2. What makes a credible and convincing speaker in the target culture?
3. How well do I know my accustomed public speaking style, in particular with regard to verbal and non-verbal signals?
4. How well can I direct it during a presentation?
5. How flexible am I in my rhetorical possibilities?
6. Does the prepared presentation meet the criteria of intelligibility?
7. What meaning and impact do my arguments take on in the target culture?
8. How is feedback given in the target culture? How well am I able to assess this feedback?

An outside view of the personal rhetorical style can be obtained via video feedback in presentation trainings or on-the-job coaching. Together with a trainer team consisting of one trainer from the target culture and one from the native culture, personal style can be reviewed while exploring and trying out alternative approaches for different target groups and occasions. The idea here is not to replace the individual presentation style that he or she has acquired over the course of his or her socialization process by a collection of cultural do's and don'ts in order to reconstruct a "cultural show". Ultimately, the goal is to expand the personal repertoire of behavioral alternatives, allowing the presenter to express his intentions in terms that will reach and be understood by the other-culture audience.

References

Allhoff, D.-W.; Allhoff, W. (2000): Rhetorik und Kommunikation. Regensburg.

Aristoteles: Rhetorik. München, 1995.

Axtell, R. E. (1994): Reden mit Händen und Füßen. Körpersprache in aller Welt. München.

Ekman, P.; Friesen, W. V. (1978): Facial Action Coding System. Palo Alto.

Frey, S. (1999): Die Macht des Bildes. Der Einfluß der nonverbalen Kommunikation auf Kultur und Politik. Bern.

Frey, S.; Raveau, A.; Kempter, G.; Darnaud, C.; Argentin, G. (1993): Mise en évidence du traitment cognitif et affectif du non-verbal. msh-informations. Bulletin de la Fondation Maison des sciences de l'hommes 70: 4–23.

Galtung, J. (1983): Struktur, Kultur und intellektueller Stil. Ein vergleichender Essay über sachsonische, teutonische, gallische und nipponische Wissenschaft.

Geissner, H. (1981): Rhetorik und politische Bildung. 2nd ed. Königstein/Taunus.

Gudykunst, W. B. (1994): Bridging Differences. Thousand Oaks.
Hovland, C. I.; Weiss, W. (1951): The influence of source credibility on communication effectiveness. Public Opinion Quarterly 15: 635–650.
Langer, I.; Schulz v. Thun, F.; Tausch, R. (1990): Sich verständlich ausdrücken. München.
Lewis, R. D. (2000): Handbuch internationale Kompetenz. Frankfurt a. M.
Okabe, R. (1983): Cultural assumptions of east and west: Japan and the United States. In: Gudykunst, W. B. (Ed.), Intercultural Communication Theory. Beverly Hills.
Thomas, A.; Layes, G.; Kammhuber, S. (1998): Sensibilisierungs- und Orientierungstraining für die kulturallgemeine und kulturspezifische Vorbereitung von Soldaten für Auslandseinsätze. Untersuchungen des Psychologischen Dienstes der Bundeswehr, 33. München.
Thomas, A.; Schenk, E. (2001): Beruflich in China. Trainingsprogramm für Manager, Fach- und Führungskräfte. Göttingen.
Toulmin, S. (1996): Der Gebrauch von Argumenten. Weinheim.
Trompenaars, F. (1993): Handbuch Globales Managen. Düsseldorf.
Ueding, G.; Steinbrink, B. (1994): Grundriß der Rhetorik. Stuttgart.

Stefan Kammhuber

2.2 Intercultural Negotiation

2.2.1 Culture and Negotiation Strategies

When Chancellor of the Federal Republic of Germany, Gerhard Schröder, took office in 1998, he proclaimed in allusion to his predecessor, Helmut Kohl, that he did not intend to conduct international politics by languishing in the sauna with the Russian president. Three years later the same chancellor headed an extremely successful economic delegation that resulted in billion dollar business deals in the People's Republic of China. The success of this venture was largely attributed to the good personal rapport between Schröder and Premier Zhu Rongji, which is illustrated in the following negotiation opening:

"Once the delegations were seated across from each other, as was the custom, and Zhu had ended his welcoming speech, Schröder announced his greeting emphasizing that, even more than attending the economic delegation, he looked forward to his wife's arrival the next day. Here Schröder alluded to an extraordinary meeting between the couples in the Schröders' private residence in Hannover the year before, whereupon Zhu sidetracked from the official agenda and responded: 'What a pity that your daughter is unable to attend this time'. Schröder responded: 'As you know, we are very disciplined'. The Schröders' daughter was attending school at the time and could not miss classes" (Süddeutsche Zeitung, 11.2.2001).

This example out of the arena of international economic policy offers insight into the influence that cultural norms and values exert on a negotiation situation. Schröder's statement at the beginning of his term in office is typical in the German cultural sphere, where the attitude prevails that creating personal rapport with the negotiation partner has no place in a negotiation. This would tend to undermine the negotiator's flexibility in directing a rational, task-oriented negotiation process toward a successful outcome. In many other cultures, such as China, for instance, creating sustainable personal rapport with negotiation partners is a key factor in successful negotiating as well as reaching and implementing agreements.

A situation can be referred to as a negotiation if the following criteria are met (Rubin and Brown, 1975):

- At least two people are involved.
- There is a conflict of interest.
- The parties voluntarily enter a relationship over a certain period of time.
- This relationship deals with dividing or exchanging specific resources and/or resolving problematic issues between the parties or those whom they represent.
- The negotiation process usually comprises a presentation of demands or offers from one party followed by agreement or counteroffers. This process proceeds sequentially rather than simultaneously.

The influence of cultural factors on the negotiation process is often underestimated. An international negotiation culture has evolved as a result of the impact of globalization on many business sectors. Other factors, such as national, political and specific organizational interests or proportion of power, take priority over cultural aspects (e.g., Zartmann 1993). In fact, the negotiation process is determined by a multitude of outside influences, and there is such a thing as an international agreement regarding how international negotiations are to proceed. This argument, however, ignores the fact that every negotiation is also a social encounter during which people communicate with each other at all times. These individuals inevitably bring in their cultural biography, which they cannot simply shed but must more or less painstakingly adapt to a particular negotiation model that was created in a specific cultural environment. The prerequisite here is that they are familiar with the negotiation model to which they are called upon to adapt. If there is no standardized negotiation culture, the more likely it is that culture-specific norms, values and rules will begin to take hold, possibly causing misunderstanding or conflict, and eventually lead to a sub-optimal result or even outright failure.

Military personnel who were on a KFOR-mission in Croatia reported on an incident involving the rental of a warehouse from a local:

"... we weren't ready to commit to a price at such short notice, but wanted to stall for time. Well, the stalling then came from the other side in that he simply did not show up, missed appointments, cancelled price agreements the very next day or refused to remember what had been previously agreed upon. Right from the beginning, he either arrived late or did not show up at all. When he did finally show up, he let us know that he was strapped for time and would meet with us the next day. The following day was no different. We are not used to these kinds of negotiation practices and, as soldiers, have never experienced this before. I have never been in a situation where I have had to haggle and there it was simply the order of the day. We were made fools of" (Thomas et al. 1997, p. 123).

2.2.2 Elements of a Negotiation Situation

Preparing for a successful negotiation in the international context involves good planning and examining the structure of the negotiation in advance to determine possible cultural influences. The following basic components can be differentiated: negotiation context, actors, object of the negotiation, strategy, process and interpreter/mediator (Thomas et al 1997; Faure and Sjöstedt 1993).

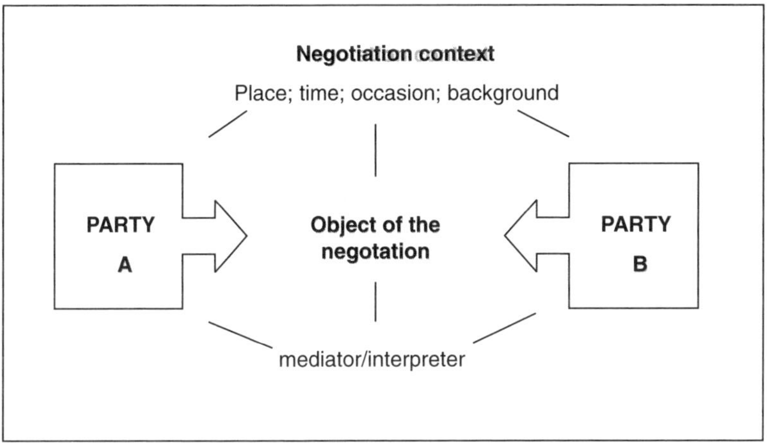

Figure 14

The Negotiation Context

Negotiations take place in predetermined situational contexts that are determined by time, place and the persons involved in the negotiation as well as the negotiation partners, the social, political and economic interest groups or the media. In mono-cultural negotiations, one can be sure that all involved have more or less the same expectations regarding the context. In intercultural negotiations, the partners can certainly have different expectations of the negotiation situation. Hence, depending on where the negotiation takes place, the location may take on a culture-specific symbolism that defines a particular relationship between the negotiation partners. Timing also plays an important role, such as in the case of a negotiation taking place in the People's Republic of China around Christmas time. The German delegation will, no doubt, feel pressured to reach a quicker decision (Thomas and Schenk 2001). Another consideration is how long a negotiation is usually expected to last in a given culture, how many people are involved in the negotiating and what language is spoken.

Actors

Each negotiation partner contributes his unique company-specific, social or national system of orientation that determines thinking, judgment, feeling and action. If one judges the behavior of other partners according to one's own system of orientation, then there is a good chance that this will result in misunderstanding or conflict and eventually cause negotiations to fail. In German/Chinese joint ventures, important decisions must be reviewed by many individuals within a complicated hierarchical structure, which often leads to elaborate and drawn-out discussions.

If the channels of decision-making are misinterpreted because the approach is unfamiliar and construed as a maneuver to "wear the Germans down", then the ambience surrounding the negotiation is likely to turn negative, which in turn can cause behavioral reactions on the part of the Germans that are interpreted as rude or inflexible by the Chinese. Included in such behavior is demanding criteria or tight deadlines.

The lesson here is that in order to negotiate successfully, it is extremely important to examine one's own culturally conditioned negotiation style, in advance, for appropriateness and strategies or behavioral quirks that are likely to be problematic and influence the ambience negatively. This requires an in-depth understanding of the other-culture negotiation style. The more information there is about one's own and the other cultures' modus operandi, the more alternatives for action become available, allowing for more flexibility during negotiations. This information includes knowledge of culture-typical decision-making processes, strategies, (non-verbal) communication habits in presentations and discussions concerning offers and counteroffers and/or recording results from the encounter.

The way in which the negotiation delegation is represented is already subject to cultural influences such as whether or not women assume a significant role or whether competence, position in the hierarchy or party membership are the decisive criteria for a higher position within the negotiation team. Ignoring or not addressing these factors as well as the hierarchical structures appropriately in cultures where there is emphasis on very formal hierarchical levels, such as in Japan, may lead to a strained, if not embarrassing, situation.

Interpreters/Mediators

The role of interpreters in negotiations is usually limited to translating the language rather than acting as envoys for other-culture systems of orientation ("Cultural Interpreter", q.v. Ch. 1, 1.5). Interpreters, in particular, could be of invaluable help in securing a successful negotiation outcome as the following story of a Japanese interpreter illustrates:

"I was in Kyoto with my German delegation where the topics of discussion were youth employment, environmental protection and more. The Germans were already arguing among themselves about the issues even while discussions were going on with the Japanese. So, actually this was an internal issue that had nothing to do with the Japanese. A short break followed during which the argumentation between the Germans escalated and became increasingly verbose. They called each other names in front of their Japanese hosts. The Japanese hate such loud disputes and feel embarrassed in such situations. They would prefer to disappear from the scene entirely. They pretended nothing had happened as the others became increasingly louder. I said, 'That's enough now . . . not one more word! You can do your fighting later but not in front of the Japanese . . .' and they were, in fact, silent. I think it's good that the Germans are so open and can express their opinions but the Japanese are not used to this. They may, after work and a few drinks, become more boisterous and even begin criticizing . . . but certainly not in public."

Interpreters are aware of the culture-specific connotation of expressions and are able to clarify these for both parties when the linguistic translation no longer suffices. They can directly influence the negotiation parties' behavior as in the case above, or modify formulations to avoid misunderstandings or infringement on norms of etiquette. To limit such highly qualified interpreters to routine translation work is a waste of a valuable resource. Selecting an interculturally competent and trustworthy interpreter during the preparation phase is extremely important.

The Negotiation Process

The course of the negotiation can be simplified by dividing it into three phases, which can be interpreted and filled out differently according to the different cultural habits.

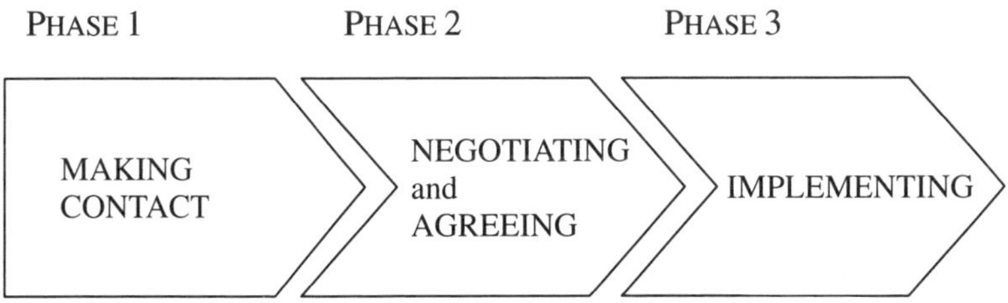

Figure 15: The Three Phases of Negotiating

Establishing Contact and Building Trust

Initiating contact with the intent of opening negotiations is followed by a critical analysis of market conditions and the selection of potential negotiation partners. Already in this phase, different cultural perspectives influence the further course of events. Who might be a "suitable partner"? From a Western perspective, factual criteria, such as competence, cost-containment and quality, qualify an organization as an appropriate negotiation partner. In cultures that tend toward collectivism and whose members, groups or corporations are part of a grown network, such as in Asian countries, partners are often selected on the basis of previous mutual obligation that must now be fulfilled even if other offers are more attractive.

Once initial contact has been made, the priority for both parties is to begin building a mutual trust basis to provide the foundation for successful negotiating. If there is no mutual trust, deception and maneuvering is bound to take its place and the negotiation turns competitive. Furthermore, each culture has different trust-building and trust-maintaining behavior and symbols. In more person-oriented cultures (Thomas et al. 1998), such as in Arab countries or Latin America, it is important to bond with the negotiation partner as a person instead of merely the role he represents for his company. This is often expressed in, what seems to Germans as, long and very personal small talk that has nothing to do with the topic of the negotiation. The trust basis that is created here, however, plays a decisive role in the later successful negotiation outcome. Individuals from very task-oriented cultures, such as Germany, find initial contact rituals and establishing a mutual liking quite difficult. There is not much leeway for interpersonal etiquette in dealing appropriately, elegantly and humorously with such situations. Here, trust tends to arise from the shared understanding of the issue involved and a clear indication of interest and processes.

Negotiating and Agreeing

A negotiation consists of many negotiation sequences comprising suggesting, agreeing/disagreeing/discussion and a summary of agreed-upon points. In this communication process, the cultural aspects of presenting an offer, discussing in favor of own interests, negotiating and non-verbal communication are a priority.

This aspect affects the negotiation span between maximal and minimal demands within which an agreement must be reached and offers and counteroffers are exchanged. German negotiation partners are often perceived as inflexible because the negotiation span is kept quite narrow and the pain threshold is reached after only a few negotiation sequences. Arab countries, on the other hand, tend to go through considerably more negotiation sequences. Negotiating is seen less as a rational pro and con trade-off that must be completed as quickly and effectively as possible, than as a time-consuming procedure designed to create personal relationships.

Implementing Results

The most important goal of a negotiation is the implementation of mutually agreed results. However, this phase may preempt misunderstanding due to mutual distrust. German negotiation parties are more likely to trust their negotiation partners after arriving at a consensus during discussions, which is confirmed in writing and verifiable. The negotiation party merits trust when it becomes evident that conditions have been meticulously followed. Trust is revoked, however, if the partner does not conform to certain conditions or interprets them too generously. This is where the Roman code of law, *Pacta sunt servanda* (contracts must be honored), plays a role. From the perspective of other cultures, the mutual and meticulously drawn up contract is signed at the beginning of the business relationship, not at the end, which led a German lawyer in Shanghai to observe: "Once the contract has been signed, the real problems start". In this sense, contracts hamper the flexibility required for adapting appropriately to ever-changing circumstances. Moreover, a very detailed contract is more likely to be grounds for mistrusting the negotiation partner, who may be pursuing an alternative motive by insisting on such concreteness. Long-term business partnerships, in these cases, are less dependent on the contractual layout than on the rapport that has been established between the partners and which must be cared for.

2.2.3 What Makes a Good Intercultural Negotiation Partner?

Is there such as thing as a born negotiator? Research has revealed that successful and cooperative negotiators have the following abilities and characteristics (Rubin and Brown 1975):
- Controlled risk behavior
- Ability to perceive and judge events in their complexity
- Ambiguity tolerance
- Positive self-image
- Cooperative and nonauthoritarian attitude

In addition, international negotiations require intercultural negotiation competence (q.v. Ch. I, 1.9). The negotiator should know what culture-specific expectations the partners have regarding the setting and the negotiation process. Consequently, a negotiation situation can be created in which all parties can cooperate on a win-win basis. The ability to modify perception is indispensable. The more intensively own and other-culture negotiation interests and their cause and effect patterns have been explored, the more likely it is that when a conflict of interests occurs, alternative solutions will be perceived and put to use for the benefit of both parties.

A successful negotiation is based on thorough preparation, which should include the following questions:

Negotiation context
- What are the expectations with respect to space, time, duration and procedure?
- – How is the outcome of the negotiation recorded?
- How binding are written contracts in a specific culture?
- What is the language of negotiation?

The negotiation issue
- How does the other party define the negotiation issue?
- Must one's own position be modified in order to avoid misunderstanding?

Other-culture negotiation party
- What cultural standards, in particular, influence negotiation behavior?
- What communication style does the other-culture party have?
- How are offers presented in different cultures?
- What culture-specific principles determine the selection of delegates?
- What is the hierarchical structure of the delegation?
- To what extent must behavior be modified to comply with the hierarchy?
- To what extent are the negotiation partners competent and authorized in their scope of responsibility?

One's own negotiation party
- What cultural standards determine one's own negotiation behavior?
- What communication style predominates in the own party?
- Must the style be modified depending on the negotiation partners?
- How is one's own position presented?
- What effect does my presentation have on the target group?
- How is one's own delegation composed?
- Does something need to be changed in the way the delegation is composed in order to avoid misunderstanding and potential conflict?
- Have one's own competencies and responsibilities been clarified in advance?

Role of interpreters and mediators

- Is an interpreter required?
- How competent and trustworthy is the selected interpreter?
- Does he/she have a bi-cultural background in addition to intercultural competence?
- What leeway does the interpreter have to act according to cultural appropriateness?

Improving individual intercultural negotiation skill requires intensive reflection of the negotiation process rather than a focus on the outcome. Qualified interpreters or intercultural coaches can accompany the reflection process as mentors and provide important insight into the development of an operational strategy. Because it is considered an unproductive use of time, organizations are rarely willing to take the time to review their own modus operandi. On the other hand, international collaborations focus mainly on the mid to long term due to the substantial initial investment. A rewarding collaboration can only be created on a solid basis of trust and only if the cultural norms and values of participants are adequately addressed.

References

Fang, T. (1998): Chinese Business Negotiating Style. Thousand Oaks.

Faure, G. O.; Sjöstedt, G. (1993): Culture and Negotiation. An introduction. In: Faure, G. O.; Rubin, J. Z. (Eds.), Culture and Negotiation. Newbury Park, pp. 1–13.

Rubin, J. Z.; Brown, B. R. (1975): The Social Psychology of Bargaining and Negotiation. New York.

Thomas, A.; Schenk, E. (2001): Beruflich in China. Trainingsprogramm für Manager, Fach- und Führungskräfte. Göttingen.

Thomas, A.; Kammhuber, S.; Layes, G. (1997): Interkulturelle Kompetenz: Ein Handbuch für internationale Einsätze der Bundeswehr. Untersuchungen des Psychologischen Dienstes der Bundeswehr, 32. München.

Thomas, A.; Layes, G.; Kammhuber, S. (1998): Sensibilisierungs- und Orientierungstraining für die kulturallgemeine und kulturspezifische Vorbereitung von Soldaten für Auslandseinsätze. Untersuchungen des Psychologischen Dienstes der Bundeswehr, 33. München.

Zartmann, I. W. (1993): International Negotiation: Does culture make a difference? A skeptics view. In: Faure, G. O.; Rubin, J. Z. (Eds.), Culture and Negotiation, 17–22. Newbury Park.

Stefan Kammhuber

2.3 Intercultural Conflict Management and Mediation

Conflict is inevitable where there is human interaction. It originates in situations where the goals of an action appear irreconcilable. The discrepancies can become evident in incompatible individual interests, different objectives, value orientation or how the relationship is defined. Dealing with such conflict productively requires a high level of social competence. Overcoming the conflict situation becomes particularly complex when different cultural systems of orientation are involved and the conflict itself is perceived and integrated differently.

The conflict can differ according to whether only one person (intrapersonal) or two people (interpersonal) are involved. In an intrapersonal conflict the individual experiences contradiction between internalized goals, interests and norms that are not compatible with each other. This condition is a result of the clash of different systems of orientation that make up identity. Thus, the four-year international assignment to Mexico may enhance career perspectives and be the fulfillment of a cherished exotic dream. However, for a father with the responsibility of a family who yanks his child out of its social network or as a friend who leaves his circle of friends behind, this decision might be differently weighted. The result is inner conflict. The intensity with which this conflict is experienced depends on how the action alternatives are weighted in relation to the norms and values of this inner system of orientation. In an encounter with other cultures, in particular, individuals often experience habitual behavior that is contrary to their own and which they feel compelled to reject. Globalization has created new fields of work that challenge or can even threaten the cultural identity of its workforce as illustrated in the example below describing the creation of call centers in India.

"In order to offer competitive customer service, so-called call centers were established by U. S. firms in India, in which young Indians meet the requests of American customers without the customer knowing that his request is processed outside the U. S. in another time zone. Agents at call centers in India are trained, required to assume an American identity complete with a new name and to deny their own identity during working hours. The result of this approach leads to an increasing number of psychosomatic illnesses. According to an Indian psychiatrist, 'most of the people we see here are psycho cases. This job changes the young people psychologically, emotionally and socially. Most of them are unable to cast off their work personality. You just don't walk back out on the streets and become a Hindu'" (SZ, No. 300, Dec. 31, 2001).

A clash of particular goals ignites interpersonal conflict. Because the interaction partners are oblivious of each other's systems of orientation and the different patterns of perception, feeling, thinking and action, misunderstanding is a natural outcome. Trying to clarify misunderstanding invariably leads to further misunderstanding, escalating in an all-out conflict.

2.3.1 Conflict Assessment

Managing conflict situations depends to a large extent on how negatively conflict is viewed in the culture in general because it threatens social harmony, such as is the case in many Asian countries, or if it can even be advantageous and should therefore be carried out openly (a "cleansing storm"). The socialization process in the occidental tradition of dialectic, through which controversial opinions pave the way toward reaching solutions at the next level, leads to acknowledging openly articulated and logically convincing argumentation patterns. Conflict from this perspective can only be applied in a setting where those involved can distinguish between the issue under discussion and personal factors. This approach is often mentioned in reference books on conflict management and negotiation strategies, such as the bestseller by Fisher, Ury and Patton (1995) in which the basic premise is: "Separate the person from the issue!" In collectivist cultures, this is not quite as easy because they are not affected by the Cartesian separation between spirit and matter. Every confrontation with the issue is synonymous with an attack on the person, the relationship and the intrinsic order and harmony within a larger context.

In collectivist societies, in which the separation of the issue and the person does not take place ... and this is the case in most cultures ..., voicing differences of opinion explicitly tends to be frowned upon. The example of a foreign language instructor at an Indonesian university illustrates this situation in a debating session she experienced on the pros and cons of an issue:

"I initiated a pros and cons discussion during class that prompted the class to engage in a lively discussion without any interference on my part.

I facilitated from behind the lines. Suddenly one of the students cried out in alarm: 'We are arguing! We are arguing!' Everyone was shocked as they realized they were engaging in something that is uncommon or actually forbidden in Indonesian culture" (Thomas et al. 1998, p. 285).

A debate will provoke a rift in the group and disrupt the relationship, which in turn is experienced as unpleasant, resulting in silence as a strategy to avoid conflict.

2.3.2 Perceiving Conflict

Individuals with different systems of orientation will systematically perceive and focus on different aspects of a conflict situation. Individuals from more individualist societies tend to perceive the issue as the source of conflict while collectivist societies tend to see a tension in the group as the trigger (Gudykunst 1994).

Most people experience conflict as unpleasant because perception of self is threatened if own interests are not adequately addressed. This desire to "save face" is a universal phenomenon that expresses itself in culture-specific forms. It has been observed that a number of different forms of "face work" influence the course of a conflict situation (Ting-Toomey 1988). While individualist societies emphasize the consistency between the personal and public self and strive to hold the balance, collectivist societies are geared toward fulfilling social obligation within a social network. The former strives to maintain his/her own face, while the latter is concerned with face-giving and face-maintaining actions in relation to one or more persons involved in an encounter (Gelfand et al 2001).

2.3.3 Conflict Behavior

Once the conflict has become unavoidable, the parties involved determine its further course. Members of collectivist cultures, in particular, will usually try to avoid conflict altogether before it occurs. They consider this factor by meticulously planning official events involving participants, seating order etc. In this way, they ensure against possible embarrassment or conflict that may be caused by not positioning a person appropriately according to his status. In an effort to recognize and avoid impending conflict, members will concentrate intensely on verbal and especially non-verbal signals of well-being or discomfort shown by their conversation partner (Tjitra 2001). If, for example, a Japanese employee wishes to express his reservation regarding his superior's request, he will hesitate for a moment before asking for clarification (Nihida 1996). A more indirect conversational style is observed in face-to-face communication behavior that interprets the message in a number of different ways in order to gain flexibility and avoid conflict.

If conflict is unavoidable, an effort will be made to change the subject, withdraw from the situation or remain silent to take off the edge. This behavior contrasts with the Western concept that a conflict must be addressed before reaching a reasonable solution. In order to minimize conflict potential in intercultural encounters, it is important that people from "low-context cultures" (Hall 1959), who emphasize explicit verbalization, are able to read between the lines and listen carefully. More particularly, they will do well to listen and hear what is *not* being said and to closely observe their conversation partner's non-verbal signals. People from "high-context cultures" (Hall 1959), who tend to glean information from content-based observation and have a more indirect communication style, need to understand that a direct communication style does not automatically limit their freedom of action and is focused on the task rather than the person. Both groups can benefit from the valuable learning potential inherent in this experience.

A German manager in Beijing reports: "At the beginning of my assignment as an engineer in China, I had a slight disagreement with a Chinese colleague about a technical detail. I just kept after him to prove that I was right about a certain point and all the facts were absolutely clear, so that I could finally just drive him into a corner giving him no other choice but to agree with me. However, this did not happen. Instead, my colleague began responding to my questions with answers that had nothing to do with the question. While I talked about the short circuit, he spoke about the weather. This continued for a while until I finally gave up" (Thomas and Schenk 2001, p. 98).

Emotions arising in a conflict are expressed in a culture-specific manner and are easily misunderstood by over- or underestimating or simply misjudging their significance. Consequently, it is imperative in Asian cultures to literally "save face" in public by maintaining an expression of harmony in spite of inner turmoil. By contrast, we feel threatened very quickly by the exaggerated gesturing, mimicry and the high-pitched velocity of speech exhibited by Southern Europeans at even the slightest disagreement, and tend to misinterpret this behavior as highly aggressive.

Conflict can arise due to different communication habits relative to proxemics that may infringe on respective "comfort zones". There is evidence that a felt sense of too little interpersonal distance from the conversation partner can trigger a physiologically proven stress reaction to the point where the "cornered" person tries to reestablish the distance to which he/she is accustomed (Middlemist et al. 1976). If the person cannot avoid this situation, the conversation partner may be perceived as invasive or too distant and affect the ambience of the encounter, increasing the probability of an all-out conflict.

2.3.4 Conflict Resolution

The cultural perspective regarding a conflict setting also determines its approach to resolution. In a study on conflict resolution strategies applied by Germans, Americans and Japanese conducted by Tinsley (2001), he was able to show that different strategies were regarded as effective according to where cultural socialization took place. While the Americans focused on integrating the interests of individual conflict parties pragmatically, the Germans concentrated on regularity and standard procedures including compiling explicitly formulated contractual backup information. The Japanese were, in turn, interested in a rapid resolution to the conflict while emphasizing the social status of the people involved.

Clearly the culturally preferred strategies are bound to elicit difficulties in an intercultural situation when, for instance, an explicit contract model designed by Germans with the intention of avoiding vagueness and grounds for mistrust, is perceived by the Japanese, for precisely this reason, as lacking in trust in the personal relationship.

Accordingly, conflict resolution depends on the extent to which the conflict parties are prepared to find a mutually acceptable agreement or if a third party has to be consulted to mediate and assist in resolving the conflict.

The mediation process, involving assistance from a third party, entails additional cultural characteristics depending on the point at which a third party intervenes, the choice of mediator and what influence he or she has and the way in which the process proceeds. Many studies have shown that a third party quickly intervened in impending conflict situations in cultures tending toward collective systems of orientation in order to safeguard or reestablish social harmony or to avoid a threat to a person's honor as, for example, in Muslim cultures (Wall and Callister 1999). In many Asian societies, institutionalized processes exist in which previously appointed mediators assume responsibility for conflict resolution and whose verdict is binding for the parties. Going to court within this context is the least preferred alternative as it documents the failure to uphold social harmony, or in the words of a Chinese author: "Peace is best, lawsuit is the worst" (Huang 1996). Individualist societies, such as Germany for instance, assume that the conflicting parties will resolve differences between each other on their own. A third party is called only if it becomes absolutely necessary. In such cases, the usual procedure is to resort to official arbitration or court, which provide a legally binding verdict. Meanwhile, however, mediation is becoming a popular option for conflict resolution in Germany, which is partially due to an overloaded public legal system (Kals and Webers 2001). Here, the mediator is an "external communication expert and often simultaneously a field expert, who mediates between the parties and helps them to develop a sustainable and future-oriented solution. He has a background function without prescribing solutions" (Kals and Webers 2001, p. 13). In comparison, other cultures apply different criteria, such as social status in community affairs, religious affiliation or age, when selecting a mediator or a group of mediators. These individuals, who are respected by everyone in the community, can present a resolution after having clarified the cause (Jandt and Pedersen 1996, p. 257 ff.).

Western oriented literature recommends assembling all involved in the conflict in a moderated workshop session during the mediation process, binding them contractually to decisions reached, and then to proceed with a clear cause and effect analysis to arrive at a solution.

Collectivist communities tend to refrain from direct confrontation. A solution is prepared in many face-to-face meetings with the conflicting parties, which is then presented and decided upon in a meeting with all involved parties. Seen metaphorically, this scenario resembles a setting in which the mediation workshop is the stage upon which the piece is played out, having been meticulously worked out in advance behind the scenes. The individualist approach, on the other hand, resembles improvisational theater, where the audience observes the play during its development. From the collectivist perspective, this poses a considerable threat to the "face" factor of all involved ... a danger that must be averted in advance.

2.3.5 Overcoming Conflict Competently

A prerequisite of overcoming conflict productively in general is the ability to respect the people and individuals on the other side; to create rapport between the parties and to look for creative solutions together, which will ensure mutual satisfaction with the process itself as well as its outcome. In order to do this, the conflicting parties must be able to modify their perspective and to discuss the conflict process. In other words, they must be able to communicate on a meta-level. Applied intercultural competence, including the required knowledge of other and own cultural standards in conflict situations and the ability to follow the course of a critical interaction so that it can be successfully negotiated, is extremely important for operating in the international arena.

Individuals active in intercultural fields might find it useful to address the following questions in advance, if necessary with the help of experts:

- How is conflict perceived in one's own culture and how do other cultures relate to conflict?
- What are the preferred modes of behavior for resolving conflict?
- At what point is a conflict considered resolved?
- How is "fairness" or "justice" interpreted by the conflicting parties?
- How can the rapport necessary for solving the conflict be created?
- What means are considered legitimate by the respective cultures?
- What persuasion strategies (rational argumentation, threats, promises etc.) are considered appropriate?
- What significance do third party mediators play in a given culture and what social status and authority do they hold?
- How do mediation processes proceed in a given culture?
- What are the characteristics of a mutually acceptable mediator?
- How binding is the outcome of mediation?

If you have read and understood this chapter, then the explanation of the following authentic case study should hardly present a problem.

A traditional and former monopolist German company is meanwhile globally active and very successful in its market sector. The subsidiary in Singapore, however, has been causing headquarters a headache for some time. Many qualified employees are leaving the company and some are resigning en masse. Headquarters decides to counter this development and organizes a workshop in Germany to look into the problem areas relative to cooperation und to develop sustainable solutions together. A professional external moderator is commissioned for the workshop to ensure the best possible results. Shortly before the workshop, the local CEO sends an e-mail containing the agenda, according to which the moderator is to team up with an HR manager from Singapore. The workshop participants were to be divided into an "inner circle" consisting of department heads and an "outer circle" made up of the remaining participants. While the "inner circle" discusses cooperation, individuals from the "outer circle" can be included if they have the information that is needed.

The German organizers are perplexed by the proposal. Can you give an idea of how this suggestion is to be understood and what the best approach is to the situation based on what you have read in this chapter?

References

Fisher, R.; Ury, W.; Patton, B. (1995): Das Harvard-Konzept. Sachgerecht verhandeln – erfolgreich verhandeln. Frankfurt a. M.

Gelfand, M.; Nishii, L. H.; Holcombe, K. M.; Dyer, N. (2001): Cultural influences on Cognitive Representations of Conflict: Interpretations of Conflict Episodes in the United States and Japan. Journal of Applied Psychology 86 (6): 1059–1074.

Gudykunst, W. B. (1994): Bridging Differences. Effective Intergroup Communication. Thousand Oaks.

Hall, E. T. (1959): The Silent Language. New York.

Huang, S.-S. (1996): The reconciliation system of the Republic of China. In: Jandt, F. E.; Pedersen, P. B. (Eds.), Constructive Conflict Management: Asia-Pacific Cases. Thousand Oaks, pp. 43–51.

Jandt, F. E.; Pedersen, P. B. (Eds.) (1996): Constructive Conflict Management: Asia-Pacific Cases. Thousand Oaks.

Kals, E.; Webers, T. (2001): Wirtschaftsmediation als alternative Konfliktlösung. Wirtschaftspsychologie 2: 10–16.

Middlemist, R. D.; Knowles, E.; Matter, C. F. (1976): Personal space invasions in the lavatory: Suggestive evidence for arousal. Journal of Personality and Social Psychology 33 (5): 541–546.

Montada, L.; Kals, E. (2001): Mediation. Lehrbuch für Psychologen und Juristen. Weinheim.

Nishida, T. (1996): Communication in Personal Relationships in Japan. In: Gudykunst, W. B.; Ting-Toomey, S.; Nishida, T.: Communication in Personal Relationships Across Cultures. Thousand Oaks, pp. 102–121.

Thomas, A.; Schenk, E. (2001): Beruflich in China. Trainingsprogramm für Manager, Fach- und Führungskräfte. Göttingen.

Thomas, A., Layes, G.; Kammhuber, S. (1998): Sensibilisierungs- und Orientierungstraining für die kulturallgemeine und kulturspezifische Vorbereitung von Soldaten auf internationale Einsätze der Bundeswehr. Untersuchungen des Psychologischen Dienstes der Bundeswehr, 33. München.

Ting-Toomey, S. (1988): Intercultural Conflict Styles. A face-negotiation theory. In: Kim, Y. Y.; Gudykunst, W. B. (Eds.), Theories in Intercultural Communication. Newbury Park, pp. 213–235.

Tinsley, C. H. (2001): How negotiators get to yes: Predicting the constellations of strategies used across cultures to negotiate conflict. Journal of Applied Psychology 86 (4): 583–593.

Tjitra, H. W. (2001): Synergiepotenziale und interkulturelle Probleme. Chancen und Herausforderungen am Beispiel deutsch-indonesischer Arbeitsgruppen. Wiesbaden.

Wall, J. A.; Callister, R. R. (1999): Malaysian community mediation. Journal of Conflict Resolution 42: 343–365.

Ulrich Zeutschel

2.4 Intercultural Project Management

2.4.1 Culturally Diverse Project Teams: A Working Method

Over the last decades, project work as a comprehensive means of solving problems and a both field-specific and organizational form of team cooperation has increased in importance. Largely independent team cooperation without hierarchical limitation has replaced ingrained structures of line organization in many different areas of the service and production sectors. This is due to technological challenges, such as increasing integration of workflow and shorter production cycles on the one hand, and on the other with the necessity of developing comprehensive solutions for increasingly complex problem settings.

At the same time, the consequences of globalization such as deregulation, international competition, multinational mergers and work-related migration are among the reasons for an increase in culturally diverse project teams. This can be the result of strategic management decisions in an effort to include regionally diverse interests in a multinational operation, for example, to ensure acceptance of work-related results in different target countries or to integrate a number of different culture-specific perspectives into a creative problem-solving approach. In other cases, international teams are created "automatically" by recruiting highly specialized experts or, quite simply, they reflect the cultural diversity among employees.

2.4.2 Particular Challenges and Opportunities in Intercultural Project Work

Even culturally homogeneous teams, whose members share similar socialization processes with similar expectations, convictions, perspectives and plans of action, have their hands full with agreeing on what standard to apply to tasks and how to interact with other team members upon joining a project team. Not only is the consensus span narrower in culturally diverse teams, but expectations and habituated approaches to creating a common basis for work differ to a great extent:

- Language skills required for communicating effectively are not sufficient because of work-related terminology, which is spoken at different levels of proficiency.
- There is no consensus of central value standards, the "secondary virtues" of work life, such as personal responsibility, competition, openness to criticism, harmony in the group or formal/informal contact.
- Team members may differ on their understanding of their role in the team with regard to leadership, initiative, and obligation to deliver and collect information.
- Different approaches to problem solving, time management or meeting management must be first recognized and then coordinated among the members.
- The institutions involved have unclear or contradictory expectations regarding commissioning and project scope.

On the other hand, project work offers a number of opportunities of intercultural cooperation:

- A clearly defined scope of work can serve as a common point of departure.
- The usual flat hierarchy in teams leaves room for actualizing potential.
- Valuable professional contributions by competent experts who are not members of the dominant cultural group can question previously assumed derogatory assessment of the respective culture.
- Freedom from (also culture-specifically determined) rules and standards of line organization offers room to create new forms of communication and cooperation.
- The project's limited timeframe facilitates and encourages "experimentation".

Experts who lead coordinated and coached international project teams were able to provide the following information on useful conditions and interventions for effective cooperation in culturally diverse teams (Zeutschel 1999a, 1999b).

Basic Conditions

- The partner country's positive image in society in general as conveyed in the media
- International cooperation is an integral part of corporate policy
- The perspective of long-term team cooperation

Contacts

- Upper management acknowledges the team, symbolized by their attendance at a kick-off workshop
- Headquarters maintains regular contact with team members abroad
- Interest and feedback on the part of the host company

Team Organization

- Assigning clear tasks and agreeing on goals at the beginning of the co-operation
- Room for personal networking and informal contact early on
- Availability of a mediator with background knowledge about the participating cultures
- An equal balance of power and influence between the team's sub-groups
- Alternating team leadership and moderation
- Mutual input on determining rules that are to apply to the teamwork

Group Dynamic

- Mutual acknowledgment and respect regarding expertise and social competence
- Dealing with latent conflict early on instead of ignoring or withdrawing from controversial issues
- After-work contact including family members and partners
- Clarifying key work-related expressions via translation and feedback
- Pioneer spirit: discovering, exploring and honoring common interests at a deeper level, such as values, lifestyles and biographies
- Enhanced motivation through a deep sense of satisfaction with the process and outcome of the group endeavor

Personal Characteristics

- Familiarity with cultural or geographic diversity, for instance due to family background or attending international schools
- Awareness of own cultural standards and maintenance of fundamental own-culture orientation
- Good listening skills and empathy
- Willingness to learn and curiosity about different ways of seeing and behaving

Suggested training and consulting measures are mentioned at the end of this chapter.

2.4.3 Stages of Development: Intercultural Cooperation in Project Groups

At the beginning of a project composed of culturally diverse members, orientation and coordinating leadership functions is a priority, similar to finding one's way in unfamiliar territory. Moosmüller (1997) describes this development as creating a team culture in which the team's "intuitive intercultural knowledge" comes into action.

Examples of effective intercultural cooperation mentioned in the interviews with experts were divided into four categories according to the action contingency model developed by Jones and Gerard (1967):

- *Dominance:* The entire team assumes the customs and standards of one of the participating sub-groups, such as the use of English as the working language, addressing each other on a first-name basis, punctuality, and the explicit meaning of yes and no answers.
- *Co-action:* Each sub-group works parallel or consecutively on separate parts of the assigned task according to where their strengths lie. One example in a German-American development team that was under time pressure showed that the American sub-group worked on a number of possible solutions and tested their applicability, while the German members followed up with precision planning and specific details of implementation.
- *Integration:* A stronger interdependence develops when elements from the repertoire of participating national sub-teams merge to create a new work form. The elements may be modified in their intensity to correspond to the compromises required; however, their origins remain identifiable.

  Two examples from a German-British joint venture underline this aspect: (a) Work meetings were arranged regularly according to German custom but were limited to the most important subjects in holding with British custom, (b) Time lines, priorities and action plans were scheduled according to the British modus operandi and followed up with German precision analysis.
- *Innovation:* This form of cultural synergy in cooperating teams is, in fact, characterized by a mutual development of forms of interaction, which result in a qualitative modification of culture-specific elements. Only very few examples of this category were mentioned in the experts' reports, one of which describes the creation of a workspace by a German-British team in the automobile industry. Although all departments responsible for development were familiar with the ideal open space offices instead of the individual office variety, they took the initiative

during their nine-month cooperative stint to implement community-generating elements, such as a styling model to serve as a focal point for interaction in the center of the workspace.

Casmir (1999) terms the above-mentioned innovation the *third culture* and Fontaine (1996, p. 269) calls it an *international microculture* (IMC):

Rather than select specific "our way", "their way", or "compromise" strategies, "this ... requires a more generic strategy, in which these – or frequently, other – specific strategies are selected on the basis of which is best accommodated to the new task ecologies encountered abroad. These latter often include ways beyond those typically preferred by the participants within their cultures".

The basic assumption in the systematic model outlined here is that the interaction categories mentioned in the experts' reports are combined in alternating time increments, although not necessarily at the level of culturally synergetic innovation, but rather via detour possibilities that may lead to a developmental "dead-end", which is not to say that the team has failed in their cooperation. The transition from one step to the next is subject to specific conditions required for moving on to the next level, as is the unproductive or destructive standstill at one level due to critically misguided development.

Step 1: Dominance/Adaptation

Insisting on one culture-specific interaction style over other styles can be a conscious and mutually agreed-upon rule of conduct or it can be the result of a majority decision based on status, "home-turf" advantage or manipulation by those in power. In addition, the rule can be demarcated by time or scope to test a particular area of interaction, can be applied to one aspect or alternate.

- *Productive:* The more conscious persons are of alternating dominance and adaptation within a given framework, the less the cultural slant becomes fixed between subgroups within the team and the clearer the specific strengths and advantages of diverse cultural styles can be perceived. This is the prerequisite for proceeding on to the next phase.
- *Destructive:* One-sided dominance can lead to a general "halo effect" in an effort to avoid dissonance on the part of the submissive parties ("the others are just all around better than we are, therefore they should have the say"). On the other hand, they may react with a desire to counter the

imposed superiority ("we will prove to you that this 'imported' approach is not suitable").

Step 2: Co-action

Team members may view the co-action phase as liberating them from a relationship based on dominance/adaptation between sub-groups or as initiating the collabortion directly if the different approaches and working styles are familiar and predictable. This phase is characterized by strict division of work between culturally homogeneous sub-teams, which take on partial problem areas simultaneously or one at a time while adhering to their specific styles and bringing in their culture-specific strengths. This form of working in tandem can be competitive or complementary in nature. Participants can plan their approaches consciously and share common goals or individual team members may act impulsively without reflection and withdraw back into the familiar sub-group. Working together on a group task in this manner can vary in terms of time and scope.

- *Productive:* The more the co-action evolves consciously, is limited in time and is oriented toward complementary endeavor, the more likely it is that there is an uninterrupted exchange of information and the more probable it is that the benefit of the respective culture-specific approaches to a common task or problem-solving effort will be acknowledged. Acknowledging and honoring other forms of dealing with issues tends to lead to the involved parties' modifying their own repertoire to accommodate different approaches.
- *Destructive:* Ongoing co-action may, under circumstances, intensify the feeling that one "simply can't see eye to eye on issues" and may result in members avoiding each other during the course of the collaboration. Reluctance to share information is likely to obscure the common goal and enforce stereotyping. Competition is often set in motion to manifest individual superiority.

Step 3: Integration

Once the team has become aware of the culture-specific strengths and their advantage in setting common goals, culturally diverse elements merge to form a new, mutually beneficial modus operandi. Core cultural elements are still evident and members must adjust their leadership styles accordingly. The combined elements are either binding for all involved or alternate between groups (contingent). Integration can be negotiated and its elements included according to a path of least resistance. Otherwise, a balance must be found between obstacles and conditions required by the changes involved. Ideally, members will evolve a mutually acceptable approach to optimize the respective advantages of the individual elements in striving for the higher goal. The integration process itself can vary depending on the affected domain.

- *Productive:* Binding, mutually accepted processes and values within the team contribute to a sense of security, guarantee identification with group norms, initiate learning and change processes. The more integration is consciously and more comprehensively oriented toward a mutually defined overriding goal, the sooner more scope of action becomes available to serve the common goal and to pave the road to entering the fourth phase.
- *Destructive:* If team members feel that the integration is being forced on them or "mechanically" negotiated, then they might perceive some sort of "foul play" in action and refuse to cooperate over the long term.

Step 4: Innovation

The own-culture frame of reference and behavioral repertoire can unfold freely if participants have generated enough trust and familiarity in the team and look forward to further development. Team members begin creating new behavioral patterns that go beyond any culture-specific repertoires and become unique to their particular team.

- *Productive:* This is the highest level of cooperation, in which the team transforms itself into a "learning organization" and develops its own team-specific working style and behavioral repertoire. In this ideal situation, the culture-specific competences and team potential merge in a functional modus operandi.
- *Destructive:* The project team may purposely distance itself from the corporate setting and other teams at this stage of development. This will increase the danger of "splendid isolation" and impact cooperation within the organizational context. The future of the team may even be at risk if they become too autonomous and uncontrollable in the eyes of corporate management.

2.4.4 Managing Culturally Diverse Project Groups Constructively

Mayrshofer and Kröger (1999) cite five clearly defined tasks to be accomplished during the course of a project in the form of an orientation grid containing hints and suggestions for intercultural project management.

Clarifying Tasks and Goals

Defining the steps involved in the project in advance does not differ substantially from clarifying steps in mono-cultural settings. They include:
- defining problems and needs,
- determining and substantiating stakeholder expectations and goals,
- deciding on a statement of purpose and concrete project goals,
- setting realistic benchmarks, expectations and specifying anticipated results,
- reflecting upon own expectations and presumptions in the project leadership,
- and clarifying the time factor and available resources.

These routine tasks in setting up the project become more complex as the project takes on intercultural dimensions. Here, organization requires consideration of different expectations and customs regarding project management. Often the participating project members and cooperation partners are separated geographically. Establishing a project advisory council or contracting a mentor to help tie the project team in with the corporate setting is highly recommended. The preliminary project development team should make a point of including the cultural groups that will participate in the following project team. Moreover, the developmental team should take the time to reach an agreement regarding common goals and terminology for the project.

Teamwork as a Mutual Initiative

Kick-off meetings have proved to be effective in initiating project cooperation and conveying its significance to all team members. Topics often include developing a common understanding of where the team stands at the outset and what the goal expectations are, planning both the steps and delegation of tasks in detail and defining a coordinated system of information distribution and decision-making, especially if not all team members are on site. Furthermore, the kick-off meeting signals a vote of confidence given to the organizers by upper management or even the employer. The event provides a chance to develop a team identity and is frequently expressed in a motto, a symbol or a catchy team name. Members of a development team in the lighting industry even went as far as to create an acrylic glass pyramid that was lit up to illuminate the engraved team rules and served as a table decoration in the conference room.

Before starting work on the assigned task, team members should have enough time to become acquainted, if possible, apart from the work-related setting. Here, participants have the opportunity to explore other-culture backgrounds, experience, interests, fields of expertise, expectations and special skills and to establish rapport based on common interests.

Work segments should be assigned to mixed sub-teams based on their abilities and previous experience with focus groups instead of grouping members according to nationality.

Ensuring Information Flow and Coordination

Regular meetings allow for an exchange of information within the team, arranging schedules, discussing deadlines, sharing resources and building team spirit. Differences in working styles should be addressed in an effort to avoid "tolerating differences in silence" if matters are not clear. Progress should be made transparent and problems in relation to individual tasks should be solved as a team. The team members' suitability (competence and motivation) for the task must be evaluated on a regular basis to avoid work overload and consequent frustration.

Key questions to gauge cooperation within the scope of regular meetings could be:

- How goal-oriented and creative are our problem-solving and decision-making strategies?
- How do we deal with different opinions, values and work styles?
- How do we synergize our differences?
- To what extent does the distribution of roles and tasks conform to our respective strengths and requirements of the situation?
- How supportive and goal-directed is our relationship with other teams? With the organization?

Language-based communication difficulties in meetings can be ameliorated by (cf. Kopper 1992, p. 232) (q.v. Ch. I, 1.5):

- using simple language and speaking clearly and simply,
- clarifying key expressions together and exploring different meanings in translation,

- structuring subjects and presenting them in small increments,
- formulating short sentences and using active verbs,
- summarizing and re-emphasizing key points,
- organizing an interpreter to whisper translations during a presentation,
- using visuals, noting key expressions and using body language for clarification,
- planning in enough time and frequent breaks,
- switching into another working language in order to give minorities the floor,
- and encouraging active participation.

Especially those teams who do not work together in the same area need to make room for communicating informally and clarifying issues apart from the regular business meetings. It is advisable that the project leaders prepare the setting so that informal communication and an exchange of experience between the regular team meetings can take place.

Benchmarking and Optimizing Cooperation

A larger scale assessment of the process makes sense between benchmarks set for the task. During such reviews, the technical and content-based aspects are in the foreground. Intercultural teams, in particular, need to consider the *how* of the collaboration, that is, the quality of communication and cooperation, in order to recognize dissonance and latent conflict in advance, instead of the *what* of the project. Being aware of the quality of communication can lead to optimizing integration or even synergetic cooperation. Existing strengths and weaknesses need to be systematically combined and examined under the aspect of cultural relativity: How are strengths acknowledged among team members, and how do they contribute to reaching the common goal? How can weaknesses be overcome? Achievements should be communicated to the team. The team should be acknowledged for their achievements and these achievements communicated appropriately.

Standardized checklists, such as the Cross-Cultural Team Performance Survey (Moran et al 1993, pp. 83–85) help in reviewing processes.

Regular meetings apart from the routine tasks should be scheduled to allow team members to view the process from a different angle. These benchmarking meetings are ideally prepared and facilitated by an external or previously designated in-company moderator. An example of a moderation sequence prepared in this fashion is included at the end of this section.

Securing Results and Evaluating Results

Similar to the initial kick-off meeting, the end of the project is an event of both in-company and public significance. An end-of-project event should set a clear signal to the outside that the project has been completed. The presentation of results should include all members of other-culture subgroups involved in the project. Performance and valuable experience gained during the collaboration should be included and useful work procedures such as methods and aids developed during the process of working together emphasized in addition to the official task-related results. Benefits of the methods and means of working together gleaned from the collaboration can conceivably be transferred to other areas of work.

All team members involved in the project should have the chance to celebrate their success at the end of the project (at the latest!). Informal celebration among colleagues allows members to acknowledge each other's contributions to the collegial atmosphere in the team and achievements in their respective fields. Separating and letting go of the ties that bonded the team members together for the duration of the project are issues that can be treated within the scope of a farewell workshop rather than during a regular workday meeting. Famous last words include bilateral feedback discussions and a review of common experiences to clarify possible residual conflict issues that could otherwise affect other areas adversely.

An overall assessment of the collaboration with a particular view to integrative and innovative work forms, should include suggestions for future teams and communicate these to new work groups. However, the mutually created work culture is the work of the team members' collective memory and cannot be transferred one-to-one to different team constellations. Well-rehearsed teams are a valuable resource for further project work, and if possible, should be included in future project constellations. On the other hand, they could also join culturally diverse project groups as multiplicators and have a "crystallizing" effect on stabilizing team structures.

2.4.5 Possibilities for Support

According to Clackworthy (1996), training and coaching for culturally diverse project teams are offered along the lines of intercultural learning on five different levels:

- *Language training*, including culturally appropriate forms of behavior such as body language and discourse depending on the context, e.g., business or informal,

- *Cultural awareness training,* including country-specific information, clarification of values and related norms of behavior,
- *Intercultural communication training* behavioral training based on experience and implemented via exercises and role plays,
- *Interaction training:* in culturally mixed groups,
- *On-the-job coaching:* observing project teams, advising project leadership and moderating process outcomes in the teams according to need.

These components should be available to support the development of the project team:
- Language training according to individual needs,
- Separate orientation workshops for national sub-groups (if possible by the same trainer) combined with cultural awareness training to sensitize members to own-culture standards and the cultural differences that are to be expected,
- A kick-off training providing background information on the project and the partners including a presentation of methods of team organization and cooperative problem solving,
- Externally moderated team development workshops, for instance, as benchmarkers for work in progress to gauge the ongoing cooperation and group dynamic and to benefit from the new forms of culture-specific cooperation and productive synergies,
- An external coach with personal experience in cooperating with the cultural groups involved,
- Final review sessions with an external moderator to reflect on the cooperation process, to obtain process results and to formulate recommendations for future teams.

Annex: Questions Used to Encourage Reflection and Integration of Culture-specific Communication and Cooperation Styles

Step 1: Perception and Description

Culturally homogeneous sub-groups within the team work side-by-side on the following tasks:
- What differences did you notice between the working and communication styles within the project team?
- Please select two of the most important differences and present your views to the entire team: Select a recent prototype situation, in which

the differences are clear. Describe the behavior of those involved in a diagram, a cartoon or in a short role play.

Following each presentation to the entire group, the rest of the team members are asked to take a stance and give an interpretation of what they saw:
- What specific behavioral differences were evident?
- How might those involved feel and what might they be thinking?
- What title or motto could you give the scenario?

Following the presentations held by the sub-teams, the significant differences are selected for further consideration according to the following criteria:
- *Visible:* Which differences required the most time and energy during the course of cooperation?
- *Fundamental:* Which differences are likely to impact other areas of cooperation?
- *Consistent:* Which differences were significant for cultural sub-groups rather than for individuals and appear consistently so that a pattern becomes evident?
- *Obstructive:* What differences obstructed team performance, constructive cooperation or personal satisfaction?
- *Escalating:* Which differences resulted in increased emotionality during the course of cooperation, or were more controlled or suppressed when dealing with "the other side"?

Step 2: Analyzing

Culturally homogeneous mini-groups create a brief presentation based on the selected style differences and the key question:
- How do we explain our distinct cultural style to persons outside of our cultural sphere? What values and reasoning do we associate with it?

Following each presentation, the values mentioned are recorded to make the corresponding style elements transparent.

Step 3: Reassessing

In a third round in mono-cultural sub-teams, the following questions are addressed to reassess differences in style and presented to the entire group:

- What risks and disadvantages do you see in insisting on maintaining or even exaggerating our own style?
- What advantages do you see in a complementary style that could offset the limitations of our own?
- In what kind of work setting would an integration of both styles seem reasonable and beneficial?

The most "advantageous" suggestions for integration situations are selected according to the following criteria:
- *Balance:* The need and extent of behavior modification is equally indicated for all participants,
- *Urgency:* Without compromise and necessary changes in this area, both team performance and ambience will suffer,
- *Achievable:* The desired integration has already been achieved in work models outside of the team or in individual situations within the team,
- *Advantageous:* The expected gain is in relation to the required effort required by the change,
- *Tangible:* Successful change becomes evident as it evolves.

Step 4: Negotiating

Culturally homogeneous mini-groups map out areas of compromise and areas where they believe there is a need for change relative to the integration topics that were previously selected:
- What do we wish to change about our behavior in order to accommodate the values and interests of other team members?
- What aspects of our behavior can we not do without?
- What changes in behavior would we appreciate from the other members?

The sub-groups also present a rough draft of the changed behavior and act it out in a role play. Agreement on the insights gleaned from the presentations and rough drafts on each topic are recorded in a change protocol. Divergent views are considered in light of the common goal and discussed in culturally mixed mini-groups. These views, together with the areas in which the participants desire change and the points already agreed upon, will be included in the protocol.

Step 5: Planning Implementation

After negotiating the integration topics, team members make sure that they all agree on the steps to be implemented in the change process before taking measures to ensure sustainability:

- How can we tell that we have succeeded in integrating our different styles in this area?
- What rules, signals and adaptation aids can be of help in sustaining the changes?
- When and how will we begin integrating the changes we have agreed upon?

References

Casmir, F. L. (1999): Foundations for the study of intercultural communication based on a third-culture building model. International Journal of Intercultural Relations 23 (1): 91–116.

Clackworthy, D. (1996): Training Germans and Americans in conflict management. In: Berger, M. (Ed.), Cross-Cultural Team Building: Guidelines for More Effective Communication and Negotiation. Maidenhead.

Fontaine, G. (1996): Social support and the challenges of international assignments. In: Landis, D.; Bhagat, R. S. (Eds.), Handbook of Intercultural Training. 2nd ed. Thousand Oaks, CA, pp. 264–281.

Jones, E. E.; Gerard, H. B. (1967): Foundations of Social Psychology. New York.

Kopper, E. (1992): Multicultural workgroups and project teams. In: Bergemann, N.; Sourisseaux, A. L. J. (Eds.), Interkulturelles Management. Heidelberg, pp. 229–251.

Mayrshofer, D.; Kröger, H. A. (1999): Prozesskompetenz in der Projektarbeit. Hamburg.

Moosmüller, A. (1997): Kommunikationsprobleme in amerikanisch-japanisch-deutschen Teams: Kulturelle Synergie durch interkulturelles Training? Zeitschrift für Personalforschung 3: 282–297.

Moran, R. T.; Harris, P. R.; Stripp, W. G. (1993): Developing the Global Organization: Strategies for Human Resource Professionals. Houston/London u. a.

Zeutschel, U. (1999a): Interkulturelle Synergie auf dem Weg: Erkenntnisse aus deutsch/US-amerikanischen Problemlösegruppen. Gruppendynamik 30(2): 131–149.

Zeutschel, U. (1999b): Intercultural synergy in professional teams: Views based on practical experience. In: Knapp, K.; Kappel, B.; Eubel-Kasper, K.; Salo-Lee, L. (Eds.), Meeting the Intercultural Challenge. Sternenfels, pp. 191–199.

Siegfried Stumpf

2.5 Intercultural Leadership and Management

2.5.1 Introductory Remark

The concepts of leadership and management are closely related. The term "manager" was borrowed from the Anglo-American linguistic area and found its way into the German language during the 20th century. In German, the term refers to a managing director, leader or supervisor. The meaning of the English verb "to manage" translates into German as "handling", "accomplishing", "leading", and "directing", which goes back to the Italian word *maneggiare,* of which the stem is *manus* and translated into German means "hand" (Drosdowski et al. 1963). The act of "accomplishing" often corresponds to the manager's task of supervising and leading. The aim the manager aspires to requires much in the way of employee support, which must be harnessed, coordinated and directed.

There are many different definitions for the concept of leadership in academic literature (cf. Neuberger, p. 5), rendering the term somewhat unclear and ambiguous: "Leadership is one of the most confusing terms that exists in organizational behavior literature. It is a general term that means such things as power, authority, administration, control and supervision, depending on who is asked. There are many definitions of leadership in the literature" (Erez and Earley 1993, p. 172).

According to von Rosenstiel (1993), "leadership" seen from the perspective of organizational psychology is a direct, intentional and goal-oriented act by those with authority to exert influence over subordinates. This rather narrow interpretation of leadership, which refers to the direct interaction between supervisor and employee, contrasts with the concept of leadership in a broader sense, which is based on a range of roles that characterize such positions. In this sense, leadership in an organization comprises an entire scope of activities that are derived from different expectations a person of authority is confronted with. Mintzberg (1991) describes this range by listing ten different roles ranging from representative, observer, information disseminator and mediator (q.v. Ch. II, 1.1). Mintzberg's diagram illustrates the diverse roles a manager is expected to fulfill.

Leading and managing are always imbedded in a cultural context. The corporate culture directly reflects the structure of basic assumptions that developed out of the involvement with internal and external expectations that guide the members of the organization in their thinking, values, feeling and action (cf. Schein 1995). The culture of the organization's social system influences the development of a specific organizational culture. It may be assumed that elements of the organizational culture that are closely interwoven with the history of a culture, a society, country or nation are the most difficult to change (cf. Hofstede 1997, p. 245 ff.). This means that culture, in the sense of a system of orientation (cf. Thomas 1993) typical for a society, nation or country, is a fundamental prerequisite for leading and managing organizations.

2.5.2 Basics of Intercultural Leadership and Management

A variety of theories and models on conditions, processes and effects of leadership have been developed within the scope of psychological research on leadership (cf. Thomas and Stumpf 2002). The model below describes the basic interdependencies pertaining to leadership while emphasizing cultural aspects (Figure 16).

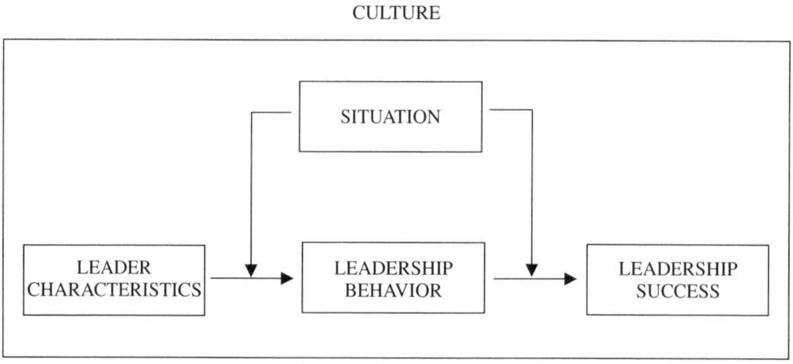

Figure 16: A framework model of leadership

The model shown in Figure 16 illustrates the following connections:

- Leadership behavior and its impact are subject to two forms of situational influence (cf. v. Rosenstiel 1999, p. 418): On the one hand, the situation determines how the leader's personal characteristics manifest in his leadership behavior, and on the other, it depends on the situation in how far specific leadership behavior leads to successful leadership. The term "situation" refers to a complex construct of conditions comprising the nature of the task, the characteristics of individuals being led, their relationship to the leader (cf. also Graen and Scandura 1987) and the leader's level of authority.

- The co-action between leadership characteristics, the nature of the situation, leadership success and behavior unfolds against the backdrop of a specific culture, whereby culture is referred to here in the sense of a system of orientation (Thomas 1993). The key role assumed by culture can be linked to aspects of symbolical leadership (Neuberger 1988, 1990), which assume that leadership stimulates a sense of potential in the employees and offers meaning in an effort to reduce the complexity imposed by the construct of conditions and to establish a binding sense of orientation for all members of the organization.
- The psychological process of perception and interpretation determine the effect the situation has on leadership behavior: the manager perceives certain aspects while others remain in the background. These elements imbue the situation with meaning and significance. It is precisely these images and interpretations that become the psychological reality that directs and forms leadership behavior. Culture, as a system of orientation typical of a society, constitutes an important factor in determining specific perception and interpretation of the momentary situation and what is still required. Leadership orients, consciously or not, along the lines of a societal system of organization that is considered binding and self-evident.
- Successful leadership depends largely on how those being led react to their leader's behavior. Here too, perception and interpretation processes play a key role. Those being led will perceive leadership behavior in a particular way and correlate it with a meaning, which in turn influences their own behavior. Culture plays a major part in this process: leadership becomes meaningful and relevant against the backdrop of a culture's system of orientation within the society to which it belongs.
- Successful leadership is no criteria in itself. Instead, it is dependent on a large number of evaluation processes, which in turn are co-determined by the respective culture. Research conducted to measure leadership success already points to the fact that there is no universally accepted criteria for leadership success. In this case, experts resort to a variety of different criteria, such as how effectively the task is managed and to what extent the organization's goal has been attained. For instance, has the market share or profit margin been increased? Has employee performance and satisfaction strengthened the emotional bond to the organization or improved the quality of cooperation within the organization (cf. Yuki and van Fleet 1992, p. 179 ff.)? The definition of "success" and what is perceived as "success" criteria can vary from culture to culture.

2.5.3 Cultural Influences and the Specific Functions of Leadership and Management

In the following discussion, we will illustrate the influence culture has on leadership and management in organizations with a view to key leadership and management functions. These include personnel management, setting and agreeing on goals, decision making, problem solving and creating the conditions for a motivating work environment.

Personnel Management

Researchers of the Ohio study group under Hemphill, Fleishman, Stogdill and Shartle (cf. Fleishman 1973) found two separate dimensions of leadership behavior based on the interviews they conducted:
- *Employee orientation:* Leadership behavior that takes into consideration different employee needs
- *Task orientation:* Behavior that focuses on employee tasks and structures their scope of work.

A manager's leadership style depends on how pronounced the two dimensions are. Thus, a task-oriented style of leadership can be differentiated from an employee-oriented style. However, due to the distinct nature of these leadership styles, a manager can be both employee oriented and task oriented, or he can be neither employee nor task oriented in the sense of a *laissez-faire* leadership style. Empirical studies on the effects of these styles have shown that there is a positive interrelation between employee orientation, leadership and employee satisfaction and a positive correlation between the manager's task orientation and employee output. Managers whose strengths lie equally in both domains are most successful in terms of satisfied employees and productivity (cf. Frey and Spielmann 1994).

The research conducted by the Ohio study group reflects a predominantly Western mindset. Empirical studies on the basic dimensions of leadership behavior were also conducted in other cultures. Misumi (e.g., 1985), for instance, conducted significant long-term research studies on leadership in Japan, whereas Sinha (e.g., 1984) headed a comprehensive research project to study leadership behavior in India. Both researchers also found two basic dimensions of leadership behavior:
- Misumi developed a PM leadership theory geared toward conditions in Japan. Here, "P" stands for "performance", in other words, performance-oriented leadership behavior that emphasizes goal achievement. "M"

stands for "maintenance" and emphasizes harmony and relationship-oriented, cohesive and integrative leadership behavior. According to this theory, a manager in the Japanese cultural context is particularly successful if he manages to adopt a leadership style that strongly reflects both dimensions.

- Sinha developed the NT leadership style and adapted it to conditions in India. Here, "N" stands for "nurturant" and refers to caring, relationship-oriented leadership behavior. "T" stands for "task-oriented" and refers to a manager's behavior in his approach to work. Again, it is precisely the combination of both dimensions in an NT style that proves most successful. According to Sinha, this condition paves the way for increased employee participation and involvement in the decision-making process.

The approaches developed by Misumi and Sinha are very similar to the Ohio school's two-dimensional approach. This indicates that leadership behavior is based on an underlying universal dimension. Specific behavior characteristics, however, are expressed and signalized through relationship or task-oriented approaches that differ according to the culture. If a Chinese boss tries to solve his subordinates' problems both tactfully and indirectly, he is showing typical maintenance behavior. In the U. S., on the other hand, the manager shows maintenance behavior if he refrains from criticizing his employees for being late for work (cf. Smith et al., 1989, p. 107).

A central aspect of leadership style involves the issue of "participation" in the sense of employee involvement in problem-solving and decision-making processes (Antoni 1999). Employee participation has the effect that it reduces resistance to change in the organization (Erez and Earley 1993, p. 104). According to Smith and Noakes (1996), employee participation is more effective in individualist nations than in collectivist cultures with high power distance (q.v. Ch. I, 1.4). The custom in the U. S. of granting employees active participation in projects involving organizational development has proven effective, while in Puerto Rico, a Latin culture with high power distance, the invitation to participate is interpreted as a sign that management is at a loss about how to proceed. Under such circumstances, employees prefer to leave the company.

The effectiveness of a participatory leadership style depends on employee expectations. Expectations are subject to change during the course of establishing rapport between employees and need to be taken into consideration. According to empirical studies conducted by Sinha (e.g., 1984, 1994) relative to an Indian cultural environment, a "nurturant task-oriented" (NT) leadership without employee involvement is indicated. Within the scope of this particular employee-supervisor relationship, employees gain work experience, develop their competencies and skills and build their self-confidence. At the same time, expectations regarding the relationship with the supervisor change when a need for more creative space and participation develops. If the relationship reaches this level of quality, the supervisor must adapt his leadership behavior to meet the need for participation in order to remain effective. According to Sinha, however, not every employee will reach the level required by the supervisor, who must then adapt to the respective employee-supervisor relationship (cf. Graen and Scandura 1987).

Setting and Agreeing on Goals

From the standpoint that organizations are perceived as social systems, one can assume that processes of goal setting and agreement play a significant role and constitute an important part of management (cf. Locke and Latham 1990; Nerdinger 2001).

Goal setting and agreeing on the terms can take many different forms. A manager can, for instance, impose goals on his employees without further explanation. He can stipulate the terms of the goal according to a "tell and sell" approach in a way that appeals and seems plausible or he can adopt a participative approach by including employee perspectives and interests and negotiate goals cooperatively. The outcomes of the different approaches and their effect on the development of the employees' commitment to the goals largely depend on the cultural system of orientation, on the basis of which the process of goal attainment is perceived and judged. Erez and Earley (1987) examined effects of different approaches to goal setting on employee performance in a comparative study between American and Israeli students. Goals were prescribed under the following three different experimental conditions: The goals were agreed upon in a group discussion (participative goal agreement) or negotiated between the manager and a representative of the group (representative goal agreement). There was no difference in performance between the groups during the participatory goal setting, while the Israelis' performance decreased significantly when the goals were simply prescribed. The authors trace this back to the Israelis' more collectivist orientation and their low power distance, giving rise to their negative feedback on the authoritarian approach to designating goals and causing them to reject it. For Israelis who were members of a Kibbutz, this tendency increased significantly, attesting to their high expectation of participatory goal setting. Another study by Erez (1986) documents that applying these results to all Israelis is difficult. Different cultural orientations according to the ethnic or social sub-group can render the available methods of goal setting effective in different ways. Employees working in the Israeli private sector, for instance, react positively to having goals prescribed to them. This shows that in transferring management techniques, for instance approaches to reaching an agreement on the goals, from one working and living environment to another, the entire socio-culture network must be taken into consideration to avoid generalization and attribution.

Deciding

According to the event management theory of leadership developed by Smith and Peterson (1988), events occurring in organizations are initially ambiguous and require interpretation. In order to make appropriate decisions, management must strive for unambiguous and reliable interpretations of such events, as far as this is possible. Here, they can resort to a number of different sources of orientation, such as how the events are perceived and assessed by their colleagues, their own experience or the organization's rules. It can be expected that the choice of orientation sources will be influenced by cultural factors according to the cultural system to which the manager belongs and the specific source of orientation he prefers. Other sources of orientation will then be secondary and play a minor role.

Smith, Peterson and Schwartz (1998) conducted a study consisting of a questionnaire designed for managers from over 40 countries (cf. also Smith 1999) exploring the connection between cultural belonging and preferences for specific sources of orientation in the decision-making process. Each country was represented by approximately 100 managers from state-run and private organizations. The managers were asked to indicate which of the following sources of orientation they used for decision making in work-related situations (e.g., dealing with differences of opinion within the department): either own experience, perspective and opinions of persons at a higher level, perspective and opinions of colleagues on the same hierarchical level, opinions of external specialist, official rules or unwritten organizational laws or according to what is considered to be an appropriate approach in the respective country. After the preference values were averaged for managers of one country and the parameters calculated accordingly, the parameters for each country were compared to each other. Figures 17 and 18 show the differences between France and Germany, as well as between China and Germany.

Figure 17 shows that French managers orient more toward the company's unwritten rules than German managers. For the Germans, on the other hand, the perspectives and opinions of specialists outside of the department are significantly more important. The emphasis on specialists' perspectives and opinions becomes evident in comparison with Chinese man-

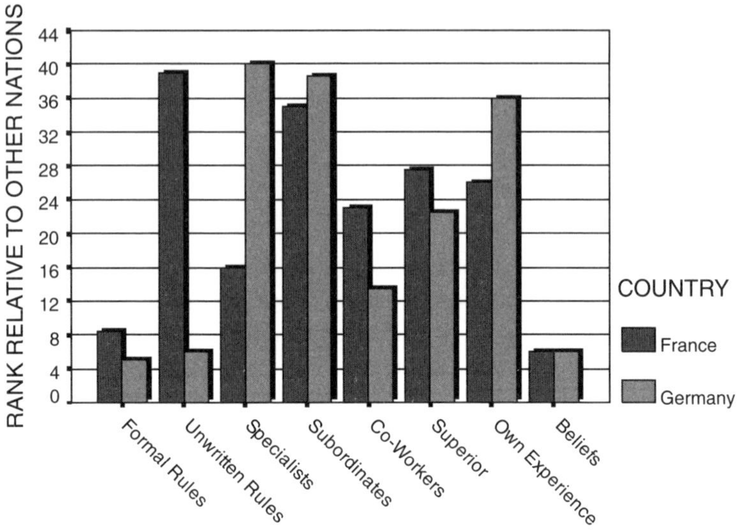

Figure 17: Event management according to French and German managers (Smith 1999). Higher ranking indicates a stronger orientation toward the respective source.

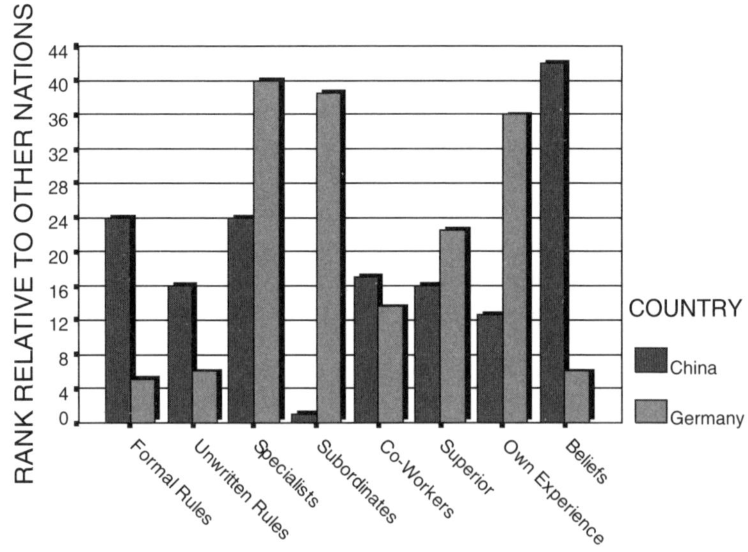

Figure 18: Event management according to Chinese and German managers (Smith 1999). Higher ranking indicates a stronger orientation toward the respective source.

agers in Figure 18. German managers tend to consider opinions of employees who are lower down in the hierarchy and rely more on their own experience than do Chinese managers. In turn, established convictions have more clout for Chinese managers than they do for German managers.

Problem Solving

Problem-solving issues in organizations are often complex. The way people deal with complex demands is a subject of study in the field of cognitive psychology under the designation complex problem solving (cf. Dörner et al. 1983). Related studies were conducted in which people direct complex computer-simulated systems. These systems depict realistic scenarios (e.g., a business operation in a given market) and include the following characteristics (Dörner 1989): *diversity of variables,* or the number of variables the system consists of; *interrelatedness,* forming the different connections between these variables; *lack of transparency* of the connections between the variables or the system itself; *momentum,* i.e., conditions within the system can change by themselves; and *polytely,* in the sense of multiple goal setting for directing the system.

Strohschneider (2001) compared problem-solving behavior and performance demonstrated by both Indians and Germans and found that significant differences were displayed in the complex MORO scenario, a system that simulates problems encountered in developmental aid. German test-persons take more initiative in trying to obtain more information and controlling system functions. Their Indian counterparts are less inclined to explore the scenario in depth, are less prone to react to cause and effect situations, are less likely to adapt their behavior to changing circumstances, make decisions more often without the necessary background information and tend to more frequently forget to monitor the effects of measures taken. The German subjects scored higher on the problem-solving rating than the Indians. Strohschneider interprets these results on the basis of different learning experiences during their respective socialization processes. In India, independent and proactive problem-solving performance is not expected and parental guidance and control is more prevalent. This results in different problem-solving strategies, which are less suited to the MORO-simulation (cf. Strohschneider 2001, p. 141).

In another study involving the complex MANUTEX scenario that simulates a small business operation, Strohschneider found indications of different culturally based management strategies. While German test-persons embarked on assertive and expansive strategies, the Indian subjects tended to prefer more defensive and risk-avoiding decisions. According to

MANUTEX, the former approach is more effective than the latter. Nevertheless, Strohschneider points out accurately that, based on his findings, one cannot deduce that the assertive-expansive approach demonstrated by the Germans is more effective under all circumstances than the defensive low-risk strategy. Instead, he claims, it can be assumed that both strategies reflect appropriate adaptation to the respective business environments:

"Considering the prevailing uncertain market conditions, undependable infrastructure and procurement of raw materials typical for India, a careful, step-by-step approach is more successful in the long run. In contrast, the German approach of taking calculated risks and making large investments makes more sense in the long run considering the "typically German" conditions of a predictable and dependable business environment" (Strohschneider 2001, p. 195).

Creating Motivating Working Conditions

Working independently and in groups is seen and weighted differently depending on the culture. The *model of the social group* (cf. Kashima and Callan 1994) prevalent in a collectivist culture such as Japan, holds that the group constitutes the main work unit in an organization. Consequently, tasks are not assigned to individuals but rather to groups. While the organization clearly defines group tasks, the roles played by individual group members are not defined by the organization, but rather are negotiated within the group. Group performance, not individual achievement, is rewarded. Thus, by rewarding the group rather than individual members, the work group is motivated to continue to work together effectively. In the *model of the rationally operating individual,* the individual plays a key role in the organization's work unit. Thus, as a rule, tasks are assigned primarily to individuals, not to a group as a whole. Individual achievement is rewarded and good personal performance is more highly valued than weak performance. The higher the individual performance, the less group support is considered to have played a role. The group merely provides the contextual conditions or the tools that the individual can resort to in the process of striving for the goal. This is not to say that group-oriented work and leadership only occurs and is effective in collectivist cultures. Ideas for workgroup constellations have been gaining momentum in Western cultures as well. An example here is the idea of a partially autonomous workgroup derived from thoughts on the humanization of working conditions leading to the economically motivated basic principle of "lean management" in the1990's (cf. Antoni 1994, 2000; Benders et al. 1999). According to Kashima and Callan (1994, p. 636; cf. also Antoni 2000), primary con-

ditions for the transferability of group-oriented working models according to a western context of work are:
- Group goals must be clearly defined.
- Group members must have the necessary know-how and skills to define the required steps toward reaching the goal.
- Group members must have the specific social competence enabling them to clarify and negotiate their role within the group.
- Group members must be motivated enough to implement the steps agreed upon and to fulfill the assigned tasks.

Leadership and management means taking the work-related needs of employees into consideration. According to an international study conducted by Ronen (1994), four types of work-related needs can be differentiated:
- Collective, material needs (e.g., secure conditions of employment, good physical working conditions);
- Collective, human needs (e.g., creating positive working relationships with colleagues and supervisors);
- Individual material needs (e.g., career, salary, prestige);
- Individual human needs (e.g., achievement, developing and implementing know-how, autonomy).

Even if there are plausible reasons for adopting a universal framework of needs, there will always be differences in emphasis on specific needs that are influenced by culture and reflect both work-related and general living conditions in the respective countries (cf. Hui and Luk 1997). In developed countries, having an "interesting" job constitutes an important need. In a more collectivist culture like Israel, the quality of interpersonal relationship takes priority. In contrast, developed countries emphasize basic existential security, for example the need for material income. Essentially, this indicates that Maslow's pyramid of needs (1954) is indeed applicable, causing Hui and Luk to summarize an overview of their research on different culture-based work needs in terms of: "Where basic needs have not been satisfied, other higher level motivators would not work" (1997, p. 376).

2.5.4 Developing Interculturally Competent Leadership and Management

The discussions above show that cultural factors influence leadership behavior and its effects to a great extent. Cultural characteristics determine what specific leadership behavior is perceived and judged as task- or employee-oriented behavior. The effects of different approaches to goal setting and agreement depend on the cultural context in which these events occur. Managers from different cultures emphasize different perspectives for making corporate decisions and they apply different approaches and strategies for overcoming complex problems. What is considered motivating by those being led also differs from one culture to the next. These differences in intercultural overlap situations are significant from a practical perspective. If the manager and the employee come from different cultures, or if a work group for managers is culturally diverse, it poses both risks and offers opportunities. The positive side would be if culturally different experiences and behavioral patterns merge and ultimately complement each other. On the other hand, there are risks involved if different experiences and behavioral patterns are not understood by either party, the interaction is experienced as unsatisfactory, is judged negatively and an acceptable form of integrating diversity does not take place. In order to profit from intercultural cooperation, it is indispensable to selectively target and develop managers with a view to applied intercultural competence. According to Thomas, Kammhuber and Layes (1997, p. 67f.), applied intercultural competence comprises the ability to be aware of cultural conditions and influencing factors in perception, judgment, feeling and action as they apply to one's self and others. Moreover, it includes the ability to actively honor and respect in the sense of alternating adaptation, to tolerate incompatibilities and to develop synergetic forms of co-existence and a world view. Selecting and developing personnel accordingly requires what is defined as intercultural leadership and management requirements. Methods must be implemented to assess appropriate candidate selection according to their applied intercultural competence. In addition, measures must be taken to develop personnel in applied intercultural competence, for example, through training and coaching in these areas.

References

Antoni, C. H. (Ed.) (1994): Gruppenarbeit in Unternehmen. Konzepte, Erfahrungen, Perspektiven. Weinheim.

Antoni, C. H. (1999): Konzepte der Mitarbeiterbeteiligung: Delegation und Partizipation. In: Hoyos, C. G.; Frey, D. (Eds.), Arbeits- und Organisationspsychologie. Ein Lehrbuch. Weinheim, pp. 569–583.

Antoni, C. H. (2000): Teamarbeit gestalten. Grundlagen, Analysen, Lösungen. Weinheim und Basel.

Benders, J.; Huijgen, F.; Pekruhl, U.; O'Kelly, K. P. (1999): Useful but Unused – Group Work in Europe. Luxemburg.
Drosdowski, G.; Grebe, P.; Köster, R.; Müller, W.; Scholze-Stubenrecht, W. (Eds.) (1963): Duden, Band 7: Das Herkunftswörterbuch. Mannheim.
Dörner, D. (1989): Die Logik des Mißlingens. Reinbek.
Dörner, D.; Kreuzig, H. W.; Reither, F.; Stäudel, T. (Eds.). (1983). Lohhausen: Vom Umgang mit Unbestimmtheit und Komplexität. Bern.
Erez, M. (1986): The congruence of goal setting strategies with socio-cultural values, and its effect on performance. Journal of Management 12: 588–592.
Erez, M.; Earley, P. C. (1987): Comparative analysis of goal-setting-strategies across cultures. Journal of Applied Psychology 72: 658–665.
Erez, M.; Earley, P. C. (1993): Culture, Self-Identity and Work. New York.
Fleishman, E. (1973): Twenty years of consideration and structure. In: Fleishman, E. A.; Hunt, J. G. (Eds.), Current Developments in the Study of Leadership. Carbondale, pp. 1–37.
Frey, D.; Spielmann, U. (1994): Führung – Konzepte und Theorien. In: Frey, D.; Greif, S. (Eds.), Sozialpsychologie. Ein Handbuch in Schlüsselbegriffen. 3rd ed. Weinheim, pp. 164–173.
Graen, G. B.; Scandura, T. A. (1987): Theorie der Führungsdyaden. In: Kieser, A.; Reber, G.; Wunderer, R. (Eds.), Handwörterbuch der Führung. Stuttgart, pp. 377–389.
Hofstede, G. (1997). Lokales Denken, globales Handeln. Kulturen, Zusammenarbeit und Management. München.
Hui, C. H.; Luk, C. L. (1997): Industrial/organizational psychology. In: Berry, J. W.; Segall, M. H.; Kagitcibasi, C. (Eds.), Handbook of Cross-Cultural Psychology, Vol. 3: Social Behavior and Applications. 2nd ed. Needham Heights, MA, pp. 371–411.
Kashima, Y.; Callan, V. J. (1994): The japanese work group. In: Triandis, H. C.; Dunnette, M. D.; Hough, L. M. (Eds.), Handbook of Industrial and Organizational Psychology, Vol. 4. 2nd ed. Palo Alto, CA, pp. 609–646.
Locke, E. A.; Latham, G. P. (1990): A Theory of Goal Setting and Task Performance. Englewood Cliffs, NJ.
Maslow, A. H. (1954): Motivation and Personality. New York.
Mintzberg, H. (1991): Mintzberg über Management. Wiesbaden.
Misumi, J. (1985): The Behavioral Science of Leadership. An Interdisciplinary Japanese Research Program. Ann Arbor.
Nerdinger, F. W. (2001): Motivierung. In: Schuler, H. (Ed.), Lehrbuch der Personalpsychologie. Göttingen, pp. 349–371.
Neuberger, O. (1988): Führung (ist) symbolisiert. Plädoyer für eine sinnvolle Führungsforschung. In: Neuberger, O. (Ed.), Augsburger Beiträge zur Organisationspsychologie und Personalwesen, Heft 2. Universität Augsburg.
Neuberger, O. (1990): Führen und geführt werden. Stuttgart.
Ronen, S. (1994): An underlying structure of motivational need taxonomies: A cross-cultural confirmation. In: Triandis, H. C.; Dunnette, M. D.; Hough, L. M. (Eds.), Handbook of Industrial and Organizational Psychology. Vol. 4. 2nd ed. Palo Alto, CA, pp. 241–269.
Rosenstiel, L. v. (1993): Kommunikation und Führung in Arbeitsgruppen. In: Schuler, H. (Ed.), Lehrbuch Organisationspsychologie. Bern, pp. 321–351.

Rosenstiel, L. v. (1999): Führung und Macht. In: Hoyos, C. G.; Frey, D. (Eds.), Arbeits- und Organisationspsychologie. Ein Lehrbuch. Weinheim, pp. 412–428.
Schein, E. H. (1995): Unternehmenskultur. Ein Handbuch für Führungskräfte. Frankfurt a. M.
Sinha, J. B. P. (1984): A model of effective leadership styles in India. International Studies of Management; Organization 14(3): 86–98.
Sinha, J. B. P. (1994): The Cultural Context of Leadership and Power. New Delhi.
Smith, P. B. (1999): Predicting process difficulties in multicultural teams. Psychologische Beiträge 41(3): 356–367.
Smith, P. B.; Misumi, J.; Tayeb, M.; Peterson, M. F.; Bond, M. (1989): On the generality of leadership style measures across cultures. Journal of Occupational Psychology 62: 97–109.
Smith, P. B.; Noakes, J. (1996): Cultural differences in group processes. In: West, M. A. (Ed.), Handbook of Work Group Psychology. Baffins Lane, Chichester, pp. 477–501.
Smith, P. B.; Peterson, M. F. (1988): Leadership, Organizations and Culture. London.
Smith, P. B.; Peterson, M. F.; Schwartz, S. H. (1998): Cultural values and making sense of work events: A 40-nation study. Submitted paper. University of Sussex, School of Social Sciences.
Strohschneider, S. (2001): Kultur – Denken – Strategie. Eine indische Suite. Bern.
Thomas, A. (1993): Psychologie interkulturellen Lernen und Handelns. In: Thomas, A. (Ed.), Kulturvergleichende Psychologie. Eine Einführung. Göttingen, pp. 377–424.
Thomas, A.; Kammhuber, S.; Layes, G. (1997): Interkulturelle Kompetenz. Bonn, Bundesministerium für Verteidigung.
Thomas, A.; Stumpf, S. (2002). Aspekte interkulturellen Führungsverhaltens. In: Bergemann, N. J.; Sourisseaux, A. L. J. (Eds.), Interkulturelles Management. 3rd ed. Heidelberg, pp. 69–107.
Yukl, G.; van Fleet, D. D. (1992): Theory and research on leadership in organizations. In: Dunnette, M. D.; Hough, L. M. (Eds.), Handbook of Industrial and Organizational Psychology, Vol. 3. 2nd ed. Palo Alto, CA, pp. 147–197.

Siegfried Stumpf

2.6 Intercultural Teams

2.6.1 Intercultural Teams: A Key Success Factor in Organizations

For many organizations regardless of size and task orientation, international activity is part of the daily agenda. Production sites are established abroad, foreign markets are developed and partnerships with other organizations are formed, such as the merger between Daimler-Benz and Chrysler or between Bankers Trust and Deutsche Bank. Global business is no longer limited to conglomerates but is increasingly the domain of successful small and medium-sized businesses (Simon 1996, p. 65). International contacts and relations are essential for both business operations and many other nonbusiness-oriented organizations. Included in this category are sector-specific organizations such as trade unions, scientific communities and military organizations involved in international peacekeeping missions. Even life in our own countries has become more international. The many foreign subsidiaries based in Germany and immigration of peoples from other countries and continents give us the impression that Europe is converging. We encounter cultural otherness everyday in schools, hospitals, universities, companies or at public events. These developments confront us with challenges that we must learn to cope with constructively.

A diversity of tasks in production, service or administration are managed by work groups or, in more modern usage of the term, teams. Despite the differences in the nature of the team in terms of lifecycle or autonomy, their common denominator is their commitment to the task and striving toward a common goal. Responsibility lies with the group rather than the individual, while the latter provides the framework for cooperation. Work groups of this kind have become a permanent fixture within organizations. On the one hand, the idea is to create more flexibility and efficiency, for instance in production, by introducing group-oriented forms of work. On the other, the complexity of tasks requires the combined efforts of group members with their diverse abilities, expertise and perspective in solving the problems they encounter. In the future, the success of an organization will depend on the productivity of its work groups.

Due to increased internationalization, we will be seeing more intercultural work groups with members of diverse cultural backgrounds. In the following discourse, we will discuss what this means for the team process and performance. The key question here is, are we dealing with a negligible dimension or an important challenge for those in an organization who build, lead, support or function within a team?

2.6.2 Chances and Risks Involved in Intercultural Work Groups

According to the heterogeneity model created by McGrath, Berdahl and Arrow (1995), the differences in social categories such as nationality or ethnic affiliation significantly impact the course of group processes and performance. Two causal connections are emphasized here:

- *Culture-specific socialization processes:* From a psychological perspective, a culture that reflects the characteristics of a specific nation or ethnic affiliation can be understood as a system or orientation that forms and influences the perception, thinking, values and actions of individuals living in this culture during the course of their socialization process (Thomas 1996). Accordingly, culture conveys and develops fundamental values, attitudes, action and thought patterns as well as task-specific abilities and skills.
- *Activating national stereotypes:* Because social categories such as nationality or ethnic belonging are easily recognized, these characteristics can activate stereotyping. Stereotyping in this sense refers to a cognitive scheme that includes assumptions about the characteristics of the people belonging to this social group (Jackson 1996, p. 57 f.). These assumptions give rise to expectations about the interaction partner's characteristics and behavior, which in turn calibrate the way one behaves, reciprocally influencing the partner's behavior.

What effects do culturally diverse groups have on group performance? Based on a comprehensive analysis of research literature, Steiner (1972) suggests the following formula for group performance:

$$\text{Actual productivity of group (AP)} = \\ \text{Potential productivity of group (PP)} - \text{process loss (PV)}$$

Potential productivity is determined by aligning the group's resources, that is the group members' skills and knowledge with the task requirements.

Actual productivity is created out of potential productivity minus what is lost during the process, which may manifest in the form of decreased motivation and coordination. Motivation deficits occur as a result of a decrease of effort on the part of group members in the group situation, similar to the "getting a free ride" effect. Coordination deficits occur when the group's existing resources are not coordinated effectively, for instance, when members are not assigned tasks commensurate with their strengths.

Steiner's formula does not include possible process advantages such as synergy effects. This does not appear to be unwarranted, according to the state of research based on group performance. Groups would do well to reduce what is lost in process work and utilize the potential inherent in their members (cf. Hackman 1998, p. 246). There is very little empirical proof for process gains that go beyond the actual process work, for example the phenomenon known as "synergy" (cf. Stumpf and Zeutschel 2000).

The effects of increased team diversity due to more culturally disparate group combinations become clear based on Steiner's formula (cf. Adler 1997, p. 131):

- The team's' *potential productivity* increases because the team is able to resort to diverse experiences, ideas and perspectives. Specific and general increases in potential differ here (cf. Maznevski 1994, p. 533 f.). A particular increase in potential occurs when members of a culture contribute direct advantages in the form of task-related expertise and ability to particular aspects of the task. This is the case, for instance, when a team whose members are natives of the respective countries and whose background is based on diverse cultural experiences in addition to their knowledge about the product attempts to introduce a product on the U. S., German and Chinese markets. In addition, a general increase in potential already results from the diversity of perception and ideas, opening up a larger playing field for action and decision making and generating controversy that can stimulate creativity within the team (cf. Johnson and Johnson 1982, Tjosvold 1985).
- The *risk of loss during the process* increases the more the diversity of perception-based biases, such as mistrust or antagonism, are present, activating stereotyping and causing miscommunication (cf. Scholl 1996).
- The increase in potential productivity can be transformed into *actual productivity* or, contrastingly, the team experiences repeated loss depending on how the group deals with *diversity management*: "Highly productive and less productive teams differ in how they manage their diversity, not, as is commonly believed, in the presence or absence of diversity. When well managed, diversity becomes an asset and productive resource for the team. When ignored, diversity causes problems that diminish the team's productivity" (Adler 1997, p. 138). The diversity

within the team should not lead to the team's disintegration. Despite all diversity, the team must be managed in a way that will sustain it as an integrated unit (cf. Maznevski 1994, A. Thomas 1999). One approach to achieve this might be to create a strategy for integration, for instance, a role structure headed by an integrative team leader (Maier 1967) and tapping into the team members' (Maznevski 1994) communication skills.

The following section introduces empirical studies on the effects of team composition on team performance.

2.6.3 Empirical Studies on the Effectiveness of International Teams

In spite of the increasing practical importance of the performance potential inherent in intercultural teams, there are only a few empirical studies that tackle this issue and in the overall scope of research in this area their share is still minimal (cf. D. C. Thomas, p. 242).

Schroll-Machl (1996), Thomas and Zeutschel (1998), Zeutschel (1999) and Tjitra (2001) conducted studies demonstrating that differences in cultural affiliation can be linked to the team's varying orientation characteristics. According to studies by Thomas, Zeutschel and Tjitra, multi- and mono-cultural teams consisting of American, Indonesian and German students were asked to join a simulated corporate business game. An analysis of group processes show that there were clear, culture-specific differences in dealing with the task and the way in which relationships were created within the team. These variables can be defined as adaptive differences (cf. Demorgon and Molz 1996) that evolved in the respective cultures and which, when effectively combined, could lead to enhanced performance. In Table 10, some of these adaptive differences are categorized into different aspects of orientation (cf. Thomas and Zeutschel 1998).

A number of studies focus on the question of whether intercultural teams are more effective than mono-cultural workgroups (cf. Watson et al. 1993; Thomas et al. 1996; D. C. Thomas 1999). Studies conducted by Watson, Kumar and Michaelsen (1993) stand out because they were conducted within the scope of a field experiment, observing authentic teams over a longer time period instead of resorting to the popular snapshot method of assembling an "artificial" team for experimental laboratory purposes. Watson, Kumar and Michaelsen (1993) assembled culturally heterogeneous

Table 10: Adaptation oppositions in behavior and perception among American, German and Indonesian team members.

Task Orientation	
Focus on recognition	Focus on action
Strive for an ideal approach that is binding for all involved (G)	Trial and error (I) Accept provisional decisions with frequent checkups (US)
Relationship Orientation	
Polarization	Harmony
Attribute success and lack of success to the individual (US, G)	Attribute success and lack of success to the collective (I)
Address conflict directly (G)	Avoid conflict (I)
Deal with differences of opinion (G)	Seek compromise (US, I)
Structural Orientation	
Exclusion	Openness
Accept unequal proportion of power (I)	Consider all team members equal (G)
Designate clear tasks (G)	Responsibilities are transparent (I)
Process Orientation	
Long-term approach	Short-term approach
Focus on continuity (G)	Focus on change (I)
Proceed consecutively (US, G)	Proceed simultaneously (I)

Note: US = American behavioral style; G = German behavioral style; I = Indonesian Style of behavior

and homogeneous teams, consisting of four or five participants, respectively. Caucasian Americans made up the mono-cultural team. The intercultural team was composed of two or more nationalities (e.g., U. S. and another country in Asia, Africa, Latin America or the Middle East) and several with ethnic backgrounds (e.g., persons of African or Spanish origin). In total 173 persons took part in the study and were divided into 17 monocultural and 19 intercultural teams. The team study lasted 17 weeks, during which time the participants had plenty of opportunity to interact with each other. The task consisted of business case studies that were evaluated upon completing the task. The process was measured at four time points: t_1 and t_4 in the fifth, ninth, thirteenth and seventeenth week. Group performance was evaluated according to each team's written response to the case studies, after which experts measured team performance according to four criteria. A grade was given for each criterion, from one (very bad) to five (very good). Then, the average of the sum was used as an indicator for the team's overall performance. Participants filled out a questionnaire separately, assessing their opinion of the team's performance at specified intervals. The team members' individual evaluation determined the performance of the team process. After each interval assessment, the teams received feedback on strengths and weaknesses relative to the group's process and performance. In follow up, the groups were invited to implement the measures discussed in the feedback discussions on their own. The study results show that the longer the team is together, the more both the process and performance are enhanced in intercultural and mono-cultural teams. This indicates that over time, team members learn to interact more confidently with each other and to fulfill the performance requirements. Initially, intercultural teams lag behind their mono-cultural counterparts. This evens out, however, the longer the team is together. By the time the fourth and last evaluation has been reached, the intercultural teams have achieved the same total performance level as their mono-cultural counterparts. The intercultural teams actually performed significantly better on two performance criteria relative to tasks dealing with a variety of different perspectives and on a task in which they were asked to generate different alternatives for a solution. However, this did not have a statistically significant effect on overall performance. These findings indicate that intercultural teams tend to have more difficulty integrating in the beginning phase, which they are able to overcome over the course of time.

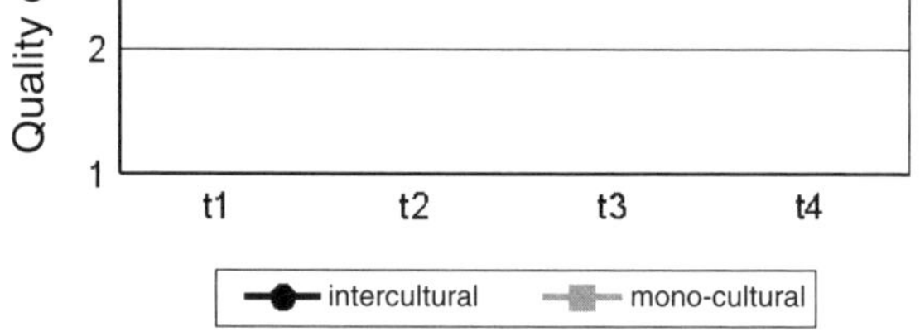

Figure 19: Illustrates the course of the statistical effectiveness value

Similar studies have been conducted by Thomas, Ravlin and Wallace (1996) and D.C. Thomas (1999). The former found that cultural heterogeneity has a positive effect on team effectiveness. In contrast to Watson, Kumar and Michaelsen, the pattern of effectiveness values evolving over time show that the effectiveness of intercultural teams is consistently higher than that of mono-cultural teams at all points of evaluation, although the mono-cultural teams were able to make up the difference for the most part at the fifth and last evaluation interval. Another pattern of findings appears in D. C. Thomas (1999), in which cultural homogeneity exerts a positive effect on the team. At all five evaluation points, the mono-cultural teams showed higher team effectiveness but, unlike the studies by Watson, Kumar and Michaelsen (1993), the intercultural group was able to reduce the gap to the mono-cultural teams near the end.

In view of the varying results, it can be assumed that the study conducted by Watson, Kumar and Michaelsen is closely connected to the specific conditions required of the team. The teams received periodic feedback on the quality of their progress and performance and were encouraged to reflect on the information they received and implement it constructively. This may have generated learning processes in the group (cf. West 1996) and contributed to the ability of intercultural teams to overcome deficits in the team process and effectiveness toward the end of the study, allowing them to catch up with the mono-cultural team (cf. Watson et al. 1998). The study conducted by Thomas, Ravlin and Wallace (1996) and D. C. Thomas 1999, p. 258) did not include this feedback loop, which may have made learning from the team experience more difficult. Furthermore, differences in the specific task characteristics may have been responsible for the different results (cf. D. C. Thomas 1999, p. 257 f.).

The following conclusions can be drawn based on these findings: Teams are unlikely to show peak performance from the moment of their conception. Instead, they require time for team members to come together, get to know each other and begin discovering mutual orientation and a shared normative idea about how the team is to proceed (q.v. Ch. II, 2.4). Traditional models of team development, such as Tuckman's (1965) model, have already dealt with this issue, in which the "performing phase" is not reached until the prerequisite phases in the team process, namely "forming", "storming" and "norming", have been completed.

- The more culturally diverse the team is, including the respective members' abilities and their disparate ideas of "norming", the more important it is to allow enough time for the "forming" stage. It is unrealistic to expect peak performance from intercultural teams from the very beginning. These teams require more time for interacting and finding their own within the team and might, as a result, find more difficulties in getting the team up and running. This is especially true when tasks require close collaboration among members (cf. also McGrath et al. 1995, p. 32 f.).
- Time alone, however, is not the only factor. It depends on how team members manage their time. Watson, Kumar and Michaelsen (1993) suggest that the required integration process is more effective if the

teams receive regular feedback on the team process and performance, can reflect on the information, as well as come up with a constructive modus operandi, cf. also Kleinbeck and Kleinbeck 1999). Targeted HR and training measures sponsored by the organization can further enhance the process of intercultural team development. This issue will be discussed in the next section.

2.6.4 Recommendations for Managing Intercultural Teams

According to a model by Maznevski and DiStefano (2000), the building block phases of *mapping, bridging and integrating* can be regarded as a success factor in the process of developing intercultural teams. The focus during the mapping phase is on encouraging the team members to recognize the relevant differences and similarities between them and how it may benefit team processes and performance. Communication processes must be established during the bridging phase to ensure adequate interaction despite the differences: "When the world views of the speaker and the listener are very different from each other, as they usually are among members of global teams, these perspectives must be bridged with very explicit attention paid to the communication processes ... Team members ... need to use their maps of differences to develop bicultural tongues and ears" (Maznevski and DiStefano 2000, p. 199).

The integration phase builds on the awareness and understanding of intercultural differences and gap-bridging communication processes. Once the team is aware of different perspectives and preferences among the team members, members must come together and solve the discrepancies resulting from the differences so that the team can develop mutually satisfying methods that will allow them to accomplish the task adequately and effectively (q.v. 2.6.3). It can be assumed that a successful integration process includes both maintaining important differences and strengthening similarities among members. The idea here is to create an understanding shared by all members of the group on how to deal constructively with existing differences among team members, which can then be mobilized to achieve the common goal.

In order to successfully negotiate the phases of mapping, bridging and integrating, the teams need support from the organization. Effective team processes and performance do not happen spontaneously in culturally diverse teams. According to Zeutschel (1999): "Synergy is not for free". The following training measures offered by organizations and designed to assist intercultural teams during the developmental phase to enhance performance are described below.

Training to enhance intercultural competence (q.v Ch. I, 2.2). The success of mapping, bridging and integration processes depends on intercultural competence, including an insight into cultural differences to support the mapping processes. Bridging processes are not possible without the required communicative ability, and integration processes require the knowledge and ability to deal effectively with intercultural conflict. It stands to reason that an organization's HR development program include measures to strengthen the employees' intercultural competence. Intercultural trainings play an important role within this framework (cf. Thomas et al. 1999). There are many different training methods that emphasize the transferal of applied intercultural know-how, and work through intercultural experiences (cf. Thomas et al. 2002).

Selecting candidates with applied intercultural competence (q.v. Ch. I, 2.1). Both intercultural competence and specialist expertise should be considered in the selection process. This applies in particular to team or project leaders, as they are responsible for directing team processes and integrating culturally based differences. In order for intercultural competence to be included in the selection process, a thorough analysis and realistic description of the concept is necessary. Culture assimilator trainings have been proven effective as a diagnostic tool for identifying leadership competence (cf. Arbeitskreis Assessment Center 1992; Neubauer 1980). Concrete intercultural requirements can be assessed for their "real life" value in different intercultural exercises (cf. Bolton 2001, Kühlmann and Stahl 1996).

Team development measures: These refer to systematic steps taken to improve the performance, quality of team work and interaction within the scope of new or already existing teams under the guidance of qualified facilitators (cf. Comelli 1994, Dyer 1995, Stumpf and Thomas 2003). Team development activities are best conducted in two phases:

- At the *beginning:* During this forming phase for teamwork activities, measures are taken to create optimal conditions. Here the relevant inter-individual differences and similarities of team members can be explored and their significance for the team brought to light (mapping). At the same time, the team can experiment with effective communication within the team (bridging). Once this foundation has been established, team members can proceed to integrate differences, such as agreeing on a modus operandi for teamwork (integrating).
- *During* the norming phase: It is not enough to simply plan the integration process in advance. Additional, previously unrecognized inter-individual differences can also emerge while working together. This stands in contrast to the idea of a predetermined interaction process that can be "solved" in advanced. In addition, previously applied measures that have proven ineffective as well as novel integration issues can arise in the

course of the team endeavor. In cases such as these, the support of an external expert may be helpful in assisting to resolve these issues.

Person-focused, on-the-job development also encourages learning while performing relevant tasks (McCall et al. 1995). Work in intercultural groups offers an excellent opportunity to acquire intercultural competence in a work context. This is especially true for managers, who, while enhancing their intercultural competence, can in this way prepare for future international assignments (Maznevski and DiStefano 2000). Here, it is advisable to integrate many feedback and reflection sessions during the team process. Many authors (e.g., Boud et al. 1985, Kolb 1984, Schön 1983) refer to the importance of reflection within the scope of experience-based learning. If reflection processes are not systematically supported, learners risk not profiting from their experience as much as they could. Put to the point, one could even say: "Experience itself does not teach, people learn from reflecting on their experience" (Tjosvold 1991, p. 189).

Learning organizations: The experiences an organization makes with intercultural learning and cooperation processes constitute an important resource, which profit from regular feedback on "real-life" experience (cf. Jackson 1996, p. 68, Thomas et al. 1999). This requires systematically compiling, evaluating and preparing the information so that the acquired knowledge can be passed on. In this way, information relevant to problems arising in intercultural groups and experience with problem-solving endeavors in both the positive and negative sense can contribute to the design of selection processes and personal development measures (training, team development and personal development measures).

References

Adler, N. J. (1997): International Dimensions of Organizational Behavior. 3rd ed. Boston

Arbeitskreis Assessment Center (Ed.) (1992): Standards der Assessment Center Technik. München.

Bolten, J. (2001): Interkulturelle Assessment Center. In: Sarges, W. (Ed.), Weiterentwicklungen der Assessment Center-Methode. 2nd ed. Göttingen, pp. 213– 218.

Boud, D.; Keogh, R.; Walker, D. (1985): Promoting reflection in learning: A model. In: Boud, D.; Keogh, R.; Walker, D. (Eds.), Reflection: Turning Experience into Learning. London, pp. 18–40.

Comelli, G. (1994): Teamentwicklung – Training von »family groups«. In: Hofmann, L. M.; Regnet, E. (Eds.), Innovative Weiterbildungskonzepte. Trends, Inhalte und Methoden der Personalentwicklung in Unternehmen. Göttingen, pp. 61–84.

Demorgon, J.; Molz, M. (1996): Bedingungen und Auswirkungen der Analyse von

Kultur(en) und interkulturellen Interaktionen. In: Thomas, A. (Ed.), Psychologie interkulturellen Handelns. Göttingen, pp. 43–86.

Dyer, W. G. (1995): Team Building. Current Issues and New Alternatives. 3rd ed. Reading, Mass.

Hackman, J. R. (1998): Why teams don't work. In: Tindale, R. S.; Heath, L.; Edwards, J.; Posavac, E. J.; Bryant, F. B.; Suarez-Balcazar, Y.; Henderson-King, E.; Myers, J. (Eds.), Social Psychological Applications to Social Issues, Vol. 4, Theory and Research on Small Groups. New York, pp. 245–267.

Jackson, S. E. (1996): The consequences of diversity in multidisciplinary work teams. In: West, M. A. (Ed.), Handbook of Work Group Psychology. Baffins Lane/Chichester, pp. 53–75.

Johnson, D. W.; Johnson, F. P. (1982): Joining Together: Group Theory and Group Skills. 2nd ed. Englewood Cliffs/NJ.

Kleinbeck, U.; Kleinbeck, T. (1999): Anreiz- und Zielsetzungssysteme. In: Hoyos, C. Graf; Frey, D. (Eds.), Arbeits- und Organisationspsychologie. Ein Lehrbuch. Weinheim, pp. 526–536.

Kolb, D. A. (1984): Experiential Learning. Englewood Cliffs.

Kühlmann, T. M.; Stahl, G. K. (1996): Fachkompetenz allein genügt nicht – Interkulturelle Assessment Center unterstützen die gezielte Personalauswahl. Personalführung Plus, 22–24.

Maier, N. R. F. (1967): Assets and liabilities in group problem solving: The need for an integrative function. Psychological Review 74: 239–249.

Maznevski, M. L. (1994): Understanding our differences: Performance in decision-making groups with diverse members. Human Relations 47: 531–552.

Maznevski, M. L.; DiStefano, J. J. (2000): Global leaders are team players: Developing global leaders through membership on global teams. Human Resource Management 39: 195–208.

McCall, M. W. Jr.; Lombardo, M. M.; Morrison, A. M. (1995): Erfolg aus Erfahrung. Effiziente Lernstrategien für Manager. Stuttgart.

McGrath, J. E.; Berdahl, J. L.; Arrow, H. (1995): Traits, expectations, culture and clout: The dynamics of diversity in work groups. In: Jackson, S. E.; Ruderman, M. N. (Ed.), Diversity in Work Teams. Research Paradigms for a Changing Workplace. Washington, DC, pp. 17–45.

Neubauer, R. (1980): Die Assessment Center Technik: Ein verhaltensorientierter Ansatz zur Führungskräfteauswahl. In: Neubauer, R.; Rosenstiel, L. v. (Eds.), Handbuch der angewandten Psychologie, Band 1: Arbeit und Organisation. München, pp. 122–158.

Scholl, W. (1996): Effective teamwork – a theoretical model and a test in the field. In: Witte, E.; Davis, J. H. (Eds.), Understanding Group Behavior. Vol. 2: Small Group Processes and Interpersonal Relations. Mahwah/NJ, pp. 127–146.

Schön, D. A. (1983): The Reflective Practitioner. How Professionals Think in Action. New York.

Schroll-Machl, S. (1996): Kulturbedingte Unterschiede im Problemlöseprozeß bei deutsch-amerikanischen Arbeitsgruppen. In: Thomas, A. (Ed.), Psychologie interkulturellen Handelns. Göttingen, pp. 383–409.

Simon, H. (1996): Die heimlichen Gewinner (Hidden Champions). Die Erfolgsstrategien unbekannter Weltmarktführer. Frankfurt a. M.

Steiner, I. D. (1972): Group Process and Productivity. New York.

Stumpf, S.; Thomas, A. (Eds.) (2003): Teamarbeit und Teamentwicklung. Göttingen.

Stumpf, S.; Zeutschel, U. (2000): Synergy effects in multinational work groups: What we know and what we don't know. In: Mendenhall, M. E.; Kühlmann, T. M.; Stahl, G. K. (Eds.), Developing Global Business Leaders: Policies, Processes, and Innovations. Westport, pp. 175–194.

Thomas, A. (1996): Analyse der Handlungswirksamkeit von Kulturstandards. In: Thomas, A. (Ed.), Psychologie interkulturellen Handelns. Göttingen, pp. 107–135.

Thomas, A. (1999): Gruppeneffektivität: Balance zwischen Heterogenität und Homogenität. Gruppendynamik 30 (2): 117–129.

Thomas, A.; Hagemann, K.; Stumpf, S. (2002): Training interkultureller Kompetenz. In: Bergemann, N. J.; Sourisseaux, A. L. J. (Eds.), Interkulturelles Management. 3rd ed. Heidelberg, pp. 237–272.

Thomas, A.; Kinast, E.-U.; Schroll-Machl, S. (1999): Entwicklung interkultureller Handlungskompetenz von international tätigen Fach- und Führungskräften durch interkulturelle Trainings. In: Götz, K. (Ed.), Interkulturelles Lernen/Interkulturelles Training. München/Mering, pp. 97–122.

Thomas, A.; Zeutschel, U. (1998): Interkulturelle Synergie in Arbeitsgruppen: Projektabschlußbericht. Institut für Psychologie, Universität Regensburg.

Thomas, D. C. (1999): Cultural diversity and work group effectiveness. Journal of Cross-Cultural Psychology 30 (2): 242–263.

Thomas, D. C.; Ravlin, E. C.; Wallace, A. W. (1996): Effect of cultural diversity in work groups. In: Bamberger, P. A.; Erez, M.; Bacharach, S. B. (Eds.), Research in the Sociology of Organizations. Vol. 14: Cross-Cultural Analysis of Organizations. Greenwich/Connecticut, pp. 1–33.

Tjitra, H. W. (2001): Synergiepotenziale und interkulturelle Probleme. Chancen und Herausforderungen am Beispiel deutsch-indonesischer Arbeitsgruppen. Wiesbaden.

Tjosvold, D. (1985): Implications of controversy research for management. Journal of Management 11: 21–37.

Tjosvold, D. (1991): Team Organization. An Enduring Competitive Advantage. Chichester.

Tuckman, B. W. (1965): Developmental sequence in small groups. Psychological Bulletin 63: 384–399.

Watson, W. E.; Johnson, L.; Kumar, K.; Critelli, J. (1998): Process gain and process loss: Comparing interpersonal processes and performance of culturally diverse and non-diverse teams across time. International Journal of Intercultural Relations 22 (4): 409–430.

Watson, W. E.; Kumar, K.; Michaelsen, L. K. (1993): Cultural diversity's impact on interaction process and performance: Comparing homogeneous and diverse task groups. Academy of Management Journal 36 (3): 590–602.

West, M. A. (1996): Reflexivity and work group effectiveness: a conceptual integration. In: West, M. A. (Ed.), Handbook of Work Group Psychology. Baffins Lane/Chichester, pp. 555–579.

Zeutschel, U. (1999): Interkulturelle Synergie auf dem Weg: Erkenntnisse aus deutschen/US-amerikanischen Problemlösegruppen. Gruppendynamik 30 (2): 131–149.

Alexander Thomas/Detmar Grosse-Leege

2.7 Managing Intercultural Aspects of Mergers and Acquisitions

2.7.1 Situation and Problem Areas

International mergers and acquisitions are a must in globally aligned markets in order to maintain, stabilize and sustain a competitive edge. Global operations of this nature are faced with an entirely new set of challenges than national or regionally based companies. National and international sources differentiate between a *merger* and an *acquisition.* A merger refers to the merging of two or more operations within a national context. An international merger, on the other hand, refers to the merging of two formerly national and independent companies into a new transnational operation. An acquisition takes place when a company is bought up by another, usually larger, operation within which it is gradually integrated. In both cases, regardless of their economic differences in various areas, the goal is to heighten the productivity of the entire operation and to create a proactive cooperation adapted to the needs of the company and its representatives. Four success factors are frequently mentioned in connection with merger and acquisition projects:

"1. A clear strategy is required for the planned merger. 2. Aside from the thorough analysis of both the legal and financial aspects, the corporate culture and staffing must be extensively re-examined. 3. Proactive communication must be sought with all participants early on. 4. Management must be focused on the integration phase, which will ultimately determine the success of the merger: Human Resources is in a position to make a significant contribution to success. This is particularly true for the integration phase when the employees must reorient and be encouraged to embrace the new company and accept its goals" (Vahs and Wuth 2001, p. 6).

Research, interviews and systematic analysis have unanimously shown that over half of all mergers do not fulfill the expectations they started out with, that many fail within the first four years and are then quietly laid to rest (Hofstede 1993). Although many mistakes are made in handling mergers and acquisitions, and a number of them are condemned to fail from the start, there are, nevertheless, a number of proven technical, organizational and economic "hard facts" involved before the possibility of success can even be considered (Gut-Villa 1997, Cooper et al. 1996).

"The probability of success can be considerably enhanced by involving HR in each of the merger and acquisition phases. It is precisely in the more in-depth and more comprehensive transitions that the "soft" factor, in other words the human aspect, plays such a significant role in reaching the desired goal. Therefore, it seems reasonable that organizations planning a merger or acquisition begin thinking in advance about aspects of culture, communication and staff" (Vahs and Wuth 2001, p. 673).

Research literature about mergers focuses almost exclusively on these merger and acquisition phases and the problems they encounter. The post-merger integration phase in business-related research and studies in international management, on the other hand, is almost entirely ignored. This is certainly due to the fact that long-term developmental and growth processes are more difficult to monitor objectively in terms of numbers and measures than decision-making processes. Furthermore, there is very little information on long-term postmerger integration phases. Longitudinal studies would be required here to recreate the phases of development and to develop specific methodologies that could document the soft factors in management development more precisely. This is also the reason why many managers currently believe that things will take off on their own once a merger has been accomplished, with much planning and calculation, media coverage and the consequent approval ratings on the stock market.

An important factor to keep in mind in managing a merger process is that mergers and acquisitions pose different challenges from those required for securing and strengthening an accomplished merger (Gersten et al. 1998). Wucknitz (2001) offers a good overview of the most important factors of human capital. Stahl (2001) explores the effect of cultural factors on the integration process during a merger in detail in relevant studies.

2.7.2 Demands Faced by Management During the Merger Process

Following an accomplished merger and the initial productive phase, everyone involved seems to be satisfied provided that the results increase profit and achieve synergy effects via cost-effective purchasing, opening new sales venues, cutting back on personnel costs and reducing hierarchical structures, for example. As long as this development continues, management and the stakeholders give little thought to its further course, in spite of the fact that sustaining merger activities is a highly complicated process in need of continual attention and maintenance. Success factors and the human risk factor play a key role in this process. Every member of the corporation, from top management through every department down to the factory floor worker, must internalize the conviction that the merger carries benefits for them individually and for the entire company. The merger must fit the bill for *everyone* involved and its benefits must be translatable into experience.

It may be expected that not all managers are prepared to take responsibility for all the changes. If a person feels that the merger is contributing to a corporate culture he cannot support or in which he no longer feels at ease and cannot realize his full potential, he should leave the company, a step he is likely to take on his own sooner or later.

Resignations at the management level are therefore not a sign of a failed merger but on the contrary, a sign of its strength. Individuals who are unable to find purpose and meaning in the merger and are not prepared to shoulder the accompanying consequences are well advised to seek out another field of activity. A merger cannot keep managers who are just waiting for the unpopular merger to fail, as they will inevitably actively promote its downfall. It is just as illogical to try to keep managers who, while seeming to go along with the required changes, are not emotionally committed.

Although global mergers are on the rise, they are still relatively rare and little information is available on how large-scale mergers develop over time. Thus, research findings and practical experience base their results on the experience gained from national mergers. This data has then been applied to global mergers, a move which is only partially valid.

As early as 1991, Bergemann found that insights gained about the structure, strategy, culture and leadership of domestic mergers can indeed be transferred to cross-boundary mergers. This version, however, involves more complexity. Recently, more studies have shown that changes in the corporate structure and culture of domestic mergers take place within a specified framework. When corporate cultures of different countries come together, the organizational cultures do not share a common foundation. Rather, they are products of different national and corporation-specific patterns of socialization. Not only does this pose a threat to habituated practices, but also questions the key orientation structures of own-culture and corporate-culture conditioning that have evolved into fixed conventions (Hofstede 1993). Thus Schnapper (1996) found:

"Many mergers and acquisitions have failed within national borders because of incompatible organizational cultures. Sometimes one organization has norms or dominant behavioral tendencies that have been a "culture shock" to the acquired corporate environment. Since organizational culture reflects many things, the chances for incompatibility are likely. ...

When the strength of this corporate culture clashes with the weaker, equally opposite set of beliefs, behavioral norms etc., there is the likelihood of the more powerful elements to triumph, usually after months or even years of wasteful, acrimonious conflict. There are many examples of these cultural battles exacting extreme costs in terms of energy, productivity, creativity and emotions (Vansina 1974).

When corporate cultural differences are combined with national cultural differences, the conflicts are even more exacerbated with less mutual understanding and chance for resolution. If a company has a cultural norm supportive of lifetime employment, and the acquiring company originates from a country where employees are 'fired at will', laying people off even for legitimate business reasons (such as redundant staff restructuring, re-distribution along different organizing principles, etc.) will be seen as ruthless, heartless and exploitative. The acquiring personnel will think their processes are legitimate and a natural and normal way to conduct business" (p. 270 f.).

Not only is this precisely what makes the integration process more complex but it also creates new challenges on a qualitative level. In a first step, the newly merged organizations must form a common basis or "interculture" (national and corporate culture) that interacts to generate new and creative potential (Forstmann 1998).

Merging two operations into one and sustaining the "marriage", requires utmost attention during the course of the merger process. The goal is to achieve long-term synergetic effects that, in contrast to domestic mergers, are not based on a shared national culture. Not only do the companies have a different historical background, and this is no different from domestic mergers, but they also feature significant differences in all areas of daily work due to their distinct cultural conditioning. Jung (2001) offers help in this respect in his comprehensive work on the subject of culture and identity work:

"By reflecting on personal feelings in relation to corporate culture, employees are more readily able to consciously find their place within the new organization and thus free up energy to take on the task at hand. Through an initial confrontation with the 'novelty' of it, positive connotations emerge in the mind and motivate the employees to step up their performance. Completing tasks on the level of values and personal identity inspires a willingness to engage in dialogue designed to address questions of an 'everyday' operative nature. Participants often expose conflict at the operative level as a proxy war, after deliberating on the identity and value level. Identity work creates the space required for more choice of action and encourages participants to tackle imminent integration issues constructively. The participants' commitment is essential for merging synergetically and sustaining a strong competitive edge" (p. 683).

A German-American global merger has more in common in terms of economically relevant values and beliefs due to shared cultural traditions than, for instance, a German-Chinese merger. One might reach the conclusion here that German-American mergers are easier to manage than German-Chinese mergers.

Interestingly, literature often refers to national cultural similarities and consequently corporate culture-specific similarities that facilitate the integration process. In contrast, very different national and corporate cultures increase the complexity and the nature of the problem. Harris and Moran (1996) cite five success factors for international mergers. Within the merger these are: *variability, complexity* and *reliability.* Among the different cultures, these are *heterogeneity* and *mutual interdependence.* Others disagree with the opinion that a high degree of heterogeneity and mutual interdependence lead to a successful organizational fit, since greater cultural differences are bound to achieve more synergy. Schnapper (1996) came up with the following findings in connection with the development of a national company in a merger process:

"... we can now talk about the evolution of a national company increasing its international operations to the extent that those operations merit its modest cultural adaptation. At some point, its international operations may demand greater flexibility and cultural diversity in its management practices so that it is multinational. It may finally reach the stage of a transnational company, where its national origin and focus is hardly recognizable, except by some historians.

At any stage of this evolutionary process, which is not necessarily predictable, there will be interfaces between procedures, practices, policies and, ultimately, the personnel who carry them out. When these staff represent different countries and national cultures, conflict is almost inevitable."

2.7.3 Intercultural Aspects of the Merger Process

Individuals involved in the integration process play a significant role in solving the integration issue by defining common goals and demonstrating a willingness to work together in a way that promotes integration despite different cultural and corporate culture values, norms and behavioral patterns (Schreyögg).

Without a doubt, chances of achieving this goal relatively quickly are particularly good in a German-American joint venture if both partners have experience with international and globally oriented business relations and both are familiar with the other's cultural idiosyncrasies. Further advantages include a high level of flexibility and the ability to act quickly and effectively while absorbing unfamiliar elements, to assess these for their applicability and to integrate them into their own thought patterns and behavioral repertoire. Developing mindfulness and mutual esteem as a fundamental value is of utmost importance (Thomas 1999; 2003b).

Observation has shown that members of different nations and cultures differ considerably in the required abilities mentioned above. It may be assumed that due to historical developments in Europe and Germany, the postwar generation in Germany faced challenges and learned to adapt to other cultures, earn the respect of business partners and to interact with others on equal footing. Germany is geographically situated in the center of Europe and its economy has a long tradition in the export of goods and services. This brought forth a large number of qualified specialists and business leaders and has developed a corporate culture that facilitates international and global mergers.

Thus one can, for example, assume that the long-standing familiarity with American culture as well as American management and corporate concepts can be considered a success factor. The Daimler-Chrysler merger and, even more so, the EADS merger certainly profit from the extensive cooperation between German, British, French and Spanish corporations as well as from the intensive, long-standing collaboration between German and American experts in technical, administrative and marketing aspects of the aerospace industry. However, judging from the developments of European, transatlantic and global mergers, these experiences alone do not suffice. Apparently, there is no all-encompassing remedy for success to date. A stronger emphasis on the action-related human factor, particularly in the field of Personnel and Human Resource Management, combined with their mutual support of intercultural trainings may promote productive cooperation initially within multicultural teams and eventually carry over to the entire corporation.

Experiences of this nature are extremely important for overcoming postmerger problems for two main reasons:

- Many specialists and executives in an operation are aware of the culture-specific problems and conflicts that can arise with foreign partners and know how to deal with them.
- Individuals with US-specific experience and internationally experienced specialists and executives can rely on their own experience in dealing with postmerger integration issues.

Close cooperation between German and American managers and the close bonds between their respective economies may suggest that a German-

American globally oriented merger is spared the challenges posed by intercultural issues. According to research findings on German-American cooperation, however, this assumption is an illusion (Hall and Hall 1993; Copper 1996; Thomas 2003a).

There are a number of significant differences between Germans and Americans, ranging from simple, everyday communication to ideas on how to solve problems productively within the team all the way to the fixed, internalized concept of product presentation. In contrast to Germans, Americans excel in initiating and conducting small talk in an effort to create a pleasant conversational atmosphere. Germans tend to be irritated by excessive small talk, considering it chitchat and an unnecessary side attraction. In teamwork, Americans tend to be extremely goal and action oriented as opposed to Germans, who tend to focus on details of the problem and prefer sticking to the task at hand. In production and product presentation, Americans emphasize customer needs in terms of functionality. Germans, on the other hand, focus on functional and technical perfection, assuming that a good product will "speak for itself".

Culture-specifically distinct systems of orientation are fixed in the respective national cultures and become even more specific in the corporate cultures. Of course there are companies in Germany, in the software industry for example, that nurture a corporate culture similar to that of the U. S. and whose employees appreciate precisely this aspect about the company. Contrarily, traditional German organizations such as Daimler-Benz or Siemens sustain very specific, deeply rooted national German values in their corporate culture. Employees in these traditional organizations gravitate strongly, at least where their job-related personal development is concerned, toward such exceptional characteristics of corporate culture. The employees' professional identity, their performance-related self-concept, job satisfaction, motivation and future expectations of what they can offer the company and vice versa are impacted by the compatibility between personal goals and expectations, and those of the organization.

In the case of a globally oriented merger between a German and an American operation, the initiators of the merger-acquisition put themselves at risk in an effort to win wide approval from both organizations by launching into an overly euphoric announcement at the outset and claiming that now everything will be different. They might further announce that the merger heralds a new era for the traditional operations and that everyone must contribute to the change process. The employees, however, orient according to their culture-specific socialization, individual life experience and development.

All members of the corporation, from the newly hired trainee to the junior executive all the way up to the board of directors, have completed their socialization and are quite able to tell right from wrong and know how to behave (Thomas 1991). Basically, it can be maintained that the more significant the changes are that are demanded of people in terms of thinking, feeling and behaving in areas that are intrinsic to their personality, the less inclined they will be to muster the willingness and ability to actively embrace change. On the other hand, change is relatively easy to bring about if only the peripheral areas are affected. This includes everything that affects personal identity, such as the fact that a person has an awareness of self or ego and has thus developed a specific concept of self apart from others. Personal identity includes the totality of attributes that a person ascribes to self, including the core content of the self-concept and with it the professional self-concept (Thomas 1992). Included here is the social identity that comprises most other attributes, for example abilities, needs, attitudes, social assessment of status, role, and prestige, that are determined by a person's social environment. In addition, personal and social identities are closely linked. In the case discussed here, intercultural identity plays an additional, more specific role. This role consists of a person's characteristics, in which are embedded the fundamental experiences of selfhood and form the system of orientation of the affiliated group to which a person feels culturally bound.

Consequently, a global merger must ask the following questions: What will be expected of employees in terms of readjustment and change in the near future, in which positions, and in what related functions? How deeply do these required changes affect a person's social, for instance job-specific or cultural, orientation and ultimately his personality?

2.7.4 Developments in the Post-merger Phase

A key factor during the postmerger phase is time. In particular, time to adjust to the changes. Human beings are basically adaptable but they need time for this process and it is a mistake to ask too much too quickly. If employees so much as suspect that they are required to meet certain expectations that could be difficult or almost impossible to fulfill during the merger-integration and merger-life phase, in other words, that evoke excessive demands in key areas, they will be intimidated, demotivated and withdraw from the situation (Very et al. 1998). Creating merger-integration teams shortly after the merger is a good way to avoid personal overload and to provide timely support for dealing with problems.

Assuming that executives who work together in such postmerger integration teams are experienced team builders and managers, and are convinced that teamwork can generate productive energy, then the team can provide support and backup in high-risk problem-solving situations. This scenario is probably much more self-evident for American executives due to their culture-specific tradition than for their German counterparts, who first attempt to achieve a consensus on how to approach tasks and to avert extreme and nonviable developments. In this way, the individual can profit from direct and group feedback and benefit from social support and enhanced feelings of self-worth.

From a socio-psychological perspective and for productive cooperation in the postmerger integration team, it is extremely important that the group be lead by a strong role model with field competency who conveys personal power and authority. A leader of this caliber is able to create a proactive atmosphere in which the team can tackle problems together, ensure the merger's viability and prosperity, and hold out against a failing stock market in times of crisis, the media and a general slump in the economy (Thomas 1991).

Because there are no concrete role models for successful global mergers in corporate history to date, it is difficult to say with absolute certainty how mergers are most likely to prosper and how they can survive economic crises.

An issue frequently under discussion is what language is to be used for communication (q.v. Ch. I, 1.5). Since English is the recognized lingua franca, it stands to reason that English should be introduced as the company language. This is already the case for international mergers, a situation that tips the balance of power, of course. For Germans, English is a foreign language and will remain so, even if it is spoken very well. For Americans, American English is the native tongue, which inevitably gives them a communicative edge. Both sides should be aware of and develop a deeper understanding of the possible communication and interaction difficulties this may cause.

Experience shows that specific and complex tasks are best discussed in one's native language, even if the foreign language is spoken very well.

If English (American English) is introduced as a company language, then teams and employees should be allowed to converse in their native language with each other as well if this is necessary for specifying ideas and concepts. In addition, a rule might be agreed upon to use English in written communication to include any English-speaking partners. Concerning the use of German as the native language and English as the foreign language, it is necessary to make a clear distinction between written and oral communication. Communicating in German is essentially included as long as the partners understand what is being said. The language itself and the level at which this is accomplished is secondary. Observers of international teams found that partners switch from one language to another without much difficulty, or speak a language that others may understand but do not speak themselves if this serves the purpose of general understanding. Using the familiar German native language to keep information from the American partners or to exclude them in any way may not be used under any circumstances. Part of the integration effort within the postmerger integration team should include a willingness to learn at least the basics of the partner's language. This encourages mutual respect and esteem, enhances integration and increases the prospects for success.

2.7.5 Practical Consequences of Managing Mergers and Acquisitions

A number of well-founded hypotheses and outcomes have been voiced in connection with the manifold problems faced by postmerger integration processes, in spite of the unsatisfactory state of research on the subject. Such hypotheses are helpful in providing management with relatively safe orientation in dealing with complex decision-making issues and motivate experts in the field to explore the subject further.

- Resolving the power issue gives the merger a better chance of survival. Both partners must be convinced and able to experience that a one-sided, asymmetrical relationship cannot bear fruit. Instead, both must be intrinsically committed and sensitive to a symmetrical balance of power and open to reciprocal influence.
- Seen from a culture-specific perspective, an international merger may not succumb to a cultural melting pot. There will always be, at least over the long term, areas within such a joint operation in which cultural idiosyncrasies will predominate.

  These culture-specific differences remain visible and will be experienced and tolerated by the employees to an extent. In the meantime, concerted effort is required to encourage all employees to internalize the message that culture-specific differences are not necessarily an extra burden, but on the contrary, might offer chances to work together more constructively or even create synergetic effects. Employees approaching cultural differences with honest esteem and willingness to weigh the positive features of both own- and other-culture modus operandi and find advantages in each can achieve this. In a next step, they can harness initially unfamiliar perspectives and cognitive and behavioral patterns successfully with the positive attributes of their own cultural orientation to create goal-oriented team synergy.

- Research on the topic of "intercultural synergy" in teams has shown that "synergy is not for free" (Zeutschel 1999; Stumpf and Thomas 1999). This means that culturally diverse individuals may well achieve synergetic effects if, equipped with reciprocal intercultural esteem, they can judge which own- and other-culture elements are likely to prove constructive and will contribute to problem solving and the ability to assess tasks. In cases where partners interact with this quality of mindfulness and honor each other's culture-specific differences, the chances are good that they will achieve the synergetic effects required for developing entirely new problem-solving strategies, conflict-free negotiating and forms of interaction. Interaction in this form is capable of generating both conscious and subliminal building blocks on the way to creating a new and specific corporate culture that will carry the merger on into the future.
- Creating an atmosphere of basic intercultural esteem and nurturing the ability to create intercultural synergy is also "not for free", as it requires sensitizing individuals to their own and other cultures' idiosyncrasies and training them to implement this ability constructively. Intercultural sensitivity training and intercultural training in international mergers, in particular with regard to specifically national-culture systems of orientation and their related corporate cultures, must begin at the management level and then gradually include the entire workforce.
- Managers involved in intercultural encounters on a regular basis require a more extensive training spectrum including cultural sensitization than employees who are not directly involved with other-culture partners. However, lower level employees also benefit from trainings providing them with the necessary intercultural knowledge. Research findings and experiences designed to create appropriate training programs are available (Thomas 1998a, 1998b; Thomas and Schroll-Machl 1998; Thomas 2003b; Landis and Bhagat 1996).
- Partners gather the most experience in departmental and function-specific areas during their interaction in the postmerger integration phase. Such experiences touch upon the perception of foreign and unaccustomed thought, judgment and reaction patterns and, at the same time, teach how to deal productively with culture-specific problems. These experiences provide the raw material for creating a pool of experts that can accomplish the following: firstly, they contribute up-to-date authentic material for the design of training programs that target current problems in the company and secondly, management gets an overview of the concrete issues with which the employees are confronted during the merger-life process.

The symbolic leadership required in support of the postmerger integration phase or the merger-life process, including its design, leadership style and the interpersonal communication between supervisors and employees, can be drawn from the expert pool and undergo stringent evaluation. The merger-life process can only be rendered viable if the common effort develops into a learning organization and can pass on productive and merger-relevant experience to employees in the form of tried-and-tested knowledge. This is where company-specific concepts of knowledge management come in (Lehner 2000).

- Studies on teams and team development, particularly in the field of social psychology, give rise to the hypothesis that teams that evolve greater productivity tend to deliberate more (West 1996). In this context, reflection or deliberation pertains to the ability to distance oneself from the issue to create objectivity on the one hand, and to become deeply involved in the development, grasp the intention, reflect on the target-performance comparison in the team and to bring these issues up for discussion on the other. A high level of reflexivity is, no doubt, a success factor for teams dealing with complex problem-solving tasks. Sustaining a high level of reflexivity on the part of management and staff is likely to set the integration process on track toward promising and stable cooperation.
- In an international merger and particularly during the postmerger integration phase, upper management must make every effort to demonstrate symbolically the absolute conviction that the path taken has a unique quality and is of utmost significance for both parties. They must show that problems can be solved with determination and an unwavering belief in the common goal. It is extremely important for management, experts and all employees to keep on course, to maintain a dependable sense of orientation and to have tangible indications that will satisfy their identity needs. This behavior must be demonstrated by a convincing and pro-active leader.
- An awareness of the differences in communication habits between Germans and Americans in an international merger is vital. Americans tend to communicate more, having a greater need for verbal communication and social exchanges than Germans. Observations in German-American work groups have repeatedly shown that Americans are used to giving personal reinforcement. Every statement and every contribution is received with enthusiasm and listeners respond with positive feedback. American employees expect their supervisors to give them regular feedback on the status of their work. Germans, on the other hand, have developed different cultural traditions. Praise is reserved for exceptional performance and not given out freely. Communication is focused on important matters related to the task.

- Although there are many arguments in favor of immediately implementing decisions regarding the international merger, and experience has shown that a delay in the implementation process can hamper success, both merger-life and postmerger integration processes require particular attention and careful long-term support. To date, there is still a lack of reliable know-how, in particular research findings, regarding these processes. However, information gathered from experience and failed merger and acquisition processes can be extremely useful. International research interested in the organizational "soft facts" and the human factor in organizations in addition to the economic "hard facts" is still lacking appropriate data for analyzing purposes, especially differentiated case and process descriptions.
- Aside from the many similarities between merger processes and acquisitions, there are, no doubt, considerable differences. Because of its complexity and the uniqueness of what it stands for, a merger has a higher risk factor and is more cost intensive, particularly in the domain of Human Resource Management. A national or international acquisition, on the other hand, involves "only" relatively little change- or adaptation-related stress for managers and employees of the acquired company. Over the mid and long term, however, measures must be introduced to encourage employees to accept the changes so that the pressure is not experienced as overly one-sided and can be distributed more evenly. In this way, a maximum of potential within the personnel department can be realized in the new (former but now changed) operation.

Implementing findings from organizational and personnel development research more consistently to solve specific problems related to merger and acquisition processes is likely to bring definite advantages in the future.

References

Bergemann, N. J. (1991): Kritische Erfolgsfaktoren im grenzüberschreitenden Fusionsprozess von Unternehmen in strategischer, struktureller und kultureller Hinsicht – eine integrierende Vorgehensmethodik. Heidelberg.

Cooper, C. L.; Liukonen, P.; Cartwright, S. (1996): Stress prevention in the workplace. Luxemburg.

Copper, E. (1996): Multicultural workgroups and project-teams. In: Bergemann, N.; Sourisseaux, A. L. J. (Eds.), Interkulturelles Management. Heidelberg, pp. 229–259.

Forstmann, S. (1998): Managing cultural differences in cross-cultural Mergers and

Acquisitions. In: Gertsen, M. C.; Soederberg, A.-M.; Torp, J. E. (Eds.), Cultural Dimensions of International Mergers and Acquisitions. Berlin, pp. 57–83.
Gertsen, M. C.; Soederberg, A.-M.; Torp, J. E. (Eds.) (1998): Cultural Dimensions of International Mergers and Acquisitions. Berlin.
Gut-Villa, C. (1997): Human Resource Management bei Mergers & Acquisition. Bern.
Hall, E. T.; Hall, M. R. (1993): Hidden Differences: Studies in International Communication. Hamburg.
Harris, P. R.; Moran, R. T. (1996): Managing Cultural Differences. Houston.
Hofstede, G. (1993): Interkulturelle Zusammenarbeit: Kulturen – Organisationen – Management. Wiesbaden.
Jung, T. (2001): Post Merger Identity. Zeitschrift für Human Resource Management 53: 683.
Landis, D.; Bhagat, R. S. (Eds.) (1996): Handbook of Intercultural Training. 2nd ed. London.
Lehner, F. (2000): Lernen und das Wissensmanagement. München.
Mauritz, M. (1996): Interkulturelle Geschäftsbeziehungen: eine interkulturelle Perspektive für das Marketing. Wiesbaden.
Schnapper, M. (1996): Multicultural/multinational teambuilding after international Mergers and Acquisitions. In: Bergemann, N.; Sourisseaux, A. L. J. (Eds.), Interkulturelles Management. Heidelberg.
Schreyögg, G. (1998): Grundlagen moderner Organisationsgestaltung. Wiesbaden.
Stahl, G. K. (2001): Management der sozio-kulturellen Integration bei Unternehmenszusammenschlüssen und -übernahmen. Die Betriebswirtschaft 1: 61–80.
Stumpf, S.; Thomas, A. (1999): Diversity in Group-effectiveness. Lengerich.
Thomas, A. (1991): Grundriß der Sozialpsychologie. Band 1: Grundlegende Begriffe und Prozesse. Göttingen.
Thomas, A. (1992): Grundriß der Sozialpsychologie. Band 2: Individuum – Gruppe – Gesellschaft. Göttingen.
Thomas, A. (1998a): Training von Fach- und Führungskräften für den Auslandseinsatz. In: Kühlmann, T. M. (Ed.), Mittelstand und Betriebswirtschaft. Universität Bayreuth.
Thomas, A. (1998b): Scientific and Practical Aspects of cross-cultural cooperation and management in the context of European Integration. In: Institut für den Donauraum und Mitteleuropa. Wirtschaftsuniversität Wien.
Thomas, A. (1999): Psychologische Probleme der Mitarbeiterführung in interkulturellen Gruppen. In: Rosenstiel, L. v.; Regnet, E.; Domsch, M. E. (Eds.), Führung von Mitarbeitern. Handbuch für erfolgreiches Personalmanagement. 4th ed. Stuttgart.
Thomas, A. (2003a): Psychologie interkulturellen Lernens und Handelns. In: Thomas, A. (Ed.), Kulturvergleichende Psychologie – Eine Einführung. 2nd ed. Göttingen, pp. 433–485.
Thomas, A. (Ed.) (2003b): Psychologie interkulturellen Handelns. 2nd ed. Göttingen, pp. 518–532.
Thomas, A.; Schroll-Machl, S. (1998): Mittel- und längerfristige Auslandseinsätze als Meilensteine der Personalentwicklung von Führungs(nachwuchs)kräften. In: Brühl, R.; Groenewald, H.; Weitkamp, J. (Eds.), Betriebswirtschaftliche Ausbildung und internationales Personalmanagement. Wiesbaden, pp. 282–311.

Vahs, D.; Wuth, S. (2001): Kritischer Erfolgsfaktor: Personalmanagement. Zeitschrift für Human Resource Management: 53.

Vansina, E. L. (1974): Grundlagen der Methodik des marxistisch-leninistischen Grundlagenstudiums. (O. O.).

Very, P.; Lubatkin, M.; Calori, R. (1998): A cross-national assessment of acculturative stress in recent European Mergers. In: Gertsen, M. C.; Soederberg, A.-M.; Torp, J. E. (Eds.), Cultural Dimensions of International Mergers and Acquisitions. Berlin, pp. 85–110.

West, M. A. (1996): Reflexivity and work group effectiveness: A conceptual integration. In: West, M. A. (Ed.), Handbook of Work Group Psychology. Baffins Lane, Chichester, pp. 555–579.

Wucknitz, U. (2001): Mitarbeiter-Marketing. Göttingen.

Zeutschel, U. (Ed.) (1999): Interkulturelle Synergie in Arbeitsgruppen. Lengerich.

Alexander Thomas

2.8 Global Corporate Communication

2.8.1 Describing the Situation

Ongoing progress in technology, data storage, duplication and transfer of diverse data (text, sound, picture, video, graphic art) are revolutionizing the way knowledge is generated, reproduced and disseminated worldwide. Similarly, technology plays a key role in applying and developing existing knowledge. Knowledge and skills have become the raw material for economic growth, which can be accessed simultaneously by an ever-increasing number of people. One could refer to these developments as the motor for global change. Creating and applying knowledge is central to gaining and maintaining a competitive edge.

Electronic media and modern means of communication are gradually replacing monopolies on knowledge, largely concentrated among individuals and capital. Knowledge can be transferred and more innovative locations can be selected without relocating competent employees. The "digital revolution" transcends boundaries between continents, countries and regions, facilitates understanding between governments and international organizations, opens new channels of communication all over the world and democratizes access to information, creating a rapprochement between individuals and governments. The global network creates a situation that will eliminate national and protectionist attempts at delineation in the mid to long term. Nations that rely on technological progress to encourage social change and the transition to a knowledge-based society will emerge as the international market leaders.

Electronic media, the Internet in particular, offers global players the benefit of strategic sales channels, means of communication and research services. Worldwide dialogue and access to information is enormously facilitated (UNCTAD).

However, what may be technically possible, does not automatically become reality. Many technological developments are not implemented because introducing them would be extremely costly or because there is a resistance to change. Resistance to innovation is linked to a strong psychological need for control over self and the environment and orientation security.

Once the euphoria over computer-mediated communication and the sensation of "a beautiful new world" subsides, paving the way for a more down-to-earth evaluation of its pros and cons, the general acceptance and strategic implementation within the context of global corporate communication can be achieved. This point has already been reached, as a computer-aided working environment has evolved into an indispensable facet of both private and work life. In addition, research related to the application and use of digitally transferred communication is no longer limited to substantiating universal application. Rather, efforts are underway to analyze the specific significance of information transferred via multimedia within the context of human communication (Döring 1999).

2.8.2 Internet Application as a Medium for Global Communication

Over the years, research into the application of electronic means of communication has given rise to controversial discussion between proponents and skeptics. Remarkably, both base their emphasis on the pros and cons of digitally transferred communication on conventional and interpersonal face-to-face communication. Within this context, Wehner (1997) states:

"In principle, users of network-bound communication can access media-bound processes. This factor is a prerequisite for creating a culture of communication based on equality and free expression while adhering to own norms and rules of cooperation. Aside from the traditional mailbox-scene, the Internet is regarded by many as a technical basis for "a culture of the universal", in which everyone can communicate with anyone anytime about anything. While the system of mass communication has been criticized because technical intervention critically disrupts the conditions of communicative interaction between sender and receiver, electronic networks are now celebrated because they make forms of authentic conversation possible. Seen from this perspective, the Internet allows individuals to approximate natural communication practices more than any other communication technology. Reference is continually made to long-distance electronic communication in terms of the Internet's global reach, speed and related temporal and spatial effects" (pp. 131 f.).

The correlation between telecommunications and data processing has given rise to the conviction that the Internet has become an interactive medium that facilitates the transferal of information between an unlimited number of participants. So-called computer forums, newsgroups, mail groups and other communication services offer users the opportunity to carry on a dialogue in spite of temporal and spatial separation.

The function of computer-mediated information analyzed within the framework of global corporate communication emphasizes advantages such as speed, spatial and temporal flexibility, as well as unlimited access to a medium for global information and interaction.

The Internet provides a means of registering supply and demand on the global market. Only those global players who manifest a strong regional presence in world markets and are quick to react to market developments and changing client needs will maintain their competitive edge. In the process, international corporations operating abroad must be well versed in the host country's local customs and cultural characteristics in order to align their communication strategies with local practices to ensure acceptance and mutual understanding.

Corporate employees must be highly qualified and able to communicate directly with clients all over the world via Internet in order to facilitate the exchange of information, discuss problems, make changes and keep abreast of developments in regional markets. The rapid exchange of pertinent information allows corporations to adapt and improve products and services in time to meet customer needs and ultimately to ensure the competitive edge.

The Internet offers globally operating companies nearly unlimited storage capacity and the opportunity to access detailed information on all subject-specific material, videos and documentation with the help of a clearly structured user interface. Moreover, the Internet facilitates customer-specific care for a highly specialized customer base. The company can react immediately to pressing issues and can take an uncensored stance in response to critical reports that find their way to the public. Due to the nearly unlimited storage capacity, information is accessible over a longer time period regardless of time differences. Ranging from image and product advertising to specific product offers, individual consulting and customer care to installation, implementation, repair and maintenance, the Internet is indispensable to global communication (Gackenbach 1998).

The different facets of corporate communication must be integrated into an overall concept of communication within the organization. Respective teams, for instance, benefit by the implementation of such a global communication strategy as do company representatives and specialists who are free to adapt the communication strategy to meet their cooperating partners' needs. This means that within a certain scope, decisions can be made on the operative level with a view to local markets and customer needs. Internet-based information and communication strategies play a key role in decentralized decision processes worldwide and can be managed from international locations.

2.8.3 Intranet for Internal Communication

Globally operating organizations with global corporate communication requirements can hardly get around introducing a standardized e-mail system to some extent that will facilitate exchange between headquarters and regional centers. The advantages of using a sophisticated intranet system are clear in that time-consuming business trips and written communication can be kept to a minimum. No doubt, an efficient internal communication network via intranet is essential to exchanging information and functioning competitively. This is particularly true for global processes involving implementation and supervision across regions, time zones, departments, hierarchies and corporate boundaries.

A further time-saving technology is work group application. Work group systems facilitate time-delayed, global cooperation on joint documents. Information and decision-making processes are accessible to all participants. Digital information banks and chat rooms support virtual teamwork. Regardless of where they are in the world, partners can be coordinated for project work. In addition, the Internet facilitates immediate access to external sources of know-how, such as consulting firms, service providers and suppliers.

The possibilities of global cooperation have created new trans-national and trans-continental communities, creating entirely new forms of social cohesion. Especially where the company has not grown together over time, but has recently emerged as a result of a fusion with a large-scale enterprise, media-supported communication can create a novel, social network between the different corporate cultures and mentalities, the particular quality of which has still to be determined (Boos et al. 1999).

Internal news platforms providing access to current global and local news for all employees is another facet of global corporate culture. Experience has shown that the platform is used more frequently if it is regularly updated and accessible around the clock.

Employee potential and competence can be enhanced by means of high-quality information management based on intranet information. This evolution expedites instant information exchange, immediate and high-quality feedback processes and incentives for new developments. If a company succeeds in integrating its employees, or at least the highly skilled and indispensable specialists, into a mutually beneficial communication process, then this translates into a great step forward in terms of productivity and competitive advantage. In this way, expertise, professional competence, overall motivation and employee commitment are harnessed to the ongoing creation of innovative knowledge.

The success of such an intranet system depends on the employees' willingness to accept and actively apply this form of communication. In turn, it is important that management is prepared to provide information relative to corporate philosophy and decision making. This will require changes in conventional forms of information policy: in particular, moving away from the practice of providing specific information to specialized experts to a more democratic approach of disseminating company-relevant information (Baltinic 1999).

2.8.4 Features of Media Use

According to Ball-Rokeach and Reardon (1988) and Höflich (1997), three core dimensions of computer application relative to Internet and intranet can be identified:

- *Information retrieval and exchange:* On the one hand, data, news, information, services etc. can be retrieved regardless of timechanges between continents and different working and business hours. On the other, the data pool can be enriched by individual feed-ins. No doubt, this application is a clearly limited form of interaction, since the primary concern is the selective processing and distribution of information without interacting directly with other information providers.
- *Discussion forums:* This form of Internet and intranet use is extremely important, as aside from content-related aspects of information, relationship factors enter into electronically mediated communication. Electronically mediated dialogues "can thus occur in time-delayed fashion such as with Internet user groups or 'live', as in Internet relay chats. The difference to the above dimension is that the user not only 'receives', in Internet language, a so-called 'LURKER', but also provides input within the scope of public discussion. Thus, he receives and sends simultaneously. Moreover, such forums are the vision of a new 'electronic agora' and are dependent on the activity of users. This collective of users of multi-faceted communication forums no longer constitutes dispersed groups, instead it is safe to refer to them as an 'electronic community' that characterizes itself through joint use, norms and rules as the smallest common denominator" (Höflich 1998, p. 116; cf. Diehl and Ziegler 1999).
- *Interpersonal communication and social relations:* This form of computer use functions as a medium for technically mediated interpersonal communication, "which includes possibilities of delayed communication (electronic mail), as well as the simultaneous communication between

> two or more users (online chat, multi-user chat). In the terminology of Ball-Rokeach and Reardon (1988), reference is made to a telelog where the relationship among users is in the foreground. The difference to the previous dimensions is that a telelog tends to have an exclusive (private) character. The similarities between the dimension is that use is only possible together with others, i.e., requires a mutual frame of reference between communication partners (commonality and reciprocity of media use in contrast to dispersed and one-sided mass communication)" (Höflich 1998, p. 116).

A further decisive advantage of computer use as a hybrid medium is the fact, "that one can change between frames seamlessly within the same medium. With reference to Ball-Rokeach and Reardon's (1988) differentiation between forums for continuing education via computer-mediated communication, an exchange, for example, can evolve into a debate (such as when news items become the topic of discussion in electronic discourse) and can lead on to an association (in personal, technically transferred contacts). In addition, any number of different telelogs (social communication spaces) can occur simultaneously. This means that through exclusion of others, public information is transferred into the private sphere and vice versa, private information can be made public. In this sense, one is dealing with a graded form of computer-mediated e-learning that can access both public and private domains (Flichy 1994)" (Höflich 1998, p. 117; cf. Boos et al. 1999).

What about individuals who prefer communicating internationally via electronic communication for efficiency and economic reasons to other forms of media? What changes at the cognitive, emotional and behavioral level take place? What effect do the users believe they have on the receiver of their messages and on their interacting partners? How do they believe they are influenced by others? What kind of pressure are they subjected to from the Internet community in the way they present news and information, receiver reactions to their messages and established rules of behavior pertaining to Internet and intranet use?

2.8.5 Consequences of Computer-Mediated Communication

On the basis of previous research, a number of computer-mediated theoretical models can be identified through which the characteristics of this form of communication can be systematized. The models offer an expla-

Table 11: Core messages of the ten most important computer-mediated communication models (according to Döring 1999, p. 240).

Theoretical Model	Core Message
1. Channel reduction	Due to nonexistent sensory channels compared to face-to-face communication, CmC is deficient and impersonal.
2. Filtering out social clues	Due to its anonymity, CmC leads to disinhibition and encourages pro-social as well as anti-social behaviour.
3. Rational choice of media	CmC is suited to specific communication situations, not to others. Correctly applied, computer-mediated communication is an enrichment.
4. Normative choice of media	CmC is influenced through social norms in the environment and is therefore often irrational and dysfunctional.
5. Interpersonal choice of media	CmC is co-influenced by the communication partner's media-specific communication pattern.
6. Information processing on the social level	CmC is just as lively as face-to-face communication as nonverbal messages can be verbalized.
7. Simulation	CmC offers a range of freedom of self-expression, thus decreasing the sense of reality, change and realization.
8. Imagination	Since CmC lacks sensory channels, projection is stimulated and evokes fantasy images.
9. Digitalization	Due to the ability of digital word processing, CmC can change the production, dissemination and reception of messages.
10. Cultural influence	CmC is influenced by the culture that operates within the respective computer network (jargon, traditions, values etc.).

nation of how such characteristics came about and what psycho-social consequences they entail. Nicola Döring identified ten models of computer-mediated communication in her monograph entitled "Social Psychology and the Internet" (1999), on the basis of which she developed an ecological media framework for her model. We will take a closer look at this model, since it is very useful as a guideline for the development of concepts of global corporate communication.

Table 11 provides an overview of the ten theoretical models of computer-mediated communication (CmC) and their core messages.

Models three, four, five and ten are interesting within the context of corporate communication. For practical application in global corporate communication, the normative media choice model, the interpersonal choice model and the cultural choice model are relevant and will be examined further.

Model of Normative Media Choices

This model assumes that the choice of media in private and in the work place are by no means subject to cost-effective considerations or decided in accordance with rational models, but rather are predetermined by specific conditions, prerequisites and social norms. This model further assumes that the evaluation of media, according to usefulness and efficiency, for example, is not so much determined by the media's functional characteristics as by social constructs. Consequently, Schmitz and Fulk (1999) could show evidence for e-mail communication, "that persons with more media experience (e-mail-experience, computer skills, keyboard skills) rate e-mail use as more practical and also use it more. At the same time, it was found that the e-mail-related social influence a person was subjected to (usefulness rating of e-mail and the use of e-mail by colleagues and supervisors), corresponded positively with a person's own usefulness rating and e-mail usage" (Döring 1999, p. 223, cf. Boos et al. 1999).

Model of Interpersonal Media Choice

This model emphasizes the potential communication partner's behavior: "On the basis of the action perspective, face-to-face communication and mediated interpersonal communication are subject to social norms and rules of communication. Seen from this perspective, it is not the fade-out expressions, especially the nonverbal variety, that are primarily responsible for communication deficits, but the lack of standard reference, including poorly administrated rules. Procedural rules pertain to formal communication processes, while so-called media regulations facilitate the adequate, situation-based use of media, based on a common definition of the media situation and the coordination of communication partners. Media regulations reflect an accepted standard of application and lead to the gratification of user expectations" (Höflich 1996).

Model of the Cultural Sphere

The cultural sphere is central to the mutual activity of media users. The communication networks form net-specific, symbolic expressions, develop a specific knowledge, and share and develop new social rules and values on how to deal with information and communication processes. In this sense, "cultural spheres" can be understood as computer networks (cf. Helmers et al. 1995).

"The model pertaining to spheres of cultural influence sheds light on the fact that significant aspects of computer-mediated communication are also influenced by the shared knowledge, tradition, social norms and values of individuals active within the communication network. This includes unintended impingement on traditions and values and may lead to conflict. Studies related to net culture often use ethnographic methods. In addition to the general characterization of features pertaining to Internet culture, the methods also describe subcultures within the Internet system" (Döring 1999).

Global business communication in all its facets is further influenced by differences in national culture. Research into this criteria and its influence on particular user groups within the context of economic and corporate communication processes, including the relevant media choices, is incomplete in view of the knowledge that is still required. Research related to the sphere of cultural influence is largely limited to what has been developed, stabilized or has already blended into tradition in the form of shared rules, norms and values within the Internet community. Research to date assumes that this Internet community operates in a sort of culture-free zone and creates entirely new culturally relevant rules out of this no-man's land, aside from the preference for English language terminology (Birnbaum 2000).

Looking at it from the perspective of global corporate communication, these studies are lacking the vital determinant of culture-specific characterization inherent in all human activity. All users have been socialized in a specific culture and have internalized the culture-specific system of orientation. Their culture provides them with a sense of meaning on all levels of action and in their thinking and feeling. Culture creates possible courses of action, action impulses and boundaries (Thomas 2003).

These cultural ties develop through orientation patterns specific to national culture, organizational culture, group culture, family culture and individual culture. An individual may well not be cognizant of dissimilar patterns of action and directed behavior because they have become an automatic part of the behavioral repertoire. Media choices and user habits will depend on national and regional cultural preferences and play a significant role within the context of corporate communication culture.

In a research summary covering the conditions of productive behavior of globally operating business teams, Hofner Saphiere (1996) compared the use of electronic media to direct, interpersonal communication and drew the following conclusions: Face-to-face communication, especially at the beginning of business relations, is extremely important for creating conditions that will enhance successful intercultural management. A phone call to initiate business relations will not have the same effect. All studies on this subject to date substantiate this. A special analysis conducted on a total of twelve globally operating work teams from different corporations, business sectors and countries showed that high-performing teams depended on face-to-face communication and communicated more in general compared to the less productive teams, who tended to communicate via e-mail. Regardless of the level of performance, all teams rated e-mail communication as the most useful communication medium, although the high-performing teams were skeptical about its unrestricted use. Like others before it, this study too showed that electronic communication media is better suited to information transfer, whereas face-to-face communication is indispensable where problem solving and cooperation is involved. Members of productive teams are more likely to communicate informally in face-to-face situations, appear to be more task-oriented *and* show more social behavior. They prefer discussing critical issues as a major part of their work and are careful to maintain a nonjudgmental communication style in performing tasks. These teams showed a high level of sensitivity toward culture-specific differences, which they tried to interpret and clarify from the partner's perspective. Ultimately, the members of this group unanimously expressed an interest in continued cooperation.

The continual increase in the amount of data and its rapid proliferation is by no means on a par with higher management efficiency, nor does it provide more goal-oriented and efficient feedback. This development is detrimental to communication on all levels as an "information overload" is likely to impede productivity. Since selection and information diversity cannot be evaluated automatically, universal availability of information and the ensuing overload is extremely difficult to cope with. An increase in information will not bring increased productivity. The key is the right information at the right time and at the right location via both the intranet and the Internet, with a view to achieving an appropriate and satisfying form of communication through high-quality editing and meaningful contextualization. The success of internal and external corporate communication depends not only on technology and its application, but also on the quality of its content. The technological availability of information does not appear to be the problem in the context of global corporate communication, but rather the quality of its content.

2.8.6 Hypotheses on the Development of Global Corporate Communication

In the future, all direct and electronically mediated forms of communication, ranging from face-to-face communication, with its significant element of nonverbal communication, paperbound verbal communication and conventional mass communication, to computer-mediated communication, are here to stay within the scope of global corporate communication. In dealing with corporate trainings for communication competence, it is important to keep in mind that trainings must include qualification in all these areas and not just in the application of electronic media.

Preferences for the type of media used depends largely on the availability of appropriate technical and economic resources, but presumably also on culture-specific habits, traditional values and religious traditions. Progressive and effective global corporate communication would therefore do well to base its approach on openness and esteem toward forms of communication developed in different cultures and withhold immediate judgment on the differences and their culture-specific functionality. Accordingly, a standardized means of communication for all individuals in the corporation would prove unproductive. It is not the role of top management at headquarters to decide what, when, how much and to what purpose computer-mediated methods should be used. The communication partners on site must have the necessary communication skills to be able to identify a suitable means for meeting communication requirements and to develop and convey a corresponding communication culture.

A range of hypotheses based on the use of electronic media in global corporate communication have been formulated to date on the strength of research findings. Initial research results are available within a limited scope.

- Media-conveyed communication, more so than face-to-face communication, facilitates communication without the limitations imposed by hierarchies: Interpersonal communication barriers fall away or are reduced. The bottom-up transfer of information is simplified (Straus 1996).
- Media-conveyed communication is less inclined to take interpersonal issues into account: barriers due to interpersonal animosity regarding personal impressions (primacy effect, halo effect etc.) are eliminated (Walther 1999).
- Media-conveyed communication facilitates critical feedback: it is easier to write and send critical feedback than to present it personally at the risk of inviting argument or critical questions and creating a problematic interpersonal relationship.
- Media-conveyed communication creates around-the-clock availability. This can lead to a consolidation of media and a self-imposed obligation to process and react to diverse, incoming information at short notice, thereby reducing the capacity of sensory input while creating stress and resistance. This will ultimately affect the quality of how the information is processed.

- Direct interpersonal communication opens the way for social influence through exercising personal power and persuasion. This important leadership tool loses its effectiveness in computer-mediated communication (Döring 1999).
- Direct interpersonal communication facilitates "learning according to a model" and is an important means of effective social learning. This capacity is greatly reduced through the use of computer-mediated communication.
- Media-conveyed communication frequently leads to information overload without providing the necessary orientation aids. This may result in an impending or actual loss of orientation.
- An information overload can be avoided by combining direct interpersonal communication and media-conveyed communication.
- Media-conveyed communication leads to a loss of orientation. In contrast, the communication partner in an interpersonal encounter provides this orientation in the form of a highly complex, albeit solid and "good gestalt" that embodies orientation-relevant information (Utz 1999).
- An optimal combination of direct interpersonal communication and media-conveyed communication within the context of modern corporate management depends on each individual situation at the corporate, departmental and group level.
- Global corporate communication will not be able to use all available means of media-conveyed communication, the cost factor being only one aspect. Diverse cultural habits, traditions, values and behavioral norms will play a role and will have to be considered. The introduction, acceptance, and application of new forms of (electronic) media that were previously unknown in a culture, are inevitably influenced by cultural factors. The current methods of communication are adapted to the new media forms through the process of assimilation. The methods of media application are adapted to traditional information and communication customs through a process of accommodation. A closer look shows how this process evolves.
- Computer-aided communication is effective for generating ideas in a group. Group coordination, on the other hand, is more effective when conducted via face-to-face communication (Boos et al. 1999).
- Tasks requiring a high level of coordination are more effectively completed on a face-to-face basis rather than by group communication via electronic media (Straus and McGrath 1994).

2.8.7 Global Corporate Communication in the Intercultural Context

Similar to other areas of global technological and economic developments, practical application in global corporate communication is ahead of (academic) theory. The pressure to react to market demands requires implementing multi-faceted means of communication, despite the inadequate knowledge of how they work and what effect they may have on such things as work performance and job satisfaction. The search for optimal solutions to the problems related to global corporate communication becomes more difficult with the use of modern electronic media because corporate and national cultural differences demand attention.

After studying the literature and conducting her own studies on the subject of productivity of global business teams, Hofner Saphiere (1996) concludes: "Findings from this study indicated the need for additional research in five key areas: factors beyond national culture, problem solving across cultures, communication in the absence of regular face-to-face contact, the ideal role of a global business team leader, and the function of cultural interpretation and mediation" (p. 250).

No doubt, globally operating business teams, especially those that are productive, are making efforts to find new forms of cooperation that all members will find beneficial, regardless of their cultural background. These efforts still raise a number of unanswered questions: What problem-solving processes and group decision-making behavior are most productive for globally operating teams? Do methods of information exchange, development of mutual decision-making processes, feedback, fair performance evaluation and conflict management exist that are equally acceptable to many different cultures while guaranteeing high team performance and team viability? How do individuals from collectivist cultures, who rely on a more indirect style of communication for giving negative feedback and tend to depend on instructions combined with a strong need for harmony, get along with individuals from individualistic cultures, who are accustomed to clear and direct instructions, criticism, and performance evaluations? Since the team members themselves have to develop forms of behavior that will lead to effective teamwork, it would be important to know whether productive work teams tend to prefer media-conveyed methods to exchange work-related information, and, on the other hand, tend to clarify questions related to interpersonal cooperation via face-to-face communication.

Meanwhile, it is clear that simple comparisons between the advantages and disadvantages of different methods of communication are of little use to global corporate communication; Each method has its specific strengths and weaknesses. It is not yet completely clear which ones they are and how they can be effectively combined. Even if studies find (Hofner Saphiere 1996) that written communication is conducive to the precise description of a circumstance, while communication over the telephone addresses and intensifies the emotional aspect, then it is still not clear if this pertains to all contextual conditions of global corporate communication. More specifically, contextual conditions referring to familiarity among communication partners, corporate-specific customs, corporate and national culture differences, language of communication, the communication partners' expectations, differences in status and positions in the hierarchy. For example, how can humor be used to lighten up a tense situation without unleashing total chaos?

The role of globally operating team leaders is more one of process facilitator, rather than that of an all-knowing leader and expert.

"In many global business teams today, the team members may be technical experts in different fields and their expertise critical to project success. It is the team leader's role to guide the team to a decision as a process facilitator. In addition to authority or content expertise, team leaders must be able to structure information-sharing and decision-making to include multiple perspectives. Yet it is not clear how this is best accomplished. Specific research questions for future studies are: What role should leaders of productive, geographically dispersed teams play, particularly when their technical/business expertise as well as their team leadership is required? How do leaders contribute opinion and information without unduly influencing a multicultural team's decision? How do leaders provide sufficient structure to allow all members of a multicultural team to contribute, but not so much structure as to stifle the contributions of others? How do global business team leaders facilitate open information exchange and disagreement without creating a threatening or tense situation for some team members?" (Hofner Saphiere, p. 252).

All experts agree that efficient global corporate communication cannot be adapted from textbooks or "how to" literature. Methods must be individually fitted to each situation within a given corporation. This can only be effective if top management and team members within a global organization are acutely aware of their own specific system of orientation, have developed a high level of sensitivity for other-culture orientation systems, and are able to deal productively with culture-based diversity. A core competence within this scope includes well-founded intercultural competence, acquired through task-oriented dialogue and a close interaction between intercultural research and organization-specific responsibilities.

References

Ball-Rokeach, S. J.; Reardon, K. (1988): Monologue, dialogue, and telelog. Comparing an emerge form of communication with traditional forms. In: Hawkins, R. P.; Wieman, J. M.; Pingree, S. (Eds.), Advancing Communication Science: Merging Mass and Interpersonal Processes. Newbury Park, pp. 135–161.

Batinic, B. (1999). Einführung und Nutzungsmöglichkeiten eines Intranet. In: Boos, M.; Jonas, K. J.; Sassenberg, K. (Eds.), Computervermittelte Kommunikation in Organisationen. Göttingen.

Birnbaum, M. (2000): Psychological Experiments on the Internet. London.

Boos, M.; Jonas, K. J.; Sassenberg, K. (Eds.), (1999): Computervermittelte Kommunikation in Organisationen. Göttingen.

Diehl, M.; Ziegler, R. (1999): Informationsaustausch und Ideensammlung in Gruppen. In: Boos, M.; Jonas, K. J.; Sassenberg, K. (Eds.), Computervermittelte Kommunikation in Organisationen. Göttingen.

Döring, N. (1999): Sozialpsychologie des Internet. Göttingen.

Flichy, P. (1994): Tele. Geschichte der modernen Kommunikation. Frankfurt a. M./New York.

Gackenbach, J. (1998): Psychology and the Internet. San Diego.

Helmers, S.; Hoffmann, U.; Hofmann, J. (1995): Offene Datennetze als gesellschaftlicher Raum. Das Modell Internet. In EU-Kommission, Vertretung der BRD – Vertretung in Berlin (Ed.), Europartner Information, Sonderheft April. Berlin: Berliner Vertretung der EU (Online.Dokument URL http://duplox.wz-berlin.de/texte/eu/).

Höflich, J. R. (1996): Technisch vermittelte interpersonale Kommunikation. Grundlagen, Organisatorische Medienverwendung, Konstitution »Elektronischer Gemeinschaften«. Opladen.

Höflich, J. R. (1997): »Electronic communities« as social worlds: Toward a socio-semiotic analysis of computer mediated communication. In: Nöth, W. (Ed.), Semiotics of the Media. State of the Art, Projects, and Perspectives. Berlin/New York, pp. 507–517.

Höflich, J. R. (1998): Computerrahmen und Kommunikation. In: Prommer, E.; Vowe, G. (Eds.), Computervermittelte Kommunikation – Öffentlichkeit im Wandel. München, pp. 141–174.

Hofner Saphiere, D. M. (1996): Productive behaviors of global business teams. International Journal of Intercultural Relations 20 (2): 227–259. New York.

Schmitz, J.; Fulk, J. (1991): Organizational colleagues, media richness, and electronic mail. A test of the social influence model of technology use. Communication Research 18 (4): 487–523.

Straus, S. G. (1996): Getting a clue. The effects of communication media and information distribution on participation and performance in computer mediated and face to face groups. Small Group Research 27 (1): 115–142.

Straus, S. G.; McGrath, J. E. (1994): Does the medium matter? The interaction of task type and technology on group performance and member reactions. Journal of Applied Psychology 79 (1): 87–97.

Thomas, A. (Ed.) (2003): Psychologie interkulturellen Handelns. 2nd ed. Göttingen.

UNCTAD (Ed.) (1996): Transnational Corporations and World Development. London.

Utz, S. (1999): Identifikation mit virtuellen Arbeitsgruppen und Organisationen. In: Boos, M.; Jonas, K. J.; Sassenberg, K. (Eds.), Computervermittelte Kommunikation in Organisationen. Göttingen.

Walther, J. B. (1999): Die Beziehungsdynamik in virtuellen Teams. In: Boos, M.; Jonas, K. J.; Sassenberg, K. (Eds.), Computervermittelte Kommunikation in Organisationen. Göttingen.

Wehner, J. (1997): Medien als Kommunikationspartner – Zur Entstehung elektronischer Schriftlichkeit im Internet. In: Gräf, L.; Krajewski, M. (Eds.), Soziologie des Internet. Handeln im Elektronischen Web-Werk. Frankfurt a. M., pp. 125–150.

Alexander Thomas/Sylvia Schroll-Machl

2.9 The International Assignment: Expatriates and Their Families

2.9.1 Stating the Problem

Employees who are willing to relocate are very much in demand in this era of globalization. Judging from job advertisements, career development is hardly possible without mobility. For young, unmarried professionals, such offers may sound attractive and promising. However, once the family is involved, the prospect of job-hopping takes on different dimensions and challenges.

The typical pattern is: The husband receives an offer from his company for an international assignment and it is expected that his spouse and the children will join him. However, the move abroad means that each family member must deal with very specific challenges.

> Actually, the transition was easy for me. The company itself is similar all over the world so my work environment was familiar to me. My daughter, however, had to leave her friends. She couldn't attend a German school, having instead to attend a Brazilian school, which meant a double workload. She had to master a 37-hour week and half her courses were in Portuguese. In addition, the core subjects were repeated in German. This was extremely difficult for her and there were many tears. Although she couldn't fail the course, she was intent on performing well. After a year, she was able to pass all subjects in the foreign language. As an avid horsewoman, it was a great comfort to her that she was able to keep two horses in Brazil and participate in horse shows. A further disadvantage was that we had to curtail her freedom, which is difficult for a 15- to 18-year-old girl (this is how long we were in Brazil). Without a doubt, this had to do with our concern for her safety. We never let her go anywhere alone, but drove or brought her to places. Since her parents were always present, it was difficult to make friends, not to mention have a boyfriend. We realized this, of course, but what should we have done? My wife had given up her job in Germany, which she had worked hard for. After the birth of our daughter, she had gone back to school and worked her way up to a cushy position. She promptly experienced an extremely serious bout of culture shock, which was exacerbated by metal poisoning. It took her a long time to overcome her health problems, a condition which is typical for culture shock. She found herself in a crisis during which time her only wish was to return to Germany. Another problem was the service personnel, who simply took complete

advantage of my fair-minded wife. Initially, she felt caged because she was stuck at home, had neither friends, nor job and was not able to speak the language.

The family constellation plays a decisive role in every international assignment. This is true not only for the well-being of the employee being sent abroad during and after his assignment, but also for his career success in general (Adler 1997; Black et al. 1992; Black and Gregersen 1990; 1991; Harvey 1985). The ultimate success of the international assignment is directly linked to how well the family (spouse, children and family members remaining at home) is prepared for the move. Is the circumstance fully accepted or merely tolerated or do they see advantages in the situation? Most employees leave on international assignments at a stage in their lives when they are settled in with a family. Although there is no official evidence supporting this statement, it can be assumed that if an international assignment is accepted against the will of the other family members, there is a strong likelihood that the spouses will eventually separate. Research findings and practical evidence relative to this issue are discussed below. According to traditional role distribution, the husband is chosen for the international assignment and his wife accompanies him. The opposite constellation, where the wife is sent abroad with her spouse and children is quite rare. The basic dynamic in role distribution (company employee, accompanying person, child) is practically identical (for further information on women on international assignment, see Ch. I, 2.10).

2.9.2 Stress Factors

Each international assignment leads to more or less pronounced psychological and physical strain caused by the new work environment and social setting. The term *culture shock*, in this regard, refers to a form of emotional disorientation caused by a constant confrontation with unexpected and unfamiliar reactions in the new setting, a feeling of being misunderstood, and no longer knowing how to act "appropriately" (Triandis 1994; Bochner 1994; Harris and Moran 1991; Furnham and Bochner 1986; Oberg 1960). Aside from these well-documented episodes of culture shock and acculturation stress, there are a number of social, socio-cultural and professional stress factors, the effects of which should not be underestimated (Wirths 1996; Schröder 1995; Debrus 1995; Medrano-Kreidler 1995; Gregersen and Black 1990). Adjusting to the host country is a challenge not only for the employee, but for each family member as well. The success or failure of this process can either facilitate or complicate the life of the entire family, depending on the ability of individual family members to adapt to the new circumstances. The situation is further aggravated by the fact that family members are more dependent on each other in a foreign environment than they are at home, setting in motion an intense interaction dynamic that did not exist in the home environment. It is extremely important for family members to have a healthy psychological foundation in order to provide the necessary mutual support. Embarking on an international assignment to escape problems at home usually leads to a rude awakening (Ward 1996; Martin and Harrell 1996; Jackson 1996; Bergemann and Sourisseaux 1996; Kühlmann 1995; Schroll-machl 1997).

Stress Factors for Expatriates

Social Strain

The employee on an international assignment may feel the strain of shouldering the responsibility for the family's welfare, knowing that his wife has given up her job at home and the children are taken out of their familiar environment (school, friends). He worries about whether the family will be able to adapt and if the move will be beneficial for everyone involved. On the one hand, the presence of the family can provide psychological support, on the other, however, it can develop into an endurance test if one member of the family has difficulty adapting. Moreover, a feeling of responsibility towards parents at home or property that cannot be attended to personally, among other commitments, add to the general strain.

Some choose to maintain a weekend marriage in order not to disrupt the spouse's career or the children's schooling. The separation of the family, however, poses special challenges and frequently excessive demands. Such expatriates are usually unpopular among colleagues because they have much time during the week and can work at night. On the home front, they may feel superfluous and inadequate, as the family has learned to take care of things on their own. Maintaining a weekend relationship is difficult enough for adults and becomes more so once children are involved. Marital stress is likely to increase if even weekend visits become impossible due to distance and family life is limited to holidays.

This is not to say that an unmarried employee has an easier time or is more successful in his job than an expatriate with family. In many cultures, unmarried employees are the exception, which can be a source of irritation for overseas partners. They are also more likely to suffer from feelings of loneliness. In the beginning, this is likely to lead to heightened acculturation stress. Seen from a positive perspective, however, single expatriates tend to establish close contacts relatively quickly to avoid feelings of isolation. The typical reaction for men is to look for a partner for the duration of their stay, which of course creates new problems. The risk that feelings of loneliness intensify with time is a realistic scenario. While under the strain of acculturation stress, there is a need to talk to others about the difficulties one is experiencing in the unfamiliar culture. Discussing difficulties with one's family or a group of colleagues at work can lead to an intensification of negative feelings, low morale and even aggressiveness toward local partners.

Some expatriates feel that their company sends them on an assignment but then leaves them to fend for themselves (Tung 1988; Thomas 2001). Employees sent on assignment must often organize the move themselves (accommodation, furniture, means of transport, insurance and more) without help from the company. The company frequently expects the employee "to finally get to work" without consideration for the time involved in getting settled. Relocation services in many countries offer invaluable support under such circumstances.

Socio-Cultural Strain

Socio-cultural strain may occur as a result of changes in everyday life and in the workplace in the host country, such as climate, rural and urban cultures, corporate culture, line of work or adapting to service personnel.

Establishing professional or personal contact with locals may prove difficult, while the loss of neighbors, acquaintances and friends back home creates a need to connect with people in the host country. An international assignment may promise the prospect of exploring the host country, its local customs and people. Efforts to establish friendly relationships or even friendships with locals may, however, eventually result in disappointment due to the difficulties involved in recognizing and understanding cultural differences.

Stress factors due to the unexpectedly difficult relationship between employees on international assignment and colleagues at headquarters back home are also frequently mentioned. Over time, the typically German behavioral patterns become less pronounced, causing the expatriates to feel misunderstood. During the course of the international assignment, the expatriate has gradually adopted some of the foreign behavioral patterns, for example concepts of time, space and quality standards, to the point where they seem quite natural to him. Communication partners at headquarters are, however, still oblivious to this acquired, culture-specific knowledge regarding norms and rules, which gives rise to misunderstandings between colleagues who got along quite well before the assignment. Another cause for dissonance is the asymmetrical constellation between the Western European and North American "expert", who is well equipped with financial backing and pertinent know-how, and local partners who do not yet have comparable valuable resources at their disposal. Consequently, feelings of superiority and a display of dominant behavior on the part of the expatriates and visiting members from headquarters may develop and further impede cooperation with local nationals.

Work-Related Stress

Most international assignments exact tremendous demands in terms of time and performance. Pressure builds with the task of dealing with local skepticism toward the "new" situation and the visitor's own fears of being exploited by locals who, because of being on their "own turf" in terms of insider knowledge, have a clear power advantage. To top it off, the expatriate often experiences a sense of alienation and gradually begins to feel abandoned by his colleagues at headquarters in Germany.

Much of what was expected in terms of professional modus operandi at headquarters, from the economical use of material, maintenance and care of equipment and machinery to forms of business etiquette between superiors and subordinates (praising and criticizing, personal responsibility, professional ethic or quality control), suddenly no longer apply during cooperation in the host country. The expatriate must reorient from his former familiar professional pattern and learn new rules.

Moreover, once he has successfully acculturated, he is likely to experience a conflict of loyalties. On the one hand, he is expected to represent company interests or those at headquarters and on the other, he now sees the situation from the perspective of the local nationals and is critical of decisions from above. He is expected to move easily between behaviorally effective and culturally specific orientation systems. He is able to accomplish this balancing act because he has learned to understand the intrinsic workings of both systems. To avoid burn-out in this process, however, he will need a strategic framework.

Reintegration Stress

When the company sends an employee abroad, the adaptation process is monitored in terms of adaptation to work overseas and living conditions. In contrast, relatively little time is invested in reintegration measures on the part of both the expat and his supervisors at headquarters (Black and Mendenhal 1991a, 1991b). Meanwhile, many studies on problems of integration show that becoming re-accustomed to life and work at home is at least just as difficult as the previous adaptation to the guest country

(Kuehlmann and Stahl 1995; Hickson 1994; Winter 1996; Napier and Peterson 1994; Harvey 1989; Gundlach and Hilmes 1987; Gomez-Mejia and Balkin 1987; Martin 1986; Austin 1986). Returning expatriates often experience emotional duress when they find that no one else is really interested in their life abroad, and that relationships at work and among friends and acquaintances have become one-sided, making it difficult to pick up where they left off before the international assignment. Returnees compensate for such unexpected feelings of alienation by judging those at home as boring and provincial against the backdrop of their international experience.

Moreover, upon returning home and with the loss of his exalted position as a "chosen" employee, the expatriate might feel that he has forfeited some of his former status. He is no longer considered to be a member of the upper crust of management and the business elite, as he might have been in the host country. Instead, he has returned to the ranks of an average employee on a par with his colleagues. Back at home, the expatriate realizes that the leadership status he may have enjoyed in terms of independence, diversity in his work and decision-making leeway no longer apply. In short, many returning expatriates refer to reverse culture shock as they recount the psychological effects of living and working in the host country in retrospect.

Studies on job reintegration repeatedly mention the stress component involved when, upon returning, the expatriate expects a job advancement on the basis of his international posting (Kühlmann and Stahl 1995; Hickson 1994; Winter 1996; Napier and Peterson 1994; Harvey 1989; Gundlach and Hilmes 1987; Gomez-Mejia and Balkin 1987; Martin 1986; Austin 1986), only to find that the sought-after position has meanwhile been filled by someone else. The qualifications acquired abroad do not meet with the expected acknowledgment. Upper management often argues that since the company has meanwhile undergone many changes, they could not commit to keeping the position open for the returning expatriate.

When jobs in middle management have been cut and entire divisions have been eliminated or sold, then the position the returnee may have coveted before his assignment may no longer exist. The discrepancy between statements made by top management, to the effect that only people with international experience can move up the corporate ladder, and the reality experienced in some cases by returning expatriates who then expect to "cash in" on this promise, leads to further disappointment and strain. Even if the sought-after position cannot be filled, reintegration could be made less stressful by allowing the expatriate to put key skills and qualifications acquired during an international assignment to good use. For the following reasons this is not often the case:

- The company is subject to operational restrictions, and there is simply no position open in which the expatriate's acquired skills could be put to good use.
- "Out of sight – out of mind" – this is the reality for returning expatriates. If they do not make an effort to reconnect with their departments and personnel during regular stopovers at home base, then they risk being overlooked when promotion time rolls around.
- The influence wielded by HR is limited. Often they are limited to supporting employees on international assignments at the administrative level only. In addition, HR does not maintain a database of company employees with international experience, nor are they involved in finding suitable candidates for international projects until the last minute.
- If HR is not charged with the responsibility of providing support in the reintegration process, then efforts to reintegrate the returnee are hampered and he might not be optimally placed due to departmental politics.
- Perhaps the information flow is not up to par so that the returnee's vitae cannot be "passed on" although he might be a prime candidate for a job.
- HR staff changes during the course of an international assignment and therefore loses sight of contacts and information.
- Employees leaving on assignment often overestimate the impact of what might have been mentioned by headquarters in terms of career enhancement upon their return. They rely on "promises" without checking in regularly.

Neither the international assignment in itself nor the acquired skills and experience counts for career advancement, but rather it is having a relatively good handle on developments at headquarters, maintaining a personal network and being able to demonstrate a proven track record during the assignment.

The duress experienced by expatriates returning from an international assignment is caused by a discrepancy between HR management expectations (e.g., "broadening of horizons", "learning a foreign language", "a stronger customer focus", "an international and global mindset and planning strategies", "cosmopolitanism") and how he is seen by colleagues and supervisors in his department.

While the expatriate might have acquired qualities as a result of a successful assignment, these may not be of central importance depending on the perspective of the employees in the department to which he returns.

Consequently, cases of double disqualification occur: On the one hand, the expatriate feels disqualified by headquarters with regard to the abilities and skills he acquired abroad. On the other, his supervisors might feel that he has lost ground as a result of his international assignment, is not sufficiently up to date on the developments that have taken place during his absence, and that his new antics are irritating. The expatriate's supervisors deny him any kind of special status, expecting him instead to readapt and play by the rules of the game back home and to "get his feet back on the ground". In addition, the expatriate might attract both envy and admiration for his success abroad because he enjoyed "a good time", "earned a fortune" and was regarded as a "hotshot" at his posting abroad.

Stress Factors for the Accompanying Spouse

Spouses who are unwilling to embark on an international assignment are often the crux of the problem. Human resource managers assume that many suitable candidates for an international assignment either turn down the offer, don't extend their contracts or terminate the assignment prematurely because of their spouses. And it actually is the spouses who bear the brunt of the burden of an international assignment, considering that they are faced with giving up their jobs, their social network at home, and contact to parents and relatives, without any kind of compensation. She is to provide her husband with a reliable back-up system. Furthermore, as cynical as this may sound, it is the women who actually *live* in the host country while their husbands spend most of their time ensconced within the company. In spite of this, the company rarely takes accompanying spouses into account in either their preparations for sending an employee abroad or for those already on an international assignment. The common opinion, especially in Germany, seems to be that family affairs are the employee's private business and do not concern the company. In contrast to working on home turf, the international assignment impacts every aspect of life, conflicting sharply with the German business ethic of keeping business and personal life strictly separate. In fact, the situation calls for a responsible move on the part of HR. However, in reality, this is rarely the case and many companies have much room for improvement in this area.

The change of circumstances brought about by the move abroad and a different way of life, including the resulting problems and challenges faced by accompanying spouses, are well documented in international research literature and empirical studies conducted by Meier (1999) and can be categorized accordingly:

Geographical and Country-Specific Conditions

Accompanying spouses must come to terms with the following conditions:

- Location/life space; urban/rural
- Climate, seasons and rural setting
- Environmental pollution, noise and overpopulation
- Possibility of unpredictable natural catastrophes
- State of technology and its availability
- Time change
- Hygienic standard, level of pollution
- Lack of infrastructure: streets, shopping opportunities, energy supply
- Limited range of food products and consumer goods
- Nutritional deficiencies

Difficulties are likely to increase if the spouse is pregnant or gets pregnant during the international assignment. Many couples combine the stay abroad with maternity leave.

Organizational and Work-Specific Conditions

The decisive factor for women who were employed at home is that they are no longer able to work in the host country (FAZ 2000, p. 24) and are limited to housewife and perhaps motherhood roles. Consequently, an important source of self-fulfillment and independence is no longer available. This is particularly difficult in a new environment in which there are initially no social or support networks. The feeling of dependency can evolve into an identity crisis, which, if not taken seriously, can cause severe marital stress until the spouse finds other means of reaffirming her individuality.

Because many spouses are tied to the house to care of the children, they are unable to acquire the necessary language skills to improve their ability to communicate and frequently suffer from feelings of insecurity and inferiority. The feelings intensify when locals turn to the husband for work-related reasons or simply because he generally has a better command of the language.

Regardless of whether there are children, the accompanying spouses usually suffer from extreme loneliness, as their working husbands tend to put in longer working hours and are locked into a six-day work week. Furthermore, the husband must take on representational duties. In other words, the husband has little time for the family. The care of young, school-aged children is so all-consuming that the spouse is likely to find it difficult to make initial contact and maintain a social network. They most often make contact with other compatriots in a similarly difficult predicament.

Table 12: Areas of difficulty for accompanying partners

Authorities in the host country	– language difficulties
	– official authorizations
	– medical care
	– finding the right schools
Living, housekeeping, shopping	– stress due to relocation
	– sub-standard living conditions
	– household coordination
	– coordinating household personnel
	– shopping habits
Limited mobility	– time management, different infrastructure
	– urban traffic
	– gender separation in Muslim countries
	– high crime rate
General living conditions	– lack of leisure and cultural activities
	– lack of work opportunities
	– lack of intellectual challenge
	– timing of the international assignment
Available information	– lack of readily available information
	– distance from home
	– absence of familiar and competent people

Table 12 enumerates the frequently mentioned problems faced by spouses in terms of underlying organizational and work-specific conditions.

The expatriate's home company most often does not provide organizational backing, personal support or involvement in the decision-making process or financial support for unmarried couples. Such factors do not make matters easier.

The Social Setting

Here too, there is a wide range of challenges that must be faced (Table 13).

In addition, the German custom of separating work and personal life becomes obsolete in a foreign environment. Women are much more obliged to take on representational duties, organize invitations and receptions, act as hosts, get involved in organized social commitments and diverse networking activities. All of these duties, in one way or another, support the husband's position and the family documents his success on a social level. Beneath the socializing, his professional work plays an integral role.

Table 13: Demands placed on accompanying partners

Living with spouse or partner	– job-related stress factors (increased work load)
	– partner's job-related difficulties
	– different gender-based role expectations under different cultural conditions
	– position of women in the host country
Living with children	– children's adaptation difficulty
	– medical care
	– sense of security (crime rate)
	– children's reactions to new living and educational conditions
Discrepancies with the company	– the husband's workload
	– conflict between family and company interests
Familiar environment at home	– problems with relatives and friends
	– envy and resentment
	– missing friends
Dealing with the local population	– physical differences
	– political situation
	– religion and religious practices
	– culture: values, norms, behavioural differences
	– socio-economic situation, belonging to a social class
	– poverty, criminality, race discrimination
	– gender roles, traditions and behavior
	– language and communication
	– unfamiliar reactions
Dealing with other people from the Western hemisphere	– initiating, maintaining and intensifying social relationships
	– rumors, gossip, social discrimination
	– expatriate colleague and supervisor disinterest in one's well-being.

Personal Conditions

Other pre-existing personal issues may arise and be exacerbated under conditions in the host country such as:

- unrealistic expectations,
- negative attitude regarding the international assignment and the host country, difficulties with the change in circumstances and routines,
- little motivation to prepare, gather information, prepare mentally and to adapt,
- an introvert personality, inhibitions, shyness,

- low self-worth and self-confidence,
- ethnocentrism,
- inability to adapt to different circumstances,
- psychological instability,
- little self-discipline,
- little aptitude for managing life-change situations.

Repatriation

Upon returning to Germany, the spouses experience similar reintegration problems to their husbands, only more pronounced. While the husband continues his work, the spouse is often unable to continue with her career. Many feel insecure about their professional qualifications and unqualified to resume their former work. Having foregone their former status, they now find that they have no right to reclaim it and there is no help from the administrative side (e.g., unemployment compensation). The main burden of moving and resettling the family rests with the spouse (finding accommodations, setting up the home and everyday organization), reintegrating into a social network (neighborhood, friends) and settling the children in schools.

If spouses are sensitized to the difficulties that might confront them abroad by involving them as equal partners prior to their departure, then they could develop more realistic expectations regarding the country and the life that awaits them. Contrary to the fears expressed by many companies, this does not lead to a change of mind about moving abroad. The gap between expectations and reality is much more likely to be bridged by sensitization, leading to the development of effective problem-solving strategies. Studies done on this topic (Black and Gregersen 1990, 1991) and experiences compiled by Schroll-Machl discuss this problem.

Stress Factors for Children

Many expatriates travel abroad with families of one or more children, who in their turn must undergo an adaptation process. It is worth mentioning that there is hardly any literature documenting the children's situation. Only three relevant analyses made in 1994 are mentioned in German-speaking literature (Binkama, O. J.; Lamberts 1984; Simon-Hohn 1992), whereby these were not results of systematic studies, but rather a collection of observations, experiences and discussion results. International literature points to the situation of accompanying children in an analytical context of developing aspects of intercultural identity (Kim 1995) and cultural adaptation (Torbiörn 1982). The authors of these studies assume that, based on the stages of development of a personal and social identity, children under the age of nine adapt to a foreign culture with relative ease, as their core identity is not yet fixed. Furthermore, their parents are their primary role models. If parents are able to create a trust-based relationship, then the children's emotional makeup is likely to be positive. In contrast, older children and adolescents who underwent such an extreme change of environment and loss of their familiar social network experienced considerable social and cognitive problems. The challenge of finding new friends and adapting to a new school system is not be underestimated.

Gaschik (1999) compiled the experiences of children and adolescents during the process of acculturation in their fathers' respective foreign postings, including the relevant adaptation difficulties, and identified six different areas of acculturation (Table 14).

Problems in the area of the *physical environment* were experienced as only slightly stressful. These are aspects over which the children and adolescents have no control, such as climate, living quarters, house personnel,

Table 14: Acculturation of children and adolescents

Areas of Acculturation	Acculturation Difficulties
Physical setting	– adapting to climate
	– nutrition
	– traffic and increased pollution
	– spacial orientation
Social setting	– social isolation
	– establishing friendships
	– change of the expatriate community
School setting	– integration into the class community
	– scholastic performance
Area of individual lifestyle	– social status
	– domestic employees
	– limited freedom of movement due to restrictions imposed from the outside
	– limitations on independence
Unfamiliar environment	– recognizing and learning other-culture rules of behavior
	– phenotypic difference
	– acceptance of "extreme" customs and traditions
Linguistic acculturation	– general language difficulties
	– language difficulties within a social context
	– language difficulties in the academic context
	– language difficulties in a cultural context

etc. Difficulties here are most often countered by resistance, habituation, acceptance or resigned tolerance. Problems relative to the *social setting* and language acculturation are experienced by children and adolescents as extremely stressful and detrimental to their emotional well-being, which is highly dependent on the ability to establish satisfactory social contacts. Children and adolescents feel the burden during the preparatory and the adaptation phase most acutely, as they fear leaving their familiar environment, social setting, friends and playmates and are anxious about whether they will be able to make new friends in their new home abroad. Experience shows that school is the most likely place to make new friends and establish social contacts. This is one reason why it is important to coordinate the international assignment with the beginning of the school year. If children change location frequently with their parents, experience shows that it is difficult for them to have friends spread all over the world. Occasional visits and long-distance telephoning cannot compensate. Problems in the area of *individual lifestyle* and the *educational setting* involve some adjustment. Although these aspects are a daily part of life, they are not of primary importance to the children's emotional well-being. Adolescents in particular suffer from a lack of freedom. However, culturally specific restrictions, local infrastructure and real physical danger make such restrictions inevitable.

The *other-culture setting* actually plays a less significant role once adolescents find a sense of belonging within the sub-cultures in the host country (e.g., expatriate communities). However, where such communities do not exist, they must exert an effort to adapt and learn how to cope. Children quite obviously have an easier time adapting to unfamiliar patterns of behavior than their parents. They tend to be more open and flexible in dealing with the foreign culture and are more willing to modify their behavior accordingly. The areas of acculturation tend to have a reciprocal effect on each other:

- Based on opinion polls, the key to managing acculturation difficulties and general progress depends on the children's and adolescents' competency in the language spoken in the expatriate community (mostly English). Consequently, overcoming acculturation difficulties in the social and educational setting as well as in nonacademic social situations is closely linked to (English) language competency.
- Aside from acquiring (English) language competency, building a social network is a core requirement for successful acculturation among adolescents. (As mentioned earlier, this is only possible if they speak the language of the expatriate community.) According to many studies, satisfactory social networks contribute to the child's emotional stability, have a positive effect on the psychological adaptation and are instrumental in overcoming general acculturation difficulties in the areas already mentioned.

Children who have moved with their parents several times are likely to be multilingual: German, English and at least one other language. This poses an additional problem: they are not really fluent in any language, least of all German. This issue becomes even more acute as graduation approaches. Many parents consciously invest in a boarding school for several years to allow their teenage children to "get grounded".

In addition to the problems typically experienced by children, the family itself may be a source of stress. Children also suffer if the parents experience acculturation difficulties or if the inability to acculturate negatively impacts the marriage during the stay abroad. In such cases, the children often become symptom carriers for parental problems.

Adolescent children are most often affected by reintegration difficulties upon returning home after an assignment, which usually have to do with re-entry into the German school system and having school grades and diplomas from non-German institutions be officially recognized. Often children have to forfeit an entire school year. Like their parents, the adolescents are disappointed that their language fluency and their experience acquired abroad is not sufficiently acknowledged. In addition, having experienced another style of education and an entirely different culture leads to comparisons and a critical attitude toward German behavioral patterns. For example, the scholastic ambience in German schools is experienced as aggressive, competitive and unfriendly, an aspect that does not make reintegration any easier. Perhaps the children and adolescents have become accustomed to belonging to the privileged class, attending schools for the privileged and feeling generally a cut above their peers. Back in Germany, they have to attend regular state schools and face the fact that they are now just another face in the crowd.

2.9.3 Support Factors

What Helps? Strategies for Acculturation Management

Aside from the stress factors mentioned, scientific literature and interviews conducted by Schroll-Machl (1997; 2002) cite personal factors and social influences that are instrumental in dealing successfully with preparations for the international assignment and reintegration stress (Kühlmann and Stahl 1995; Hickson 1994; Winter 1996; Napier and Peterson 1994; Harvey 1989; Austin 1986). Among these are:

- an ongoing conscious awareness of how to deal with unexpected, perplexing and contradictory behavior.

- learning to attend to physical and emotional well-being to ameliorate the effects of culture shock.
- making a conscious effort to seek out social contacts and support within the family setting itself, the neighborhood and the work-related environment among both German and international expatriate groups, as well as among the local nationals.
- using focused strategies to maintain and strengthen self-awareness and control in dealing with a new work-life balance and to take measures to maintain a balanced sense of self in encounters with new and unfamiliar circumstances. Such strategies include learning the language, finding out about the host country and its culture-specific system of orientation and learning to adapt to its culturally acceptable pattern of behavior.
- activating effective cognitive restructuring processes in an effort to achieve a mutually beneficial learning experience, and ultimately a synergy between familiar patterns and new, unfamiliar and unexpected situations.

Much has been written about strategies for dealing with acculturation problems and culture shock in both literature and in first-hand experiences. Key factors are such personal characteristics as a natural empathy and sensitivity to the needs of others, a high tolerance threshold, patience and perseverance, respecting and honoring otherness in the form of unfamiliar and unusual behavior (ambiguity tolerance), openness together with an element of humility and restraint.

Adapting to life changes does not happen overnight, but rather it proceeds as a development over time. From an everyday work perspective, the following elements may support the expatriate's efforts to adapt to the unfamiliar environment:
- Taking a sincere interest in the country and local customs does not go unnoticed by local business partners. It is appreciated and helps to create rapport.
- The company, colleagues and compatriots provide feedback and have an open ear.
- Appreciating the benefits of work abroad, such as more independence in their work and the opportunity for personal enrichment.

Accompanying partners and spouses cite the following strategies for dealing with their difficult situation:
- Decorating the living space to create a feeling of familiarity.
- Accepting the role of spouse or partner and learning to achieve a higher level of self-worth instead of relying on outside approval.
- Reasserting a sense of self-confidence and self-respect by tackling different, purposeful challenges and gaining competency.

- Discovering a meaningful personal goal while abroad. Many women manage to find creative solutions for some kind of work. Others rediscover hobbies they have neglected and appreciate the time they now have to cultivate them or enjoy discovering the host country. Some among them manage to get a job through the embassy or an organization.
- Contacts are extremely important for getting involved in activities, e.g., compatriots, other expatriates, locals, clubs, neighbors, company employees and acquaintances.
- Some spouses become cultural experts on the host country through travel, literature and their service personnel, who provide them with an insider's view of daily life and contacts through which they can experience the host country from a different perspective.

The following support factors for children and adolescents dealing with acculturation were identified:
- Support and acceptance within the family network and the peer group.
- Participating in fulfilling and interesting activities.
- Cultivating such personal attributes as being open to new and unfamiliar situations and events and flexible in dealing with otherness (Meier 1999).

In any case, the bottom line for a successful international assignment is a big "yes" from all involved. This must be clear for all members of the family and the company.

> As an HR specialist, I interview many candidates chosen for international assignments. I am astounded at how often the family is not included in the candidate's decision. It seems to me that in many cases the husband makes the choice without including his family in the decision to relocate. They don't seem to be aware of what such a move means for the family. I think this is a mistake. I am quite aware of the difficulties the family has to face. We understand if a candidate decides to refuse the offer! We realize that there are phases of mobility and of immobility in life.

What remains? – An Evaluation of the International Assignment in Retrospect

An international assignment is not all strain. Instead, it can be an important step in personal development. This even holds true for international assignments that did not prove successful from a career perspective. Frequently, expats experience a form of broadening of horizons or *personal enrichment.* The positive effects of personal development are described as increased self-confidence and self-worth, composure, optimism, flexibility, tolerance, self-reliance and perseverance. Research studies and frequently mentioned accounts point to enhanced social competence, the ability to empathize and a heightened sensitivity to unfamiliar thought and behavioral patterns (Eder 1996).

Related assets include thinking in global terms, the ability to *modify perspective* and a deeper understanding of international cooperation and other-culture settings (e.g., experiencing a Third World Country), experience with other perspectives including one's own, and a new perspective of Germany in a global context.

A further aspect within this range of topics emphasizes a keen sense of curiosity and *adventure* with regard to exploring similarities and differences between self and otherness and learning to deal effectively with unfamiliar events and encounters.

Children too, profit from a number of advantages as a result of the time spent abroad: they speak a *foreign language* fluently and have grown in their *personal development* during the process of living in another culture and experiencing its diverse values, norms and behavioral patterns relative to wealth and poverty, which may contrast sharply with German customs. Foreign language competency and personal experience in a very different cultural setting is considered integral to the development of interests and abilities for assignments abroad.

Qualification

The international assignment might lead to career enhancement but it is by no means a guarantee. Many expatriates see their assignment abroad as having contributed to both personal development and further qualification in their area of specialization as a result of the new tasks that had to be mastered.

> My perspective has changed. Due to my international background, I now make decisions differently, estimate costs in a different light and have reassessed my understanding of competitiveness. I now view the concept of Germany as a "business location" from the outside.

A further asset includes the ability to assess other-culture partners' problem areas, needs and demands upon return to German headquarters.

> Now I can better understand the reasons behind some of the enquiries from our partners in China because I understand the big picture. I can now reply from a new perspective of understanding and I feel I am making a valuable contribution.

Enhanced management skills contribute to a shift in leadership priorities, more emphasis on social competence and confidence in dealing with more complex management and administrative assignments – especially under difficult conditions – and to managing employees from diverse cultural backgrounds more effectively.

> I learned how to communicate with people and to view them as resources. I am more open toward individuals from different backgrounds and now consider different points of view. I ask more questions and don't assume to have immediate answers. In this way, I find it easier to accept different people the way they are. I have become more patient and indirect. It's amazing how useful that is in Germany too!

It is interesting to note to what extent one international assignment qualifies a person for the next assignment abroad, that is, to what extent the strain of acculturation has subsided. Some expatriates actually experience an addiction to embarking on one international assignment after the other, usually because they experience extreme reintegration stress or no longer feel at home in Germany. On the other hand, they feel challenged by the assignment in the host country and enjoy a pleasant and exotic lifestyle with quite a bit of independence in their work. In the course of repeated international assignments, acculturation strain diminishes and the integration/reintegration process becomes part of the routine. Culture shock loses its bite, the loss of self-confidence is bolstered by the knowledge that this situation can also be successfully managed. Of course, the cost of this sort of life may be a gradual move away from social contacts in Germany. The death of parents and relatives due to old age and grown children moving out to lead their own lives may lead to "burning the bridges" to Germany and leave no other choice but to remain abroad.

2.9.4 Final Comments

Each international assignment constitutes a unique event when considered from the perspective of conditions at home and in the host country, the nature of the work and assignment, the family constellation, environmental factors, age factors, phases of life, life plans, as well as each individual's attitude and expectations with regard to moving abroad. There is a difference between a couple without children accepting the assignment or an expat and his wife with two school-aged children. Quite often, the assignment comes at a time when career development is at a standstill or family planning is either not yet an issue or is already in full swing. Frequently, a first or second pregnancy exacts unexpected and excessive demands when it coincides with the international assignment. Starting a family, strain due to pregnancy, birth and caring for the newborn, the move, acculturation in the host country, loss of work and starting over in a foreign culture all lead to an accumulation of demands, which are hardly possible to surmount alone. In such cases, a one-shot preparation training is not enough. Here, intercultural coaching sessions tailored to individual needs are required to deal with problem clusters and their overall dynamic. On the one hand, the organization is obligated to support cost-intensive expatriates and, seen from another perspective, the organization indirectly enhances its training and development program by supporting the expatriate and paving his way to further qualification, which will ultimately serve the organization. Moreover, offering support is bound to strengthen the expatriate's sense of job commitment and loyalty to the company.

Professional help during this time of critical reorientation is a good investment in terms of long-term personnel development. Support in this form makes sense not only for large, international companies, but also for smaller and medium-sized, internationally active enterprises. Relevant training and coaching providers offering individualized training programs are meanwhile widely available (IKO 2001).

Of course, not every international assignment is a "hard-luck story". What may seem an insurmountable problem for one person might be an enriching experience for another. Each person has a different stress threshold. All stress factors mentioned here by no means apply to every international assignment. A bottom-line maxim, however, is that the entire family will benefit from the experience abroad if acculturation issues can be mastered together and if each family member (spouse and each child) adapt well to new circumstances in the host country. In this case, the stay abroad is bound to be an enriching experience for everyone involved.

Interview results and literature on the subject support the realization that a comprehensive and systematic preparation for the international assignment, including reintegration support for the entire family upon their return, constitutes a high priority. A key consideration here is that individually designed intercultural training programs in preparation for the international assignment be offered in tandem with field and industry-specific topics (Thomas 1995) (q.v. Ch. I, 2.2). Many people have vague or mistaken notions about what awaits them when they decide in favor of the international assignment. This may not hold as true for the purely work-related demands as it does for the psychological and emotional aspects involved in working with locals in the host country, living in a foreign country under unaccustomed climatic conditions and shouldering the responsibility of the decision and its consequences for the family.

Sending an employee on an international assignment is a costly affair and involves a risk to the company. Consequently, the decision must be carefully planned in order to minimize the chances of failure. Under such circumstances, one might expect the companies to offer large-scale support for their employees since they otherwise risk polarizing specialists and top management: the one group choosing mobility over a traditional lifestyle with the family, and the other choosing to stay at home at the risk of forfeiting upward mobility. According to the widely read German newspaper "Die Zeit" (1999), potential candidates for an international assignment most frequently reject the posting because their spouses or partners are unable to find work.

References

Adler, N. J. (1997): International Dimensions of Organizational Behavior. Cincinnati.

Austin, C. N. (Ed.) (1986): Cross-Cultural Reentry: A Book of Readings. Abilene, TX.

Bergemann, N. J.; Sourisseaux, A. L. J. (Eds.) (1996): Interkulturelles Management. Heidelberg.

Black, J. S.; Gregersen, H. B.; Mendenhall, M. E. (1992): Toward a theoretical framework of repatriation adjustment. Journal of International Business Studies 23 (4): 737–760.

Black, J. S.; Gregersen, H. B. (1990): The other half of the picture: Antecedents of spouse cross-cultural adjustment. Journal of International Business Studies 22 (1): 461–477.

Black, J. S.; Gregersen, H. B. (1991): When Yankee comes home: Factors related to expatriate and spouse repatriation adjustment. Journal of International Business Studies 22 (1): 671–694.

Black, J. S.; Mendenhall, M. E. (1991a): The U-curve adjustment hypothesis revisited: A review and theoretical framework. Journal of International Business Studies 22 (1): 225–247.

Black, J. S.; Mendenhall, M. E. (1991b): A practical but theory-based framework for selecting cross-cultural training methods. Human Resource Management 28 (4): 511–539.

Bochner, S. (1994): Culture shock. In: Lonner, W. J.; Malpass, R. S. (Eds.), Psychology and Culture. Boston, pp. 245–251.

Brinkama, A. (o. J.): Mit Kindern und Jugendlichen im Ausland. Hinweise zu Problemen und Wirkungen. Institut für Interkulturelles Management. Königswinter. (Unveröffentlichtes Manuskript)

Debrus, C. (1995): Die Vorbereitung von Mitarbeitern auf den Auslandseinsatz: Aus der Praxis der Henkel KGaA. In: Kühlmann, T. M. (Ed.), Mitarbeiterentsendung ins Ausland. Göttingen, pp. 119–141.

Eder, G. (1996): »Soziale Handlungskompetenz« als Bedingung und Wirkung interkultureller Begegnungen. In: Thomas, A. (Ed.), Psychologie interkulturellen Handelns. Göttingen, pp. 411–422.

FAZ – Frankfurter Allgemeine Zeitung (2000): Beim Auslandseinsatz die Interessen des Ehepartners berücksichtigen? – Die Entsendepraxis der Allianz Versicherung und der Deutschen Bank/»Bodenständige Nachwuchskräfte«. Frankfurt Nr. 1, 3.1.2000, p. 24.

Furnham, A.; Bochner, S. (1986): Culture Shock. London.

Gaschick, A. (1999): Akkulturationsprozesse mitausreisender Kinder im Kontext betrieblicher Auslandsentsendungen. Universität Regensburg. (Unveröffentlichte Diplomarbeit)

Gomez-Mejia, L.; Balkin, D. B. (1987): The determinants of managerial satisfaction with the expatriation and repatriation process. Journal of Management Development 6 (1): 7–17.

Gregersen, H. B.; Black, J. S. (1990): A multifaceted approach to expatriate retention in international assignments. Group/Organization Studies 15 (4): 461–485.

Gundlach, F. W.; Hilmes, M. (1987): Wiedereingliederung von Auslandsrückkehrern. Personalführung 20 (7): 490–493.

Harris, P. R.; Moran, R. T. (1991): Managing Cultural Differences. Houston.

Harvey, M. G. (1985): The executive family: An overlooked variable in international assignments. Columbia Journal of World Business 20 (2): 84–92.

Harvey, M. G. (1989): Repatriation of corporate executives: An empirical study. Journal of International Business Studies 20: 131–144.

Hickson, J. (1994): Re-entry shock: Coming »home« again. In: Lonner, W. J.; Malpass, R. S. (Eds.), Psychology and Culture. Boston, pp. 251–258.

IKO (2001): Institut für Kooperationsmanagement an der Universität Regensburg: Qualifizierungsangebot. Regensburg, IKO-consult.de.

Jackson, T. (1996): Cross Cultural Management. Oxford.

Kim, Y. Y. (1995): Cross-cultural adaption. An Integrative Theory. In: Wiseman, R. L. (Ed.), Intercultural Communication Theory. Thousand Oaks, pp. 170–193.

Kühlmann, T. M. (Ed.) (1995): Mitarbeiterentsendung ins Ausland. Göttingen.

Kühlmann, T. M.; Stahl, G. K. (1995): Die Wiedereingliederung von Mitarbeitern nach einem Auslandseinsatz: Wissenschaftliche Grundlagen. In: Kühlmann, T. M. (Ed.), Mitarbeiterentsendung ins Ausland. Göttingen, pp. 177–215.

Lamberts, K. (1984): Mit Kindern im Ausland leben. Protokoll eines Fachgesprächs in der Zentralstelle für Auslandskunde. Bad Honnef.

Martin, J. N. (1986): Orientation for the reentry experience: Conceptual overview and implications for researchers and practitioners. In: Paige, M. (Ed.), Cross-Cultural Orientation. Lanham.

Martin, J. N.; Harrell, T. (1996): Reentry training for intercultural sojourners. In: Landis, D.; Bhagat, R. S. (Eds.), Handbook of Intercultural Training. London, pp. 307–326

Medrano-Kreidler, M. del C. (1995): Bedingungen für das Wohlbefinden von Mitarbeitern bei Auslandseinsätzen. Frankfurt a. M.

Meier, C. (1999): Akkulturationsprobleme und -strategien der mitausreisenden PartnerInnen im Kontext betrieblicher Auslandsentsendungen. Regensburg. (Unveröffentlichte Diplomarbeit)

Napier, N. K.; Peterson, R. B. (1994): Expatriate re-entry: What do repatriates have to say? Human Resource Planning 14: 19–28.

Oberg, K. (1960): Cultural shock: Adjustment to new cultural environments. Practical Anthropology 7: 170–182.

Schröder, A. (1995): Die Betreuung von Mitarbeitern während des Auslandseinsatzes: Wissenschaftliche Grundlagen. In: Kühlmann, T. M. (Ed.), Mitarbeiterentsendung ins Ausland. Göttingen, pp. 143–160.

Schroll-Machl, S. (1997): Bilanz-Gespräche mit Expatriates über Integrationsprobleme im Gastland. Deggendorf. (Unveröffentlichtes Manuskript)

Schroll-Machl, S. (2002): Frauen als Expatriates in Führungspositionen. Eine Untersuchung am Goethe-Institut InterNationes. München/Deggendorf. (Unveröffentlichtes Manuskript)

Simon-Hohn, H. (1992): Auslandsaufenthalt mit Kindern. Erfahrungen von Familien deutscher Fachkräfte der Entwicklungszusammenarbeit. Bad Honnef.

Thomas, A. (1995): Die Vorbereitung von Mitarbeitern für den Auslandseinsatz: Wissenschaftliche Grundlagen. In: Kühlmann, T. M. (Ed.), Mitarbeiterentsendung ins Ausland. Göttingen, pp. 85–118

Thomas, A. (2001): Going global! Und wo bleibt die Familie? Personalzeitschrift für Human Resource Management 53/1: 700–703.

Torbiörn, I. (1982): Living Abroad: Personal Adjustment and Personnel Policy in the Overseas Setting. New York.

Triandis, H. C. (1994): Cross cultural industrial and organizational psychology. In: Duvette, M. D.; Hough, L. M.; Triandis, H. C. (Eds.), Handbook of Industrial and Organizational Psychology, 4. Palo Alto, S.103–172.

Tung, R. L. (1988): The New Expatriates: Managing Human Resources Abroad. Cambridge.

Ward, C. (1996): Acculturation. In: Landis, D.; Bhagat, R. S. (Eds.), Handbook of Intercultural Training. 2nd ed. London, pp. 124–147.

Winter, G. (1996): Reintegrationsproblematik: Vom Heimkehren in die Fremde und vom Wiedererlernen des Vertrauten. In: Thomas, A. (Ed.), Psychologie interkulturellen Handelns. Göttingen, pp. 365–381.

Wirth, E. (1996): Mitarbeiter im Auslandseinsatz: Planung und Gestaltung. Wiesbaden.

Die Zeit (1999): Lieber hier als dort. Mobil sein ist alles. Doch nicht mehr alle machen mit. 8.7.1999, p. 28.

Iris C. Fischlmayr/Sylvia Schroll-Machl

2.10 Women in International Management

2.10.1 Expatriate Women – Still a Minority

Proliferating global alliances, the founding of foreign subsidiaries and international joint ventures virtually force multinational organizations to consider the most qualified employees for an international assignment ... regardless of gender. "In a ferociously competitive global economy, no company can afford to waste valuable brainpower simply because it is wearing a skirt" (Adler 1997, p. 310). Contrary to this statement, however, women are in the minority when it comes to international assignments. Over the last years, research studies pertaining to expatriate women have increased (Adler 1984a; 1984b; 1987; 1994a; Tung 1997; Smith 1999; Harris 1993; 1995; Westwood and Leung 1994; Marshall 1984; Domsch and Lieberum 1997; Caligiuri and Tung 1999; Caligiuri and Cascio 1998; Linehan 2000; Fischlmayr 2001; Schroll-Machl 2002; Fischlmayr 2002; Mayrhofer and Scullion 2002). Despite the increasing interest, international women managers are still a scarcely researched phenomenon. One reason is certainly that women in management positions are still the exception. Relative to the already low number of women in international management, expatriate women are even more underrepresented. In the U. S., the number of women in management positions has "already" reached 40 percent (Hantschel 2000), yet expatriate women make up a mere ten to twelve percent (Tung 1997). According to a study on mobility (ECA 1996), only nine percent of European expatriates are women, whereby no difference is made between those in managerial and nonmanagerial positions. Finding data on the proportion of women in management and on those selected for international assignments in Austria and Germany is a difficult task. According to studies, five to eight percent of the managers abroad are women (KF-Uni-Graz 1998; Fishlmayr 2001) while twenty-two percent hold positions in administration and management (ILO 1998). In Germany, 25.1 percent of all managers across corporate levels are women (Hantschel 2000). Only 8.2 percent are found in mid-management (Schaufler 2000) and hardly any women are found in the top echelons (Assig 2002). There is no data available for the proportion of women chosen for international assignments although, relatively speaking, the tendency should be around five percent at best.

Articles on "female expatriates" are generally written by women for women and tend to attract little attention. Another characteristic of these studies is that they are compiled primarily by American authors and thus tend to be biased. Studies conducted in European countries are difficult to find. In both Germany and Austria, only a few research studies exist in the area of expatriate women (Domsch and Lieberum 1997; Fischlmayr 1999; Fischlmayr 2001; Hofbauer 2002; Schroll-Machl 2002; Fischlmayr 2002; Mayrhofer and Scullion 2002). Research findings and data include the dispatch process (from recruitment to the return to home base) and experiences of women in international business (gender comparisons, challenges, comparison to circumstances at home base, examples of everyday situations).

In the following discourse, we will treat only themes relative to expatriate women. A more general discussion on the subject of expatriation is included in Chapter 9.

2.10.2 Key Results of Gender Studies

English language research differentiates between the term "sex" as the biological designation and "gender" as the role assumed in the course of a socially conditioned learning process. The terms are frequently confused in everyday usage, i.e., "gender" is equated with "sex" and vice versa. Hence, many people judge others purely on the basis of their biological designation ("sex"). Seen from this perspective, a woman's role is less advantageous compared to that of her male counterpart's. Such gender-specific stereotyping attributes particular roles, behavior, characteristics and lifestyles to both men and women. For instance, emotionality, team orientation, friendliness, warm-heartedness, understanding, supportiveness, sensitivity, intuition and tactfulness are characteristics that are usually associated with women. Men, on the other hand, are often characterized as aggressive, strong, rational, independent, competitive, self-assured, analytical and determined (Bern 1974; Wilson 1995). From childhood on, both men and women demonstrate an awareness of their roles in society and reflect this in their perception and view of self. Gender-determined conformity and behavior that has been learned during the course of socialization confirms and reinforces general stereotyping.

Self-perception and the role ascribed by society are strongly reflected in language. Men tend to talk about numbers, facts and results and present others with a *fait accompli*. From a professional standpoint, they often act according to the maxim "first come, first serve" or "what counts is getting the job". Once this has been achieved, men tend to believe there will be enough time to prove oneself. Women often use the passive voice, more indirect formulations and ask many questions, all of which points to a lack of assertiveness. Women in management positions confirm this claim that "it is difficult getting admitted to the selection process. One is virtually forced into coming across as arrogant" (Opermann and Weber 1995; Ehrhardt 2000).

The Significance of Candidate Selection for Management Positions

HR managers tend to select candidates who resemble themselves. Since men usually hold top-level positions, this not only explains male predominance, but also reinforces it. Men are considered the "in-group", so to speak, and women make up the "out-group" (Schein 1975; Aronson 1994; Harris 1995). Factors such as the percentage of women in the entire applicant pool also have an influence on the personnel manager's decision. In addition, management is reluctant to select women who are not members of a power network. These informal intrigues play a significant role in the selection process both at home and abroad. Traditionally, women have not had access to such groups and find it difficult to join, even today. However, since it was not deemed necessary to promote or to consider women as candidates for top positions, there was no reason for men to include them in their networks (Rizzo and Mendez 1990; Harris 1995). It is assumed that with increasing international experience, women will move into top positions at home, which in turn will raise the percentage of women on international assignments (Fischlmayr 2001).

Conclusion: HR managers are often subconsciously influenced by gender stereotyping, which significantly affects their choice of candidates.

The Significance of Self-perception and Self-portrayal of Female Expatriates

Aside from the bias shown by HR managers, women's reluctance to accept international assignments and gender-consistent behavior are demonstrated reasons why they are still the exception in management positions. Reports based on various experiences and analyses of decision-making processes of those women selected, despite the obstacles mentioned, show that if women were able to modify their attitudes, the ratio of women expatriates would increase significantly. The following examples illustrate this.

When women expatriates are asked why it is that they, in particular, were chosen, the answers are predominantly comments such as "sheer luck", "good timing" or "there was no one else". The words "competence", "know-how" or "best person for the job" are rarely part of women's vocabulary in contrast to men, who often describe the reason behind their selection in these terms. In this way, women tend to undermine their own professional image.

Moreover, women tend to adapt their professional life to private life or more clearly stated, to that of their spouse. This becomes evident in statements like: "I wouldn't mind being sent abroad by the company for a few months but this would mean leaving my partner/spouse for a longer period of time and is therefore out of the question for me". One female manager described the situation quite accurately and pointedly from her perspective, stating that "married women tend to organize their life around their husbands. Generally, there is no discussion if the husband is the one who wants to go abroad. However, if the woman is the one to go abroad, things change" (Fischlmayr 2002).

When men speak about their past successes, they proudly expound on their abilities and skills that brought them financial rewards and a step up on the corporate ladder. "I can ..." and "I know ..." typically reflect male attitudes. On the other hand, statements like "I believe that I could possibly ...", or "Perhaps we should ..." tend to reflect the female stance. In this way, women often belittle themselves by emphasizing coincidence, luck or the simplicity of the task over their actual ability (Fischlmayr 2001; 2002). When women speak about past successes, they tend to use less personal and more subdued descriptions. In so doing they convey a weaker self-image instead of highlighting their individual achievements.

Time and again women succumb to a misleading self-concept and show a lack of self-confidence. Some women rely on their charm and then worry about having exposed emotions and fears (Marshall 1984; Wilson 1995; Oppermann and Weber 1995), with the result that they negate their feelings, communication skill and empathy (Rizzo and Mendez 1990). These women will adapt their behavior and assume other's opinions while rejecting their own. They deny their feelings and lose their spontaneous creativity, contributing to an appearance of helplessness. Often women do not realize that their competitive edge lies precisely in their eloquence and sensitivity, their ability to read between the lines, their intuition and networking mentality and in their interest in others. They prefer to be seen as modest, downplay their accomplishments and have difficulty accepting compliments. Women could enhance their self-respect by "merely" learning to accept praise and acknowledgment and developing a self-confident personality (Aronson 1994; Ehrhardt 2000). These characteristics are particularly important requirements for international assignments. The positive correlation between self-confidence, cultural adaptability and professional achievement is a known fact (Caligiuri and Cascio 1998). Thus it stands to reason that self-effacing behavior prevents women from being chosen for an international assignment.

Conclusion: Women often obstruct their own career advancement, particularly if they act according to their gender-specific roles. Their behavior confirms and reinforces gender roles in the minds of others.

2.10.3 Accepting the International Assignment

The most well-known discourse on expatriate women, based on studies conducted by Nancy Adler, exposes three myths why women managers are not sent abroad:

1. Women are not willing to accept a position abroad for the sake of pursuing an international career.
2. Companies refuse to send women abroad.
3. The bias against women in foreign countries renders them ineffective.

While myth number one concerns the motives, myths number two and three address the obstacles that women actually encounter.

Adler herself rejects myth number 1, since her study on both male and female MBA students indicated the same interest in an international assignment. Yurkiewicz and Rosen (1995), on the other hand, tested the general willingness to accept an international assignment and found that men are quicker to decide and less complicated about their decision to accept the offer. These different results may also reflect the students' circumstances, as it is easier for them to signal a general willingness than for a candidate with a family and a secure job. Grounds for rejecting international assignments are usually for family reasons, such as the partner's unwillingness to come along, the partner's own career ambitions, uncertainty about the children's education and the partner's cultural preparation (Yurkiewicz and Rosen 1995; Brett and Stroh 1995; Fischlmayr 2001). The fact that this problem concerns both men and women, especially in view of the increasing number of dual career couples, is rarely considered (Reynolds and Bennett 1991; Smith 1999).

Conclusion: Regardless of gender, the willingness to accept an international assignment depends on numerous factors and not only on the basic willingness to go abroad.

2.10.4 The Selection Process

The selection process is mentioned as one reason why women are underrepresented in international management. To this effect, Harris (1999) examined the conditions under which women have equal opportunity in the selection process. Results show that the greatest probability for equal opportunity lies in closed formal and informal systems. This means that the clearer the criteria and the more HR is involved in the selection of candidates, the more often women are sent on international assignments.

Other studies (Fischlmayr 2002) indicate, however, that reality seems to deviate from theory. Hardly any women were selected on the basis of a formal application process consisting of an official proposal, a job application, an interview and selection of the most suited candidate. Candidates for international assignments are chosen predominantly in informal processes. Many women ask to be sent abroad to a certain subsidiary: "I was not selected for an international posting and asked repeatedly to be sent to Italy since my husband is Italian". The fact that women ask and men are asked, automatically puts women at a disadvantage.

Conclusion: Men are asked and women ask to be sent on an international assignment.

2.10.5 Expatriate Women's Situation

Adler's second "myth", stating that companies hesitate to send women abroad, is actually true (Adler 1994a). Asked why, the answers are:

- Women encounter particularly strong bias abroad from supervisors, employees, colleagues and customers.
- The problems faced by dual career couples are insurmountable.
- There is concern for the physical welfare and safety of single women.

Myth number three concerning the ineffectiveness of women due to prejudices against women in foreign countries turns out to be unfounded (Adler 1984b; 1987). On the contrary, most expatriate women are very successful. Not only are they accepted, they use their interpersonal skills to their advantage and benefit from being women. Moreover, other compatriots abroad tend to be more prejudiced than the locals in the host country are. The following section discusses research findings on the exceptions contained in these myths. We will treat questions concerning the actual problems encountered by women on international assignment, how they are dealt with and what aspects prove to be most helpful in the process.

The Dual-Career Issue

More and more couples live in partnerships in which both have a career they are not willing to give up (dual-career couples). A closer look shows that if the man has a dual-career conflict, companies tend to look for solutions, whereas a woman with the same problem encounters reluctance on the part of management to send her abroad (Harris 1995; Adler 1984b; Smith 1999). Without a doubt, the dual-career issue presents a significant problem since hardly any country outside of the EU will grant spouses a work permit. Coordinating two careers while trying to manage a family is extremely complex, although coping successfully in this respect is not unheard of (Punnet et al. 1992; Cagliguiri and Cascio 1998; Westwood and Leung 1994; Fischlmayr 2000). A woman is expected to give up her career when her partner/husband is selected for an international assignment. Accompanying husbands, on the other hand, are very seldom; not only are they rarely the main breadwinners, but they are also "relegated" to the role of househusbands.

Prejudices against Professional Women at Work

While companies hesitate to send women to specific countries because they suspect particular prejudices against women (Adler 1984a; Caligiuri and Tung 1999), studies indicated a different scenario:

- It is a premature conclusion to assume that expatriate women will not be accepted in cases where there are no local women to fill the position.
- Performance is the crucial factor, not gender (Taylor and Napier 1996; Adler 1984a, 1987; Westwood and Leung 1994; Izraeli et al. 1980).

Finally, the unexpected and striking result is: an expatriate woman in management in a foreign company is undeniably accepted and acknowledged!

The solution to the puzzle lies in the definition of the role of either "guest" or "manager" (Schroll-Machl 2002). An expatriate woman is perceived first and foremost as a foreigner in a high position and as a woman in second place (Adler 1984a). This tends to shift the perspective with respect to her role as a woman (Izraeli et al 1980) and, provided she does her job, there is no reason whatsoever not to respect her.

- As a foreigner, the expatriate woman is initially considered a visitor. This means that she is not perceived as part of the local culture and is granted special status as a guest. She enjoys the additional benefit as a foreigner and is granted more leeway and is tolerated in matters of lifestyle (e.g., clothing, hairstyle, accommodation), which may deviate considerably from local cultural norms. People know that she comes from abroad and has experienced a different socialization process. This role script contains attributions such as "white", "European", "Western" and "privileged" and evokes corresponding behavior. The fact that she is a woman is of secondary importance since, in any case, she is "totally different" (Schroll-Machl 2002).
- The power position (manager) is reinforced by the status of expatriate (guest). Official invitations to professional events pose no problems whatsoever. The woman is considered a representative, interacts with other representatives and may even have access to country-typical, official and professional men's groups because the combination of roles "foreign manager" gives her license (even in some Islamic countries) (Schroll-Machl 2002).

Women are less prone to voice problems with local employers and colleagues than they are about difficulties with headquarters at home, their position, the duration of their assignment, communication networks and a position upon their return (Adler 1994a; Harris 1995). While the women felt accepted and thoroughly supported by local men (Adler 1994a; Fischlmayr 2001), male expatriate colleagues had difficulty acknowledging women in leadership positions (Grove and Hallowell 1997). Women managers, especially the younger ones, report many power struggles with colleagues and supervisors (Schroll-Machl 2002). The younger the woman, the more she is seen and treated as an "object" and "female being", only to be regarded as an individual in her own right in later years (Fischlmayr 2000).

Furthermore, German and Austrian supervisors and colleagues set the stage for the treatment of their female counterparts, thereby influencing the behavior of local men toward the expatriate women. Many men tend to focus attention on themselves under certain circumstances, ignoring their female colleagues in the course of the discussion in an effort to demonstrate their importance. Seeing that the German or Austrian woman seems to receive less respect from her own (German/Austrian) colleagues and supervisors and is apparently not as important as previously assumed, local men follow suit and pay the woman less respect (Schroll-Machl 2002).

Conclusion: Women tend to experience prejudice from male compatriots, rather than from men in the host country.

Women Are Successful

Adler (1994b) reports that ninety-seven percent of the women she interviewed were successful in their overseas positions – according to their own estimation as well as to objective criteria for success.

Women's leadership style, with an emphasis on the social component, is considered a success factor in many countries. The women interviewed (Adler 1979; 1994a; Schroll-Machl 2000) pointed out that their leadership style relies on two-way communication and a caring attitude. The women tried to see the situation from the other's perspective (empathy), showed respect and addressed others on both the task and relationship level. They allowed time for these aspects and considered circumstances from a number of different angles, all of which, they claimed, are key components for successful leadership. They talked to the employees and listened to their problems. They were concerned about fairness and cooperative teamwork, integrated the experiences of local colleagues and tried to coordinate the different points of view as far as possible. Furthermore, they reported having fewer qualms about making concessions (Schroll-Machl 2002). Considering that this concerned style of leadership provides an important supplement to the concept of task orientation (see Thomas et al 2003, q.v. Ch. 2.2.3 Schroll-Machl), demonstrated by German executives in particular, this is a key success factor in terms of corporate climate and consequently, for employee motivation. The feedback obtained from local employees regarding their female supervisors supports this standpoint. This approach is often criticized as too soft, a view that is not generally shared abroad.

A woman in a management position in a German company is conspicuous because it is unusual that Germans would send a woman in this position abroad. This leads to the following results (Schroll-Machl, 2002): (1) A woman receives advance credit. She must be good, otherwise she would not be in this position (cf. also Adler 1994a). (2) She comes across as more convincing, leading others to have higher expectations of her, for example, expecting her to create new structures and overcome particular difficulties. This image corresponds well to her unique job profile and perhaps even contributes to the support and optimism she encounters. Employees are even willing to swerve from the usual routine and try new approaches under the auspices of their new supervisor. While men tend to conform to predetermined expectations, women in management positions are generally freer to create in the space that is created, thanks to the employees' inexperience with and the novelty of the experience. A woman in the top echelons is still something exotic and is therefore not obliged to conform to existing ideals.

Women expatriates are extremely successful in Scandinavia and France, where they are accepted in every field of work (Caligiuri and Tung 1999). This is hardly surprising, since women are backed by informal support factors (networks, access to social strata, etc.) that can be used for professional purposes.

Conclusion: Women in international leadership positions and especially on international assignments are successful. The key to their success is a direct result of their feminine characteristics and the simple fact that they are women.

Difficulties Encountered as Individuals and in their Private Lives

Biases held against women expatriates in their professional roles mentioned by Adler were refuted in the studies cited above. Nevertheless, difficulties do exist on the individual level and in private life, as reported by expatriate women:

Women tend to suffer more from loneliness and isolation than men (Adler 1994a; Mendenhall and Oddou 1985; Linehan 2000, Fischlmayr 2002). The more the emphasis is on her role as "guest", the greater the gap is between her and the local population and the sharper the sense of loneliness is felt. The woman is not perceived as the person she is, but rather as a representative of a company, a country and a function, and is treated accordingly (Schroll-Machl 2002). The position of influence in the company adds to the feeling of isolation. Private friendships with employees are often not compatible with her professional image and may even lead to bouts of jealousy. In many countries, the supervisor is not invited to private events in order to maintain a distance. It is expected, however, that the supervisor invites employees and the invitation is gladly accepted. Frequently, a woman is not able to meet with female counterparts simply because there are none (Schroll-Machl 2002). Although the same dynamic applies to both men and women, women tend to suffer more from its effects. This may be because the majority of expatriate women are single, in which case loneliness is felt more intensely.

Cultural variables in the host country, such as religion, traditions and regulations, can make a woman's stay in the country difficult (Caligiuri and Tung 1999; Solomon 1994; Fischlmayr 2000; Schroll-Machl 2002).

- In order to establish contacts, it is crucial to abide by the role scripts required by the host country. Two patterns of lifestyle are generally advantageous: life as a family or as a couple. Two-way invitations are acceptable in these cases since men can always talk to men and women to women and the children can play with each other. Everyone functions within a role and the structure is not threatened. Following the rules of behavior facilitates any kind of social life or, for that matter, makes it possible in the first place.
- Single status is considered very unusual and even strange in many cultures throughout all social classes, educational levels and professional positions. Questions about marital status are inevitably raised. There is no code of conduct on how to deal with unmarried persons. Where there is no partner at one's side, an imbalance is created. Consequently, it is extremely difficult to make and maintain private contact. Invitations may even be entirely unacceptable.
- Furthermore, women may find it stressful to have to assert themselves on a daily basis in a country where women have relatively little freedom of movement. Culture-specific rules limit independence, making travel or even simply going out alone to a cinema or restaurant extremely difficult. Expatriate women often find that they are alone in taking such liberties. It takes courage to pioneer new terrain.
- Women on their own can also awaken the protector instinct in men – at least in situations where security is an issue. Under these circumstances, men may assume their protector role, offering support and fatherly care. It is important to deactivate the belief among HR professionals that women are likely to encounter danger while abroad and must be protected!
- In addition, women in top positions with a good salary do not have the higher market value in terms of sex appeal (at home and abroad) that men do. The high-ranking position, and the corresponding position of power, makes it difficult for women to enter a relationship with locals. Friendships with local men would be unusual not to mention scandalous. An intimate relationship would be entirely out of the question. In contrast, unattached men are invited more spontaneously, more often and with more ease, generally because of the greater freedom of movement they enjoy, but also intentionally, for more obvious reasons.
- Single mothers represent a kind of hybrid form in this context. Although

they are single, they do, however, signalize "something akin to a family", so that by virtue of having children a certain female norm is created, which permits friendship with other women.

A woman who lives abroad together with her partner or family is not only directly confronted with the host country's role expectations for a woman, but also with the expectations she associates with her role as a German woman (Schroll-Machl 2002). It is her job to coordinate roles regarding partnership, children and household within her nuclear family. Women are especially attuned to an accompanying spouse's sense of well-being and worry about his feelings of inadequacy because he may be feeling under-challenged and overly dependent. In addition, the couple's socially conditioned environment (parents, parents-in-law, acquaintances and friends, the German expatriate community, etc.) consider the woman, the couple and the family exotic, causing enormous pressure for the couple to clarify and justify such "unconventionality". The male solution, to assume the purely professional role, is much more difficult for a woman because she tends to perceive her life more within an overall context, where her career constitutes *only* one aspect. Many women do not consider a career successful if they have to risk their marriage or the family breaks up.

Outcome: While expatriate women may enjoy professional merit, they have to cope with a number of difficulties in their personal lives. In this respect, the usual family-related gender roles apply in one's own culture as much as they do in the host country.

2.10.6 Coping Strategies and Support Factors

Expatriate women are essentially confronted with the same coping stress as men when it comes to being sent on an international assignment. However, women are faced with additional gender-specific problems.

Coping With Professional Difficulties

German and Austrian women often do not convey an image commensurate with their leadership status. Once they feel comfortable in their leadership role and have aligned their professional goals with those of local staff needs and expectations, they are less prone to displays of authority and control. This is to a woman's advantage as overt attempts to take control could lead to employees rejecting her authority. Employees not familiar with a participative leadership approach are often tempted to step into the space that is created and take advantage of the situation. In contrast, factors such as prestigious appearance (mainly clothes), academic titles (e.g., a doctorate) or presenting oneself exclusively in a professional role will impact her message and render her professionally competent. Often the rule is to accept conflicts that are inevitably linked to the role, to bear them and to steer them toward a solution. In interactions with German colleagues and supervisors, women should appear self-confident and "prepared for confrontation", should reduce their inclination toward harmony and double-check their trust in the goodwill of others from case to case. They must be prepared to defend their position and to avoid the victim trap (Schroll-Machl 2002).

Individuals in leadership positions join support networks. While men have access to such networks, i.e., begin to create such networks at the beginning of the international assignment, women rarely have networks of this kind and are excluded from the typical informal male-dominated networks (Adler 1994a; Mendenhall and Oddou 1985; Linehan 2000; Fischlmayr 2002). Frequently, women must first try to gain access to existing power networks and then learn to use them to their advantage. Women's networks are very rare and are a great help wherever they exist (Schroll-Machl 2002).

Managing General Difficulties

Women are more likely to admit to having difficulties and to seek support in keeping with the well-known self-help stereotypes (Schroll-Machl 2002). Women seem to be more attuned to areas in which they have problems, are able to assess their difficulties more objectively and to take the necessary steps toward reaching a solution. Their confidants are usually a spouse or partner, family, friends at home and trusted colleagues in similar situations or health professionals. The interaction can take place in person, via telephone or e-mail. In general it appears that women have substantially less time than men do. Whether married or not, women in many countries are simply less flexible in terms of time due to stronger family commitments.

One advantage of living abroad is often mentioned (Fischlmayr 2000; Schroll-Machl 2002): Compared to Germany or Austria, practically all other countries offer more child-care facilities and live-in help. This makes life for working (married or single) mothers from both a practical and psychological standpoint much easier and alleviates the omnipresent guilty conscious.

Furthermore, women tend to enjoy widespread courtesy, consideration and other characteristics of goodwill, which they may not be accustomed to from home (Adler 1994a; Fischlmayr 2000; Schroll-Machl 2002).

2.10.7 Conclusion

Women tend to be less represented in international management than in management positions in general, although, from a professional perspective, there is absolutely no reason why this should be the case. Women are successful and acknowledged as such, even in many countries where HR professionals in German and Austrian firms might think differently (e.g., Asia, Islamic countries). Furthermore, women contribute leadership qualities that focus on the person, a much-needed addition to the predominant emphasis on task orientation. The added challenges (single) women face outside of their professional environment can be dealt with by providing mentoring for the duration of the international assignment.

Professional women striving to keep abreast of developments in international organizations should have access to relevant information of this nature. Once such subliminal obstacles are removed, women will take their place among the increasing pool of managers in Germany and Austria who conduct international business on a daily basis at home and abroad.

References

Adler, N. J. (1979): Women as androgynous managers. A conceptualisation of the potential for American women in international management. Journal of Intercultural Relations 3: 407–436.

Adler, N. J. (1984a): Women do not want international careers: and other myths about international management. Organizational Dynamics 13 (2): 66–79.

Adler, N. J. (1984b): Women in international management: Where are they? California Management Review 26 (4): 78–89.

Adler, N. J. (1987): Pacific Basin managers: a Gaijin, not a woman. Human Resource Management 26.

Adler, N. J. (1994a): Competitive frontiers: Women managing across borders. In: Nancy, J.; Izraeli, D. N. (Eds.), Competitive Frontiers: Women Managers in a Global Economy. Cambridge/Mass., pp. 22–40.

Adler, N. J. (1994b): Women managing across borders. Journal of Management Development 13: 24–41.

Adler, N. J. (1997): International Dimensions of Organizational Behavior. 3rd ed. Cincinnati, OH.

Aronson, E. (1994): Sozialpsychologie. Heidelberg/Berlin/Oxford.

Assig, D. (Ed.) (2002): Frauen in Führungspositionen. München.
Bem, S. (1974): Measurement of psychological androgyny. Journal of Counseling and Clinical Psychology 42: 155–162.
Brett, J. M.; Stroh, L. K. (1995): Willingness to relocate internationally. Human Resource Management 34 (3): 405–424.
Caligiuri, P. M.; Cascio, W. F. (1998): Can we send her there? Maximizing the success of western women on global assignments. Journal of World Business 33 (4): 394–416.
Caligiuri, P. M.; Tung, R. L. (1999): Comparing the success of male and female expatriates from a US-based multinational company. International Journal of Human Resource Management 10 (5): 763–782.
Domsch, M. E.; Lieberum, U. B. (1997): Weibliche Führungskräfte im Ausland. Personalwirtschaft 9: 18–21.
ECA (1996): Women on the Move. Managing Mobility Survey.
Ehrhardt, U. (2000): Die Klügere gibt nicht mehr nach. Frauen sind einfach besser. Frankfurt/Main.
Fischlmayr, I. C. (1999): Female Expatriates in International Management. In: Freisler-Traub, A.; Innreiter-Mooser, C. (Eds.), Zerreißproben. Linzer Schriften zur Frauenforschung. Band 11. Linz, pp. 107–134.
Fischlmayr, I. C. (2000): Expatriation in Österreich – Empirische Untersuchung unter Personalmanagern und ehemaligen Auslandsentsandten. Linz. (Unveröffentlicht)
Fischlmayr, I. C. (2001): In Search of the Best Suited Expatriate. An Empirical Study on the Applicability of Literature. Dissertation, Universität Linz.
Fischlmayr, I. C. (2002): Female self perception as barrier to international careers? International Journal of Human Resource Management 13 (3): 773–783.
Grove, C. L.; Hallowell, W. (1997): Female assignees: lessons learned. Runzenheimer Reports on Relocation October 1997.
Hantschel, G. (2000): Frauen in Führungspositionen – Ein europäischer Vergleich mit Perspektiven zur Personalentwicklung. In: Regnet, E.; Hofmann, L. M. (Eds.), Personalmanagement in Europa. Göttingen.
Harris, H. (1993): Women in management: opportunity or threat? Women in Management Review 8: 9–14.
Harris, H. (1995): Organizational influences on women's career opportunities in international management. Women in Management Review 10 (3): 26–31.
Harris, H. (1999): Women in international management: Why are they not selected? In: Brewster, C.; Harris, H. (Eds.), International HRM. Contemporary Issues in Europe, 258–276.
Heilmann, M. E. (1980): The impact of situational factors on personnel decisions concerning women: varying sex composition of the applicant pool. Organizational Behavior and Human Performance 26: 386–395.
Hofbauer, J. (2002): Kontinuität und Wandel in betrieblichen Geschlechterbeziehungen an Beispielen der Mobilitäts- und Zeitkonkurrenz im Management. In: Goldberg, C.; Rosenberger, S. (Eds.), Karriere Frauen Konkurrenz. Innsbrucker Studienverlag, Innsbruck, pp. 15–40.
ILO – International Labour Organisation (1998): World of Work. 23 (8). ILO, Switzerland.
Izraeli, D. N.; Banai, M.; Zeira, Y. (1980): Women executives in MNC subsidiaries. California Management Review 23: 53–63.

KF-Uni Graz (1998): Expatriates – Luxury or Necessity – Aspekte des internationalen Personaleinsatzes. Studie am Institut für Internationales Management. Universität Graz.

Linehan, M. (2000): Senior Female International Managers: Why so few? Aldershot, GB.

Marshall, J. (1984): Women Managers: Travellers in a Male World. Chichester.

Mayrhofer, W.; Scullion, H. (2002): Female expatriates in international business. empirical evidence from the German clothing industry. International Journal of Human Resource Management 13 (3), 815–836.

Mendenhall, M.E.; Oddou, G. (1985): The dimensions of expatriate acculturation: a review. Academy of Management Review 10 (1): 39–47.

Oppermann, K.; Weber, E. (1995): Frauensprache – Männersprache. Zürich.

Perry, E. L. et al. (1994): Explaining gender based selection decisions: a synthesis of contextual and cognitive approaches. Academy of Management Review 19 (4): 786–820.

Punnett, B. J. et al. (1992): The challenge for women expatriates and spouses: some empirical evidence. The International Journal of Human Resource Management 3 (3): 585–592.

Reynolds, C.; Bennett, R. (1991): The career couple challenge. Personnel Journal Vol. 70 (3): 46–48.

Rizzo, A.-M.; Mendez, C. (1990): The Integration of Women in Management. Westport.

Schaufler, B. (2000): Frauen in Führung! Bern.

Schein, V. E. (1975): Relationships between sex role stereotypes and requisite management characteristics among female managers. Journal of Applied Psychology 60 (3): 340–344.

Schroll-Machl, S. (2002): Frauen als Expatriates in Führungspositionen. Eine Untersuchung am Goethe-Institut Inter Nationes. München/Deggendorf. (Unveröffentlicht)

Smith, C. (1999): Managing the Dual Career Expatriate. Paper presented at the EIASM (European Institute for Advanced Studies in Management). Workshop on Expatriation. September 24–25.

Solomon, C. M. (1994): Success abroad depends on more than job skills. Personnel Journal Vol. 73 (4): 51–59.

Taylor, S.; Napier, N. K. (1996): Working in Japan: lessons from western expatriates. Sloan Management Review 37: 76–84.

Thomas, A.; Kammhuber, S.; Schroll-Machl, S. (Eds.) (2003): Handbuch Interkulturelle Kommunikation und Kooperation, Bd. 2: Länder, Kulturen und interkulturelle Berufstätigkeit. Göttingen.

Tung, R. L. (1997): Canadian Expatriates in Asia-Pacific: An Analysis of their Attitude Toward and Experience in International Assignments. Paper presented at the Meeting of Society for Industrial and Organizational Psychology, St. Louis, MO.

Westwood, R. I.; Leung, S. M. (1994): The female expatriate manager experience. International Studies of Management and Organization 24 (3): 64–85.

Wilson, F. M. (1995). Organizational Behavior & Gender. Berkshire/GB.

Yurkiewicz, J.; Rosen, B. (1995): Increasing receptivity to expatriate assignments. In: Selmer, J. (Eds.), Expatriate Management. Westport (CT), pp. 37–56.

3. A Strategic Overall Concept for Introducing Interculturality in Organizations

Eva-Ulrike Kinast/Sylvia Schroll-Machl

Not all international organizations in Germany have a basic strategy for managing international activities. This may well indicate that top management is unaware of the consequences this is likely to have on the cooperation between employees at headquarters and those at partner organizations abroad (including international customers and competitors). In this final chapter, we will attempt to illustrate the influence of basic corporate strategies for international activities on employees and the way they deal with interculturality. In addition, we will explore the reasons why intercultural trainings frequently do not bring the desired results in the absence of an overall comprehensive strategy.

The Intercultural Encounter: The Function of Interaction between the Individual, the Situation and the Culture

The previous chapters showed that:

- The *action* that takes place during an intercultural encounter determines the function of the interaction between the person, the situation and the culture (Figure 20).
- One *person* always influences an action on the basis on his/her psychological condition including perception, thought, feeling and behavior. The importance of applied intercultural competence becomes evident as the international dimension increases. Intercultural training has a track record in developing applied intercultural competence.
- A *situation* comprises tangible events in terms of economy, ecology, materialism or culture. Among these are key areas of management such as negotiations, teams, mergers and acquisitions, intercultural fields and practical application, for example, HR development, scientific cooperation, military and police missions, as well as typical functions within the organizations such as research and development, production, sales and personnel.

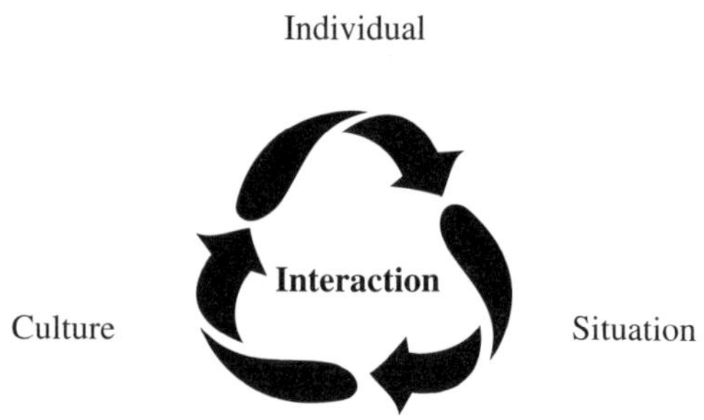

Figure 20: The function of the interaction between the individual, the situation and the culture

- Every *culture* includes a specific system of orientation with specific cultural standards. The content and extent of the given cultural standards differ according to the culture.

Internationally active employees find themselves caught between these poles of tension where their own idiosyncrasies, abilities and situational demands clash with their partner's *(individual)*. This happens when faced with certain aspects and challenges demanded by the *situation* including any discrepancies that may arise between their own and their partner's cultural standards *(culture)*. The result of the interaction can take any number of forms depending on the tension configuration.

Strategies for Interculturality

According to a systematic scheme developed by Schroll-Machl and Nový (2000), the internationally active employee and his/her other-culture partner have the option of four strategies on how to deal with culture-specific differences in perception, thought, feeling and behavior between themselves and another individual in cultural overlap situations. Figure 21 illustrates the strategies for interculturality.

The illustration describes the following interculturality strategies:

Dominance/Adaptation
Here one individual's culture dominates the other individual's culture. The dominant culture's cultural standards become the standard of behavior that is binding for both. Individuals belonging to the dominated culture are asked to adapt to these standards.

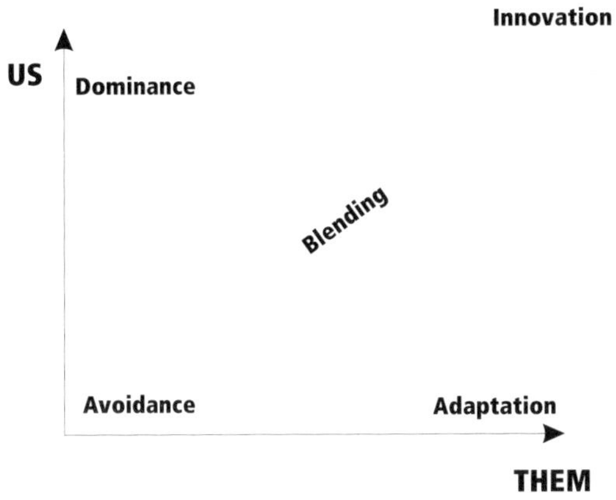

Figure 21: Interculturality strategies according to Schroll-Machl and Nový (2000, p. 170)

Blending
According to this strategy, the cultural standards of both cultures involved intermingle, offering the participants three options: 1.) Either they find a *compromise* by agreeing on the smallest common denominator, designate a framework within which interaction takes place, allowing the actions of the participating cultures to unfold without a preference for either culture; 2.) Or they bring the cultures together in a form of co-action, i.e., task sharing, whereby each individual does what he/she is good at *(combination)* (cf. Zeutschel 1998); 3.) Or the participating cultures group into an alternating contingency by interlocking significant behavioral characteristics and establishing the newly created standards as a maxim for simultaneous interaction *(integration)* (cf. Zeutschel 1998).

Innovation/Synergy
This strategy requires both individuals to have an awareness of their own and their partner's culture. They define the values, norms, rules etc. of the respective cultural standards and work out similarities and differences. Having created this basis, both individuals define a *new* behavioral alternative and supplement their behavioral repertoire by a third, innovative element that serves as a mutual point of departure for their interaction.

Avoidance
This strategy is particularly recommended for Germans who tend to have a rather direct communication style. According to this strategy, the person acting remains in the background and is passive without contributing in the way of reaction or criticism. This strategy can have a deescalating effect and may therefore prove more effective than other strategies.

The interculturality strategy an employee chooses does not depend on the individual or on the clash between the different cultural standards (culture), but rather on the intercultural latitude granted by his/her corporation, supervisor, function and task. The degree of freedom in this area plays a significant role in the overall *situation*. This aspect will be discussed further in the following sections.

Basic Strategies for Conducting International Business in Global Organizations

Intercultural considerations are dependent on an organization's underlying corporate strategy for international activities. A key question here is to what extent headquarters influences the foreign subsidiary and vice versa. According to Heenan and Perlmutter (1979; similar: Reineke 1989), there are five types of basic strategies, which are illustrated in Figure 22.

Ethnocentric Strategy
Corporations with an ethnocentric leadership style espouse a one-sided relationship between headquarters and the foreign subsidiary. This basic strategy is often the choice during the initial phase of the internationalization of an operation, when there is only one foreign subsidiary. Ethnocentrically led organizations designate the corporate strategy and philosophy and transfer these to the foreign subsidiary, which has little autonomy in the matter. Top management holds key positions at both headquarters and

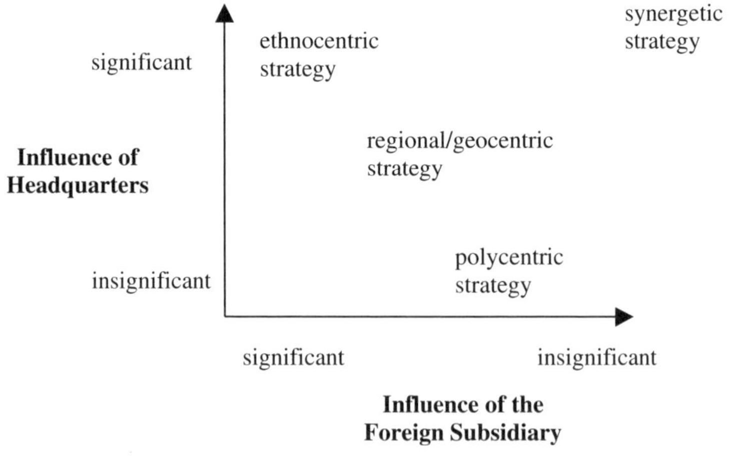

Figure 22: Basic strategies for conducting international business in global organizations

at the foreign subsidiary. Cultural differences are often ignored in favor of standardization, an approach that can culminate in pent up conflict potential between headquarters and the foreign subsidiary, suggesting something akin to "cultural colonization" (Scholz 1993).

Polycentric Strategy

Organizations with polycentric leadership grant their foreign subsidiaries autonomy to a large extent. Corporate strategies and philosophies are developed at the overseas site and adapted to its specific requirements. Accordingly, headquarters and the foreign subsidiary can each maintain their individual image. This strategy often applies where the foreign subsidiaries are located in distant countries where local managers run the operation but rarely move up to management positions at headquarters. Cultural differences play an important role, although synergetic effects often go under in the process. Difficulties in coordination between headquarters and the foreign subsidiary are the flip side of the advantages offered by autonomy and the ability to fine-tune decisions between the foreign subsidiary and environmental stipulations.

Geocentric Strategy

Organizations with geocentric leadership blend the corporate strategies and philosophies from both headquarters and the foreign subsidiary, and then implement the blended strategy at the foreign subsidiary. The executives' nationality plays a minor role in filling positions. Their (intercultural) competence, on the other hand, is a decisive factor. Cultural differences and similarities are taken into consideration.

Synergetic Strategy

The synergetic strategy is an extension of the geocentric strategy. Synergetically managed corporations develop a third, innovative approach consisting of the combined elements at headquarters and the foreign subsidiary. According to the principle of "the whole is more than the sum of its parts", management implements the new concept at the foreign sites. Synergetically led operations appreciate the diverse cultural characteristics displayed by both representatives from headquarters and local managers and consider this aspect a valuable resource. Again, cultural differences and similarities are taken into consideration.

Regiocentric Strategy

Regiocentric leadership adapts headquarters' corporate strategy and philosophy to the requirements of the foreign subsidiary. In contrast to the geocentric strategy, however, the individual foreign subsidiaries have less influence. The prefix "regio" suggests that this strategy and its newly defined elements pertain to foreign subsidiaries in a region such as, for example, Europe or Asia. The regiocentric strategy is often applied in operations with small-scale cross-border contacts such as Germany/Austria/Switzerland and Germany/Czech Republic. A key characteristic of this strategy is that headquarters might well adopt the corporate strategies and philosophies of these subsidiaries, thus aligning management at headquarters with that of the subsidiary. Executives are recruited locally and sent to headquarters at short intervals.

A further attribute of geocentric, synergetic and regiocentric strategies is evident in the attempt to find a balance between the different cultures and the advantage of a method of overall optimization (e.g., standardized controlling systems and production processes, comparative hierarchies) as well as to weigh the pros and cons of the most suitable compatibility with local requirements at the foreign subsidiary. Only the regiocentric strategy allows for solutions that are beneficial to headquarters and to the organization as a whole. In this way, headquarters profits from new ideas that never would have been created if the organizations had not been open to outside influence.

The type of interculturality strategy that is actually applied by individuals in the international arena, an aspect which to date has found little response, depends decisively on the corporation's basic strategy for dealing with international business relations, which provides the framework for the employees' intercultural activity and prescribes the choice of interculturality strategy, even if this only occurs implicitly. This situation also determines the nature of intercultural conflict. The basic strategy an international corporation chooses for dealing with its international business quite often depends on the extent and the importance of its international business operations. General opinion is that the geocentric strategy can only be used for corporations with a global network. The following examples, however, show that this basic strategy can also prove effective for a single foreign subsidiary.

The Influence of International Corporate Strategies on the Interculturality Strategy of Internationally Active Employees

The basic strategy lays down the possibilities and limits of the intercultural playing field for employees of the corporation and thereby determines how employees are *allowed* to react in response to cultural overlap situations. This means that:

- if an international organization adheres to an ethnocentric strategy, then the culture of the employee from headquarters dominates the culture of the employee from the foreign subsidiary (dominance). Intercultural interaction is limited to finding the best possible solution for integrating the other-cultural partner. Since, at best, this can only be partially successful, the dominated partner is likely to harbor some resentment over the lack of respect for his cultural attributes and demonstrate this in some form of hostility or resistance. The dominating employee will feel increasingly frustrated that, despite all efforts, he is unable to sustain commitment, criticizing intercultural training seminars for not having provided him with the tools – provocatively stated – to effectively "manipulate" the other individual.
- if the organization adheres to a polycentric strategy, then the employees from headquarters have to adapt to the culture of the employees at the foreign subsidiary (adaptation). The employee from headquarters has a difficult time with intercultural interaction and experiences moments of doubt with regard to the appropriateness of the re-orientation and change required of him and whether he will be able to fulfill expectations.
- according to the geocentric and regiocentric strategy, the cultural standards of the employees' culture at headquarters and at the foreign subsidiary are integrated (compromise, combination, integration). The intercultural interaction is experienced by both sides as a give and take situation. This is, however, time consuming and requires participants to continually negotiate options until a solution is found.
- in the case of the synergetic strategy, both employees develop new behavioral alternatives, which in turn create a new standard (innovation/synergy). Experience shows that this is rare and can also lead to controversy. In time, however, it contributes to a feeling of teamwork among individuals and enhances performance.

Basic Strategy

Interculturality Strategy	ethnocentric	polycentric	geocentric	synergetic	regiocentric
Dominance/Adaption	✓	✓			
Blending			✓		✓
Synergy/Innovation				✓	
Avoidance	✓	✓	✓	✓	✓

Figure 23: The intercultural strategy employed by international managers in relation to the organization's basic strategy for international operations

– avoidance strategies can be used as an interculturality strategy in all the basic strategies mentioned. The following examples serve to illustrate the international manager's interdependent position within the individual functions of the global operation. The goal is to demonstrate the effects on the individual level as well as the consequences for the entire organization.

Examples

The Basic Strategy's Influence on Sales at a German Sports Manufacturer in Poland

A German manufacturer of sophisticated, brand-name sports gear popular with sports enthusiasts decides that his products will be sold exclusively in specialty stores. The German manufacturer now asks his Polish sales manager to follow suit and to offer his products in specialty stores throughout Poland. The Polish sales manager is appalled, fearing that this measure will cause sales to drop drastically. The situation escalates into a conflict. From a cultural perspective, it is important to understand that in Germany, merchandise sold in specialty stores is considered to be of higher quality than what is sold in supermarkets. In Poland, on the other hand, sports gear manufacturers are considered more advanced if they sell high quality merchandise in supermarket chains (similar to a superstore or hypermarket there).

According to the choice of a basic strategy consistent with Heenans and Perlmutters (1979), the conflict as well as its solution can take a different course, as one might suspect, depending on the interculturality strategy chosen according to Schroll-Machl and Nový (2000).

In the case of the *ethnocentric strategy*, the German sports gear manufacturer dominates the Polish sales manager and the merchandise is sold in Polish specialty stores. The German manufacturer (corporate level) will most likely begin to wonder why his products are not selling and will complain about decreasing turnover. However, he will still feel a sense of self-satisfaction because his merchandise is, after all, a "quality item". The Polish sales manager, on the other hand, is likely to feel frustrated and disregarded in his role as sales expert on the Polish market. Eventually, he is likely to resign his position with the company (individual level). He might feel that he has been discriminated against and see the Germans as inflexible and authoritarian. The responsible employee from headquarters is likely to consider the Pole to be either uncooperative or easily offended and might complain that despite the Polish sales manager's arguments having been reasonable to an extent, he was *not able* to give in since he would have been acting contrary to corporate policy.

In accordance with a *polycentric strategy*, the German sports gear manufacturer *adapts* to the Polish sales manager's modus operandi and sells the articles in supermarket chains, regardless of the German sales strategy (corporate level). The German sports gear manufacturer accepts the culture-specific differences inherent in the Polish consumer's market behavior. Nevertheless, he will have considerable doubts about sustaining the image of a high-quality product and will be concerned about the threat to the corporate identity of his company. This development is bound to impact his internal image (e.g., the pride German employees take in working for a company that produces the high-quality article "XYZ") as well as the image projected to the outside (e.g., customers who buy the high-quality "XYZ" product). The Pole (individual level) is satisfied and motivated because he sees his products on a supermarket shelf and can now be considered a savvy sales manager of a state-of-the-art operation. He might now see Germans as cooperative and open to progress. The German, on the other hand, is impressed by the extent of the cultural differences and their unforeseen consequences.

The *geocentric* strategy *blends* both sales strategies: The sports gear is sold both in specialty stores and in supermarkets in Poland (corporate level). This way the German sports gear manufacturer maintains the high-quality product image and at the same time offers the up-and-coming generation of Poles with Western consumer behavior a corresponding range of sports gear in specialty shops. By the same token, the Polish sales manager realizes that he is being taken seriously and can offer the average Polish consumer high-quality sports gear in supermarkets. The only problem will be to agree on prices. The Pole and the German might engage in negotiations for some time before they have resolved this issue. However, both are likely to walk away with the feeling that they are interculturally competent and have profited from the experience.

The *synergetic strategy emphasizes* an *innovative* solution. An example here would be if the German sports gear manufacturer were to set up a huge supermarket, comparable to an American mall, for various brand-name sports gear in the capital of Poland. This way the German would get his high-end shop and the Pole his corresponding supermarket. The disadvantage is that the investment is higher than that of any of the other strategies and opponents must first warm up to the idea (corporate level). The advantage on an individual level is that both the German and the Pole feel their needs have been met and are satisfied with their collaborative efforts.

The *regiocentric strategy*, too, *blends* both sales strategies. In this case, the Polish sales strategy influences the German sales strategy in Germany (corporate level), as unlikely as this may sound. In time, the German sports gear manufacturer's goods would be sold at supermarket chains. On the individual level, this would be a significant endorsement for the Pole. The German might take pride in his ability to contribute to and be inspired by the international cooperation.

The Basic Strategy's Influence: Illustrated by Production and Quality Management Processes at a German Automobile Manufacturing Plant in Eastern Europe

A German automobile manufacturer, with a sophisticated and world renowned reputation, buys his headlights from a supplier whose production has been outsourced to Eastern Europe. Soon after, German quality management finds flaws in the headlights manufactured in Eastern Europe: only one headlight works on some of its automobiles. The cause is that, contrary to regulations, employees at the production plant do not differentiate carefully enough between different brand-name components and thus frequently install the wrong headlights. The Eastern European production manager is confronted, whereupon he replies: "The employees aren't stupid. They know what parts are required and how to assemble them and even if a mistake occurs, it's hardly worth a crisis. It's enough for one headlight to work!" A conflict ensues. From a cultural perspective, it is important to know that Eastern Europeans love to improvise and tend to ignore prescribed structures, while Germans prefer to plan each move, to organize procedures and to stick to the prescribed procedures.

Depending on the basic strategies chosen, i.e., according to Heenans and Perlmutters (1979) or the interculturality strategy according to Schroll-Machl and Nový (2000), both the course of the conflict and its resolution can differ.

According to the *ethnocentric strategy*, the German automobile manufacturer *dominates* the Eastern European production manager and the supplier withdraws the production of headlights for this manufacturer from the Eastern European production site (corporate level). In this way, the automobile manufacturer maintains his standard of quality. The Eastern European production manager, however, (individual level) is offended because his commitment and effort are not appreciated, not to mention the commitment and effort shown by his employees at the production site. He does not understand why the Germans make such a fuss about a few mistakes. The German quality assurance manager is upset as well and launches into a litany about regulations in an effort to avoid a reoccurrence of the situation.

In keeping with the *polycentric strategy*, the German automobile manufacturer *adapts* to the Eastern European production manager's strategy. According to this scenario, the potentially flawed headlights would be installed. This solution would be inconceivable, however, due to the quality requirements of this sophisticated brand and the stringent safety regulations in Germany.

The *geocentric strategy integrates* both production strategies. The German supplier, for instance, asks the Eastern European production manager for his understanding of the German quality standards and provides him with detailed information about customer demands and the reasons behind them. In addition, he offers a reward for decreasing the amount of flawed products in the form of appreciation, career opportunities and good business relations to German management, which in turn, soothes ruffled feathers (individual level). On the cultural standards level, the integration of the participant's different cultural standards proves successful because both the German's need for structure and the Eastern European's "person-centered form of control" are honored. In all likelihood, the German supplier will succeed in decreasing the margin of error (corporate level).

A *synergetic strategy* would have to come up with an *innovative* solution, which is hardly feasible due to the technical requirements (unless multi-functional headlights can be developed ...).

A *regiocentric* strategy, integrating both strategies, is also unrealistic since it is imperative that both headlights are functional according to German standards for the reasons already mentioned (luxury brand and driving safety).

The examples are purposely selected from different areas of responsibility within corporations. Basic strategies of international corporations are dependent on a number of factors that inevitably affect operations. This aspect must be taken into consideration when agreeing on a strategy and involving others.

Conclusion

The goal is to illustrate that the basic strategy that international corporations have agreed upon for pursuing their international business interests has a significant influence on the interculturality strategy practiced by management and employees. If management has not established a basic strategy, then this will impact internationally active employees' sense of orientation and they will be unclear about what exactly is expected of them in cultural overlap situations. Frequently, a group of culturally diverse employees intuit what behavior is appropriate in a given situation. These implied theories of appropriate behavior direct the employees' behavior. Believing what appropriate behavior is and knowing what behavior the company expects to be represented abroad differs significantly. The difference combined with individuals' tendency to behave ethnocentrically in situations of cultural overlap in order to dominate, regardless of their cultural belonging, aggravates the issue. This is true for both the members of the other culture(s) as well as for management at headquarters at home. The latter tends to expect its employees to be able to switch from one interculturality standard to the next, for example, from blending to dominating, which only exacerbates the conflict.

For the reasons mentioned, it is mainly up to employees in middle management to resolve conflicts created in cultural overlap situations. Top management is frequently oblivious to the intricacies involved.

Generally, HR development is asked to select appropriate training measures for individual employees. The employees do in fact learn about the cultural standards of other cultures and apply this knowledge in order to interact appropriately in a cultural overlap situation. Kinast (1998) came to this conclusion in her research (q.v. Ch. I, 2.3). However, somewhere along the line, the impression remains that many conflicts persist and that all the intercultural trainings have little effect. The fact is that intercultural training cannot (and does not want to) assume top management's responsibility for establishing a corporate basic strategy for pursuing international activities.

Recommendations and Examples of Intercultural Corporate Development

From a *strategic* point of view, it is recommended one conduct an *analysis* to determine the basic strategies (experience has shown that not only one basic strategy applies) which the entire operation and the individual departments have been working with to date and what the results were. The next step should involve organizing a workshop for executives and upper management in order to develop and agree upon an appropriate basic strategy for interacting with international business partners at both headquarters and its foreign subsidiaries. This basic strategy must be absolutely clear, have the backing of management at headquarters and the foreign subsidiaries and be communicated by management top down. Aside from the typical newsletters, workshops should be organized to introduce executives to the basic strategy agreed upon, followed by a session to elaborate on the effects the basic strategy is likely to have on the employees' interculturality strategies within their specific areas of responsibility. The managers are then assigned the task of familiarizing their employees with the basic strategy and ensuring that it is actually implemented. For this task, the managers require adequate preparation.

From a *systemic* perspective, it is recommended to hire a neutral *process consultant*, such as an experienced, external consultant with the necessary personal qualifications (assertiveness, communication skills, flexibility etc.), professional expertise (e.g., a background in psychology), methodological competence (facilitating, coaching, training, mediation) and intercultural competence (knowledge about the specific cultural standards of one or more cultures, foreign language skills etc.). Ideally, the candidate will have had several years experience as a manager in an international operation.

From a structural perspective, it is recommended to assign a project team to the task of intercultural corporate development. In larger organizations, a department could also assume this responsibility. The team could operate virtually and ideally, project members would have diverse professional backgrounds (psychology, law, business etc.) and have similar personal, methodical and intercultural skills to the external systemic consultant. If employees within the organization lack these skills, they should receive the necessary remedial training to enhance their competence. The project team is responsible for initiating the process of intercultural corporate development, for supervising and directing it.

On the individual level, HR development within an organization should be responsible for the development of intercultural personnel and once the basic strategy has been firmly installed, for the design and implementation of an overall concept for enhancement measures, such as intercultural training and intercultural coaching.

Interculturality, reflected on a strategic level within the organization followed by a decision regarding an appropriate basic strategy, opens up a wide range of possible outcomes. In closing, we list several snapshot examples:

- "Intercultural mediators" could be involved in geocentric or regiocentric strategies to prevent conflict in cultural overlap situations. These could be individuals from headquarters and the foreign subsidiary, who rotate alternately in both directions from headquarters to the foreign subsidiary and work in the respective departments. In so doing and by attending intercultural trainings, they will have acquired the necessary intercultural competence for their target country and begin acting as go-betweens and integrators (integration) between headquarters and the subsidiary, translating information in a way that is culturally appropriate and corresponds to the culture-specific mindset. Not all employees of one culture communicate with employees of the other culture. Rather, a lot of information is channeled via these key persons.

- In the case of a geocentric strategy, it may be crucial to adhere to headquarters' requirements and goals by compensating with measures on site to enhance employee motivation, even if they do not correspond to headquarters' financial policy, such as additional social benefits. In this sense, integration gains a material dimension.
- Mediators can be engaged to assist in conflict resolution within the scope of regiocentric, geocentric and synergetic strategies. These professionals mirror the respective culture-specific perception, thought patterns, feelings and behavioral characteristics between conflict partners and, in this way, lead the conflict toward a resolution.
- Once headquarters has recognized the significance of mediated contextual information in the decision-making process within the scope of a basic ethnocentric strategy, employees at headquarters will (finally) have the time and financial backing for travel to the target country in order to: a.) inform employees in depth at the foreign subsidiary about specifications from headquarters and b.) to establish a sustainable relationship with foreign colleagues and set the stage for a trust-based, genuine collaboration. Employees from the foreign subsidiary receive on-the-job training at headquarters in an effort to create transparency about the organization's background and the way it is interconnected. Consequently, domination can be tolerated and accepted because it is visible. The hidden ghost of colonialism fades in favor of the realization that certain standardized procedures are more efficient and the employees begin developing a sense of pride in working for this particular organization.

These examples illustrate individual measures within the framework of the overall concept and how they proved effective in particular cases. The discourse and the decisions taken with regard to a basic strategy for interculturality within an organization are considerably more extensive: A basic strategy for interculturality establishes the necessary and binding framework for conclusive, consistent intercultural interaction for managers and employees. Without this commitment, the corporation risks confusion, counter-productive interaction and "damage repair costs", both materially and socially, and the full potential for realizing interculturality remains untapped.

References

Heenan, D. A.; Perlmutter, H. V. (1979): Multinational Organizational Development: A Societal Approach. Reading/Mass.

Kinast, E.-U. (1998): Evaluation interkultureller Trainings. Lengerich.

Reineke, R. D. (1989): Akkulturation von Auslandsakquisitionen. Eine Untersuchung zur unternehmenskulturellen Anpassung. Schriftenreihe Unternehmensführung und Marketing, Band 23.

Scholz, C. (1993). Personalmanagement – Informationsorientierte und verhaltenstheoretische Grundlagen. München.

Schroll-Machl, S.; Nový, I. (2000): Perfekt geplant oder genial improvisiert? Kulturunterschiede in der deutsch-tschechischen Zusammenarbeit. München/Mering.

Zeutschel, U. (1998): Kooperation in internationalen Teams – Potentiale, Beobachtungen, Empfehlungen. Projektinformation 3 (Abschlusspräsentation), Universität Regensburg. (Unveröffentlichtes Arbeitspapier des Forschungsprojekts Interkulturelle Synergie in Arbeitsgruppen)

Author Index

Subject Index

The Authors

Prof. Georg Felser is a professor of business psychology at Harz College in Wernigerode, Germany.

Iris Christiane Fischlmayr Ph.D. is an assistant at the Institute of Corporate Leadership with a focus on international management research at the University of Linz, Austria.

Evelyne Glaser Ph.D. is a professor at the Institute of International Management at the University of Linz, Austria.

Detmar Grosse-Leege (†), initially a business correspondent, moved into industry in 1975 (Villeroy & Boch, Audi, Gruner + Jahr, Daimler Chrysler, Aerospace). In the last decade he collaborated with corporations and academia in the field of "Intercultural Communication". He was president of IIK in Bayreuth, Germany from 1998 to 2000.

Barbara Hatzer is a psychologist who works for the Berner Group in the field of international personnel training.

Stefan Kammhuber Ph.D. is a psychologist and professor, consultant and trainer for intercultural personnel development, corporate communication and rhetoric in industry and administration. He is co-founder of the Institute for Cooperative Management (IKO) at the University of Regensburg, Germany.

Eva-Ulrike Kinast Ph.D. is a self-employed HR management consultant and coach for corporations worldwide.

Gabriel Layes Ph.D. is a psychologist and works at the Institut für Vermögensaufbau (IVA) GmbH in München. His areas of study include intercultural psychology, social and organizational psychology.

Sylvia Schroll-Machl Ph.D. is a psychologist and freelance trainer and coach for renowned companies, organizations and ministries in the area of intercultural training and personnel development.

Siegfried Stumpf Ph.D. is a psychologist and professor at the Betriebswirtschaftliches Institut Gummersbach. He is co-founder of the Institute for Cooperative Management (IKO) at the University of Regensburg, Germany.

Alexander Thomas Ph.D. is a professor of social and organizational psychology at the University of Regensburg, Germany. He is co-founder of the

Institute for Cooperative Management (IKO) at the University of Regensburg, Germany.

Gerhard Winter Ph.D. is a psychologist. He was senior academic advisor for the Institute of Psychology at the University of Tübingen, Germany in the department of Social Psychology and the Psychology of Personality until 1998. He is honorary professor for Intercultural Communication and Understanding at the Technical University in Chemnitz, Germany.

Ulrich Zeutschel is a psychologist and is a management and research consultant in Hamburg, Germany, as well as freelance trainer and moderator.

Wenn Sie weiterlesen möchten ...

Sylvia Schroll-Machl

Doing Business with Germans

Their Perception, Our Perception

3rd edition

As globalisation becomes more pervasive in everyday life, many people are faced with challenging new situations: Cultural differences no longer fascinate only tourists and intrigue academics. The impact of globalisation has become, to a large extent, a part of our daily life, particularly in the business world.
This book sheds light on the two sides of German business partnerships in intercultural settings. On the one hand it deals with people working with Germans from their home country as well as with expatriates who have come to live and work in Germany. On the other hand it portrays Germans who have business relations all over the world negotiating with people in business meetings or via telecommunications.
What is "typically German"? How do other people perceive me as a German? This book will help you to achieve intercultural competence, that means: understanding of the cultural standards of others and insight into one's own culture.
Based on her academic training and many years of experience, Sylvia Schroll-Machl describes real-life situations that foreigners have experienced with Germans and explains, what Germans actually mean when they say and do particular things. The author also investigates the cultural and historical background which has shaped the German identity.

Sylvia Schroll-Machl

Die Deutschen – Wir Deutsche

Fremdwahrnehmung und Selbstsicht im Berufsleben

4. Auflage

Die Globalisierung ist inzwischen allgegenwärtig. Diese Tatsache stellt viele Menschen vor neue Situationen: Kulturunterschiede sind nicht mehr nur etwas, was Touristen fasziniert und Wissenschaftler anregt, sondern sie sind weitgehend Alltag geworden, insbesondere auch in beruflichen Zusammenhängen.
Das Buch wendet sich an beide Seiten dieser geschäftlichen Partnerschaft: zum einen an jene, die mit Deutschen von ihrem Heimatland aus zu tun haben, oder als Expatriate, der für einige Zeit in Deutschland lebt, zum anderen an die Deutschen, die mit Partnern aus aller Welt im Geschäftskontakt stehen, sei es per Geschäftsbesuch oder via Kommunikationsmedien. Für die erste Gruppe ist es wichtig, Informationen über Deutsche zu erhalten, um sich auf uns einstellen zu können. Für Deutsche selbst ist es hilfreich zu erfahren, wie unsere nicht-deutschen Partner uns erleben, um uns selbst im Spiegel der anderen zu sehen.
Sylvia Schroll-Machl berichtet auf dem Hintergrund langjähriger Praxis als interkulturelle Trainerin und Wissenschaftlerin über viele typische Erfahrungen mit uns Deutschen und typische Eindrücke von uns.
Es geht ihr aber auch darum, diese Erlebnisse und Erfahrungen aus deutscher Sicht zu beleuchten, damit die nicht-deutschen Partner entdecken, wie wir eigentlich das meinen, was wir sagen und tun. Zudem beschäftigt sich die Autorin auch mit den kulturhistorischen Hintergründen, die uns Deutsche prägen.

Karin Schreiner

Mit der Familie ins Ausland

Ein Wegweiser für Expatriates

Im Kontext von Globalisierung und weltweiter Mobilität brauchen künftige Expatriates ein Rüstzeug, um in interkulturellen Settings entsprechend auftreten und bestehen zu können. Dieses Buch vermittelt das theoretische und praktische Hintergrundwissen, das für einen längeren Arbeitsaufenthalt im Ausland nötig ist: Was ist Kultur? Wie kann ich Kulturen miteinander vergleichen? Was sind interkulturelle Kompetenzen? Wozu sind interkulturelle Trainings gut? Wie verläuft die Anpassung an die neue Kultur? Was ist ein Kulturschock? Wie bereitet man die Rückkehr in die Heimat vor?
Da Expatriates meist nicht allein ins Ausland gehen, liegt ein Schwerpunkt dieses Buches auf der Situation mitausreisender Angehöriger. Partner von Expatriates stehen vor wichtigen Lebens- und Karriereentscheidungen, mitausreisende Kinder werden von einem Leben im Ausland entscheidend in ihrer Entwicklung geprägt. Mitausreisenden fehlen vor Ort und nach der Rückkehr oft Struktur und Perspektive. Wie sie die Herausforderung, mit ihrer Familie ins Ausland zu gehen, erfolgreich meistern können, verrät dieses Buch. Zahlreiche kurze Fallbeispiele und Erfahrungsberichte ergänzen die Darstellungen.

Alexander Thomas / Astrid Utler / Ulrike de Ponte / Stefan Schmid

Realität und Innovation in der europäischen Begegnung

Die Autoren haben untersucht, was europäische Begegnungen, speziell von jungen Menschen, zur Entwicklung Europas beitragen und was sie unter bestimmten, innovativen Bedingungen und Dynamiken einbringen können. Dazu wurden Projekte des formellen und informellen Bildungssektors mit konkretem Europabezug erhoben und analysiert. Außerdem wurden Experten der europäischen Begegnung interviewt zu deren Einschätzungen und Erfahrungen hinsichtlich Erfolgsfaktoren, Rahmenbedingungen sowie der gewünschten Rolle der Förderer. Aus den Ergebnissen und auf Basis psychologischer Theorien konnten Empfehlungen abgeleitet werden: Zum einen wurde ein Methodenpool entwickelt, in dem eine Vielzahl an Methoden zusammengestellt und bezüglich ihrer Lernwirksamkeit eingeschätzt wurden. Zum anderen werden detaillierte Hinweise geliefert, welche Bausteine berücksichtigt werden müssen, um europäische Begegnungsprojekte möglichst nachhaltig und wirkungsvoll zu konzipieren.

Alexander Thomas (Hg.)

Psychologie des interkulturellen Dialogs

Das Europäische Jahr des interkulturellen Dialogs war Anlass genug, die Psychologie als eine für die Entwicklung des interkulturellen Dialogs zentrale wissenschaftliche Disziplin nach ihrem spezifischen Beitrag zu befragen. In diesem Sammelband werden aus verschiedenen Perspektiven heraus psychologische Erkenntnisse zur Entwicklung und Qualifizierung des interkulturellen Dialogs dargestellt und anhand empirischer Forschungsbefunde und Praxiserfahrungen analysiert.
Behandelt werden zum einen Bedingungen und Grundlagen zur Ausbildung, Gestaltung und Förderung des interkulturellen Dialogs. Welche Bedeutung der interkulturelle Dialog in der Praxis hat und wie er genau aussieht, wird anhand verschiedener Handlungsfelder gezeigt. Unter die Lupe genommen werden in diesem Zusammenhang unter anderem Profit- und Non-Profit-Organisationen, internationale und europäische Austausch- und Begegnungsprogramme, interkulturelle Trainings und Integrationsprogramme für Migranten.